GENEROUS GIVING

They
Shall Not
Go Hungry

Share
What
YOU
Have!

ASSOCIATED
JEWISH PHILANTHROPIES
1931-32 CAMPAIGN
October 25—November 6

WE DARE NOT FAIL!

# THE JEWS
## of Boston

# THE JEWS of BOSTON

*Essays on the Occasion of the Centenary (1895–1995)*
*of the Combined Jewish Philanthropies*
*of Greater Boston*

*Edited by*

Jonathan D. Sarna & Ellen Smith

COMBINED JEWISH PHILANTHROPIES OF GREATER BOSTON
1995 / 5755

First published in 1995 by
The Combined Jewish Philanthropies of Greater Boston, Inc.
126 High Street
Boston, Massachusetts 02110

Distributed by Northeastern University Press
360 Huntington Avenue
Boston, Massachusetts 02115

ISBN: 1-55553-217-9

First edition
Printed in the United States of America

# Foreword

THE TRADITION of our people and our community shaped the decision to publish *The Jews of Boston* in commemoration of the 100th anniversary of the Combined Jewish Philanthropies. What could be more fitting than to commission a book in celebration of the CJP Centennial? Our reverence for scholarship and learning is reflected in the twelve original essays that portray Boston Jewry from its earliest beginnings to the present. Each one presents a different facet of the complex totality of our history; each one illuminates an aspect of Boston Jewish life. *The Jews of Boston* is a singular achievement, for it is the first comprehensive history of our Jewish community. Reading it, we appreciate that we continue to play a dual role as makers and participants in American Jewish history. We are unique, and still our story parallels Jewish life in other cities.

Since its inception, Boston's Jewish community has been noted for its unmatched intellectual strength, its capacity for innovation, and its willingness to take risks in support of its vision and ideals. CJP was the first Jewish Federation in the country, in fact, the first federated charity of any kind. Born out of innovation, it reinvented itself many times throughout the century to meet the changing needs of the Jewish community. Today it faces new challenges, including a transformed partnership with Israel and the historic opportunity to bring hundreds of thousands of former Soviet Jews home to Israel.

Most important, the next great era of American Jewish life will bring with it the challenge of Jewish continuity and the opportunity to participate in a Jewish spiritual, intellectual, and cultural renaissance in America. Boston has already taken the first step with its communal and congregational partners in this great enterprise. Once again, Boston has the unique combination of talent, intellect, and commitment to change, to bring this educational, cultural, and religious revolution to life and serve as a catalyst for communal change throughout the country.

CJP is the product of many hands, shaped and reshaped over the course of a century to meet the changing needs of a changing community. We are grateful to each of our distinguished leaders and to all our volunteers, the men and women of this community who have steadfastly supported our Federation and all that it embodies:

> *Tzedakah*, justice, for those who are vulnerable and disadvantaged among our people in Boston, in Israel and around the world, and among our neighbors in our urban environment;

> *Torah*, Jewish education, a commitment to promoting Jewish literacy, Jewish values, and Jewish meaning for ourselves, our children, and our grandchildren from generation to generation.

CJP celebrates 100 years of service to the community, and looks forward with confidence to our second century, proud of our mantle as the first charitable Federation in the country. Greater Boston is home to America's sixth largest Jewish population; our community is vibrant and strong. Whatever new challenge our second century brings, our response will be grounded in our tradition and our vision inscribed clearly on the outer wall of our new headquarters at 126 High Street,

> *The world stands on three things:*
> *On Torah;*
> *On the service of God;*
> *And on acts of lovingkindness.*
>
> PIRKE AVOT 1:2

MICHAEL J. BOHNEN
*Chair, Board of Directors*

BARRY SHRAGE
*President*

*December 19, 1994*
*16 Tevet 5755*

# Contents

# Preface

OR THREE HUNDRED FIFTY YEARS Jews have lived in Boston, but no one has written their history. Two late 19th century surveys featured the achievements of prominent individuals; two 20th century publications provided brief popular overviews. Only Albert Ehrenfried attempted a comprehensive history of the community—and that only until 1900—but he died before the manuscript and its source notes were completed. The book was published privately, but never achieved wide distribution.

This volume seeks to provide a history of the Boston Jewish community in an accessible, scholarly fashion. Its focus is the Jews of Boston, and how from colonial to modern times, they sought to define and create identity and community among themselves and within the broader citizenry of Boston and America.

*The Jews of Boston* grew out of a fortunate conversation in 1992 among Ruth Fein, Ami Ducovny, and the staff of the Combined Jewish Philanthropies of Greater Boston. Anticipating the 1995 Centennial of the CJP, the first federated charitable organization in the United States, the group proposed commissioning a community history, rather than a history of the Federation itself, as CJP's celebratory gift to the community. Public programs, exhibitions, community oral histories, and book plans took shape.

With funding provided by the CJP, the book contract was awarded to Brandeis University. Jonathan D. Sarna, the Joseph H. & Belle R. Braun Professor of American Jewish History and Chair of the Department of Near Eastern and Judaic Studies, was selected to serve as editor, assisted by Beth Tischler. Early in the book's planning, Dr. Sarna invited Ellen Smith, Curator of the American Jewish Historical Society, to serve as the book's co-editor. Scott-Martin Kosofsky was integral to the project team from its beginning as the book's designer and producer. Susan Ebert served as the CJP liaison as well as one of the authors; her wonderful calm and wise counsel is writ large in the history of this book.

*The Jews of Boston* could not have had a more supportive or amiable sponsor than the Combined Jewish Philanthropies of Greater Boston. The CJP granted the editors full editorial control to structure the book and select the contributors. Eleven authors were chosen to represent the generational spectrum of scholarship on Jewish Boston and a wide range of views and insights. Each author was given broad license to define the content and focus of his or her essay, within the general structure outlined by the editors.

*The Jews of Boston* is organized in two parts. The first six essays provide an historic overview of the community from its early, tentative beginnings through its emergence in the 20th century as one of the most influential Jewish communities in America. In the second part, six topical essays focus on key aspects of Boston's unique role in American and Jewish history. Chapters on Boston's synagogues, Boston's Jewish neighborhoods, and Zionism present groundbreaking information by the new generation of American Jewish historians now emerging on the academic scene. Assessments of Boston Jewish philanthropy, education, and intellectual culture evaluate those movements' pioneering roles in the evolution of Jewish culture in Boston and America.

We have chosen in this volume to focus on issues of community and identity rather than on the specific histories of individual people, organizations, and congregations. As editors we are well aware that other essays might have been written, and that a great many significant names and developments have, of necessity, been omitted. Our central guideline to the authors was to address the qualities that make Boston unique in American Jewish history and to assess how those factors have helped shape the community's self-understanding and character. In that story, we believe, readers can find reflections of personal, as well as communal odysseys, and draw parallels to the experiences of other Boston communities. Beyond this, we hope that this volume serves as an introduction to Jewish Boston and as a catalyst for additional studies of its history and people.

*The Jews of Boston* is in a very real sense the product of the community it describes. We are especially grateful to Susan Ebert, Ruth Fein, Michael Bohnen, Barry Shrage, Sherman Starr, Terry Holzman, and the staff and Board of Directors at the Combined Jewish Philanthropies of Greater Boston for launching this book project and for allowing the book to develop along independent and scholarly lines.

Brandeis University provided the home for this project. Special thanks are offered to the administrative staff of the Department of Near Eastern & Judaic Studies, Ellen Hosbjor, Helene Altman, and Toby Kennen; to the office of Grants and Contracts, Joel Cohen and Roberta Nary; to the Judaica Department of the library,

Charles Cutter and his staff; and most of all to the administration of the University, particularly President Jehuda Reinharz and Provost Irving Epstein, for their enthusiastic support of scholarship in American Jewish History.

The American Jewish Historical Society, Waltham, Massachusetts, has served as unofficial home to the project, providing space, a delightful working atmosphere, and generous access to their remarkable collections. We particularly wish to thank Michael Feldberg, Executive Director, and Gina Hsin, Reference Librarian, for their intellectual contributions and patient legwork. Society President Justin L. Wyner endorsed the project early and placed the intellectual resources of the Society before us. Helpful assistance was also provided by Stanley Remsberg, Assistant Director; Holly Snyder, Archivist; Helen Sarna, Director of Cataloging; and Libby Finkelstein, Membership Secretary.

Book designer Scott-Martin Kosofsky contributed far more than his impeccable artistic and design abilities. A literate and intelligent critic, Scott's insights elevated the character and quality of the project at every turn. M. Sue Ladr contributed patient, expert design advice. David R. Godine recommended Scott for the project; both men bring a dedication to and belief in quality books, and we are grateful to them both.

Marlowe Bergendoff of Exeter, New Hampshire, turned copyediting into an art form and saved us from many errors of text and type. We also thank Maria Granfield at the Combined Jewish Philanthropies for proofreading assistance. Nahum Sarna graciously helped with the English translation of Hebrew text.

*The Jews of Boston* in many ways grew out of the research done for "On Common Ground: The Boston Jewish Experience, 1649–1980," a National Endowment for the Humanities-funded, nationally-traveling, prize-winning exhibition curated for the American Jewish Historical Society in 1980 by Ellen Smith. It is a pleasure again to thank the individuals who formed the core team of "On Common Ground:" Martha Katz-Hyman, Research Coordinator; Ellen Spencer, Project Assistant; Sylvia Kaufman, Chair of the Volunteer Research Committee and the women who worked with her; exhibition designer Gill Fishman, President of Gill Fishman Associates, Inc., Cambridge, Massachusetts; Jeffrey Kennedy, Project Designer, then of Gill Fishman Associates; and Michael Schaffer, sound and light designer for the exhibit's Sabbath Kitchen. David R. Pokross, then Chairman of the Boston Exhibition, and the late Isaac M. Fein, then Chairman of the AJHS Exhibition Committee, served as mentors and community leaders of "On Common Ground;" neither ever lost their view that eventually a book on Jewish Boston should emerge from the exhibition's pioneering efforts. We are pleased to acknowledge again the AJHS staff as constituted in 1980 who also contributed to "On Common Ground": Bernard Wax,

Director; the late Nathan Kaganoff, Librarian; Stanley Remsberg, Assistant Director; and Nehemiah Ben-Zev, Assistant Librarian.

We have enjoyed the generous support of many individuals and organizations in the preparation of this book. Beth Tischler organized the early research for the project, and her many contributions and insights inform the final result. Richard Heath, a landscape architect and historian of Roxbury, came to us early in the project with the extensive work he had done on the physical legacy of the Jewish settlement in Roxbury. Gerald Gamm gave an entire, snowbound Sunday afternoon and evening in Rochester, New York, to share his knowledge of Roxbury communities and his extensive collection of photographs. David Kaufman's capacious knowledge of Boston Jewish history guided us on many paths we might otherwise have missed.

Several individuals gave us access to their private collections. Even if we were unable to use their material, we value their generosity. Some wish to remain anonymous and we thank them privately. We publicly thank Sumner Greenberg, Arnold H. Kaplan, Joel Krensky, Peter Schweitzer, and Murray Zimiles.

We have tried in *The Jews of Boston* to present previously unpublished photographs along with the classic images of Jewish Boston. This has meant extensive photographic researches beyond those done in the past decade. For their help with this photographic research we are grateful to Gerald Gamm, David Kaufman, Mark Raider, and David Sternburg. Karen Arsenault and David Glader of The Vilna Shul Heritage Center shared their knowledge of Jewish Boston photographs. Private collectors and photographers were exceptionally generous with their knowledge and their images. We thank Jules Aarons, Harvey Fenton, Miriam Freedman, Thelma Freedman, Richard Heath, Maurice Kates and his family for access to their scrapbook of Maurice's father (the synagogue-ark maker Sam Katz), David Kaufman, Arthur Krim, Lila Levin, Martin Sandler, Bernard and Susanne Shavelson and their family, Peter Vanderwarker, Natalie Velleman, and Nick Wheeler. Photographer A. Samuel Laundon made his superb photographs of the Vilna Shul available to us. Photographer Carl Mastandrea employed his large-format camera to capture beautifully for us large buildings and small, dark places. Bruce Jones provided us with digital artwork for the two modern maps.

The staffs of many public and private institutions in Boston and beyond proved exceptionally generous with their time and their collections, willingly digging just a little deeper to find that one (or twenty) fresh new images. For their enthusiasm and professional skills we gratefully thank: Sally Pierce and Christina Slautterback, the Boston Athenæum; Sinclair Hitchings and Aaron Schmidt, Boston Public Library; Lorna Condon, Society for the Preservation of New England Antiquities; and Marc

Foley, Beacon Properties Corporation; Ruth Freiman, Beth Israel Hospital, Boston; Albert Kalman, Congregation Agudas Achim Anshei Sfard, Newton; Shalva Siegel, Hebrew College; Faye Weingarten, Jewish Community Housing for the Elderly; Melissa Wenig, Leventhal-Sidman Jewish Community Center; Martin Sandler and Michelle Marcella, Massachusetts General Hospital; Chris Steele, Massachusetts Historical Society; Michael Rosenberg, Maimonides School, Brookline; Michael Yeates, The MIT Museum; Karen Mittleman, National Museum of American Jewish History, Philadelphia; Rabbi Chaim Ciment, New England Hebrew Academy, Brookline; Jack Melcher, Spaulding Company; Edie Brown, Striar Jewish Community Center; Betsy Abrams, Temple Israel, Boston; Rabbi Dr. Ira A. Korff; and the many helpful staff members of the *Boston Globe*; the *Boston Herald*; Congregation Mishkan Tefila, Newton; Congregation Ohabei Shalom, Brookline; the Franklin D. Roosevelt Library; Harvard-Radcliffe Hillel; Harvard University Archives; The Grand Lodge of Masons, Massachusetts; The Jewish Museum, New York City; Solomon Schechter Day School of Greater Boston; Temple Emanuel, Newton; Temple Emeth, Newton; Temple Israel, Sharon; Temple Sinai, Brookline; Time/Life Publications; and the United States Supreme Court.

Even when found, the photographic remains of Jewish Boston sometimes still needed restoration. Deep appreciation is extended to Sal Lopes for his expert photographic prints from the American Jewish Historical Society's collection of glass slides; and to Norman O'Neil and Bill James at Aurora Graphics, Portsmouth, New Hampshire, for their support in scanning and imagesetting. *The Jews of Boston* was expertly printed by The Nimrod Press, Westwood, and distributed by Northeastern University Press. Our personal thanks are extended to Walter T. Tower, Jr., Chairman of Nimrod, and to John Weingartner, Senior Editor at Northeastern.

The eleven authors whose work comprises this book have been unflaggingly devoted to this project. They have responded to all queries and deadlines with promptness and good humor, turning a logistically complex project into a model of collegial cooperation.

Finally, there are our own families to thank. Loving support from our spouses, and our children's excited anticipation of seeing their names in print constantly enlivened our two years of work on this book. With much love we thank Dr. Ruth Langer, and Aaron and Leah Sarna; and Bill, Danya, and Jonathan Pastuszek.

JONATHAN D. SARNA and ELLEN SMITH
*Brandeis University*
*December 5, 1994 / 8th Day of Chanukah, 5755*

# The Jews of Boston
# in Historical Perspective

*Overleaf:* Boston and environs as viewed from the east, 1993. *Photograph by Aerial Photos International, Inc.*

JONATHAN D. SARNA

# The Jews of Boston
# in Historical Perspective

בזמן הזה הכל לפי השנים הכל לפי המקומות הכל לפי הזמן

"Nowadays, everything depends upon the years, the locations, and the season."

TALMUD BAVLI TA'ANIT 14b

OSTON, historian Sam Bass Warner once wrote, "is a unique place with its own particular natural and human history, but it is also a very ordinary American place, typical of the nation's many metropolises."[1] Jewish Boston is much the same, at once unique and ordinary, in some ways typical of America's Jewish communities and in other ways distinctive. The central themes of Boston Jewish history are familiar ones to students of American Jewish life: immigration, adaptation, socio-economic mobility, religion, education, culture, philanthropy, Zionism, assimilation, antisemitism. The expression of these themes, however, is peculiarly Bostonian, affecting the timing and character of Jewish settlement, the relationship between Jews and their Christian neighbors, and above all the life of the mind—that love of learning that sets Boston apart as the "Athens of America" and has promoted the optimistic hope that "Athens" and "Jerusalem" might ultimately be reconciled.

The roots of the Boston Jewish community extend far back into the colonial period—back as far as "Solomon Franco, the Jew" who accompanied a cargo vessel into town in 1649. For two centuries, however, only a handful of Jews settled down long enough in Boston to establish a permanent home. The rest were Jewish transients, individuals who wandered in and out of the city. Never were there enough Jews around to form a community.

This fact—the absence of any organized Jewish community in early Boston—sets the city apart from the major American port cities where Sephardic Jews settled in numbers: Savannah, Charleston, Philadelphia, New York, and Newport. One potential Ashkenazic immigrant, the learned Israel Baer Kursheedt, who arrived in

Boston in 1796 having studied under Rabbi Nathan Adler in Frankfurt, found but one Jewish family in town and no synagogue. He quickly retreated. Other immigrants bypassed Boston entirely. As a result, the frontier cities of Cincinnati, Cleveland, Louisville, and St. Louis all had synagogues and organized Jewish communities before Boston did; so did smaller cities like Easton, Pennsylvania. It was only in the 1840's that Boston finally housed a sufficient number of Jews to form a community, and in 1843 they formally organized as Kahal Kadosh Ohabei Shalom (The Holy Community Lovers of Peace). This became the third synagogue in New England, following those previously established in Newport and New Haven.

Religious, cultural, and economic factors all help to explain the general reluctance of early American Jews to settle in Boston. They preferred more open and cosmopolitan cities where opportunities and foreign immigrants abounded—hence their affinity for New York and the cities of the frontier. Boston, by contrast, projected an image of formidable homogeneity; for a time it held the dubious distinction of being America's most homogenous city.[2] Until the coming of the Irish, most immigrants, and certainly most Jews, sought their fortunes elsewhere.

Students of American Jewish communities have discovered that "the degree to which Jews were involved in the early growth of a city and had achieved a notable and respected place in public and private life . . . directly influenced how later generations of Jews were received." Where Jews won "pioneer" status, as in Indianapolis, Cincinnati, and San Francisco, they generally fared better. Where they were seen as latecomers and interlopers, they generally fared worse.[3] Boston Jews fell into this latter category. Notwithstanding the pious Hebraism of the Puritans and the occasional intrusion of intrepid Israelites bent on trade, Jews remained an alien presence in early Boston. They were not among the city's founders, and they were not particularly welcome.

The great migration from Germany in the 19th century, a migration that transformed many American cities and spread Jews where none had lived before, largely passed Boston by. Only three percent of Boston's immigrant population was German in 1850 and six percent in 1870. Perhaps fearing to compete with the Irish, the mass of German immigrants, Jews and gentiles alike, settled south and west of Boston in a belt that stretched from Connecticut, New York, New Jersey, Delaware, and Maryland through Pennsylvania and into the Midwest.[4] One of the most striking features of Boston Jewish history, as a result, is the absence of an entrenched, well-organized German-Jewish community of the type found in cities like New York, Cincinnati, and San Francisco. This reluctance on the part of German Jews to settle in "the Hub of the universe" explains both the Boston Jewish community's failure to thrive in the way that Jewish communities in these other cities did during the central decades of German-Jewish immigration and the comparative lack of internal tension between Central and East European Jews later on.

Boston's Jewish population did nevertheless grow from less than forty Jews in 1840 to approximately one thousand Jews on the eve of the Civil War. While spectacular in percentage terms, the actual growth is far less than that experienced by other major cities where Jews settled. Keeping in mind that all Jewish population figures from this period are approximations at best, it is estimated that during this same period New York City's Jewish population grew from 7,000 to 40,000; Philadelphia's from 1,500 to 10,000; Cincinnati's from 1,000 to 10,000; and San Francisco's from no Jews at all to 5,000.[5]

Even the small number of Jews who did immigrate to Boston during these years were more often Polish than German in origin. Fleeing economic privation and religious persecution, they stemmed particularly from the province of Posen, then under Prussian sovereignty. A statistical analysis reveals that no less than forty-four percent of Boston's Jews during this period were born in "East and West Prussia, Poland, Posen, and Pomerania"; the birthplace of another twenty-nine percent within the German-Polish lands remains uncertain. Eight percent more came from other countries, including a small but distinctive group that immigrated from Holland. Only nineteen percent hailed specifically from Southwest Germany and Bavaria. This surprising preponderance of Polish Jews stands in stark contrast to the situation in the Midwest. In Milwaukee, for example, only four percent of Jews stemmed from Polish lands, while seventy-five percent came from Southwest Germany and Bavaria, Bohemia and Austria.[6]

The influence of Boston's Polish Jews may readily be seen within Congregation Ohabei Shalom, which from the beginning understandably followed the Polish-Jewish rite known as *Minhag Polin*. The minority that preferred the German rite, known as *Minhag Ashkenaz*, seceded in 1853, establishing what became Kahal Kadosh Adath Israel, today Temple Israel. Henceforward, Ohabei Shalom became known in Boston as the Polish Congregation, and Adath Israel as the German one. As late as 1878, the Polish congregation was the largest in town, boasting almost two and a half times as many members as its German rival.[7]

The Polish character of Jewish Boston also manifested itself in other ways. Not having experienced the same historical conditions that paved the way for Reform Judaism's rise, Polish Jews in America tended to be more religiously conservative than their German counterparts; Reform spread far more slowly among them. So it was in Boston. "While all over the United States reformed Judaism began to assert itself, the Jews of Boston, of the Hub of the Universe, of the literary centre of America, took no part whatsoever."[8] The author of this statement, Rabbi Solomon Schindler, was himself a Reform rabbi, and it was he who introduced religious reforms into the "German Congregation" beginning in 1874, fifty years after the emergence of religious reforms in Charleston and thirty years after the first Reform congregations developed in Baltimore and New York. As for the "Polish Congregation," although it, too, introduced religious reforms in the 1870's, seeking to stem the flow of younger members to Adath Israel, it did not formally affiliate with the Reform Movement for another twenty-five years.

All of these factors—the small size of the early Boston Jewish community, its Polish character, and its religious conservatism—affected the relationship between the "established" Jewish community of Boston and the new wave of East European immigrants who made their presence felt as early as the 1870's. Victims of economic privation and political oppression, these new immigrants came initially from Lithuania, then under Russian sovereignty. They settled in the poorest sections of the North End and established new Orthodox synagogues: Shomre Shabbes ("Sabbath Observers") and Beth Abraham. Even as they lived across town from one another, however, the new Russian Jews and the older Polish ones found much in common. The leader of the new immigrant community, Baruch Isaac Reinherz, looked upon the rabbi of Ohabei Shalom, Falk Vidaver, as a *landsman,* a fellow "Russian-Pole." Both men wrote frequently for the European Hebrew press, and both wrote glowingly about America as a land where Jews could be free and succeed. Even when the two men fired polemics at one another, their dispute ended with a call for communal unity and joint efforts on behalf of Jewish education. For the most part, the size and composition of the 19th-century community kept intra-Jewish tensions to a minimum.[9]

The massive East European immigration of the 1880's and 1890's heightened intra-Jewish tensions in Boston. The city's Jewish population multiplied approximately eight-fold during these two decades, from about 5,000 to 40,000. Understandably, the small established community felt overwhelmed. Putting aside their differences, Boston's German and Polish Jews came together to meet this crisis. The East European immigrants, quite mistakenly, viewed them all as "Germans" and treated them with suspicion. What is remarkable in retrospect, however, is not the ugly tensions that developed between old and new immigrants or the unfortunate decision in 1882 to ship a group of 415 impoverished refugees back to New York, but rather the speed with which the manifold problems posed by immigration were overcome. Led by the wealthy German Jews of Adath Israel, particularly the Bavarian-born Jacob Hecht and his American-born wife Lina, the community mobilized to aid the refugees, creating a panoply of benevolent institutions to receive and assist them. In 1891, when the city's Russian Jews founded their own institution, the Benoth Israel Sheltering Home, to offer immigrants temporary shelter and food, the established community offered support. "We have to take care of the thousands coming to our shore," Edward Goulston, Adath Israel's former president, declared at the dedication. "We must help them to become good citizens . . . We must certainly treat the immigrants with kindness and toleration."[10] In 1895 the establishment of America's first federation, the Federation of Jewish Charities, underscored the community's resolve to work together to solve communal problems; its list of charter subscribers included a sprinkling of Russian Jews. In 1908, the Federation expanded to embrace charitable societies recently established by these Russian Jews. As a result, years before such cooperation was effected in cities like New York and Cincinnati, Boston Jews of different immigrant backgrounds—Polish, German, Russian, and more—regularly interacted at the federation's meetings.[11]

By World War I, East European Jews dominated Boston's Jewish community. Of the estimated eighty to ninety thousand Jews in the city, all but a few thousand were recent immigrants or their children. Even the old "German Congregation," now universally known as Temple Israel, was attracting young Jews of Eastern European descent. The Temple's new rabbi, Harry Levi, was himself the child of Polish-born parents and made East European Jews feel welcome.[12] So, where other Jewish communities, including New York, continued to grapple with the legacy of misunderstanding between German Jews and their East European cousins, Boston, by and large, did not. Only disparate patterns of residence and separate country clubs kept the old social distinctions alive.

Zionism, too, proved less divisive an issue in Boston, partly again because East European Jews so dominated the community. In addition, the fact that the city's best known and most highly respected Jew, Louis Brandeis, as well as many of his intellectual friends, and Boston's *Jewish Advocate,* all strongly advocated Zionism served to undermine the movement's critics. Widespread local support for Irish nationalism strengthened the case for a Jewish homeland still further. Admittedly, earlier rabbis of Temple Israel, Solomon Schindler and Charles Fleischer, had attacked Zionism from the pulpit; for them it raised the spectre of dual loyalty. Harry Levi, however, came to support the Zionist cause, not so much for American Jews as for those living "hopeless lives" elsewhere. His successors at Temple Israel proved to be staunch Zionists, as did most of the other major rabbis in the community. By World War II, according to George Gallup, more than ninety percent of Greater Boston and New England Jews supported Zionism, a record unmatched anywhere else in the United States.[13]

Boston thus was largely spared the wearisome intra-communal battles over immigration and Zionism that divided so many American Jewish cities, particularly those rich with 19th-century history and steeped in the traditions of German Jewry. The issues that Boston Jews faced instead were those that would eventually come to the fore in most urban areas where Jews lived: tensions between immigrants and their children, between wealthier Jews and poorer ones, between Jews of different religious persuasions, Orthodox, Conservative, and Reform, and—most important of all as far as local residents were concerned—tensions between Jews and their neighbors.

Writing on the subject of Jews and their neighbors in 1889, Rabbi Solomon Schindler was still rhapsodic: "It cannot be said that the New Englanders had ever shown a spirit of intolerance to Jewish settlers . . . . Jews could never complain of ill-treatment in New England." Schindler himself maintained close ties with Boston's liberal Protestant elite, and for many years, according to his biographer, "felt more at home with non-Jews than with Jews." His portayal of inter-group harmony in the city bespoke more hope than reality.[14]

In fact, the relationship between Boston Jews and their neighbors was never so simple. For all that they professed to respect the "ancient Hebrews," most Bostonians prior to the late 19th century had, at best, a fleeting aquaintance with Jews. They heard about them more than they actually saw them, and they puzzled over how to reconcile the historically stereotyped "mythical Jew," found in their books, with the real Jew, the proverbial "Jew next door," who seemed altogether different. The poet Oliver Wendell Holmes (father of the Supreme Court justice), for example, admitted that he grew up with the "traditional idea" that Jews "were a race lying under a curse for their obstinacy in refusing the gospel." "The principal use of the Jews," he believed, "seemed to be to lend money, and to fulfill the prediction of the old prophets of their race." Later, as he came into contact with Jews, he changed his mind. As he recounted in his poem, "At the Pantomime," he moved from "silent oaths" against "the race that slew its Lord" to a recognition that Christianity emerged from Judaism and that Jews remained an extraordinary people. More important, he adopted a pluralistic view of religion—one more commonly found in the 20th century—urging Christians "to find meaning in beliefs which are different from their own."[15]

Ralph Waldo Emerson, perhaps Boston's greatest 19th-century sage (and Louis Brandeis's favorite Boston author), once compared Jewish Law to "Evil" and Judaism to a disease. Commenting on "A Sketch of a Polish Jew" shown at an 1839 Boston exhibition of pictures painted by Washington Allston, he remarked to his diary that "the Polish Jews are an offence to me; they degrade and animalize." In his public address on "Fate" he declared, foreshadowing the late 19th-century myth of a worldwide Jewish conspiracy associated with the "Elders of Zion," that "the sufference which is the badge of the Jew has made him, in these days, the ruler of rulers of the earth." Yet in a later lecture, delivered in 1869, Emerson put forth a different view: "You cannot bring me too good a word, too dazzling a hope, too penetrating an insight from the Jews," he declared. "I hail every one with delight." Just a few months earlier he had indeed hailed ("All Hail! You have written a noble poem, which I cannot enough praise") a volume by the Jewish poet Emma Lazarus, whose work he had been encouraging and whom he subsequently welcomed to his home in Concord. Emerson thus embodied the contradictions and ambivalences that quite generally characterized Brahmin views of the Jew during this period. As was also the case elsewhere in the United States, conflicting emotions, changing experiences, and divergent influences pulled people now one way concerning the Jews, now the other.[16]

Mass immigration, first of the Irish and later of the so-called "new immigrants," including Southern Italians and Jews, transformed the Boston that the city's old families knew and gradually undermined their confidence. The optimistic Yankee humanitarian belief in the power of education and democracy to effect immigrant uplift gave way to devouring fear: some members of old-line families came to believe that their race, their country, and their whole way of life was imperilled. By the late 19th century, Henry Adams and Henry James had turned venomously anti-Jewish. The poet James Russell Lowell became obsessed with Jews: he sought them out and avoided them, defended them and attacked them, admired them and feared them. His uncertainties, Barbara Solomon has pointed out, paralleled his feelings about America in general and reflected the social and intellectual concerns of his age.[17] Seeking to protect the world they had known, old-line Bostonians withdrew into themselves; their social institutions kept the Irish, the Jews, and other immigrants out. The Boston *Social Register* (1891), a listing of some 8,000 "proper Bostonians," provided a reliable guide to the chosen ones whom high society favored. Revealingly, it included fewer than a dozen Catholic families and exactly one Jewish man, Louis Brandeis. Brandeis was also the only Jewish member of the Dedham Polo Club. Yet notwithstanding his Harvard degree, his pedigreed law partner, his

Yankee ways, his intellectual eminence, and his growing wealth, Brandeis was still excluded from at least four other exclusive clubs—as was every other Boston Jew. "Antisemitism," he complained to his brother some years later, "seems to have reached its American pinnacle here."[18]

For the Jewish masses, of course, this kind of social antisemitism meant very little. They had neither the money nor the inclination to join high society and felt content to live amongst themselves. When, however, the Brahmin-dominated Immigration Restriction League promoted a literacy test to keep additional immigrants from America's shores, or when over fifty elite Bostonians signed a 1916 petition seeking to prevent Louis Brandeis, their hero, from winning Senate confirmation to the Supreme Court ("He has not the confidence of the people," they alleged), or when their own children found themselves excluded from prestigious jobs on account of their "race," they understood that "intolerance" and "ill-treatment" of the kind Schindler disclaimed had in fact come to pass. Even Mary Antin, whose paean to Boston in *The Promised Land* sought to rekindle faith that "in America everything is possible," lost some of her youthful optimism after World War I.[19]

More directly troubling to the masses of Jews in the immigrant neighborhoods of Boston was the reception that they met at the hands of their neighbors, particularly the Irish, and to a lesser extent the Italians. Both groups were Catholic, and as the Boston settlement house director Robert Woods wrote in 1902, "They can love each other for their common enmity to the Jew." In the early years of the West End, Jews and gentiles of a young age still played together. "We were a cosmopolitan gang," Isaac Goldberg recalled of his boyhood friends around the turn of the century. "There were Italians, Scotch, Irish, Bohemians, Jews, and nondescripts . . . We knew nothing of racial prejudice . . . Later our education would be completed by our parents; we would learn to hate one another as befits members of a Christian civilization." Those who grew up later, however, remembered a more Balkanized Boston, where Jews lived within their own boundaries and faced consequences if they ventured out. Journalist Theodore H. White, for example, recalled living in "an enclave surrounded by Irish" during his youth in the 1920's. The local library lay in an Irish district, and his "first fights happened en route to the library" to get books. "Pure hellishness divided us," he recollected, but looking back he concluded that "even where the friction between the groups was greatest . . . it was not intolerable."[20]

Jews, of course, were not the only targets of young toughs. Fights between the Irish and the Italians were legion as well. "For years," according to one student of the subject, "it was not considered safe for a young Italian to set foot in Charlestown, and the young Irishman who ventured into the North End found himself in similar jeopardy."[21] To a considerable degree, these battles among Boston's young people reflected the political battles then being waged by their elders over turf, power, and social advancement.

Anti-Jewish violence peaked in Boston during the hard years of the Depression and the Second World War. Fear stalked the Jewish community at that time and senseless acts of violence abounded. Nat Hentoff recalls a typical episode in his autobiography, *Boston Boy.*

> *One evening, three friends and I are walking through large, dark Franklin Park on the way to a dance at the Hebrew school. Coming toward us are four bigger boys. When they are close enough, it is clear they are not Jewish. And since they are not Italian, they are Irish. Their leader swaggers up to me and asks—what else? —"Are you Jewish?" Since there are other members of my tribe with me . . . I nod.*
>
> *"You got a light?" he asks.*
>
> *As I go to my pocket, I look down, and a stone, a huge stone, smashes into my face. Or so it feels. The shock and pain are such that it takes a few moments for me to taste the blood and feel the space where, a second ago, there had been a tooth. Their leader, rubbing his fist with satisfaction, waits for a revengeful lunge and is not surprised when it doesn't come. So few of these kikes fight back. He and his sturdy companions move on, guffawing.*[22]

Economic tensions and jealousies underlay some of this violence. Cultural and political differences between Catholics and Jews, exacerbated by the New Deal, the Spanish Civil War, Catholic isolationism, and the Church's fear of communism also played a significant role. The man who fully exploited these tensions and in the process attracted a large local following was Father Charles E. Coughlin, a demagogic radio priest from Royal Oak, Michigan. His call to "drive the Money-changers from the Temple," his scurrilous attacks upon New Dealers, and his fulminations against "International Bankers" struck sympathetic chords in Catholic Boston—as they did in many other cities where Jews and Catholics lived side by side. In 1935, Coughlin was the guest of the Boston City Council and the Massachusetts legislature; a year later his Union Party ran stronger in Boston than in any other American city. Thereafter, beginning in 1938, his antisemitism became increasingly overt and raucously strident. He linked communism and atheism with "Jewish internationalism," reprinted the *Protocols of the Elders of Zion,* and embraced fascism. He also established the Christian Front, a quasi-military pro-fascist organization whose rallies often ended with the Nazi salute. Cries of "liquidate the Jews in America" were heard at some of these rallies. The brutal attacks on local Jews that took place in Boston over the next five years were frequently carried out by Christian Front members.[23]

What particularly disappointed Boston's Jewish community at this time was the tepid response to local antisemitism on the part of politicians and Catholic church leaders. In Boston, more than in other cities, politicians, priests, and policemen shared common family ties and common roots in Irish soil. Having themselves been oppressed, both in their homeland and in Boston, the Catholic Irish and their leaders now banded together to protect their own. Their silence allowed *Social Justice*, the Coughlinite newspaper, to be sold outside of Boston's Catholic churches until the government suppressed it for sedition in 1942. Their acquiescence, also in 1942, paved the way for the notoriously antisemitic pro-Coughlin editor of the Brooklyn *Tablet*, Father Edward Lodge Curran, to appear as principal speaker at South Boston's Evacuation Day Program. Cardinal O'Connell specifically sanctioned Curran's appearance, and two thousand people turned out to greet him. Worst of all, their hands-off attitude meant that physical attacks on Jews throughout Dorchester and Mattapan continued. In October 1943, two young Jewish victims of such violence were themselves taken into custody when they protested the refusal of police officers to arrest their assailants. One was severely beaten by an officer who called him a "yellow Jew," and both were prosecuted and fined ten dollars. The incident, coming as it did against the backdrop of Nazi atrocities throughout Europe, received extensive press coverage and generated a public outcry. The young Irish dissident Frances Sweeney, editor of the *Boston City Reporter* and a courageous spokeswoman for liberal Catholics opposed to fascism and antisemitism, blamed "Governor Saltonstall, Mayor Tobin, the church and the clergy" for giving the Christian Front indirect encouragement. Reputedly, she also labelled Boston "the most anti-Semitic city in the country." As investigations multiplied and Boston's police commissioner lost his job, the local conspiracy of silence gave way to concerted action. Once that happened, incidents of antisemitism in the city dropped dramatically.[24]

The 1944 appointment of Richard Cushing to serve as Boston's Archbishop—he was, at the time, the youngest such prelate in the world—did much to improve intergroup relations throughout the city. Within months of his ascension, he vigorously condemned antisemitism and ordered his priests to oppose all forms of discrimination. Setting a personal example, he himself befriended local Jews and cooperated with the Boston Jewish Community Council. He boasted that his own sister had married a Jewish man.

A Cambridge priest, Father Leonard Feeney, dissented from Cushing's liberal policies on theological grounds. He opposed improving relations with non-Catholics and particularly rallied his followers against Jews, whom he characterized as "horrid, degenerate hook-nosed perverts." On one occasion, he publicly compared Temple Israel's Rabbi Joshua Loth Liebman to a "dog"; later, he threatened to disrupt the opening of the Catholic chapel at Brandeis University. His followers, meanwhile, perpetrated attacks against young Jews around Franklin Park. In response to Jewish pleas for help, Cushing, unlike his predecessors, acted decisively. In 1949 Feeney was dismissed from the Jesuit order; in 1954 he was excommunicated.[25]

Subsequent decades in Boston witnessed the breakup of Catholic ethnic parishes, the weakening of ethnic politics, the religious revolution wrought by Vatican II, the burgeoning impact of suburbanization, and widespread socioeconomic improvements for Jews, Irish and Italians alike. Antisemitism declined nationwide, and in Boston as well. "Today, compared to 40 years ago, there's a love affair between Jews and Catholics," Philip Perlmutter, executive director of the Jewish Community Relations Council, reported in 1985.[26] Although issues such as Sunday closing laws, state aid to parochial schools, public celebrations of Christmas, and the right to an abortion continued to divide Jews and Catholics, the commonality of political and economic interests that drew members of the two faiths together proved far more important.

The anti-Jewish violence that broke out in Dorchester and Mattapan in the late 1960's and early 1970's disrupted this improving era of community relations between Jews and their neighbors. Robberies, muggings, and assaults became daily occurrences; once again, Jews felt afraid to leave their homes. "I was held up four times," one elderly Jewish woman complained. "The first two times they only took my money; the last two times they beat me up and threw me on the street." The perpetrators of violence this time were not Irish Catholic members of the Christian Front or supporters of Father Feeney, but rather young blacks, many of them newcomers to the neighborhood. Their victims were most commonly poor and elderly Jews who remained behind in Dorchester and Mattapan after the bulk of the Jewish population had moved away to the suburbs. As had been true three decades earlier, so now Jews felt that public officials ignored their plight. The Jewish community, too, was slow to react; racial tensions in the city were bad enough, some Jewish leaders felt, without further inflaming them. In the end, the Jewish community succumbed to the inevitable. "We urged all the Jews to get the hell out of there as quickly as they can," one local Jewish leader later recalled. With help from the Combined Jewish Philanthropies, Jewish social service agencies helped the remaining few thousand Jews to relocate.[27]

If Boston never proved to be as harmonious or tolerant a place for Jews as Rabbi Solomon Schindler had expected back in 1889, it did live up to its reputation for nurturing and cultivating the life of the mind. Schindler himself described the city as "the literary centre of America." Fifteen years earlier, a Hebrew guidebook published in Berlin employed the better-known phrase, "the Athens of America," and also described the city as "the nation's foremost seat of wisdom and learning." According to a popular 19th-century aphorism, the typical query asked about someone in Boston was "How much does he know?" In time, this became the city's defining characteristic in Jewish eyes as well.[28]

As early as 1903, the social worker Frederick Bushée noticed that "among some of the Jewish families [in Boston] education seems to be more highly prized than it is by any other nationality." Himself a devoted immigration restrictionist, he was profoundly ambivalent about this discovery. Jews, by contrast, gloried in the "intellectuality" with which they were stereotyped. Mary Antin, author of Boston's best-known Jewish immigrant autobiography, for example, laid heavy stress on education as the key to the promise of the "Promised Land." School became her surrogate house of worship, while for her father, "education, culture, [and] the higher life were shining things to be worshipped from afar." By contrast—as if to confirm the adage that New Yorkers care less about what you know than about how much you are worth—the hero of Abraham Cahan's famous Jewish immigrant novel of 1917, *The Rise of David Levinsky* (set in New York), never secured his dream of higher education; he was too busy getting rich.[29]

Boston Latin School served as the first gateway for many of the young Jewish boys who prized education. Theodore White remembered it as an excellent but "cruel school." "It accepted students without discrimination, and it flunked them—Irish, Italians, Jewish, Protestant, black—with equal lack of discrimination." White was among those who struggled on, and he was not alone. A 1985 roster of ten famous Latin School students ("a distinguished gallery of old boys"), published to celebrate the schools's three hundred and fiftieth anniversary, is fifty percent Jewish. All five of the Jews listed—Bernard Berenson, Leonard Bernstein, Nat Hentoff, Robert Coles, and Theodore H. White—were among the school's recent (since

1885) graduates. Their achievements made them part of a Latin School tradition made famous by the five earlier names on the list: Cotton Mather, Ben Franklin, Sam Adams, Ralph Waldo Emerson, and Samuel P. Langley.[30]

It was Harvard, however, that truly symbolized success to the Jews of Boston. Embodying as it still does "so much of the city's body and soul," Harvard, particularly the Harvard shaped by its liberal, philosemitic president, Charles Eliot (1869–1909), became for Jews what it had long been for "Proper Bostonians"—a major part of their "total existence."[31] To enter the hallowed halls of Harvard became a sacred rite of initiation for Jews, a sign that they had been accepted into the priesthood of the intellectual elect. Even if they remained social outcasts as students, as many Harvard Jews did, the fact that they had successfully passed through the university's portals gave them a feeling of both superiority and belonging: Harvard was now their school as well. Indeed Harvard came to serve as something of a barometer of Jewish social acceptance within the city as a whole. Thus when Eliot's successor, the Judeophobic A. Lawrence Lowell, sought to place a quota on Jewish admissions in 1922, all of Boston Jewry felt the slap. When, in later years, Harvard returned to merit-based admissions, appointed more and more Jews to its faculty, added Jewish Studies courses to its curriculum, and invited Jews to fill upper level administrative positions, Boston Jews knew that for them, too, a whole new day had dawned.[32]

This relationship between Harvard University and Boston Jewry—reflecting on the one hand a marked congruence between Brahmin values and Jewish values and on the other hand an age-old tension between Hellenism and Hebraism—strikes at the heart of what is distinctive about Jewish Boston: its enchantment with the life of the mind. Boston Jewry's most enduring contributions lie in this realm, and many of its most creative intellectual figures devoted their lives to the quest for synthesis, seeking to reconcile, as it were, the two great traditions to which they fell heir.

Three examples must suffice. The Harvard Menorah Society, founded in 1906 for "the study and promotion of Hebraic ideals," explicitly sought to bridge the world of the university and the world of the Jew. Its leaders, Henry Hurwitz and Horace Kallen, both Boston-bred and Harvard-educated, sought to "make Jewish culture respectable among educated Americans." The secular Jewish culture that they envisaged formed the basis for the Intercollegiate Menorah Movement that Hurwitz promoted to his dying day.[33] Louis Brandeis, the very embodiment of those values that one associates with Jewish Boston, found in the Zionist movement the magic synthesis that could link Americanism and Judaism. His creative reinterpretation of Zionism in staunchly American terms legitimated the movement and helped pave the way for its subsequent dramatic acceptance and growth. Finally, Harry Wolfson, the pioneering Jewish scholar whom local Jews revered as "the sage of Harvard," found his synthesis in the study of philosophy. Having mastered both the Greek and the Jewish philosophic traditions, he not only delineated their harmonization, as achieved by Philo of Alexandria, but also pointed to the centrality of Judaism within the larger community of philosophic thought that included Christianity and Islam.[34]

Liberalism underlay all of these creative syntheses, and that is no accident. For it was the great 19th-century Brahmin liberals, like Charles Eliot, who seemed most welcoming to Jews, while conservative restrictionists and conservative Catholics persecuted and excluded them. Temple Israel's rabbis, Solomon Schindler and Charles Fleischer, preached liberalism in the late 19th century; Louis Brandeis and his circle helped to shape American Progressivism in the early 20th century; Louis Kirstein, the Filene brothers, David Niles, and Felix Frankfurter galvanized the forces of Boston liberalism in support of Franklin D. Roosevelt during the Great Depression; and Michael Walzer, Leonard Fein, and Steven Grossman, among others, continued to uphold the torch of liberalism into the 1990's. Liberalism, indeed, forms part of the ethos of Boston's Jews—so much so that some Boston Jews consider its values to be intrinsic to Judaism itself. While far from the truth, the assumption is nevertheless revealing, providing as it does yet another example of the local penchant for synthesizing two worlds into one.

Learning is an even more important part of the local Jewish ethos. Through the years, the great heroes of Boston Jewry have been its intellectuals and scholars—the "smart set" as Stephen Whitfield dubs them in his essay in this volume. Louis Brandeis, for example, was long remembered for having achieved the highest scholastic record of any Harvard Law School student (as well as a special dispensation from the Board of Trustees allowing him to graduate at a younger age than the rules allowed). Harry Wolfson, it was said, "dazzle[d] old John Harvard with his magnitude of brains." Rabbi Joseph B. Soloveitchik, according to an opinion cited in the *New York Times,* was one of the half dozen most brilliant rabbinic scholars "since Maimonides in the 13th century."[35] Such luminaries commanded reverential followings in Boston. Not only were their public lectures hugely attended, but they themselves became communal role models and the objects of extraordinary veneration. It was precisely this kind of veneration that a newcomer to Boston, Abram L. Sachar, drew upon when he argued that American Jews needed a new university of their own. What he and a phalanx of Boston and New England Jews envisaged in 1948 was a high quality secular university, a kind of Jewish Harvard, sponsored by the American Jewish community and named for Louis Brandeis himself—the ultimate synthesis, in short, of American and Jew.

Today, no community has more colleges and universities in its midst than Boston does, and none boasts so high a proportion of Jewish academics and students among its population. The city has become a focal point for Jewish student activities of every sort: social, political, cultural, and religious. It also serves as home to the Association for Jewish Studies, the professional organization of Jewish scholars established in 1969. For all that it is educationally well-endowed, however, we have seen that Boston is in other ways embarrassingly impoverished compared to kindred American Jewish cities of its size. It is neither as old, nor as rich, nor as invested in national Jewish institutions as most of its East Coast cousins, and the relationship between Jews and their neighbors in the city has often been deeply troubled.

What the best local Jewish minds sought nevertheless to accomplish, as Hurwitz and Kallen did through the Harvard Menorah Society and Brandeis through Zionism, was to forge a creative synthesis between Boston and Jew, a mélange that, they hoped, would combine the best features of each culture—"Athens" and "Jerusalem"—and make Jews feel welcome in both. Most of the chapters that follow in this volume are, in effect, analyses of this optimistic experiment. They explore how in different historical periods and communal settings the interaction between Boston and Jew played out. Was synthesis possible and was it effected? No final verdicts are rendered here; the question is left hanging. But even to pose the question is to suggest how the history of Jews in Boston might take on some larger significance.

# *Notes*

1. Sam Bass Warner, Jr., *Province of Reason* (Cambridge: Belknap Press of Harvard University Press, 1984), 2.

2. Oscar Handlin, *Boston's Immigrants* (New York: Atheneum, 1971), 12, 25; Gilbert Osofsky, "Abolitionists, Irish Immigrants and the Dilemmas of Romantic Nationalism," *American Historical Review* 80 (1975): 889.

3. Judith E. Endelman, *The Jewish Community of Indianapolis* (Bloomington: Indiana University Press, 1984), 3; John Higham, *Send These to Me* (Baltimore: Johns Hopkins University Press, 1984), 142–144; Jonathan D. Sarna and Nancy H. Klein, *The Jews of Cincinnati* (Cincinnati: Center for the Study of the American Jewish Experience, 1989), 7.

4. Timothy J. Meagher, "'Immigration Through the Port of Boston': A Comment," in *Forgotten Doors,* ed. M. Mark Stolarik (Philadelphia: Balch Institute Press, 1988), 27; Gunter Moltmann, "The Pattern of German Emigration to the United States in the Nineteenth Century," in *America and the Germans,* ed. Frank Trommler and Joseph McVeigh (Philadelphia: University of Pennsylvania Press, 1985), vol. 1, 21.

5. Jacob R. Marcus, *To Count a People* (Lanham, Md: University Press of America, 1990); Sarna and Klein, *Jews of Cincinnati,* 181; Stephen G. Mostov, "A Sociological Portrait of German Jewish Immigrants in Boston: 1845–1861," *AJS Review* 3 (1978): 125–26.

6. Mostov, "A Sociological Portrait," 150.

7. Albert Ehrenfried, *A Chronicle of Boston Jewry* (Boston: Privately printed, 1963), 372–73; *Statistics of the Jews of the United States* (Philadelphia: Union of American Hebrew Congregations, 1880), 7.

8. Solomon Schindler, *Israelites in Boston* (Boston: Berwick & Smith, 1889), chap. 2; Rudolf Glanz, "Vanguard to the Russians: The Poseners in America," *YIVO Annual* 18 (1983): 20–21.

9. One exchange from the Hebrew journal *Ha-Shahar* is reprinted in translation in Ehrenfried, *Chronicle of Boston Jewry,* 430–431; see also Harvey A. Richman, "The Image of America in the European Hebrew Periodicals of the Nineteenth Century" (Ph.D. diss., University of Texas, 1971). On Reinherz, see Zvi Hirsch Masliansky, *Zichronot* (New York: Hebrew Publishing Company, 1929), 196, translated in Gary P. Zola, "The People's Preacher: A Study in the Life and Writings of Zvi Hirsch Masliansky" (Ordination thesis, Hebrew Union College-Jewish Institute of Religion, 1982), 196–97; and Ben-Zion Eisenstadt, *Israel Scholars in America* (New York: A. H. Rosenberg, 1903), 102 (in Hebrew).

10. Quoted in Arthur Mann (ed.), *Growth and Achievement: Temple Israel* (Cambridge: Riverside Press, 1954), 33; see Jacob Neusner, "The Impact of Immigration and Philanthropy Upon the Boston Jewish Community (1880–1914)," *Publications of the American Jewish Historical Society* 46 (December 1956): 71–85.

11. Barbara Miller Solomon, *Pioneers in Service* (Boston: Associated Jewish Philanthropies, 1956), 12–71, 176–79.

12. Mann, *Growth and Achievement,* 35, 87.

13. See Mark Raider's essay in this volume.

14. Schindler, *Israelites in Boston,* unpaginated [p.2]; Mann, *Growth and Achievement,* 48.

15. Eugene R. Fingerhut, "Were the Massachusetts Puritans Hebraic?" *New England Quarterly* 40 (December 1967): 521–31; Oliver Wendell Holmes, *Over the Teacups* (Boston: Houghton Mifflin, 1891), 193–99; Louis Harap, *The Image of the Jew in American Literature from Early Republic to Mass Immigration* (Philadelphia: Jewish Publication Society, 1974), 87–90; see Jonathan D. Sarna, "The 'Mythical Jew' and the 'Jew Next Door' in Nineteenth Century America," in *Antisemitism in American History,* ed. David A. Gerber (Urbana: University of Illinois Press, 1986), 68–69, from which some of this paragraph is drawn.

16. Alfred R. Ferguson (ed.), *The Journals and Miscellaneous Notebooks of Ralph Waldo Emerson* (Cambridge: Belknap Press of Harvard University Press, 1964), vol. 4, 6, 8; vol. 7, 221–22; Harap, *Image of the Jew in American Literature,* 102-104; Jonathan D. Sarna, "American Antisemitism," in *History and Hate,* ed. David Berger (Philadelphia: Jewish Publication Society, 1986), 118–23; Philippa Strum, *Louis D. Brandeis* (New York: Schocken, 1984), 16.

17. Martin Duberman, *James Russell Lowell* (Boston: 1966), 307–10; Barbara M. Solomon, *Ancestors and Immigrants* (Chicago: University of Chicago Press, 1972), 17–20; Harap, *Image of the Jew,* 96–99; Sarna, "The 'Mythical Jew' and the 'Jew Next Door,'" 61.

18. Cleveland Amory, *The Proper Bostonians* (New York: Dutton, 1947), 13; Allon Gal, *Brandeis of Boston* (Cambridge: Harvard University Press, 1980), 29-43.

19. Solomon, *Ancestors and Immigrants,* 115–19, 195–202; A. L. Todd, *Justice on Trial* (New York: McGraw Hill, 1964), 106; Mary Antin, *The Promised Land* (Boston: Houghton Mifflin, 1969 [1912]), xiii, 352; Warner, *Province of Reason,* 31-33.

20. Robert Woods, quoted in Jack Beatty, *The Rascal King: The Life and Times of James Michael Curley* (Reading, Mass.: Addison-Wesley Publishing Company, 1992), 449; Isaac Goldberg, "A Boston Boyhood," in *The Many Voices of Boston,* ed. Howard Mumford Jones and Bessie Zaban Jones (Boston: Little, Brown, 1975), 347; Theodore H. White, *In Search of History* (New York: Harper & Row, 1978), 28.

21. William Foot Whyte, "Race Conflicts in the North End of Boston," in *The Many Voices of Boston,* 332.

22. Nat Hentoff, *Boston Boy* (New York: Knopf, 1986), 21.

23. John F. Stack, Jr. *International Conflict in an American City* (Westport, Conn.: Greenwood Press, 1979), 87–103, 128–42; Charles J. Tull, *Father Coughlin and the New Deal* (Syracuse: Syracuse University Press, 1965); Leonard Dinnerstein, *Antisemitism in America* (New York: Oxford Univerity Press, 1994), 115–23; Alan Brinkley, *Voices of Protest* (New York: Vintage, 1983), 121–22, 269–73.

24. Stack, *International Conflict*, 128–139; Beatty, *The Rascal King*, 449–55; Hentoff, *Boston Boy*, 17–19, 65–72.

25. Hillel Levine and Lawrence Harmon, *The Death of an American Jewish Community* (New York: Free Press, 1992), 38; *Boston Globe*, 18 February 1985, 14; James Hennesey, *American Catholics* (New York: Oxford University Press, 1981), 300; Abram L. Sachar, *A Host at Last* (Boston: Little, Brown, 1976), 71–72.

26. *Boston Globe*, 18 February 1985, 14.

27. Yona Ginsberg, *Jews in a Changing Neighborhood* (New York: Free Press, 1975), 115; Levine and Harmon, *Death of an American Jewish Community*, 319.

28. Schindler, *Israelites in Boston*, unpaginated [p.19]; Aaron Judah Loeb [Leon] Horowitz, *Tuv Artsot Ha-Berit* (Berlin: 1874), 10 [bound with his *Rumanyah ve-Amerikah*]; Morton Keller, *Historical Sources of Urban Personality: Boston, New York, Philadelphia* (London: Oxford University Press, 1982), 5.

29. Frederick Bushée, *Ethnic Factors in the Population of Boston* (New York: Arno, 1970 [1903]), 21; Solomon, *Ancestors and Immigrants*, 168–70; Antin, *Promised Land*, 204.

30. White, *In Search of History*, 34; "A Distinguished Gallery of Old Boys," *Smithsonian* (April 1985), reprinted in Hentoff, *Boston Boy*, 36.

31. Amory, *Proper Bostonians*, 292; *Imagining Boston: A Literary Landscape* (Boston: Beacon Press, 1990), 331.

32. Nitza Rosovsky, *The Jewish Experience at Harvard and Radcliffe* (Boston: 1986); Henry L. Feingold, "Investing in Themselves: The Harvard Case and the Origins of the Third American-Jewish Commercial Elite," *American Jewish History* 77 (June 1988): 530–53; Donald Altschiller, "The Veritas About Harvard's Jews," *Genesis* 2 9 (September 1977): 1,6,7.

33. Susanne Klingenstein, *Jews in the American Academy* (New Haven: Yale Univerity Press, 1991), 41–43; Elinor Grumet, "Menorah Association," in *Jewish American Voluntary Organizations*, ed. Michael N. Dobkowski (New York: Greenwood Press, 1986), 321–24; Jenna Weissman Joselit, "Without Ghettoism: A History of the Intercollegiate Menorah Association, 1906–1930," *American Jewish Archives* 30 (November 1978): 133–54.

34. Jonathan D. Sarna, "'The Greatest Jew in the World Since Jesus Christ': The Jewish Legacy of Louis D. Brandeis," *American Jewish History* 81 (Spring/Summer 1994): 346–364; Klingenstein, *Jews in the American Academy*, 18-33; Leo W. Schwartz, *Wolfson of Harvard* (Philadelphia: Jewish Publication Society, 1978).

35. Strum, *Louis D. Brandeis*, 18; Schwarz, *Wolfson of Harvard*, 225; *New York Times*, 23 June 1972, as quoted in *Jewish Action* 53 (Summer 1993): 22.

# Strangers and Sojourners:
# The Jews of Colonial Boston

*Overleaf:* Quincy Market between South
and North Market Streets, engraving.
*Private collection.*

ELLEN SMITH

# Strangers and Sojourners:
## The Jews of Colonial Boston

גר־ותושב אנכי עמבם

"I am a resident alien among you."

GENESIS 23:4

N AN EARLY SPRING DAY in April 1649, a ship docked in Boston harbor carrying cargo for Edward Gibbons, Major-General of the local militia. Accompanying Gibbons's cargo was the Jewish scholar and trader, Solomon Franco, agent for the Dutch merchant Immanuel Perada. Franco disembarked in Boston with Gibbons's supplies, but confusion arose as to whether Gibbons or Perada owed Franco his pay. The local court determined the responsibility was not Gibbons's, and when the ship left Boston for Holland, it left an angry and unpaid Solomon Franco behind.

Franco had little recourse. By law, newcomers to most English colonial towns became the town's financial responsibility if the newcomers could not support themselves. Towns therefore required "strangers" to post a bond upon their arrival. If no bond was posted, towns usually provided temporary financial support for newcomers and "warned" them out of town. Franco, with no intentions of settling in Boston permanently, posted no bond and was duly "warned out" by the Boston court. Recognizing that Franco had not received his expected salary from the Gibbons consignment, the vote allowed

> *the said Solomon Franco six shillings p weeke out of the treasury for tenn weekes for his subsistance till he cann gett his passage to Holland, so as he doe it with that time.*[1]

Franco found passage, and Boston's first Jew of record sailed off within three months of his arrival.

Yet in several respects, Solomon Franco's sojourn typifies the experience of many Jews in Boston during the 17th and 18th centuries. Like Franco, most Jews who came to the area were Sephardic traders, allied with the broad network of English, Dutch, and Italian merchants who helped link Europe, the West Indies, Africa, and the North American colonies through commerce, trade, and family connections. Like Franco, too, most of Boston's early Jewish settlers only made Boston a temporary home. And like Franco, their time in Boston was spent in the absence of a permanent Jewish community or Jewish institutions.

Solomon Franco never harbored the intention of settling permanently in the Boston area. He therefore never faced the complex issues of creating a life in Boston as both a Bostonian and a Jew. But Jewish settlers to follow continuously wrestled with the dual identity. Some would leave their Judaism behind entirely. Others would forge identities as civic and as Jewish leaders. All would know the ambiguity, as did their forefather Abraham, of being עמכם . . . גר־ותושב, "a resident alien among you."

The lack of a permanent Jewish community made Boston unique among major eastern seaboard towns in the 17th and 18th centuries, the result of a variety of contributing factors.

Jewish immigration to British North American colonies was discouraged altogether throughout most of the 17th century. The expulsion of the Jews from England in 1290 left few Jews with British citizenship available or welcome to settle in the British North American colonies even three and a half centuries later. Jews who did settle in the West generally chose the more receptive Dutch colonies in New Amsterdam and the Caribbean islands. With the English Civil War, Jews were readmitted into England and its possessions. But by then, Jews who chose to migrate to British North America tended to select cities where trade centers already linked to the trans-Atlantic trade routes were well established.

Boston, perhaps surprisingly, did not rank high on those lists. The Massachusetts Bay Colony had been founded in 1630 in part to advance British trading interests. But the colony did not succeed on the scale of New York, Pennsylvania, Virginia, Georgia, or the Carolinas. No large-scale crops or industries emerged to form the foundation of a strong export economy. Massachusetts evolved instead as a series of locally linked, agriculturally based communities. Boston thus held little economic appeal to the British or European-based Jewish trading families from whom many New World Jewish immigrants were drawn.

The Massachusetts Bay Colony had also been founded as a religious haven for Puritans, a broad community of reformed Christians who had emigrated from Holland and Britain beginning in 1629. Though probably only half the early colony's residents were Puritans, they dominated civic and church leadership. Seeking to become a model for Congregational Christianity, the Puritan community actively discouraged religious dissension. Throughout the 17th century, many dissenters and religious critics—including Roger Williams, Anne Hutchinson, Samuel Gorton, and Quakers—chose, or were forced, to leave.

Jewish settlers in the New World thus found immigration, economic, and religious opportunities more congenial in the West Indies and the port cities south of Boston. Jews established small but permanent communities in the major colonial cities along the Atlantic coast in New Amsterdam/New York City in 1654, Newport in 1658, Savannah in 1733, Philadelphia in 1737, and Charleston in the 1750's.

And so Boston, uniquely among the major seaport towns in colonial North America, developed in the 17th and 18th centuries without a permanent Jewish community. Important North American Sephardic trading networks never figured prominently in Boston's development as a colonial mercantile and maritime center. Boston's Jewish residents lived there impermanently, without the institutions and communal security of other colonial towns. The lack of a permanent Sephardic community in colonial Boston thus helped shape the city's economic and cultural character in its absence, even as it might have by its presence.

Yet despite the lack of a permanent Jewish community in Boston in the 17th and 18th centuries, New England, as Judge Samuel Sewall observed, was "seldom wholly without them."[2] Jewish traders provided a constant, though never permanent, presence. Their names are retrievable from court, census and tax records, and occasional references in surviving diaries and letters. The names of Jewish women and children are harder to come by. But a sampling of even this scanty evidence gives a sense of the life of Boston's earliest Jews in a city lacking an organized Jewish community, permanent Jewish institutions, or an evolved Jewish leadership.

Among Boston's earliest Jewish residents was Rowland Gideon, "the Jew." Gideon's ancestors were Portuguese *conversos* whose wanderings took them from Lisbon to Brazil, Amsterdam, and Hamburg where Gideon (né Rehiel Abudiente) was born. Gideon migrated to Barbados, working on the family plantations, and by 1674 he had settled in Boston, establishing himself as a merchant in partnership with Daniel Barrow (né Baruch Lousada).

Gideon and Barrow appear sporadically in city documents, including the Boston Court records. In 1674, the pair brought suit in an attempt to recover a £100 debt from a tobacco transaction. The verdict in the case does not survive, but a unique petition does. Gideon, concerned about his unusual status as a Jew in Boston, was at great pains to remind the Court that in

> *comitinge my case to the hondd court & Gentlemen of the Jurye....God command our Fathers that the Same Law should bee for the Stranger & Sowjournner—as for the Israellits.*[3]

The petition focuses the tension Gideon felt being both a Bostonian and a Jew. As a "Stranger," Gideon worried about being awarded full rights under the law. But as a resident, a "Sowjournner," Gideon committed his redress to the Boston courts, confident at some level that despite the ambiguities of his status and identity, justice would be applied. Cognizant of his status as an outsider, Gideon chose in this instance to live as an insider. But his petition expresses an awareness that such a choice yielded no assured guarantees.

Other Jews also sojourned temporarily in Boston in the 17th and 18th centuries. A mulatto Jew, Solomon, was charged in the Essex County court in 1668 for travelling on the Lord's Day. The list of inhabitants for Boston in 1695 includes "Samuel the Jew." The diaries of Samuel Sewall and Cotton Mather mention three Frazon brothers, Joseph, Samuel, and Moses, who maintained a large warehouse in Charlestown and traded with the West Indies. The 1790 list of inhabitants of Boston includes two likely Jewish widows, Mrs. Abrahams and Mrs. Decoster.[4]

More thorough biographies of some of Boston's early Jews are also retrievable. The Sephardic Jewish trader, Isaac Lopez, arrived from London in 1716 and established himself as a merchant. In 1720 he was elected as a constable and paid the customary fine excusing him from service. He erected a timber mill in 1722 on land he purchased near Boston's Wind Mill, but disappears from the records in 1728.

In the 1730's, a famous and unruly partnership was established between two Jewish merchants: Isaac Solomon and Michael Asher. Asher arrived from New York City in 1716 and lived in the South End on Newberry (now Washington) Street, where he and Solomon operated a snuff mill. The pair served as Boston agents for several New York City merchants, including Mordecai Gomez. Their religion as well as their livelihood linked them to New York: both Asher and Solomon donated regularly to New York's congregation Shearith Israel, Asher paying dues as a member.

But in 1734 their loyalties seemingly changed. The pair purchased land from Joseph Bradford on the east side of Chambers (formerly Shute) Street behind Cambridge Street. There they established a shop and set aside part of the land to be used as a burying place for "the Jewish nation."

The partnership between Asher and Solomon turned acrimonious, however, and

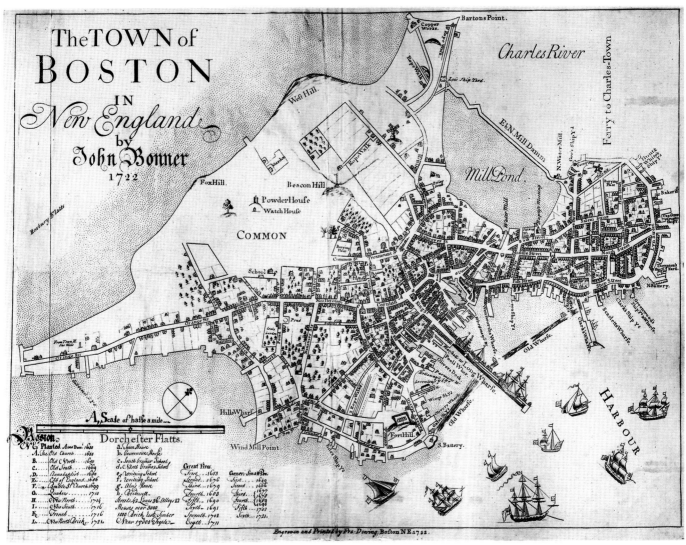

in 1735 Solomon and his wife sold their interest in the property to Asher. Asher forfeited the land, including the cemetery, in 1736. A sale of the property as late as 1750 indicated that the "Burying Ground as it is now fenced in to the Jewish nation" was still intact, but no evidence exists that it was ever used. After 1750, the Jewish cemetery is never referred to again.

Yet the cemetery proposed by Asher and Solomon provides the first surviving evidence of a desire for permanence by Boston's transient Jewish community. Virtually every early Jewish settler in Boston for whom clear records survive had business, family, and religious ties someplace else. Each seems to have been buried in Jewish cemeteries in New York, Newport, or the West Indies. Yet the concern to establish a Jewish cemetery in Boston—and by inference to establish a *chevra kadisha*, a burial society to prepare the dead, oversee their internment, and maintain the cemetery according to strict Jewish law—overrides for the first time the traditional

FIG. 1. John Bonner, "The Town of Boston in New England," Boston 1722. The Wind Mill, near Isaac Lopez's timber mill; Newberry Street, site of Michael Asher and Isaac Solomon's snuff mill; and Cambridge Street are all marked. *Boston Athenæum, Boston, Massachusetts.*

FIG. 2. Hebrew Exercises of William Bradford, ca. 1657, in the manuscript of Bradford's *History of Plimouth Plantation*. Bradford's reasons for studying Hebrew are written in the triangle at the top. *Archives of the Commonwealth of Massachusetts.*

identification with Jewish communities outside Boston. It would be another hundred years before Boston's Jews established a permanent Jewish burying ground in the city. But for the first time, the strangers had indicated a yearning to stay.

Other yearnings to stay—to make Boston a place of refuge and peace—had been expressed in the language and images of the Hebrew Bible by the Puritan founders and settlers of Massachusetts. Puritans had broken with the Church of England in the late 16th century over matters of ritual, congregational polity, and biblical authority. Hounded as dissenters throughout England, many migrated, especially to Holland and New England.

Like Jews, Puritans were men and women of The Book, who sought guidelines for their earthly and spiritual lives in the Bible. Puritan ministers and scholars, teachers and laity, studied the "Old and New Covenants," seeking evidence of the Lord's intentions for their undertakings. Puritans understood themselves to be a new Israel, a persecuted religious group led from Egypt (England) to a Promised Land (New England). Their narratives refer to their journeys as an Exodus, to New England as the New Canaan. Puritan histories described their leaders as biblical prophets and priests.[5]

But the Hebrew Bible was more than metaphor. The Puritans saw in the five Books of Moses clear predictions of the coming of the Christ and the events of the New Testament. The stories, prophesies, and promises in the Hebrew Bible prefigured, for the Puritans, their own physical and spiritual wanderings and pointed to the promises fulfilled for them in the Christian Testament.

The intensity of this study of the Hebrew Bible created among the Puritans a learned group of Hebraic linguists and scholars. When Harvard College was founded in 1636, proficiency in Hebrew was made an entrance requirement and part of the standard curriculum. Harvard's first two presidents, Henry Dunster and Charles Chauncy, were renowned Hebraicists and shared with the College tutors responsibility for instructing undergraduates in Hebrew, Syriac [Aramaic], and Greek. Commencement theses and *quæstiones* recited by the students often incorporated Hebrew or Biblical themes.[6]

Puritan ministers and Harvard students were not the only devotees of Hebrew. At the end of his life, William Bradford, the pilgrim governor of Plimouth Plantation, decided to teach himself Hebrew. On the blank pages at the front of his diary "Of Plimouth Plantation," he practiced Hebrew grammar and transcribed Hebrew texts. In front of his exercises, in the shaky hand of his old age, he explained his motivation.

> *Though I am growne aged, yet I have had a longing desire to see with my own eyes, somthing of that most ancient language, and holy tongue, in which the law and Oracles of God were write; and in which God and the angels spake to the holy patriarchs of old time, and what names were given to things from the creation. And though I cannot attaine to much herein, yet I am refreshed to have seen some glimpse hereof (as Moyses saw the land of Canan a farr of).*[7]

The Hebrew Bible also figured in Puritan worship. Sermons and treatises on "Old Covenant" themes were common throughout the 17th century. The first book published in North America was a book from the Bible: *The Whole Booke of Psalmes.* Printed in 1640 on the press at Cambridge, and more commonly known as *The Bay Psalm Book,* the volume includes rhymed English translations of all of David's psalms, to be sung in church by the congregation, not just read or preached. The Hebrew Bible also informed the Puritans' sense of law and justice. In 1636, the Reverend John Cotton composed a "Draft of the Model of Moses His Judicialls," a set of civil laws based on the Bible which he proposed for the Bay Colony. A version of them was adopted in 1641 as "A Bodie of Liberties."

Puritan interest in the Hebrew Bible was paralleled by interest in the Hebrew peoples themselves. The Puritans believed, as did most Christians of their era, that the Christ's Second Coming and the advent of the Kingdom of Christ would occur only after the conversion of the Jewish nation. Throughout the 16th and 17th centuries a fierce debate waged among Christian scholars as to the method and sequence by which this conversion would take place.

The debate took a more focused turn after the Europeans encountered the native American peoples. Many Christians—Massachusetts Bay's Puritans among them—believed that the Indian nations might be among the lost tribes of Israel. Ministers in Europe and New England corresponded throughout the 17th century

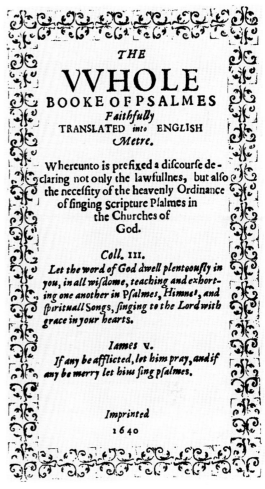

FIG. 3. *The Whole Booke of Psalmes* [Cambridge, New England, Printed by Stephen Daye], 1640. The first book published in North America, the "Bay Psalm Book" was also the first to use Hebrew type, which was specially cut for the volume. *Harvard College Library.*

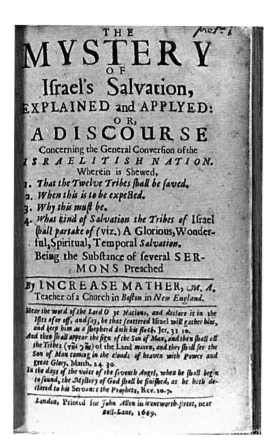

THE
MYSTERY
OF
Ifrael's Salvation,
EXPLAINED and APPLYED:
OR,
A DISCOURSE
Concerning the General Converfion of the
ISRAELITISH NATION.
Wherein is Shewed,
1. That the Twelve Tribes fhall be faved.
2. When this is to be expected.
3. Why this muft be.
4. What kind of Salvation the Tribes of Ifrael
fhall partake of (viz.) A Glorious, Wonder-
ful, Spiritual, Temporal Salvation.
Being the Subftance of feveral SER-
MONS Preached

By INCREASE MATHER, M. A.
Teacher of a Church in Bofton in New England.

Hear the word of the Lord O ye Nations, and declare it in the
Ifles of far off, and fay, he that fcattered Ifrael will gather him,
and keep him as a fhepherd doth his flock, Jer. 31. 10.
And then fhall appear the fign of the Son of Man, and then fhall all
the Tribes (THt 2 me) of the Land mourn, and they fhall fee the
Son of Man coming in the clouds of heaven with Power and
great Glory, Matth. 24. 30.
In the days of the voice of the feventh Angel, when he fhall begin
to found, the Myftery of God fhall be finifhed, as he hath declared to his Servants the Prophets, Rev. 10. 7.

London, Printed for John Allen in Wentworth-ftreet, near
Bell-Lane, 1669.

FIG. 4. Increase Mather, *The Mystery of Israel's Salvation.* London, 1669. Increase Mather's first publication reflects his life-long interest in the relationship between the conversion of the Jewish nation and the "Second Coming of Christ." *American Jewish Historical Society.*

assessing the evidence. The Reverend John Eliot spent his adult lifetime ministering to and evangelizing the Massachusetts tribes. He waivered in his belief that the native American tribes were of Hebrew origins, but never abandoned the possibility completely. In 1650, the Reverend Thomas Thorowgood of Norfolk, England published *Jewes in America* (London), exploring the "Probabilities that the Americans are of that Race" and causing enormous excitement in Europe. Eliot lent his "pro" voice to the preface of the 1660 edition.

Individual Jews in Boston were also prospects for conversion. Samuel Sewall recorded that Reverend Bradstreet baptized "Simon, the Jew" in Charlestown in 1702.[8] Cotton Mather, the grandson of two founding ministers of Boston, and his father, Increase Mather, both wrote extensively on the subject. Increase Mather's *The Mystery of Israel's Salvation* remained for a century the single most influential North American work on "the General Conversion of the Israelitish Nation."[9] Cotton also published works about—and to—the Jews. His private Diary records his "cries: For the conversion of the Jewish Nation," his joy at news of Jews successfully converted, and his bitter disappointment when his own efforts to convert Jews failed.[10] Among his failures was the relentless pursuit of one of the Frazon brothers. One of Mather's arguments for Christianity devolved into trickery, and as Samuel Sewall recorded, "The forgery was so plainly detected that Mr. C. M. confest, after which Mr. Frasier would never be persuaded to hear any more of Xianity."[11]

The 17th century, then, laid the foundation for many of the forces that would later define the Jewish experience in Boston. On the one hand, the Puritans possessed enormous admiration for the Jewish heritage: an academic dedication to the Hebrew Bible, language, and culture; a spiritual affinity for the history and wanderings of the Hebrew tribes. On the other hand, the inhabitants' experience with a living Jewish community was virtually non-existent. The few Jews who sojourned in Boston were deemed occasional prospects for hoped-for conversions. But no organized Jewish community existed to present its own face to the Christian inhabitants, or to support its individual Jews.

Into this vacuum came the Jewish scholar and Hebraicist Judah Monis. Monis's earliest years remain obscure. He was likely born in Italy in 1683, descended from a family of Portuguese *conversos* who moved to the continent in the 16th century. Educated at the Jewish academies in Leghorn, Italy and Amsterdam, Holland, Monis emigrated to British North America. By 1715 he had settled in New York City, where he was running a small store and teaching Hebrew to Christians and Jews. By 1720 he had moved again, this time to Cambridge, Massachusetts.

In Cambridge, encouraged by his friends who considered him "a great master of the Hebrew language," Monis presented his handwritten manual of Hebrew grammar to the officers of Harvard Corporation on June 29, 1720, "for Your Judicious perusall." The Corporation responded favorably, and on April 30, 1722, "Voted, That Mr. Judah Monis be improved as an instructor of the Hebrew Language in the College." Monis replaced the tutors in that role and became the first instructor in Hebrew at Harvard College.[12]

But there was a catch. From the time of his arrival in North America, Monis had corresponded with leading Puritan ministers on issues of Kabbalah, the Trinity, and Christian doctrine. These interests intensified with his move to Cambridge, and under the guidance of local ministers, Monis extended his study of the Christian faith. One month before he assumed his post at Harvard, Judah Monis converted to Christianity.

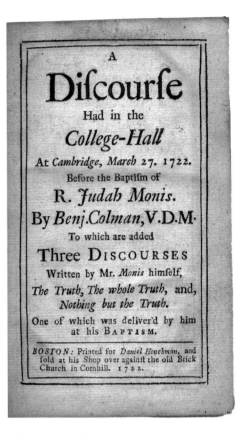

FIG. 5. Benjamin Colman and Judah Monis, *A Discourse . . . Before the Baptism of R. Judah Monis*, bound with *The Truth, The whole Truth, and Nothing but the Truth*. Boston, 1722. American Jewish Historical Society.

Monis's baptism ceremonies took place in College Hall before as "numerous an assembly as the place would admit."[13] An ailing Increase Mather was replaced by the Reverend Benjamin Colman, who delivered the sermon, "Moses a Witness unto our Lord and Saviour Jesus Christ." Monis's own lecture continued the argument. In "The Truth," Monis attempted to prove that Jesus was indeed the Messiah as foretold in the Hebrew Bible. Colman's remarks, a "Preface" by Increase Mather, and *The Truth* were published in Boston in 1722 with two more essays written by Monis: *The whole Truth* (arguing for the divinity of Jesus) and *Nothing but the Truth* (seeking to prove the doctrine of the Trinity).

Monis's conversion to Christianity garnered world-wide attention. Many ministers expressed skepticism, embittered by histories of converted Jews reverting to their original faith, and concerned that the Harvard requirement for its faculty to be Christians may have figured in Monis's decision. But Colman and Increase Mather defended Monis to the world audience. In his "Preface" to *The Truth*, Mather asserted, "There is no cause to fear that Mr. Monis will Renounce his Christianity, since he did embrace it Voluntarily and Gradually, and with much Consideration and from Scriptures in the Old-Testament."[14]

FIG. 6. William Metcalfe, "His Hebrew Grammer," 1724. Manuscript copy of Judah Monis's lectures on Hebrew grammar. Until the publication of Monis's *Grammar of the Hebrew Tongue* in 1735, Monis's students had to copy the text by hand from Monis's copy. Jonathan Belcher indicated on his copy (at the Massachusetts Historical Society) that it took him "about 4 weeks" to transcribe. *American Jewish Historical Society.*

More importantly, Monis defended himself. Recognizing that Jews would not take "the News of my Embracing the Christian Religion" to be "the best you have ever heard," Monis went on to assure them that "my embracing Christianity, was because I was persuaded it is the only Religion wherein I thought I could be saved . . . I did it not rashly, but upon mature thoughts and deliberations." [15]

Judah Monis maintained until the day he died that he converted from conviction, not convenience. He joined the First Church in Cambridge in May 1722, and he remained a lifelong member and supporter. In January 1724 he married Abigail Marret, a Christian woman. Their marriage seems to have given them both comfort, and they conducted their public lives well integrated in the Cambridge Christian community, and well regarded by it.

Monis never earned enough money to support himself and Abigail on his instructor's salary, however, and the Harvard College records track Monis's constant petitioning for increased support. Monis supplemented his income by running a small store in Cambridge, occasionally translating Spanish documents for Massachusetts and Connecticut officials, and eventually receiving grants from the legislature. But his chief concern was to educate the Harvard College students in the Hebrew tongue.

At the beginning of his appointment, all undergraduates were required to take his Hebrew course, "excepting the Freshmen, and Such others as Shalbe Exempted by the President and their respective Tutors." Hebrew was to be taught four days per week, and

> *Every Scholar shalbe obliged to have an Hebrew Bible, or at lest an Hebrew Psaltar, and also an Hebrew Lexicon. Their Hebrew Exercise shalbe as follows, vizt. one Exercise in a week shalbe the writing the Hebrew and Rabbinicall. The rest shalbe in this gradual method, That is to Say, 1. Copying the Grammar and reading. 2. Reciting it and reading. 3. Construing, 4. Parsing, 5. Translating, 6. Composing, z. reading without points.* [16]

Monis's instruction was based on the manuscript Hebrew grammar he had composed in 1720, which students had to copy painstakingly by hand each year. In 1724, Monis began petitioning the College Corporation to publish his Hebrew grammar, and after extended negotiations, the Corporation agreed to underwrite the publication. Hebrew type was sent from London and set on the Cambridge press. In 1735, one thousand copies of Judah Monis's *A Grammar of the Hebrew Tongue* were published, and for the next twenty-five years the book was a required text for Harvard students. Payments for the volume were added automatically to their quarterly bills.

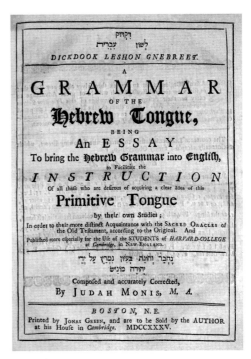

But not even the publication of the *Grammar* increased student enthusiasm for their Hebrew classes. Hebrew had never been popular at Harvard. The relatively short amount of time devoted to Hebrew each week made it difficult to learn the language well. From the 17th century onward, students complained that the exercises and grammar were boring. Surviving copies of Monis's students' manuscript grammars are full of doodles and marginal insults directed at their instructor. Monis's personal style of teaching may not have enhanced undergraduate enthusiasm either. College records show that Monis was frequently hazed by his students and that attendance in his classes was a constant problem.

FIG. 7. Judah Monis, *A Grammar of the Hebrew Tongue*. Boston, 1735. *American Jewish Historical Society.*

Nonetheless, the Corporation supported his efforts. In 1723, the Corporation recorded itself "greatly satisfied w$^{th}$ his assiduity and faithfulness in his instruction, ye surprising effects of them having ben laid before the corporation."[17] But his troubles with undergraduates persisted, and by 1724 College officials returned the teaching of undergraduate Hebrew to the tutors. Monis remained responsible only for teaching the graduate students and College tutors.

FIG. 8. William Burgis, *A Prospect of the Colledges in Cambridge in New England.* Engraving, Boston, 1726. *Boston Athenæum, Boston, Massachusetts.*

Monis produced and proposed a series of additional publications in Hebrew, both to instruct his College students and to assist in the conversion of the Jewish nation. His translations of "The Creed" and "The Lord's Prayer" into Hebrew were included in his *Grammar.* Other ongoing projects (never brought to publication) included a Hebrew-English dictionary, "Nomenclatura hebraica," and translation of the "thirty-nine Articles of the Church of England, and the Assembly's Shorter Catechism into Hebrew. And . . . the Larger Catechism."[18] He also kept a manu-

script of rabbinic Kabbalistic writings, assembled a private collection of Hebrew books, and made broad use of the Hebraic collections in the Harvard College Library.

Monis taught Hebrew at Harvard for thirty-eight years, until his wife's death in 1760. By then, his teaching had dwindled to one weekly class with graduate students and his pay with it. With his own health declining and student interest in his courses flagging, he sold most of his library and retired to the house of his wife's brother-in-law, the Reverend John Martyn, in Northboro. There he joined the Northboro Church, to which he donated three silver communion cups, and where he was voted a seat of honor. He died in Northboro on April 25, 1764, and is buried in the church cemetery. Among his bequests were a silver tankard and cup for use at the communion table, £46 to neighboring ministers, and £156 to a establish a fund for minister's widows, a fund that survived well into the 20th century.

Monis's life presents one example—if an extreme example—of how a Jewish individual made a place for himself in Boston history. Without the support of Jewish institutions, a Jewish community, or even other Jewish individuals, Monis entered the life of Cambridge as a Christian. He consciously chose to do so. Having voluntarily left a mature Jewish community in New York City, Monis came to Cambridge to teach the Hebrew tongue as a Christian. He seems never to have looked back.

But the community sometimes looked on with caution. The Cambridge First Church, contemporary diaries, and the College records often refer to Monis as "the converted Jew," "the converted rabbi," the "Christianized Jew." Church records indicated concern that Monis may have continued observing the Sabbath on Saturdays. And the headstone on his grave bears witness to the double identity by which Monis was understood in his community. The inscription reads, in part: "A native branch of Jacob see. Which, once from off its olive brook,/ Regrafted, from the living tree . . ."

Moses Michael Hays chose a different approach to being a Bostonian and a Jew. Like Judah Monis, he settled in Boston as an adult, in a city without a Jewish population and without Jewish institutions. Like Monis, his life was conducted in "the first circles of society."[19] But unlike Monis, Hays and his family lived their lives publicly as Jews, practicing and proclaiming their faith, and ultimately honored and remembered for it.

Hays was born in New York City on May 9, 1739, the fifth child and second son of Judah Hays and Rebecca Michaels Hays. His parents were Dutch immigrants who arrived in New York City about 1720. Judah was naturalized in 1729 and admitted as a Freeman of New York in 1735. His shop at the corner of Stone and Broad Streets specialized in broadcloth, velvets, linens, and general supplies.

Judah raised Moses to be a shopkeeper and trader, and in 1760, took him into his shipping and retail business. For four years they worked together until Judah's death in 1764. Judah left Moses the business and the largest share of his assets.

Judah left Moses something else as well: a firm grounding in his Jewish faith and responsibilities. Judah had joined New York's Congregation Shearith Israel in 1730, folding his family into the life of New York's Jewish community. Moses served the congregation as second *parnas* (vice-president) in 1766 and *parnas* in 1767. Even after he moved away, Moses retained an attachment to the congregation, appearing on donor lists intermittently throughout his life.

FIG. 9. E.M. Carpenter (after Gilbert Stuart), *Moses Michael Hays* (1739–1805), 1883, Richmond, oil on canvas. The original portrait burned in a house fire. *Grand Lodge of Masons in Massachusetts, Boston.*

In 1766, Moses married Rachel Myers, the younger sister of famed New York silversmith Myer Myers. Admitted as a Freeman in New York in 1769, Moses's business interests nevertheless drew him elsewhere. By 1767 he was already trading with Aaron Lopez of Newport, and by late 1769 Hays and Rachel were living there.

In Newport, Hays entered a business partnership with Meyer Pollack, specializing in shipbuilding, exports, and the manufacture of vinegar. But "by various losses at sea and other inevitable misfortunes,"[20] the partnership became insolvent, and Hays and Pollack were jailed. Under a 1771 law passed for the relief of debtors they liquidated their holdings, and in December of 1771 Hays and Pollack were acquitted and set free. Hays immediately reestablished himself in trade, and in 1772 he was again selling the full range of trans-Atlantic wares: raisins by the cask, Dutch gin and brandy in twelve-bottle cases, jamaica rum, salad oil, bar-iron, ships bread, ysam tea, cinnamon, cloves, nutmegs and mace, white bread, and small kegs of Irish beef and Burlington pork.

The American Revolution brought new sets of difficulties to Hays. In 1775, seventy-six men in Newport were asked to sign a declaration of loyalty to the Ameri-

FIG. 10. James B. Marston, *The Old State House and State Street*, Boston, c.1801, oil on canvas. Moses Michael Hays's offices and the Massachusetts Bank's offices in the American Coffee House can be seen in the right foreground. *Massachusetts Historical Society.*

FIG. 11. Advertisement for Moses Michael Hays's business enterprises. *Bank of Boston.*

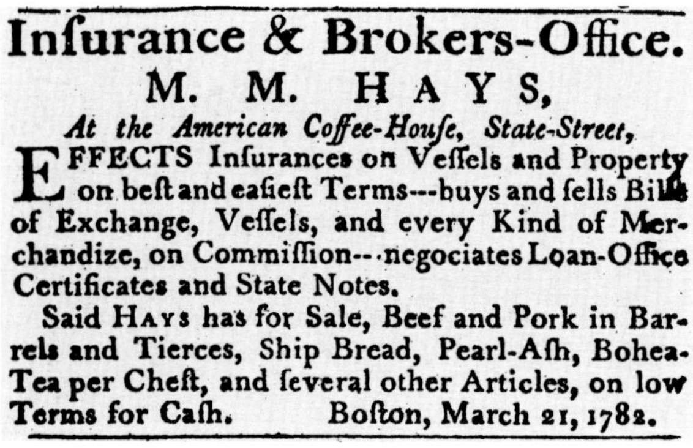

can colonies. The oath included the phrase, "upon the true faith of a Christian." Like Aaron Lopez before him and Abraham Touro to follow, Hays publicly objected to the phrase and refused to sign. A letter he offered in 1776 affirming his belief that the Revolution was a just cause did not suffice. Only when the "oath as a Christian" phrase was omitted did Hays finally agree to sign.

Hays and his family left Newport ahead of the British attack in 1776. By the fall of 1776, the Hayses were living at least part-time in Boston, and by 1782 they had settled there permanently.

Moses Michael Hays arrived in Boston at a time when the city was devastated by the physical and financial effects of the American Revolution. For the next three decades, Hays and his family would play key roles in establishing the financial and cultural institutions that would define post-Revolutionary and 19th-century Boston.

Hays opened a shipping office and warehouse on Long Wharf and an office in the American Cafe building on State Street. He was among the first Boston merchants to turn his eyes to the newly opened markets of the Far East. Hays served as the shipping agent and insurer for dozens of journeys to the Far East and brokered the wares his investments returned.

But an unstable currency and the lack of a recognized Boston bank made international commerce difficult. Hays was among Boston's top business leaders who realized that without secure financial institutions, Boston could not compete in the expanding world markets. In 1784 the Massachusetts legislature passed "An ACT to Establish a Bank." Hays was one of nine men empowered to sell stock and was himself among the bank's original stockholders. On July 5, 1784, the Massachusetts Bank (now the Bank of Boston) opened in the old Manufactory House on Long Acre (now Tremont) at the northerly corner of Hamilton Place. It was the first independent joint-stock bank in the United States and the second bank chartered in Massachusetts.

Hays wasted no time making use of the bank he had helped to create. The Bank's early 20th-century historian records:

*Even on its first business day the Massachusetts Bank received deposits and cashed checks. The first depositor was Moses Michael Hays, who by the close of business on the opening day had deposited over $14,500. The first withdrawal, on the first day, was made by Moses Michael Hays . . . The first discounter was Oliver Wendell . . . and the second was the same Moses Michael Hays, who appears to have been the man who made the greatest use of the facilities of the Massachusetts Bank at its start.[21]*

FIG. 12. The "First Banking House," precursor to the Bank of Boston, in its original location on Long Acre. *Bank of Boston.*

Indeed, the only known recorded criticism surviving against Hays was entered by a bank clerk, who wrote *"Quidnunc"* (busybody) next to a check Hays wrote to himself.[22]

Hays next turned his attention to the creation of an insurance industry. The capacity to insure vessels and their cargoes was outpacing individual merchants' financial abilities, and Hays took a lead in founding the earliest marine and fire insurance companies in Boston. His first attempt in 1784 to organize the Boston fire underwriters failed, but he was involved in 1797 with Paul Revere and fourteen other Boston businessmen in forming the second local fire insurance company, The Massachusetts Mutual Fire Insurance Company. The company was the first to employ agents to sell policies and provided compensation of firemen for distinguished effort. In various forms, the company survived until 1894. Hays was also involved with the founding of the Massachusetts Second Fire Insurance Company (1797) and the Boston Marine Insurance Company (1797).

Hays was also active in a variety of civic projects. He donated to subscriptions for beautifying Boston Common, to building bridges and turnpikes, to the establishment of theaters and banks, and to Harvard College.

FIG. 13. Masonic apron of Moses Michael Hays. *Grand Lodge of Masons in Massachusetts, Boston.*

Hays was instrumental in establishing the Masonic movement in New England. On December 6, 1768, Hays was appointed Deputy Inspector General of the Rite of Perfection for the West Indies and North America, to promote the establishment of that order in the United States. In 1769 he organized, as Master, King David's Lodge of New York City under a warrant issued to him as "a Hebrew of Masonic Distinction." He relocated the Lodge to Newport in 1780, where he served as a member until 1783. His work on behalf of Masonry also took him to Philadelphia and Jamaica, and finally, in 1782, to Boston.

FIG. 14. Paul Revere, Teapot and Creampot, Boston, 1783. Both items bear the monogram "MRH" [Moses and Rachel Hays]. Moses Michael Hays counted Paul Revere among his chief friends. Hays sponsored Revere to serve as Deputy during Hays's second term as Grand Master of the Grand Lodge of Masons. Hays commissioned at least nine pieces of silver from Revere. *American Jewish Historical Society.*

In New York and Newport, Hays led Lodges with significant Jewish membership, many of them his relatives and business partners. Hays's Boston Masonic brothers were likewise business partners and leaders. But when Hays was accepted to the Massachusetts Lodge in November 1782, he joined as the only Jew. It was the first signal that Hays would be accepted into Boston society and fraternity.

Hays served the Lodge with distinction. Between 1782 and 1792 he was elected Master, Junior Grand Warden, and Grand Master. Hays also organized the merger of the two Provincial Grand Lodges in Massachusetts in 1792, creating the Grand Lodge of the Most Ancient and Honorable Society of Free and Accepted Masons for the Commonwealth of Massachusetts.[23]

The Hays family lived on Middle (now Hanover) Street, "one of the fashionable streets of the town," in a large brick home with fifteen rooms and thirty-one windows. The  family filled it to capacity. Moses and Rachel had seven children: Judith, Rebecca, Judah, Sarah (called Sally), Solomon (who died as an infant in 1775), Catherine, and Sloe. In 1784, Moses's sister Reyna Touro, the widow of Rabbi Isaac Touro of Newport, came to live in the house with her three children, Abraham, Judah and Rebecca. When Reyna died in 1787, Moses assumed full responsibility for his nephews and niece. The 1790 Record Commissioners of Boston reports the Hays household as made up of "2 white males, 2 white males under 16, 11 females, 2 other free persons; no slaves."

Others described the heartbeat of the household. Under Hays's roof "dwelt hospitality—it was an asylum for friendship, the mansion of peace."[24] Samuel Joseph May, Louisa May Alcott's grandfather, a Unitarian minister and a leading abolitionist, also had clear memories of the family. May had been a close childhood friend of the Hays and Touro children; his father had been Moses's "friend," "comforter" and "counselor." In his *Memoirs*, May remembered "Uncle and Aunt Hays" for their love of children, their generosity, their high culture, and most importantly, for their pride in their Jewish religion and way of life. In May's recollections, many of the Hays's most admirable qualities resulted from the teachings of their faith.

*If the children of my day were taught, among other foolish things to dread, if not despise Jews, a very different lesson was impressed upon my young heart. . . .*

*[Hays's] house . . . was the abode of hospitality . . . He and his truly good wife were hospitable, not to the rich alone, but also to the poor. Many indigent families were fed regularly from his table. They would come especially after his frequent dinner parties and were sure to be made welcome, not to the crumbs only but to ampler portions of the food that might be left.*

*I was permitted to stay with them several days, and even weeks, together. . . . I witnessed their religious exercise, their fastings and their prayers, and was made to feel that they worshipped the Unseen, Almighty and All-merciful One. Of course I grew up without prejudice against Jews—or any other religionists— because they did not believe as my father and mother believed.*[25]

FIG. 15. Hebrew Bible belonging to Moses Michael Hays. Amsterdam, 1725. *Temple Israel, Boston.*

Moses and Rachel raised their children, nephews and niece as practicing Jews. They conducted regular worship services in their home and the household library contained dozens of Hebrew books. The Jewish obligation to practice charity directed much of what Hays did on behalf of Boston and its citizens.

Moses Michael Hays died intestate in Boston on May 9, 1805, on the 66th anniversary of his birth. Obituaries spoke of the esteem and affection with which Boston society held him. He was remembered as a man of strong intellect, virtue, and benevolence; as a kind husband, an indulgent father, and "a most valuable citizen."[26]

FIG. 16. William King (died ca.1809), Silhouettes of Rebecca Touro, Abraham Touro, and Judah Touro, 1805. Hollow-cut paper mounted under reverse painted glass. *The Jewish Museum/ Art Resource, New York.*

But he was not a typical citizen. The man who helped create modern Boston and was a part of its highest ranks was also recognized as a man apart. The obituaries acknowledged that difference and bridged it in his death, as Hays had bridged it in his life. "Take him for all in all, he was indeed a man. . . . He is now secure in the bosom of his Father and our Father, of his God and our God."[27]

Moses Michael Hays set a standard in late 18th-century Boston for business and civic leadership, community service, and charity. The most prominent Jew in Boston before the 1840's, he achieved what many before him could not: success as both a Bostonian and a Jew. Without the benefit of an organized Jewish community, and without legal guarantees of religious freedom, Hays was able to preserve his religious heritage and pass it on to his family as a living faith.

Hays's only son Judah grew to join his father in his ship-

THE JEWS OF BOSTON

ping and insurance business. Hays doted on Judah, and Judah perpetuated many of his father's civic and business interests. He was initiated into the Massachusetts Lodge of Masons in 1788 and elected to membership in 1790. The City of Boston elected him fireward in 1805, making him likely the first Jew to hold elected office in the city. In 1807 he became one of the original proprietors of the projected Boston Athenæum. He drowned off the coast of Florida in 1832.

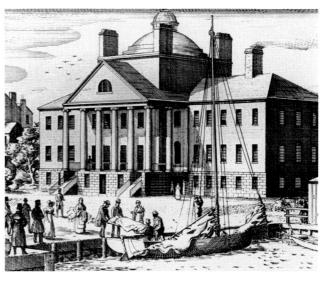

FIG. 18. Patient arriving by boat at Massachusetts General Hospital, 1821. Abraham Touro helped fund the early construction of the hospital and left it $10,000 upon his death in 1822. Judah Touro matched the bequest in his will in 1854. *Massachusetts General Hospital.*

Hays's daughters also helped consolidate the expanding Hays family networks. In 1776, Judith and Sally married their first cousins, Samuel and Moses Mears Myers, sons (by different wives) of Myer Myers, Rachel Hays's brother. The couples moved to Richmond, Virginia, where the Myers family became prominent in civic and religious affairs. Daughters Catherine and Sloe followed their sisters to Richmond. Neither married and they were buried under a single headstone in the Newport Jewish Cemetery. Rebecca Hays died unmarried in Boston at age thirty-two.

Abraham Touro remained in Boston and Medford with his sister Rebecca, serving as the Boston agent for his brother Judah, conducting his own shipping business with the West Indies, and building vessels in his Medford shipyard. He, too, was an early proprietor of the Boston Athenæum. Touro helped finance bridge companies in Malden, Charlestown, and Kennebec, turnpikes in Newburyport and Medford, the Middlesex Canal, and a theater, bath house, and riding school. He also spearheaded the 1816 fundraising effort for the Massachusetts General Hospital, helping to coordinate fundraising drives in Boston and Medford.

As his uncle before him, Abraham Touro conducted his prominent civic life as a practicing Jew. In 1816, he appeared before the Boston selectmen "to request that the town clerk set forth in the records that he was of the Jewish faith and belonged to a synagogue."[28] He paid to replace the decaying wooden fence around the Newport Jewish cemetery with a brick wall in 1822.

Touro died on October 3, 1822, from a "mortification" to a broken leg he sustained when he was thrown from his chaise. The *National Intelligencer* of October 22 remembered him as "a gentleman whose urbanity, hospitality and public spirit made him beloved and respected by all who knew him." In a will that attracted considerable national attention, he left $10,000 in trust to the State of Rhode Island for the care and preservation of the Jewish synagogue, and $5,000 for the upkeep of the

FIG. 17, *opposite.* Gilbert Stuart (1755–1828), *Abraham Touro* (1777–1822), ca.1817, oil on canvas. *Massachusetts General Hospital.*

FIG. 19. Anderson & Blessing, *Judah Touro*. Ambrotype, New Orleans, ca.1854. *American Jewish Historical Society.*

cemetery and the street leading up to it. He bequeathed $10,000 to Congregation Shearith Israel in New York; $5,000 to the Boston Humane Society; $5,000 to the Boston Female Asylum; $5,000 to Boston's Asylum for Indigent Boys, and $10,000 to Massachusetts General Hospital, a sum that "fairly took away the breath of this last organization."[29] Touro Streets in Newport and Medford still bear his name. He is buried in the Newport Jewish cemetery.

But in the civic and religious legacies of Moses Michael Hays and his descendants, his nephew Judah Touro surpassed them all. Judah Touro was born in Newport on June 16, 1775, the day before the Battle of Bunker Hill. Raised by his uncle Moses, and trained in his uncle's businesses, Touro sailed for New Orleans in 1801. He opened a shop for the sale of Yankee small-wares, and with his Boston credit and connections, built up a respectable business.

When New Orleans was acquired by the United States in 1803, Touro's business exploded. He gradually amassed a fortune, acquired, he told his friend Rabbi Isaac Leeser, "by strict economy." Frugal, reclusive, and modest, Touro avoided public gatherings and formal society, keeping only to a few close friends.

Nevertheless, Touro's life comes down through history tinctured with romance and adventure. The legend persists that in Boston he fell in love with his cousin Rebecca Hays, and that Moses opposed the marriage. Touro left Boston shortly thereafter, and neither he nor Rebecca ever married.

More certain are his two adventures in battle. During a Mediterranean trip at age twenty-two, he survived an attack by a French privateer. Touro served under General Andrew Jackson during the defense of New Orleans against the British, and on January 1, 1815, on the field of Chalmette, he took a direct hit from a twelve-pound shot. Left for dead on the river bank, he was rescued by his friend and fellow merchant Rezin D. Shepherd. He lived the rest of his days in Shepherd's household, and remembered Shepherd generously in his will "for the preservation of my life."

New Orleans, Boston, and most of world Jewry would remember Judah Touro. His extraordinary career of philanthropy began during his lifetime. He founded the first free library in New Orleans in 1830. He purchased the debt-ridden Unitarian Church of his friend Reverend Clapp and returned it to the congregation rent-free. Later, when fire destroyed the church, Touro made the largest donation to its rebuilding. Staunchly opposed to slavery, Touro would purchase slaves in order to free them, often training them and setting them up in business. At Touro's insistence, the slaves in the Shepherd house were also freed.[30]

In Boston, people took notice of Touro, too. On June 17, 1825, the fifteenth anniversary of the Battle of Bunker Hill, the cornerstone was laid for the proposed monument. But funding dwindled and the project came to a standstill. In 1839, industrialist Amos Lawrence offered $10,000 toward completion of the project if the remaining funds could be raised. In Boston, no backers appeared.

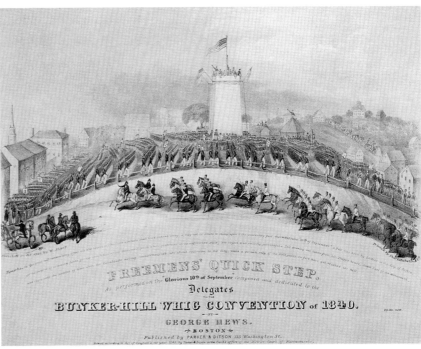

FIG. 20. William Sharp, *Freeman's Quick Step.* Boston, 1840. Tinted lithograph with hand coloring. The cover of this sheet music shows the Bunker Hill Monument half-completed at the time of the "Ladies' Fair" in September 1840. The fair was organized to help raise funds to complete the monument. Boston businessman Amos Lawrence and Judah Touro, then of New Orleans, each donated $10,000 to finish the monument and their names are inscribed on its base. *Boston Athenæum, Boston, Massachusetts.*

But in New Orleans, the man born on the day before the Battle of Bunker Hill heard of the impasse and provided the remaining $10,000. Boston responded with such an outpouring of ceremony and gratitude that Touro later told Reverend Clapp that "if it were not that his action might be misconstrued, he would have revoked his contribution to the Bunker Hill Monument Association, on account of the publicity it aroused."[31] On June 17, 1843, the monument in Charlestown was finally dedicated. The base bears an inscription recognizing differences, and the common humanity and aims, of Lawrence and Touro.

> *Amos and Judah, venerated names*
> *Patriarch and Prophet, press their equal claims . . .*
> *Christian and Jew, they carry out one plan,*
> *For though of different faith, each is in heart a man.*

Judah Touro died in New Orleans on January 18, 1854, at age seventy-eight. Touro Street and the Touro Infirmary there carry his name. His friend, Reverend Clapp, explicated the status of the entire Hays/Touro family when he wrote, "This gentleman was the humblest man whom I have ever been acquainted with . . . he was born, reared and had lived and died in the Hebrew faith. It was the faith of his father, who was a learned and most esteemed Rabbi. It was the faith that had been handed down to him by a long line of illustrious ancestors. . . . It was the faith of Jesus himself, who was a Jew, and who declared that the religion of the Old Testament contained all that is requisite to guide us to eternal joy."[32]

But if Touro had been generous in life, in death he breached all boundaries. His will set new standards worldwide in philanthropy. Touro left over $400,000, over half of it to organizations outside New Orleans and Newport. Almost half went to secular causes; the rest to Jewish organizations throughout the world. Practically every Jewish organization and congregation known to Touro in fifteen states received a bequest. Organizations in Palestine received $60,000. The brick fence that Abraham Touro had erected around the Newport cemetery was replaced by the present granite and steel fence and memorial gateway. In Boston, $5,000 went to Shepherd's daughter Mrs. Gorham Brooks and $5,000 went to Supply Clapp Thwing, Touro's business agent and lawyer. He donated $5,000 to Boston's Congregation Ohabei Shalom, and, he wrote, "I give and bequeath to the following Institutions, named in the will of my greatly beloved brother, the late Abraham Touro of Boston the following sums." Judah then matched Abraham's gifts exactly: $5,000 to the Boston Female Asylum; $5,000 to the Asylum for Orphan Boys; and $10,000 to Massachusetts General Hospital. This time the hospital Trustees voted a resolution that "in accepting the legacy of the late Judah Touro, recognize in it an act prompted by fraternal love and a philanthropy not confined within the narrow bounds of time, place, or sect."[33]

Touro's body was delivered to Newport in June 1855. His headstone bears the inscription: "By righteousness and integrity he collected his wealth, in charity and salvation he dispensed it."

With Judah Touro's death in 1854, the last connection to Boston's preeminent colonial Jewish family disappeared. By then, the foundations of a new and permanent Jewish community in Boston had been laid. Like their colonial predecessors, Boston's new Jewish citizens would struggle to define a working balance between being Jewish and being a Bostonian, between being a part of, and distinct from, their American communities. Some, like Judah Monis, would assimilate entirely. Others, like Moses Michael Hays, would carve roles for themselves as Americans and as Jews. All would benefit—knowingly or unknowingly—from the foundation laid by Puritan interest in Hebraic culture and from the persistence of Boston's early Jews, who made their way as alien residents, without the guarantee of religious freedom, or the support of a Jewish community or congregation.

1. Nathaniel B. Shurtleff, ed., *Records of the Governor and Company of the Massachusetts Bay* (Boston, 1853), vol. 2, 273; vol. 3, 159, 160.

2. Quoted in Jacob R. Marcus, *The Colonial American Jew: 1492–1776* (Detroit: Wayne State University Press, 1970), vol. 1, 303.

3. Lee M. Friedman, "Rowland Gideon, An Early Boston Jew and His Family," *Publications of the American Jewish Historical Society [PAJHS]* 39 (1939): 27. Gideon returned to London in 1693 where his descendants gained wealth, titles, political and social power, and married and converted into Christianity.

4. For more extensive lists see Leon Hühner, "The Jews of New England (Other than Rhode Island) Prior to 1800," *PAJHS* 11 (1903): 75–99 and Lee M. Friedman, "Early Jewish Residents in Massachusetts," *PAJHS* 23 (1915): 79–90. Scholars debate the use of "Jewish-sounding" names as proof of an individual's Judaism.

5. See, for example, Cotton Mather, *Magnalia Christi Americana* (London, 1702). A good overview of scholarship on Puritans and the Jews in America is found in Shalom Goldman, ed., *Hebrew and the Bible in America: The First Two Centuries* (Hanover and London: Brandeis University Press and Dartmouth College, University Press of New England, 1993).

6. Samuel Eliot Morison, *Harvard College in the Seventeenth Century* (Cambridge: Harvard University Press, 1936), especially Part 1, 140–47, 200–07 and Part 2, Appendix B.

7. As transcribed by D. De Sola Pool, "Hebrew Learning Among the Puritans of New England Prior to 1700," *PAJHS* 20 (1911): 32. See also Isidore S. Meyer, "The Hebrew Exercises of Governor William Bradford," in *Studies in Jewish Bibliography, History and Literature in honor of I. Edward Kiev* (New York: Ktav 1971): 237–88.

8. M. Halsey Thomas, ed., *The Diary of Samuel Sewall, 1671–1729* (New York: Farrar, Straus & Giroux, 1973), vol. 1, 474.

9. Increase Mather, *The Mystery of Israel's Salvation* (London, 1669).

10. *Diary of Cotton Mather* (New York: Frederick Ungar, 1975), vol. 1, 200. See also vol. 1, 298, 300, 315.

11. Quoted in Lee M. Friedman, "Cotton Mather's Ambition," in *Jewish Pioneers and Patriots* (Philadelphia: Jewish Publication Society of America, 1942), 98. Friedman is quoting from Samuel Sewall's diary as transcribed in *Collections, Massachusetts Historical Society*, series 5, vol. 6 (1879), 80. The entry is not in the Halsey edition of Sewall's *Diary*.

12. Monis was also awarded a master of arts degree by Harvard in 1723. For more on Monis, see the "Selected Bibliography" in this volume.

13. *The New-England Courant* (Boston) 26 March–2 April 1722.

14. Increase Mather, "The Preface to the Reader" in *The Truth*, by Judah Monis (London, 1722), iv. It should be noted that early correspondence and offers of employment by Harvard College *preceded* Monis's conversion. See "Judah Monis" in *Sibley's Harvard Graduates*, vol. 7, ed. Clifford K. Shipton (Boston: Massachusetts Historical Society, 1945), 640.

15. Judah Monis, "To my Brethren According to the Flesh," in *The Truth*, i–ii; iv.

16. *Harvard College Corporation Records*, 30 July 1722, 78–79.

17. Lee M. Friedman, "Judah Monis, First Instructor in Hebrew at Harvard University," *PAJHS* 22 (1914), 7.

18. Benjamin Colman, "The Preface" in *The Truth*, ii.

19. Samuel Joseph May, *Memoir of Samuel Joseph May*. (Boston: Roberts Brothers, 1873), 15.

20. Albert Ehrenfried, *A Chronicle of Boston Jewry from the Colonial Settlement to 1900* (Boston: Privately printed, 1963), 215.

21. H.S.B. Gras, *The Massachusetts First National Bank of Boston 1784–1934* (Cambridge, 1937), 15.

22. Gras, *The Massachusetts First National Bank*, 57.

23. On Hays and the Masonry see Ehrenfried, *A Chronicle of Boston Jewry*, chap. 12, and Harvey Smith, *Moses Michael Hays, Merchant—Citizen—Freemason, 1739–1805* (Boston: Moses Michael Hays Lodge, A.F. & A.M., 1937).

24. *Boston Centinel*, 11 May 1805.

25. May, *Memoir*, 15–16.

26. *Boston Centinel*, 11 May 1805.

27. *Boston Centinel*, 11 May 1805; *Columbian Centinel* (Boston), May 1805; *Newport Mercury*, 18 May 1805.

28. The synagogue was probably Shearith Israel in New York City, to which Touro contributed $666.43 in 1817.

29. Ehrenfried, *A Chronicle of Boston Jewry*, 257, quoting Oliver Wiswall, grandson of Judith Hays Myers.

30. Leon Huhner, *The Life of Judah Touro (1775–1854)* (Philadelphia: Jewish Publication Society of America, 5707–1946), 69.

31. Ehrenfried, *A Chronicle of Boston Jewry*, 265.

32. Ehrenfried, *A Chronicle of Boston Jewry*, 269.

33. For a copy of the will and an early summary of Touro's life, see Max J. Kohler, "Judah Touro, Merchant and Philanthropist," *PAJHS* 13 (1905): 93–111. Touro was partially guided in his bequests to Jewish organizations by his friend, the New Orleans Jewish leader, Gershom Kursheedt.

*Notes*

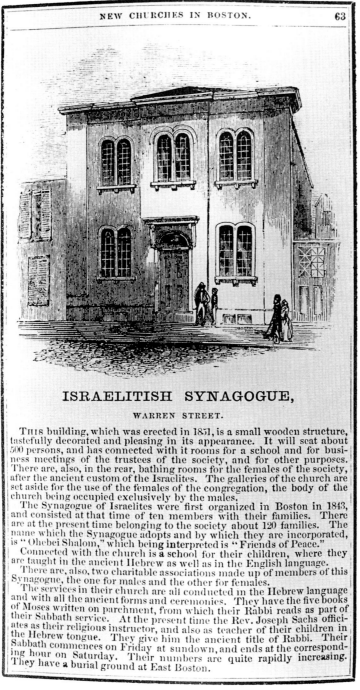

## ISRAELITISH SYNAGOGUE,

### WARREN STREET.

THIS building, which was erected in 1851, is a small wooden structure, tastefully decorated and pleasing in its appearance. It will seat about 500 persons, and has connected with it rooms for a school and for business meetings of the trustees of the society, and for other purposes. There are, also, in the rear, bathing rooms for the females of the society, after the ancient custom of the Israelites. The galleries of the church are set aside for the use of the females of the congregation, the body of the church being occupied exclusively by the males.

The Synagogue of Israelites were first organized in Boston in 1843, and consisted at that time of ten members with their families. There are at the present time belonging to the society about 120 families. The name which the Synagogue adopts and by which they are incorporated, is "Ohebei Shalom," which being interpreted is "Friends of Peace."

Connected with the church is a school for their children, where they are taught in the ancient Hebrew as well as in the English language.

There are, also, two charitable associations made up of members of this Synagogue, the one for males and the other for females.

The services in their church are all conducted in the Hebrew language and with all the ancient forms and ceremonies. They have the five books of Moses written on parchment, from which their Rabbi reads as part of their Sabbath service. At the present time the Rev. Joseph Sachs officiates as their religious instructor, and also as teacher of their children in the Hebrew tongue. They give him the ancient title of Rabbi. Their Sabbath commences on Friday at sundown, and ends at the corresponding hour on Saturday. Their numbers are quite rapidly increasing. They have a burial ground at East Boston.

*"Israelites in Boston," 1840–1880*

ELLEN SMITH

# "Israelites in Boston," 1840-1880

צדקה עשה הקדוש ברוך הוא בישראל שפזרן לבין האומות
"The Holy One, blessed be He, showed mercy unto Israel by
scattering them among the nations."
TALMUD BAVLI PESAHIM, 87b

N 1821 the Massachusetts state constitution guaranteed full rights of citizenship to the commonwealth's religious minorities, removing the last state-wide legal and political barriers to universal settlement. Jews, among others, could now settle in Boston and environs virtually without restriction. As they did, the Protestant establishment eyed them hopefully. Beginning in the early 19th century, and especially after the Second Great Awakening, Christian and missionary interest in the Jewish people accelerated. Hopeful that the conversion of the Jews would hasten the coming of God's Kingdom, writers and poets explored the history and perceived beliefs of the Jewish people. In Boston, an active press and missionary community produced a steady stream of histories, plays, and printed images concerning Jews and their culture.

The leader of this missionary effort was Hannah Adams, a fifth-generation New Englander and one of the most widely read New England authors of the late 18th and early 19th centuries. A shy woman, educated by her father and her own researches, Adams produced two influential works concerning the Jews, plus a well-regarded history of New England. Her *Dictionary of all Religions* (published in Boston in 1784 as *An Alphabetic Compendium of the Various Sects*) went through two title changes, three American and two British editions before its fourth and final version was published in Boston in 1817. Her *History of the Jews* (Boston, 1812) proved the key American text on the subject for the next half-century.[1] Striving "to be faithful to each group's self-understanding," she provided a notably sympathetic, generally unstereotyped account of Jewish history and beliefs.[2] A major focus in both volumes, however, remained the conversion of the Jews. In 1816 Adams founded "The Female Society of Boston and the Vicinity for Promoting Christianity Among the Jews," an organization that she considered to be the crowning achieve-

FIG. 1. Boston was an active center for early 19th century interest in studying and evangelizing Jews.

*Moses in the Bulrushes: A Sacred Drama in Three Parts,* by Hannah Moore. Boston: Isaiah Thomas, June 1813. Plays about the Jews attracted audiences throughout the antebellum period. *The Jew* by Cumberland was performed regularly in Boston, and as late as 1853, *The Jewess* was performed at the Boston Museum. *American Jewish Historical Society.*

*Pray for the Jews! A Sermon Preached at the Thursday Lecture in Boston, August 15, 1816,* by Thaddeus Mason Harris, preached before the Female Society of Boston and the Vicinity for Promoting Christianity Among the Jews two and a half months after its founding by Hannah Adams. *American Jewish Historical Society.*

"The Sorrowing Jew," sheet music, by George J. Webb. Boston: R.W. Thayer's Lithography, 1841. Music promoted popular interest in the Jews' history and condition. Webb's song went through at least three editions and ends, "O teach them their own pierced Messiah to view,/ And bring to His fold the poor sorrowing Jew." *American Jewish Historical Society.*

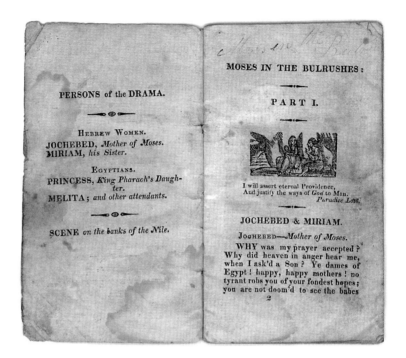

ment of her life's work. Long after she passed from the scene, she hoped, it would labor in love to bring the Jews "home."

Meanwhile, Jews abroad were being persecuted. In 1840, on the eve of the establishment of Boston's first permanent Jewish community, a Catholic priest and his Muslim servant in Damascus disappeared and the ancient libel began to circulate that Jews had kidnapped them to use their blood to bake Passover matzah. The Ottoman Turkish authorities, conspiring with the French Consul, arrested and tortured several Jews, who "confessed" falsely to the act. Numerous Jews, including sixty children, were subsequently imprisoned without food, an action that aroused national and international protests.

In Boston, a protest rally was called on September 21, 1840, at the Clarendon Street Chapel "to take into consideration the condition of the Jewish nation as respects both their present and welfare." Believing that the Jews' conversion to Christianity would end their spiritual and physical distress, Boston extended an invitation "to the suffering Jews of other nations, to come to this country, and would now particularly invite them to our city, where we presume they might do as well as in other cities in the world, though at present we have very few with us."[3] Unknown to the meeting organizers, the community they desired was less than two years away from forming. But in its Boston environs, the community would tend not so much toward Christianity as toward a strengthened Judaism, forged by new opportunities and responsive to the ambiguities of American Jewish life.

The Jews who came to Boston in the mid-19th century migrated from a broad range of Central and Eastern Europe states. In Boston, as throughout America, characterizing this migration as "German" is misleading. Beginning in the 1820's, gathering steam in the 1840's and 1850's, and continuing throughout the 1860's and 1870's, Jews left various German- and Yiddish-speaking provinces in increasing numbers to journey to America.[4] They came from the central German provinces, from Alsace in the west, from the Hapsburg and Austro-Hungarian territories in the south, and from Posen and Prussia, even Russia and Lithuania in the northeast and east.[5]

New taxes on the Jewish communities, marriage restrictions, pressures to leave their traditional trades for more "useful" occupations in agriculture and artisanry, to adopt the German language, and for Jews to send their children to German rather than Jewish schools, weighed heavily upon these Jews. Even with emancipation that granted them equality in law, Jews were not in fact uniformly accorded equal rights with non-Jews. At best, emancipation brought with it mixed blessings, raising many of the ambiguities and hard choices an integrated Jewish community faced in the European mainstream. Particularly among younger and poorer Jews, emancipation became a time to look to new opportunities in Western Europe and North America.[6]

By raw measures, the Central European migration to America was small. Compared to the more than two and a half million Jews who would arrive between 1880 and 1925, only 150,000 Jews arrived in the United States between 1820 and 1880.[7] But from this small influx, new and permanent Jewish communities across the whole country were created. Fed by continuing migration and the internal growth of the new Jewish settlements, the Central European Jews of mid-century established the character and spread of Jewish communities throughout the United States.

In Boston, the migration from Posen dominated, distinguishing Boston from other American Jewish communities. This Polish region, along with other Polish areas east of the Elbe River, had been annexed by Prussia in 1793 bringing into the "German" sphere hundreds of thousands of Yiddish-speaking *Ostjuden* (Eastern Jews). Though the Jews of 19th-century Germany never amounted to more than one percent of the total German population, by 1850 half a million Jews resided in German territories. As early as 1816, up to forty percent of Prussian Jewry actually consisted of Polish speakers from the former Polish territory.[8]

In Boston the same proportions applied. Between 1840 and 1861, forty-four percent of Jews born abroad were born in northeastern Germany, including Prussia, Poland, Posen, and Russia. Another nineteen percent were born in southwestern Germany, especially Bavaria, Baden, and Saxony. Twenty-seven percent were German-born (region unspecified), and the birthplaces of ten percent remain unidentified.[9]

While European Jewish culture provided a general uniformity between the Jews of southwestern and northeastern Germany, some differences did pertain. Generally, Jews from southwestern Germany were emancipated earlier, lived in rural villages and small towns as well as major urban centers, engaged in peddling and small businesses, spoke German, and reformed their Jewish practices earlier. Jews from the east, whose emancipation came later than in the west, tended to reside in concentrated urban settings, engage in textile trades, speak Yiddish, and be slightly more resistant to religious reform. These differences carried to the new American setting, providing the seeds of future American Jewish communal divisions.

The earliest Central European Jews seem to have settled in Boston in the early 1840's. By 1842 there is evidence that the small group had gathered into a religious community, for in September of that year, ten men gathered at the home of Peter Spitz in Fort Hill to celebrate the Jewish New Year.[10] On May 24, 1843 approximately eighteen worshippers congregated to celebrate the circumcision of Spitz's first-born son, and they decided to form a permanent congregation. They hired Henry Selling, formerly of Albany, as a combination *chazan, shochet* and *mohel*—cantor, teacher, ritual slaughterer, and circumcizer. They called themselves Congregation "Ohabei Shalom," (Lovers of Peace), Boston's first Jewish congregation.

The congregation's first act (or perhaps that of a related, but prior burial society—the original records disappeared in a fire) was to establish a Jewish burial ground. On April 29, 1844 the Congregation petitioned Boston to set aside 100

Fig. 2. "Plan of the City of Boston," 1844. Engraved by G.B. Boynton. The Central European Jews settled in the area immediately to the left (south) of the Common. *Boston Athenæum, Boston, Massachusetts.*

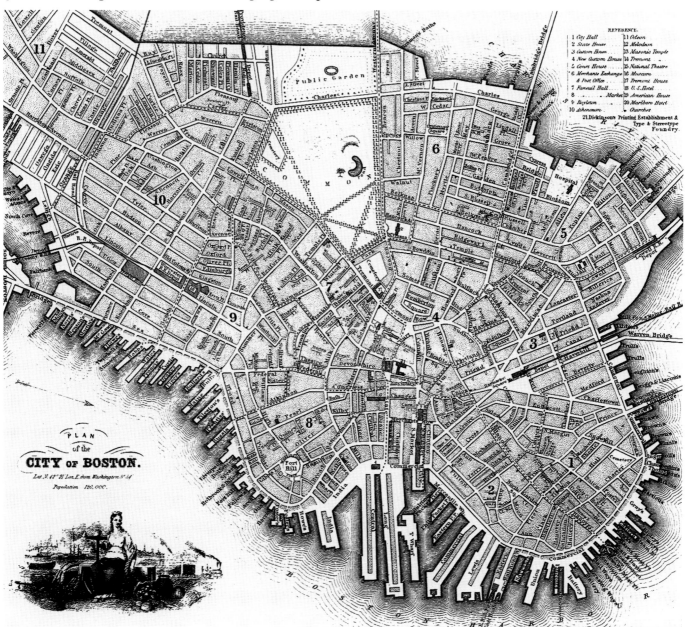

square feet in a corner of the East Boston City cemetery for its exclusive use. The petition was rejected, but a subsequent offer to purchase land for a burial ground was approved. At the corner of Byron and Homer streets in East Boston, a 10,000 square foot site was acquired for $200.00, paid for in part by a five dollar assessment on each congregation member.[11] The conversion of the property to a Jewish cemetery was formally approved by the city on October 5, 1844. For the first time in two hundred years, Boston's Jews could be buried in the city in which they lived.

Boston's Jews could now also worship together in their new American home. After the spring of 1843, enough permanent residents had settled in Boston to ensure consistent *minyanim* (the minimum ten men required for a communal service). The Boston Episcopal priest, Reverend E. M. P. Wells, invited by a "son of Abraham" to witness "the feast of trumpets," counted forty worshippers at the September 1844 Rosh Hashannah services. The congregation's learning and piety impressed him; their rented quarters in Boston's South End did not. Climbing up a set of rickety stairs he found

> *an upper room. . . . not a comfortable or decent place for the performance of that service which thousands of years ago swelled through the arches of Solomon's Temple. . . . The service was performed with more solemnity, earnestness and apparent devotion than I have seen in a far better synagogue. I was surprised that so many (there were about forty present) could read the Hebrew so fluently and in most cases with a good degree of understanding as apparent from their manner. Every man took part in their service and there was far more voice used than is often heard in the beautiful responsive service at Trinity or St. Pauls.[12]*

Believing that the congregation deserved a more appropriate and permanent facility, in part because he felt that the Jews' study of Torah would eventually lead them to accept Christianity, Wells petitioned Boston's Protestants to contribute toward a synagogue fund and to "begin to treat [the Jews] as brothers, as friends, as fellows."[13] His plans to underwrite the synagogue and convert the community never materialized, but the Jewish congregation Ohabei Shalom did. On March 26, 1852, it dedicated its own synagogue building on Warren Street, between Eliot and Tremont, paid for by congregation members and several civic contributors. The thirty by forty-six foot building encapsulated the responsibilities and aspirations of Boston's Jewish community. The seating for 400 could accommodate all of Boston's approximately 125 Jewish families. Hebrew and German instruction proceeded in the attached schoolhouse, and congregational and community business was transacted in the trustees' room above the school. A *mikveh* (ritual bath) helped ensure that ritual obligations could be met by the women and men of the community. "There is something fine and admirable even in the humble circumstances of such a spectacle," the Reverend Cyrus A. Bartol commented to his West Boston Church congregation regarding the synagogue's dedication. "The courageous and cheering rearing, upon a close street, in a low quarter of the city, of that small synagogue — that a few might worship the God of their Fathers, in the way of their Fathers," caused him to wonder whether the earnestness of Christian religious practice compared to that of the Jews.[14]

But the unity of Congregation Ohabei Shalom was relatively short-lived. From the beginning, religious and cultural differences between the southwestern and northeastern German members of the congregation strained against consensus. The adoption of the prayerbook and religious ritual used in the Bavarian city of Fürth established one of many cultural fault lines along which the congregation's "Polish" and "German" members would shortly divide. By late 1853, a break-away *chevra* (auxiliary society) formed among the majority northeastern Polish immigrants, dissatisfied with their lack of influence in the original *chevra*. The reappointment of Joseph Sachs as *chazan* further infuriated the Polish majority, who opposed his tenure. Unable to reach a compromise, the minority southwestern German members withdrew from the congregation, taking with them their *chazan*, most of the founders and officers of the congregation, the shofar, the Sefer Torah, the original record books, and the name "Ohabei Shalom," as well as their declared rights to the synagogue building, the cemetery, and the $5,000 bequest left to "Temple Ohabei Shalom of Boston" in the will of Judah Touro.[15] When the civil courts later granted the stay-behind Polish congregation rights to the Ohabei Shalom name, the Touro money, and the Warren Street synagogue, the German group took the name Adath Israel, today known as Temple Israel.[16] It leased a building on Pleasant Street, purchased its own cemetery in Wakefield, and became the preeminent "German" Jewish institution in the city. Its ranks split again in 1856 when some East Prussian members formed Die Israelitische Gemeinde Mishkan Israel.[17] Native allegiances seemed to determine religious association, even in the new land.

While religious loyalties tried the creation of a unified Jewish community in Boston, other aspects of life helped to shape and reinforce a more cohesive local identity. Ties of neighborhood, demographics, and above all business and economic life brought Jewish residents together.

The first Central European Jews settled in Boston's lower South End, in what is today's theater district. In the mid-19th century, the area was bounded by Boston Common on the north, Boston Harbor on the south, the business district on the east, and Boston neck on the west connecting Boston peninsula to Roxbury and towns beyond.[18] Built up during the first half of the 19th century, and especially in the 1850's, the area never fulfilled its promise as middle-class housing and was soon surpassed by the filling in of the Back Bay.[19] Instead, the earliest Central European Jewish immigrants settled in this area, as well as in parts of the downtown and North End. By the late 1850's, virtually all of Boston's Jews lived close to one another in the South End.[20] They concentrated in the Park Square area, a relatively undesirable section between Summer Street, the mud flats, Boston neck, and Washington Street. A few more settled in the adjacent South Cove. According to Stephen Mostov, "Between 1845 and 1861, at any one time, two-thirds of the city's Jews, in contrast to only 17 percent of all city residents, lived in the 'Park Square' area. As many as 85 percent lived in the South End, as compared to one-third generally."[21]

The community gathered first around Ohabei Shalom on Warren Street, and later Adath Israel on nearby Pleasant Street. The location of the synagogues drew new Jewish residents and immigrants to the area, as well as businesses supporting the community. Kosher butchers and provision stores concentrated in the blocks around the synagogues, as did many artisans and shopkeepers. The Jews of Boston were literally neighbors, daily sharing the same residential, business, and religious spaces. Their small numbers further encouraged their insularity. Despite their own concentration in the Park Square area, no more than 500 of the 10,248 residents of the area in 1860 were Jewish.[22] In this concentrated face-to-face society, a self-supporting and self-sustaining Jewish community first came into being.

The demographics of the early Central European Jewish settlement also worked to reinforce homogeneity and a sense of community. The Jewish migration to Boston was a young migration, consisting primarily of single men and women under thirty. They arrived steadily between 1840 and 1861, often with or after their siblings, and once settled into some kind of job, they married and began raising families.[23] Some men returned to Europe for wives, but most seem to have married immigrant women, who seem to have favored slightly older men. Mostov estimates that almost two-thirds of Boston's Jewish couples had no foreign-born children, but by 1860 these same couples already had an average of 3.8 children each.[24] The immigrant community was thus quick to marry among itself, to bear American Jewish children, and to raise them in close proximity to one another, further reinforcing the group's solidarity and interconnectedness.

But the strongest tie that bound the Central European Jewish community together was its business culture. Whereas Boston's total working force exhibited a great range of occupational diversity, Jewish Boston was intensely concentrated in its two traditional European occupations: commerce and clothing.[25] Peddlers, tailors, and clothing and dry goods merchants accounted for over one-half of Jewish employment between 1846 and 1861, compared to only twenty percent of the entire Boston work force.[26] Other occupational characteristics similarly distinguished Boston's Jews. Those Jews employed as artisans were almost exclusively tailors, opticians and watchmakers, cigarmakers, and furriers. Non-Jews, by contrast, rarely established themselves in these trades. Furthermore, as central European Jews displayed persistence in their residential patterns, so did they display persistence in their occupations. Peddlers might advance to petty shopkeepers, and tailors to clothing manufacturers, but few Jews changed their occupations completely.[27] The economic advancement of Boston's Jews was generally smooth; few "skidded" down the economic ladder, and fifty to ninety percent of sons did better than their fathers, particularly the sons of skilled workers.[28] Few Central European Jews before 1880 became laborers and few entered the white-collar professions; most remained solidly in the middle. This pattern, characterized by occupational persistence, a generally steady economic rise, and a concentration in peddling, merchandising and certain kinds of artisanship, distinguished Jews from the general labor pool in Boston, and mirrored the occupational profile of central European Jews in other mid-century American cities.[29] Like their neighborhoods and their youthfulness, the occupational status of Boston's Jews tended to isolate them from the rest of the community, unifying them instead around shared experiences and tying them to those of their own kind.

Boston's Jewish families pushed their children toward business, with the goal of self-employment being nearly universal. Sons generally entered the work force at age fifteen,[30] commonly employed by their fathers and uncles, or in a business related to the family enterprise. Marriages were often contracted with an eye toward consolidating business interests even further. By the late 1870's, Boston's Central European Jews had, as a group, advanced up the economic ladder faster than any other Boston population.[31] They had done so as a community, linked by kinship and interlocking business ventures.

Peddling was the main occupational entry point for most of Boston's Central European Jews. Yankee New England had long relied on peddlers for many of its purchases, and Jewish peddlers soon filled a niche being abandoned by native-born itinerants. Upon arrival in Boston, a man could gather clothing and other wares

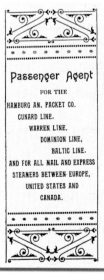

## J. WAXMAN,
Dealer in
### Diamonds, Watches, Clocks & Jewelry,
· OPTICAL GOODS ·
Of every description.
821 WASHINGTON STREET,    BOSTON.

*Repairing of Watches, French Clocks and Jewelry a Specialty.*

---

## ISRAEL COHEN & CO.
SUCCESSORS TO LOUIS & COHEN.
# CLOTHING,
## 89 Summer Street,    Boston.

ISRAEL COHEN.    JAMES H. COHEN.    LEO M. COHEN.

---

## A. BILAFSKY,
### Real Estate and Mortgages,
Auctioneer and Justice of the Peace,
### No. 27 SCHOOL STREET,
*ROOM 96.* —————    BOSTON.

Residence, 41 Main Street, Everett, Mass.

---

## H. SLOBODKIN,
Agent for B. MEIER, 64 AVENUE C, NEW YORK.
MANUFACTURER OF כשר THE CELEBRATED
### Vienna and Frankfort Sausages, Bologna,
→BEEF SMOKED CORNED TONGUE←
Home-Made Pickles a Specialty.
### 43 Lowell Street, Corner Cotting,
BOSTON.

*Orders for City or Country Promptly attended to.*

---

## J. A. HENEY & SON,

האנדלער אין
לעדער אונד שורה פיינדינגס,
זאהלען · טאפס · נאגעל · etc.
דער ביללינסטע סטאהר אין באסטאן
16 מארשאלל סטריט,
נאהע עקקע יוניאן
באסטאן,

---

## LEVIN'S
# Military Band and Orchestra
J. LEVIN, Leader and Manager.
Office, 325 Washington St.,   Room 24.
BOSTON.
Hours 9 to 4.    Residence, 104 Lenox St.

First-Class Music, Brass or String, furnished for all occasions.

The best Musicians with all the latest and most popular music, and well-known prompters at reasonable rates.

Special rates for benefits.

---

# MY SHOE STORE
IS NOT
## The Largest in the World,
but it is large enough to contain a complete line of FOOTWEAR for Ladies, Gentlemen and Children, which we sell at
**ROCK-BOTTOM PRICES.**
Give us a call.
# DAVIS COHEN,
*41 Chapman St.,* -    *Boston.*

---

FIG. 3. Advertisements for Boston Jewish businesses as they appeared in *History of the Jews of Boston and New England* (1892). *American Jewish Historical Society.*

from a small merchandiser and pay for it after the wares were sold. Credit was commonly extended by petty shopkeepers, by family members, and by various free loan associations established to help individuals set themselves up in business. The proximity of the South End to the railroad depots and the horse-railroad line to Roxbury was also an advantage to peddlers whose routes included New Hampshire, Maine, and rural Massachusetts.

Peddling also provided entré to related businesses. Lewis Levi appears in Boston records variously as a second-hand clothing dealer and in the fancy glassware business. In fact, the two businesses were one. Levi sold his chinaware and glass to peddlers and took his payment in used clothing, which he then resold.[32] Landladies often took wares from peddlers in rent; pawnbrokers relied on peddlers as well as neighborhood residents for their inventory. As individual peddlers advanced up the economic ladder to retail or wholesale businesses, new immigrants arrived to take their routes. By the time most of the Central European Jews had moved beyond peddling, the Eastern European immigration filled the gap, assuring that in Boston, as in most American cities, peddling and the Jewish population were linked for nearly a century.

Peddlers also hawked their wares in Boston's streets, shouting down customers and each other so loudly that Boston finally passed laws quieting peddlers who "would announce their sale by whatever means they could yelling in the streets, ringing bells or blowing horns," from 8 a.m. until sunset.[33]

In peddling were found many of the business lessons learned by the Boston Jewish community. Persistence and savings allowed modest and steady gains in economic status. With bank and commercial loans generally unavailable to Jews, the community constructed its own system of credit, complete with its own bankers, credit unions, and free loan societies.[34] Profits generated by successful businesses were plowed back into expanding them and then into starting related enterprises, which in turn provided employment for more Jews moving up the economic ladder. Businesses also relied heavily on family employees, further reducing costs. By the 1880's Boston boasted several extremely wealthy Jewish businessmen, particularly in the clothing and boot and shoe trades, and an overall advancing and extremely stable working population.[35]

Women's lives were bound up in the business world as well, further blurring the lines between family and work. Though generally unrecorded in City Directories and censuses, many women labored beside their husbands and children in stores, managing stock, inventories, accounts, and customers. Women earned additional income by taking in boarders in their homes and occasionally by teaching.

Besides consolidating community and kin, business also made an impact on the conduct of traditional religion. Jewish holidays and the observance of the Jewish Sabbath on Saturday, a workday in America, brought the demands of Boston and Judaism into direct confrontation. "It is a crying fact that the Sabbath could not be kept by the Israelites," Rabbi Solomon Schindler wrote in 1889, recounting congregation Adath Israel's struggle with the issue. "No matter how much they were justified in clinging to the historical Sabbath, no matter how sincerely people bemoaned that this day was so shamefully neglected . . . the men had to attend to their business; the young, if they wished to find employment in any profession, were obliged to work on that day; and thus it came that only a few elderly gentlemen who had retired from business, and a few ladies, attended the Sabbath services."[36] Schindler and his congregation experimented with Friday evening services, but the pressures of increasing distances travelled by synagogue members, the dark winter nights, and competition from "concerts and theatrical performances" forced "the so much dreaded step of introducing Sunday services."[37] The Sunday services proved successful, but the change highlighted two evolved realities of Boston Judaism in the third quarter of the 19th century: the increasing prominence of women in the synagogues and the new relationship between the religious world of Judaism and the secular world. For Schindler and other Boston Jewish reformers, changes were not made to accommodate or imitate Protestant culture so much as to ensure the strength and continuity of Judaism.

By the late 1870's, as Boston's Jews began to prosper, they began to move from the lower South End to Roxbury, Brookline, and especially the upper, "new" South End along the now-widened Boston neck.[38] These moves, too, clustered around

FIG. 4, *facing page.* Early stores of the William Filene family. William Filene (b. Posen, 1830) sailed to America at age 18, married Clara Ballin (b. Bavaria 1832), and settled in Boston in 1848. By 1851 they opened their first retail store on Hanover Street in the North End. Other stores followed in Salem (as early as 1856) and Lynn (by 1870). In 1881, Filene opened a dress trimming store in Boston on Winter Street, the forerunner of the major Filene's chain of department stores.

*Above:* "Filene's Pavilion," 45–47 Market Street, Lynn, Massachusetts, opened 1856, ca. 1880. *American Jewish Historical Society.*

*Below:* "William Filenes," possibly 18 or 32 Market Street, Lynn, Massachusetts, 1875. *American Jewish Historical Society.*

FIG. 5. A. Shuman and Company store at Shuman Corner, Boston, as illustrated in *History of the Jews of Boston and New England* (1892). Abraham Shuman (b. Prussia 1838) became the wealthiest clothing manufacturer and retailer in Boston in the 19th century. He began as a custom tailor in Roxbury; with support from other Jewish businessmen, he branched into boys and men's clothing manufacturing, retailing, and wholesale furnishing. *American Jewish Historical Society.*

newly constructed synagogues, but the new houses of worship began to spread farther apart. With the influx of Eastern European Jewish immigrants to the North and West Ends and near north cities outside of Boston in the late 19th-century, the physical unity of Jewish Boston was permanently fragmented. Neighborhoods would thereafter define subcommunities but no longer the community as a whole. Boston's Jewish community would need new definitions of its common ground.

Among the new structures of community and identity that emerged at this time were voluntary societies, as well as social and charitable clubs established to bring people together as their businesses and residences drew them apart. Foremost among the organizations founded in the 1880's and 1890's was the Elysium Club, established by members of Adath Israel. Expensive and exclusive, the club's membership closely resembled the leadership roster of Temple Israel and to a lesser degree Ohabei Shalom; the United Hebrew Benevolent Society, led by the same group of men, also met in its rooms. Other clubs and lodges founded included the Clio Club, attracting younger, rising Boston Jews; the Progress Club, the Comus Club, the New Century Club, a variety of Jewish lodges, and the Young Men's Hebrew Association, which provided classes and an employment bureau as well as social and recreational opportunities. All of these organizations highlighted a community redefining itself by voluntary associations, by specific interests, and increasingly, by class and wealth. The creation of these organizations also underscored the Central European Jews' continuing desire to associate among themselves as Jews. Excluded from many mainstream Boston establishments and businesses, the Jews of Boston chose to create structures to preserve their own identity, even as they emulated and assimilated the larger culture in many ways. The creation of this working, delicate balance, to be tested and refined in the century to come, was perhaps their most lasting legacy to the Jews of Boston who followed them.

At the beginning of the 19th century, Boston writers and missionaries had assessed the prospects of Jews in America and Boston and foreseen a good fit. Their predictions had not been wrong. In King's *Dictionary of Boston*, 1883, neatly sandwiched between entries on "Health, Board of" and "Herald (The Boston)," the article on "Hebrews in Boston" summarized the state of the Central European Jewish community at the cusp of the Eastern European Jewish migrations.

*Thirty-five years ago a Hebrew was an unusual sight in Boston; but since that period Hebrews have increased so rapidly that now they number no less than 6,000. They are to be found in all parts of the city, busily engaged in trade and traffic, and are, as a class, industrious and thrifty. . . . Some are quite wealthy, nearly all are in comfortable circumstances; none are wanting in shrewdness, and capacity for driving a good bargain, and many are educated and cultured. They are not wanting in political aspirations; several having filled municipal offices of honor and trust, and others having attained higher public positions. The more wealthy and enterprising are engaged in the clothing-trade; many are jewelers and tobacconists, and a large number are pawnbrokers. . . .There are seven congregations . . . 5 B'nai B'rith lodges . . . The order Kesher Shel Barsel has two lodges . . . The order Free Sons of Israel is represented by 2 lodges. The order Treue Schwestern is represented by Naomi Lodge. There are several Chewras connected with the congregations, and ladies' societies devoted entirely to benevolent purposes. . . . There are also a Young Men's Hebrew Association, and the Elysium Club,—the latter a social organization with spacious and quite elegant rooms on Concord Street."*[39]

FIG. 6. Solomon Schindler, as illustrated in *History of the Jews of Boston and New England* (1892). Born in Silesia in 1842, Schindler emigrated to America in 1871 and in 1874 became rabbi of Boston's Congregation Adath Israel. Gifted orator, administrator, and author, Schindler helped lead Boston's efforts toward religious and social service reform, and forged ties with leaders of the local Protestant community. *American Jewish Historical Society.*

As the century neared its close, Boston's Jewish community also took a look back on itself. Rabbi Solomon Schindler wrote his *Israelites in Boston: A Tale Describing the Development of Judaism in Boston* in 1889 as a fundraiser on behalf of the [Leopold Morse] "Home for Aged and Infirm Hebrews of Boston."[40] The book spun off only modest profits, and Schindler seems to have written it rather quickly, for he clearly did not do his history homework. But the volume provides a fascinating assessment of the community by one of its most influential and widely connected members. "From all facts which I was able to collect, it appears that about fifty years ago the good people of Boston and vicinity did not know more what a Jew was or how he looked than they were told by their pastors," Schindler wrote in wonder. "I have even the testimony of a trustworthy co-religionist that he had found people gazing at him with amazement . . . because they had imagined the Jews had horns growing out of their foreheads, and he wore none."[41] Schindler spent his Boston lifetime as rabbi of Temple Israel and later as Superintendent of the United Hebrew Benevolent Association proving to gentiles that Jews were as humane and civil and productive as the best of the Yankees, and his book consists primarily of the biographies and hornless images of his list of outstanding

FIG. 7. Leopold Morse, as illustrated in *History of the Jews of Boston and New England* (1892). Born in Bavaria in 1831, Morse was held by many Jews of his generation to be the model American businessman, politician, and philanthropist, despite his intermarriage and disavowal of Jewish practices. Arriving in 1848, he began as a peddler and eventually helped create the Leopold Morse & Co. clothing house. In 1876 he became the first Jew in Massachusetts elected to the U.S. Congress. *American Jewish Historical Society.*

Boston Jewish citizens. Most were leaders of Congregations Ohabei Shalom and Adath Israel, all were male, and all rose in the community through their business ventures.[42]

But if Schindler celebrated Boston's business leaders (mindful that the book was intended to raise funds for the Hebrew Home), he lamented the Boston Jewish community's slow pace at religious reform, how it "took no part whatsoever in the endeavor of Young America to bring Judaism abreast with the time and to win for it the respect of the Gentile world."[43] Schindler then recounted, in the third person, his own hiring by Adath Israel, his dogged efforts to introduce Reform, his eventual successes in introducing "edifying and orderly services...[and] modern ideas," and the perceived influence of his reforms on other Central European congregations.[44] He brought a harsh critique to the burgeoning congregations of the new Eastern European immigrants. "They all, however, failing to grasp the spirit of Americanism, and endeavoring to perpetuate European customs and European orthodoxy, remain unsuccessful in their work, and are unable to bring themselves to public recognition."[45] In this, history would prove Schindler a poor prophet, but he did recognize the next group around which Boston's Jewish identity would coalesce. The Jewish community in Boston would be redefined again, not by the Judaism modelled on Yankee structures that Schindler favored, but by a Judaism and Jewish community more referenced to its European sources, more self-contained and even more cloistered than its predecessor.

In charitable activities, Schindler (by 1889 the Superintendent of the United Hebrew Benevolent Association) gave Boston high marks. He particularly praised the women of Boston's Jewish community for their integration of social and charitable activities on behalf of the city's deserving poor.[46] But his model Jew of Boston was Leopold Morse, the peddler turned business magnate turned U.S. Congressman. Though married to a gentile woman, and "too broad to tie himself to any denomination," Morse nevertheless remained strongly tied to Boston's Jewish community through his charitable activities and communal advocacy. In characterizing Morse's understanding of the life of a Jew in America, Schindler was in fact stating his own conclusions: "A man must be a good citizen, a good American first; then may follow his appreciation of the land in which he first saw the light of the world; and then, and only then, his predilection for one or another religious sect."[47]

Three years after Schindler's history of the Boston Jewish community, the *History of the Jews of Boston and New England* appeared.[48] A more comprehensive but less orderly volume than Schindler's, the *History* nevertheless shares many orientations with it. Leopold Morse is held up as the model Jewish citizen; his Home for Aged and Infirm Hebrews and Orphanage is presented as the model charitable enterprise. The volume presents the history of the early Jews of Newport and Boston (though much incorrect information is given), an overview of Boston's early Jewish congregations, histories of individual business and religious leaders and Boston Jewish organizations, excerpts from newspapers and journals on Jews of other North American communities, a long article on "The Jews and the Theatre," poetry, Jewish jokes, and ennobling aphorisms. But unlike Schindler's history, the *History of the Jews of Boston* also focuses on the post-1880 Eastern European immigrants, with feature articles on their rabbis, Yiddish poetry (including "Der Juedische Peddler"), and "The Jews at the North End." The book is not so much a retrospective history or an apology for the community, as a picture in words of how it looked at century's end, a moment of transition. While Schindler's volume was a last plea for the vision and behaviors of his Central European community, the *History* recognized that this era had already passed. The book's organization—episodic, somewhat fractured, a mosaic giving a complex picture of the whole community—is in fact an accurate mirror of the community it is describing and the community to come.

What then, would be the legacy of Boston's Central European Jewish community? They established, above all, the foundation for virtually every major Boston Jewish institution and organization, including several of its leading synagogues, its charitable infrastructure, and its chief social and recreational associations. Because no Sephardic or other Jewish settlement preceded them, they were free to fashion the character of the community in their own image, focusing on family and business and the need to perpetuate both within a Jewish context adapted to American realities. They created a communal structure based on mutual aid and volunteerism, and like their brethren throughout America, established a strong role for the laity in the operation of the Jewish community. The fact that in Boston they were heavily Polish ("East-German") meant that Western and Eastern European Jews had lived together and worked together and married one another for forty years before the late 19th-century migrations began. Perhaps as a result, those migrations appeared to Boston's Jews somewhat less shocking; in any event, Boston's Central European Jews mobilized more quickly than in most other American cities to assist the immigrants. Perhaps most importantly, they attempted to pass on to them their model for living a consciously Jewish life in new ways, adapted to the advantages of Boston and America, and creative with the ambiguities that such a conjoined existence could bring.

# *Notes*

1. Thomas A. Tweed, "An American Pioneer in the Study of Religion: Hannah Adams (1755–1831) and Her *Dictionary of All Religions*," *Journal of the American Academy of Religion* 60 (1992): 437–64.

2. Tweed, "An American Pioneer," 446.

3. *Boston Mercantile Journal*, 22 September 1840, quoted in Lee M. Friedman, *Jewish Pioneers and Patriots* (Philadelphia: Jewish Publication Society of America, 1948), 118.

4. Hasia R. Diner, *A Time for Gathering: The Second Migration, 1820–1880*, (Baltimore and London: Johns Hopkins University Press, 1992). Diner argues (232) "It is much more accurate to talk about a century of migration and consider immigration from the 1820s through the 1920s as a single movement that began in western Europe and moved gradually and unevenly to the east."

5. It is more accurate to speak of "German states" than "Germany" in this period, as the unification of Germany under Bismarck was not completed until 1871. Throughout most of the century, each German-speaking region enacted its own laws, including those dealing with its Jewish population.

6. On the history and impact of emancipation on the 19th-century European Jewish community see Jacob Katz, *Out of the Ghetto: The Social Background of Jewish Emancipation, 1770–1870* (Cambridge: Harvard University Press, 1973) and Naomi Cohen, *Encounter with Emancipation: The German Jews in the United States, 1830–1914* (Philadelphia: Jewish Publication Society of America, 1984).

7. Diner, *A Time for Gathering*, 233.

8. See Avraham Barkai, "German-Jewish Migrations in the Nineteenth Century, 1830–1910," *Leo Baeck Institute Yearbook* 30 (1985), 301; and Diner, *A Time for Gathering*, 26. Emancipation proceeded more slowly for the Polish-German Jews. Prussian emancipation laws in 1812 excluded Jews from Posen and other Yiddish-speaking territories; full legal emancipation was not accorded them until 1866.

9. Stephen G. Mostov, "A Sociological Portrait of German Jewish Immigrants in Boston: 1845–1861," *AJS Review* 3 (1978), Table 4, 135. By including Württemberg, Hanover, and Hesse in his southeastern Germany estimates, Burton S. Kliman estimates 33.7% of Boston's Jews migrated from those regions and 45.3% from the northeast. See Burton S. Kliman, "The Jewish Brahmins of Boston: A Study of the German Jewish Immigrant Experience, 1860–1900," (senior thesis, Brandeis University, 1978). Typescript copy, American Jewish Historical Society.

10. Tradition records them as William Goldsmith, Moses Ehrlich, Peter Spitz, Himan Spitz, Bernard Fox, Charles Hyneman, Jacob Norton, Isaac Wolf, Abraham F. Bloch, and Peter Spitz. The original German-language records of the congregation were destroyed by fire. See S[imon] Simmons, *The History of Temple Ohabei Shalom, Principal Events from Its Organization in 1843, to the Fiftieth Anniversary Celebration on February 26th, 1893 (Boston, 1893)*, 10–11.

11. Albert Ehrenfried, *A Chronicle of Boston Jewry, From the Colonial Settlement to 1900* (Boston: Privately printed, 1963), 338–39.

12. *Boston Mercantile Journal*, 23 September 1844, as quoted in Lee M. Friedman, "The Dedication of Massachusetts' First Synagogue," in *Jewish Pioneers and Patriots* (Philadelphia: Jewish Publication Society of America, 1948), 122.

13. *Boston Mercantile Journal*, 23 September 1844, as quoted in William A. Braverman, "The Ascent of Boston's Jews, 1630–1918," (Ph.D. diss., Harvard University, 1990), 22-23.

14. Quoted in Arthur Mann, ed. *Growth and Achievement: Temple Israel 1854–1954* (Cambridge: The Riverside Press for the Board of Trustees of Temple Adath Israel, 1954), 23.

15. Ehrenfried, *A Chronicle of Boston Jewry*, 346–48.

16. For more on the founding and subsequent histories of Boston's earliest Jewish congregations, see David Kaufman's essay in this volume. See also Jeanette S. and Abraham E. Nizel, *Congregation Ohabei Shalom: Pioneers of the Boston Jewish Community—An Historical Perspective of the First One Hundred Years, 1842–1982* (Boston: By the congregation, 1982) and Stella D. Obst, *The Story of Adath Israel* (Boston: By the congregation, 1917).

17. See *Temple Mishkan Tefila: A History, 1858–1958* (Newton, Mass.: By the congregation, 1958).

18. Whitehill, Walter Muir, *Boston: A Topographical History*, 2d ed., enlarged (Cambridge: The Belknap Press of Harvard University Press, 1973), 120.

19. Whitehill, *Boston: A Topographical History*, 119-20.

20. Mostov, "A Sociological Portrait," 140.

21. Mostov, "A Sociological Portrait," 141.

22. Mostov, "A Sociological Portrait," 142. Isaac Leeser had estimated approximately 120 Jewish families in 1851, a number Mostov (131) finds probable. See also Braverman, "The Ascent of Boston's Jews," 34–44.

23. Braverman, "The Ascent of Boston's Jews," states (31) that "over half of Boston's founding generation of German Jews arrived before 1855."

24. Mostov, "A Sociological Portrait," 136, 131, 137. Mostov (128) also points out that until 1860 there was a virtual absence of all foreign-born immigrants in Boston other than Englishmen and Irishmen. The Jews, though pioneers in this regard, were numerically too insignificant to have an immediate impact on the Boston community.

25. For comparative figures on the general Boston occupational and demographic structures see Oscar Handlin, *Boston's Immigrants, 1790–1880*, 2d. ed. rev. and enl. (New York: Atheneum, 1975) and Peter Knights, *The Plain People of Boston, 1830–1860* (New York: Oxford University Press, 1971). Stephan Thernstrom's *The Other Bostonians: Poverty and Progress in the American Metropolis 1880–1970* (Cambridge: Harvard University Press,

1973) contains useful information for the end of this period. Burton Kliman also analyzes the demographics and employment patterns of Boston's central European Jews. See Kliman, "The Jewish Brahmins of Boston."

26. Mostov, "A Sociological Portrait," 145.

27. Mostov, "A Sociological Portrait," 147.

28. Kliman, "The Jewish Brahmins," 105, and Braverman, "The Ascent of Boston's Jews," 80–81.

29. Mostov, "A Sociological Portrait," 151.

30. Kliman, "The Jewish Brahmins," 98.

31. Kliman, "The Jewish Brahmins," 134 and chap. 3.

32. Kliman, "The Jewish Brahmins," 155.

33. Kliman, "The Jewish Brahmins," 168.

34. This proved especially important after the great Boston fire of 1872 razed much of the manufacturing and wholesale districts, destroying a great portion of Jewish businesses as part of the massive devastation.

35. For the stories of individual central European families that succeeded in business, including the Morse, Shuman, Spitz, Ratshesky, Reinstein, Wolf, and Filene families, see Braverman, "The Ascent of Boston's Jews," chap. 3.

36. Solomon Schindler, *Israelites in Boston: A Tale Describing the Development of Judaism in Boston, Preceded by the Jewish Calendar for the Next Decade* (Boston: Berwick & Smith, [1889]), chap. 3.

37. Schindler, *Israelites in Boston*, chap. 3.

38. For more on the evolution of these, and other Boston Jewish neighborhoods, see Gerald Gamm's chapter in this volume.

39. Edwin M. Bacon, *King's Dictionary of Boston* (Cambridge: Moses King, 1883), 224–25.

40. Schindler, *Israelites in Boston*, Preface.

41. Schindler, *Israelites in Boston*, Introduction.

42. Three women, leaders of female lodges and charitable organizations, are briefly mentioned, but not in the full-page biographies accorded the men.

43. Schindler, *Israelites in Boston*, chap. 2.

44. Schindler, *Israelites in Boston*, chap. 2. He further wrote (chap. 5), "I believe in reform, but do not stand still at the mere changing of outward forms. My endeavors have always been directed toward reforming the very spirit."

45. Schindler, *Israelites in Boston*, chap. 3.

46. For more on the development of the UHBA, the Hebrew Ladies' Sewing Circle, and other early charitable organizations in Boston, see Susan Ebert's chapter in this volume.

47. Schindler, *Israelites in Boston*, chap. 5.

48. The full title is *History of the Jews of Boston and New England. Their Financial, Professional, and Commercial Enterprises. From the Earliest Settlement of Hebrews in Boston to the Present Day. Containing a Historical and Statistical Record of Every Jewish Congregation, Fraternal Order, Benevolent Society and Social Club, Together with Biographies of Noted Men, and Other Matters of Interest* (Boston: The Jewish Chronicle Publishing Co., 1892). The volume is sometimes attributed to Abraham G. Daniels.

# The Emergence of a
# Unified Community, 1880-1917

*Overleaf:* Jewish merchants, Orleans Street,
East Boston, 1914. *Boston Athenæum,
Boston, Massachusetts.*

WILLIAM A. BRAVERMAN

# The Emergence of a Unified Community, 1880-1917

הנה מה־טוב ומה־נעים שבת אחים גם יחד

"Behold, how good and pleasant it is for brethren to dwell in unity."
PSALMS 133:1

 N JANUARY 1909, Jacob De Haas, editor of the *Boston Advocate*, invited readers to respond to the question, "What methods would tend most to unite the Jews?" He was undoubtedly discouraged by the answers. In Boston, one rabbi commented, "We may notice the distinct constituent elements of Jewry, different religions, different races, classes hopelessly out of social sympathy with one another, and far differing ideals of the necessary and the desirable."[1] Within a decade, however, Boston's Jews had made significant advances toward unity. A new spirit of cooperation and identity was evident not only in the pages of the Jewish newspapers, but also in the efforts of the community to establish a stable economic and residential base, to aid its poor, to become openly and vocally involved in the city's political life, to support a Jewish state in Palestine, and to define clearly a functional balance between being Jewish and being American. The years from 1880 through 1917 chart the coalesecence of Boston's diverse Jewish population into a self-assertive and articulate ethnic community.

Jews fled from lands controlled by the Russian Tsar in the early 1880's as a direct result of antisemitic laws and acts sanctioned by the state. A longstanding policy of repression toward Jews begun after the partition of Poland in the 18th century brought thousands of Jews under Russian control. Although the pogroms were the most obvious and vicious antisemitic acts, they did not alone stimulate the mass exodus of Jews. As immigration historian Samuel Joseph noted, the "less evident, because less spectacular, methods of restrictive law and administrative action" were more important in pushing Jews out of Russia.[2]

FIG. 1. Jewish family in rural Eastern Europe, ca. 1890. *American Jewish Historical Society.*

FIG. 2. One of the earliest known photographs of Jewish Boston, corner Prince and Salem streets, Boston's North End, ca. 1893. *Boston Public Library, Print Department.*

Between 1880 and 1914, more than 90,000 Jews informed immigration officials in ports across the United States that their final destination was Massachusetts.[3] Almost all of the Jews who actually arrived in Boston between 1880 and 1917 came from Russia, but less than half of them remained in Massachusetts; one out of three left immediately for New York City.[4] Skilled laborers, especially those who worked in the needle trades, were most likely to leave Russia for America. The typical Russian Jewish immigrant was a literate male with a skilled trade who arrived with an illiterate wife and small children.[5] Coming as families, these immigrants intended to stay. In the early 1890's, over sixty percent of the arriving Jews claimed they had a skill, and less than two percent listed themselves as professionals.[6] This trend continued into the first decade of the 20th century.

The first Russian Jews who arrived in Boston settled near their Polish and German brethren in the South End. These earlier immigrants, as if in response, began moving to better areas of the city. Old prejudices against the Orthodox and culturally distinct Russian Jews were reinforced by class differences. By the 1890's, the leading Central European Jews no longer lived in the old South End, but in Roxbury and the better areas of the new South End. Members of the Morse, Strauss, Ehrlich, and Hecht families were among the few Jews living in the Back Bay. Almost all of these Jewish elites were successful businessmen, most of whom worked in the clothing trade. Their position, both in the economic life of the city as a whole and within the Jewish community, made them stand out as their ethnic group's leading representatives.[7]

Russian Jews also moved in large numbers into the North and West Ends. After the Irish made the North End their home in the 1850's, the area became one of Boston's most important centers of first-generation immigrants. In 1880, less than one thousand Italians and a few hundred Central European Jews lived in the North End.[8] By 1895, the North End contained 7,700 Italians and 6,200 Jews. Within a twenty-year period, the once largely Irish district had

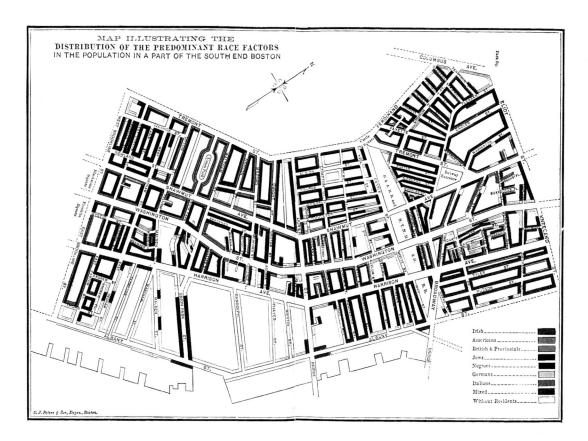

FIG. 3. "Distribution of the Predominant Race Factors in the . . . South End, Boston," as printed in Robert A. Woods, editor, *The City Wilderness: A Settlement Study by Residents and Associates of the South End House.* Boston: Houghton Mifflin, 1898.

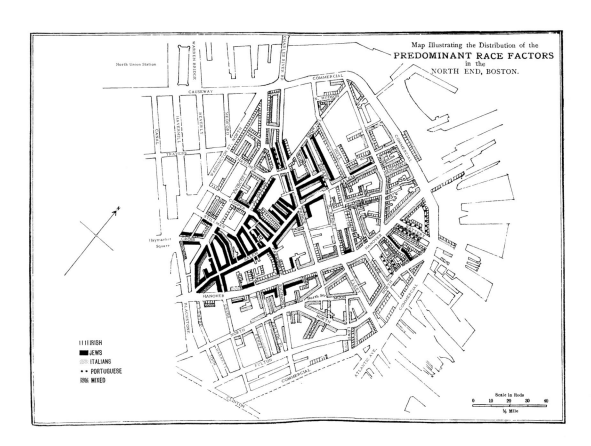

FIG. 4. "Predominant Race Factors in the North End, Boston," as printed in Robert A. Woods, editor, *Americans in Process: A Settlement House Study,* Boston: Houghton Mifflin, 1902.

FIG. 5. Jewish children at the corner of North Bennett and Salem streets, North End, Boston, ca. 1900. *Boston Public Library, Print Department.*

become one of the most cosmopolitan areas in Boston. Italians, Portuguese, Poles, Germans, and Russian Jews all lived in close proximity. The young Jewish immigrant Kevie Carmen remembered how the "noisy mixture of many languages sounded like another Tower of Babel."[9] Other Jews observed men and women dressed in "multicolored garb" and smelled the unmistakable aroma of Old World cooking.[10]

Nearly all observers commented on the unappealing conditions prevalent in the North End. Many Bostonians agreed with the Yankee settlement house pioneer Robert Woods that the central problem of the North End was "the problem of immigration, to be solved at the ports of the United States."[11] The immigrants worked to address their own needs, and by the turn of the century, the North End hosted a full array of Russian Jewish social and religious institutions ranging from Orthodox synagogues to burial societies to ladies' sewing circles to baseball teams.[12] The district housed an economic cross-section of Jews as well. Some chose to remain close to the traditional way of life made possible by the thousands of Jewish immigrants living there even after they achieved economic success. But the majority of Jews moved out of the North End when it proved financially possible to do so. For many, their destination was the West End, where streets were not as crowded and an Orthodox life could be maintained.

Historically, the West End followed the general pattern established in the older North End: it had once been an enclave of wealthy residents, then home to the middle-class and rising Irish immigrants, Boston's African-American population, and finally, and later than in the North End, home to the "new" immigrants, particularly the Jews and Italians.[13] Unlike the North End, the West End had different socio-economic enclaves. There were many respectable and comfortable areas as well as others that were as "noisome and dark" as any in the North End. Along the slope of Beacon Hill, for example, one contemporary noted that the "struggling people" and the "prosperous and responsible Boston citizens" were physically only blocks apart.[14] The rapid transformation of the area's ethnic composition is readily seen in census figures: in 1880, the West End included only 125 Italians and 100 Jews, while fifteen years later, 6,300 Jews and 1,100 Italians called the area their

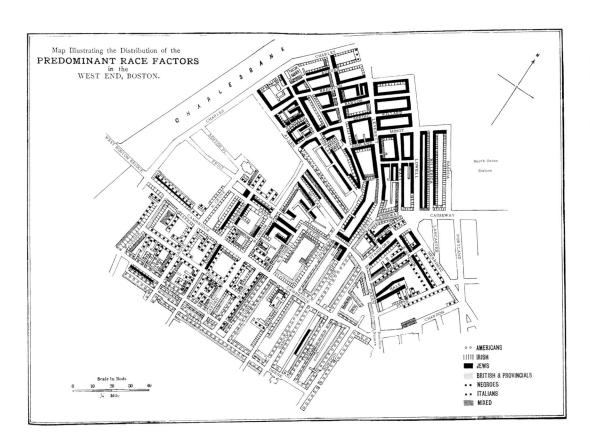

Map Illustrating the Distribution of the
**PREDOMINANT RACE FACTORS**
in the
WEST END, BOSTON.

AMERICANS
IRISH
JEWS
BRITISH & PROVINCIALS
NEGROES
ITALIANS
MIXED

Scale in Rods
0    10    20    30    40
⅛ Mile

FIG. 6. "Predominant Race Factors in the West End, Boston," as printed in Robert A. Woods, editor, *Americans in Process: A Settlement House Study*, Boston: Houghton Mifflin, 1902.

FIG. 7, *below*. Poplar Street looking toward Chambers Street, West End, Boston, 1910. *Boston Public Library, Print Department.*

FIG. 8, *left*. Corner of Chambers and Spring streets looking toward Leverett Street, West End, Boston, 1910. *Boston Public Library, Print Department.*

FIG. 9. Victims of the Chelsea Fire line up for clothing and Passover supplies in front of the Young Men's Hebrew Association, Boston's West End, April 1908. *Boston Public Library, Print Department.*

home. In 1910, as many as 40,000 Russian Jews lived in the West End.[15]

The North, West, and South Ends, along with Chelsea, were the most important Jewish immigrant neighborhoods of the late 19th and early 20th centuries. From 1892 to 1917 the more successful Jews expanded out of the downtown wards and moved to Roxbury and Dorchester. What began as a small movement of the rich became a mass exodus by 1918.[16] Within a ten-year period, Boston's Jewish population had almost completely left the North, South, and West Ends and settled in more outlying districts. Since the First World War effectively ended the influx of new immigrants, the older Jewish neighborhoods never recovered their former size. As Roxbury and Dorchester became more populated, the demand for service industries further stimulated the Jewish demographic shift. The Chelsea Fire of 1908 also contributed significantly to the number of Jews who moved into what historian Sam Bass Warner described as Boston's "streetcar suburbs."[17] Boston's Jews would never again live in such concentrated physical proximity. Community would need to be forged beyond geographic boundaries.

With their arrival in Boston, the new Russian immigrants faced the immediate necessity of making a living. The majority found such opportunities in Boston's well-developed textile and shoe industries, a segment of the economy previously entered into by Central European Jewish immigrants. But success in the clothing business was not limited to "German" Jews. Indeed it was the success of these first Jews in Boston in the clothing trade that made it possible for Russian Jews to peddle, accumulate capital, and then open their own small stores. It was also the Russian Jews who carried out most of the skilled and unskilled labor upon which the larger clothing manufacturers depended.

Part of the reason for the economic success of many Russian Jews was their ability to position themselves in sectors of the clothing industry that others had either overlooked or consciously avoided because of the unpleasantness and low status of the work.[18] Benjamin Feinberg and his sons, for example, cornered the market in the wool rag business. Feinberg was born in Pliskov, Russia, in 1840 and worked in the cattle business. He left Russia with his wife and six sons in 1888, in part for fear of having his sons drafted into the army and in part for economic betterment. The family landed at the Cunard Dock in East Boston in August, 1888, took the East Boston ferry to Fleet Street, and then hired a horse car to Tremont Street in search of a man who ran a cigar store. The cigar dealer sent the family to the home of Max Solomon who took care of them until they found three rooms on Salem Street in the North End.[19]

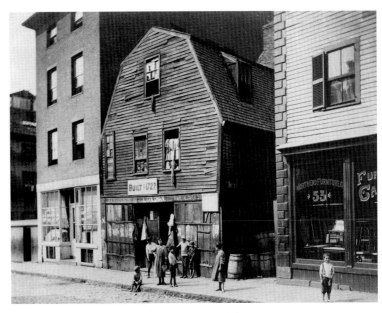

The Feinbergs bought bedding and other necessities on the installment plan and received free bread, milk, and groceries from the Jewish dealers in the North End until Mr. Feinberg started making money. With his old world skill of cattle dealing useless, Benjamin worked as a rag picker with his son William. He received three dollars a week, barely enough to pay for rent and food for a family of eight. Other sons brought home additional funds by sorting woolen clippings for clothing manufacturers. When Benjamin felt he had learned the rag business, he hired a shop in an old fire engine house and "started to prosper almost from the beginning." The family moved to Pitts Street and then to Wall Street in the West End. In the early years of the 20th century all of the brothers combined their businesses and formed B. Feinberg and Sons, which soon became New England's premier rag business.[20]

Jews also worked in businesses related to the clothing industry, including accessories and furs. Although the amount of money that could be made in this sector of the economy was not as great as in the manufacturing and retailing of regular clothing, the successful Jews who entered these trades made thousands of dollars in profits. With competition limited, and with a ready source of labor, the Jewish businesses thrived.[21]

Boston's second leading manufacturing industry was the boot and shoe business. In the 1850's, after the Howe and Singer sewing machines made it possible to stitch quickly the

FIG. 12. Shoe factory interior, probably Boston. Charles H. Currier, ca. 1890. *Library of Congress, Washington.*

FIG. 13. Peddler on Spring Street between Chambers and Poplar, West End, Boston, 1907. *Boston Public Library, Print Department*

upper leather of boots and shoes, the industry expanded at a tremendous rate. By the 1880's, Boston had become the center of the state's shoe business. Although cities such as Lynn were important shoe centers, Boston was the great market, clearing house, and financial center for the entire New England shoe industry. Two of Boston's foremost Jewish families—the Hechts and the Freidmans—were involved in the shoe business and both families had vital connections with other cities.[22]

On the other hand, Boston's Jews found it difficult in the early 20th century to break into the highest financial circles, closed to them because of their religion and lack of preparedness. In response, several Jews formed their own financial institutions. Abraham Ratshesky was already a wealthy man before he started the United States Trust Company in 1895. But some immigrants began in banking with only a few hundred dollars, catering to the specific needs of Boston's increasing Jewish immigrant population. The Hungarian-born Julius Rottenberg was one of Boston's leading bankers for immigrants. Leaving his native Eger as a youngster and working first in New York as a small banker and steamship ticket agent, he arrived in Boston in 1895 and opened the "Universal Banking House" on Salem Street. The business expanded rapidly. Rottenberg not only helped immigrants with financial matters but also acted as their advisor on personal problems. One of his employees, Kevie Carmen, left to form a rival steamship ticket and banking office in Salem, Massachusetts, and later competed with him in Salem Street in Boston's North End. With immigration reduced during the First World War and then severely limited by law, Carmen moved into commercial banking, while Rottenberg expanded his business to serve the Italian and Polish communities.[23]

But the American way of work took its toll on Boston's immigrant Orthodox Jews. They found it difficult to close their shops and businesses on the Jewish Sabbath, particularly since Massachusetts Blue Laws prohibited them from working on Sundays. As a result, many resignedly compromised and accepted at least some Saturday work. For those who did not, the cost in economic and family terms could be high. Joseph Malkin, "a slim man with a very sad face and a long black beard," was a religious Jew who did not work on Saturday. He spent twelve hours all other days of the week picking rags in Chelsea.[24]

With thousands of Orthodox Jews living in Boston in the late 19th century, there was a tremendous demand for kosher meat and other specifically Jewish businesses. Kosher shops filled the Jewish districts of Boston, especially in the North and West Ends, and later in the Blue Hill Avenue district of Roxbury and Dorchester. With competition fierce, kosher meat wars periodically wreaked havoc on the Jewish community. In response, in August 1892, a butcher trust formed in the North End to fix prices for kosher food. A mass meeting of angry consumers, many of them women, filled one of the North End synagogues to protest, accusing the butchers who had agreed to fix prices of selling non-kosher meat. The *Jewish Chronicle* attacked the complaining Jews, noting that the same tactics had been employed in an attempt to reduce the price for killing fowl. Each consumer, the paper pointed out, had the option of buying her food from whatever dealer she chose, and there was no reason to embarrass the community with hysterical accusations.[25] Meat strikes, headed by Jewish wives angry over the high price of food, broke out repeatedly in Boston, and in later years frequently received support from the *Jewish Advocate*. But with the exception of two kosher meat cooperatives in the West End, the Jewish food service industry continued to be controlled by price-fixing trusts.

Although many Jews worked in the service industries, few entered the professions. In late 19th-century Boston, there was only a handful of Jewish doctors, lawyers, and educators. In part this is explained by the overwhelming drive of Boston's early Central European Jewish immigrants to succeed in business. Fathers and sons worked together and it was expected that the children of successful business leaders would take over the family businesses. Men like Lee M. Friedman, a successful lawyer and superb amateur historian of American Jewish history and Jewish Boston, whose father Max was for a time the largest boot and shoe wholesaler in America, was the exception to the general rule. Yet it was with the influx of

FIG. 14. "Food Protestors in West End." Early 20th century photograph taken for the Boston *Herald Traveller*. *Boston Public Library, Print Department.*

FIG. 15. Boston Matzo Baking Company Office, Parmenter Street, North End, Boston, 1894. *American Jewish Historical Society.*

East European immigrants that the Jews of Boston began to branch out into the professions in significant numbers. The dramatic change is reflected in the number of Jews who attended Harvard College. Less than one percent of Harvard's student body in 1881 was Jewish; in 1908 Jews accounted for seven percent of the total; in 1922 more than one fifth of all entering freshmen were Jews, almost all of them Russian Jews.[26]

Despite the remarkable achievement of some Jewish families, most of Boston's Jews were neither large manufacturers, bankers, professionals, nor food distributors. They earned moderate wages as workers in small businesses and factories, and as independent peddlers, small retailers, second-hand clothes dealers, and even pawnbrokers. Many Jewish women also worked, largely out of necessity. The *Advocate* commented on the twin pulls of home and economic survival on traditional Jewish women, commenting in 1908 that the first allegiance for Jewish women was the home. Women's proper sphere was "fostering loyalty to Judaism in those who love them, rising above the problems of frocks and fashions, personal pleasures and enjoyments, breathing in those about them a spirit of race and a constancy to principle, a devotion and a love in the sphere of charity." The paper sympathized with the thousands of women employed in the cloak trades who were the "greatest sufferers" in the industrial army.[27]

FIG. 16. Boston sweatshop, early 20th century. Photograph given in memory of Bessie Hurwitz, one of the "sweatshop girls" pictured. *American Jewish Historical Society.*

The formation of unions and benevolent societies helped many struggling Jews move out of poverty. Boston's Russian Jewish women employed in the garment industry had a strong ally in Philip Davis, a Russian Jewish graduate of Harvard College and a leader in the North End Civic Service House, a settlement house and educational center started by another Russian Jewish graduate of Harvard, Meyer Bloomfield. Through his work in the North End, Davis learned about the Jewish women who "labored in the little sweat-shops which honeycombed the neighborhoods," working long days under filthy and dangerous conditions. Under his tutelage, these working women gained self-confidence and learned to support collective action to effect change. In the fall of 1902, Davis helped organize the Waist-makers', the Wrap-makers', and the White-goods Workers' Unions. Union negotiations failed, as did a subsequent strike. Although the women returned to work, they later affiliated with the larger International Union to bring about improved conditions.[28]

FIG. 17. Newsboys in front of the Boston Globe building, 1919. *Boston Public Library, Print Department.*

Other national unions had branches in Boston, including the Boston Tailor's Union, the Amalgamated Clothing Workers of America, and the American Federation of Labor, and many Jews were members. In addition to traditional unions, Boston's Jewish workers organized benevolent associations that cared for them and their families in case of accident or death. These associations also provided social activities for the workers and their families. Jewish newsboys, a very popular vocation for young Jews since the work could be done before and after school, also organized their own union and raised money to send one boy each year to Harvard College. Their union was affiliated with the AFL and Boston's Central Labor Union.[29]

Generally, the economic progress of Boston's Jews represents a success story. From very humble beginnings the city's Jewish population achieved moderate

FIG. 18. Winchell School, West End, Boston. Class 3, Room 12, early 20th century. *Boston Public Library, Print Department.*

and in some cases remarkable socio-economic advancement. Jews, indeed, fared better than any other ethnic group in the city's history.[30] Coming from urban settings and used to living in a capitalistic economy, they were able to adjust to Boston with less trauma than the Irish or Italians who in their homelands had almost all been agricultural workers. Status in the old country for Jews was based not just on wealth and family connections, but on education and religious training. Jews brought this traditional drive for learning with them to Boston. Jewish males won more academic dis-

tinctions in the Boston school system than any other ethnic group in part because of this traditional emphasis on education, and in part because of their parents' willingness to sacrifice their own comfort for the advancement of their children.[31]

The Jews' success in Boston was also helped by their long tradition of self-regulation, their ability to overcome prejudice through self-reliance and, as the credit agents so often reported, through their habit of looking after co-religionists. Businessmen who would otherwise not have received credit could rely on other Jews for loans. Boston's Jews also had a highly developed club life which solidified business and social ties. Excluded from Boston's preeminent social clubs, both German and Russian Jews started their own. The most exclusive was the Elysium Club, organized in the 1880's by Jacob Hecht and other leading German Jewish leaders. Young Jewish businessmen met at the club rooms after work and on weekends to play cards, talk informally, and dine. By 1893, nearly 150 Jews were members of the elegant club located at 218 Huntington Avenue. Eastern European Jews formed the New Century Club in 1900. The young lawyer Jacob Silverman along with William M. Blatt and other lawyers and doctors wanted a club where Jewish professionals could meet and discuss Jewish affairs. Although there was never a stated policy of excluding Jews from different national origins, the Elysium always remained dominated by German Jews and the New Century became the Russian social enclave. Boston had dozens of other Jewish social clubs, many of which were local offices of national organizations such as B'nai Brith.[32]

Finally, the agents of Boston Jewish culture glorified material success and rewarded those who achieved it. They emphasized the importance of making the most of this world and of moving up the socio-economic ladder. This attitude is readily seen in the Boston Jewish press. Beginning with the *Hebrew Observer* in 1883, the ideal Jew was depicted as one who, through hard work and honest business practices, made large profits and then supported those Jews still struggling economically. Every issue of the paper carried reports of Jewish businessmen and their social activities. In the eyes of Rabbi Solomon Schindler, the paper's editor, the model Jew was Leopold Morse—the very embodiment of the rise from peddler to merchant-prince. Although Schindler admitted that Morse's religious allegiance to Judaism was questionable—in fact, Morse's wife was Episcopalian—he nevertheless held him up as an example to the community of the proper role for Jewish Americans to emulate: "His good, sound common-sense has taught him the great lesson that in this our glorious country a man must be a good citizen, a good American first; then may follow his appreciation of the land in which he first saw the light of the world; and then, and only then, his predilection for one or another religious sect."[33]

The *Jewish Chronicle* continued to emphasize the importance of material achievement. Not only did much of the paper discuss the community's business history, it also introduced a regular column that provided readers with biographical vignettes of its leading men. The heroes of the community were clearly those who had not just made money but who had also helped their fellow Jews either through charity work, club activity, or political achievement. In striking contrast to the Irish Catholic newspaper the *Pilot*, where labor leaders, priests, politicians, and the common laborers received the most attention, Boston's Jewish papers, even in the 20th century, almost completely ignored the plights of labor and rarely praised or even reported on Boston Jewry's most significant labor leader, Henry Abrahams. In later years, the *Advocate* continued to highlight the community's business and professional leaders. Academic success was also highly praised in its pages. Each year, it carefully printed the names of all Jewish graduates of the Boston high schools and local colleges who had distinguished themselves with honors.[34]

It is a mistake to conclude that all of Boston's Jews managed to become middle-class citizens by the First World War. Many remained impoverished and either left the city entirely or remained locked in a life of ceaseless struggle. But comparably speaking, Boston's Jews were able to advance economically and educationally faster than any other immigrant group. They arrived at the right time, with the right skills, and with aspirations compatible to the economic and professional needs of the city and the region. Boston, as far as Jews were concerned, was a good fit.

Prior to the mass immigration of Russian Jews in the late 1880's, Boston's established Jewish community had built effective charities that took care of the community's poor and even managed to aid impoverished Jews in transit through the city. Jews took great pride in the fact that not one member of the community had received city or state aid. The appearance in Boston of thousands of Russian Jewish immigrants entirely transformed the structure of the city's Jewish charities and opened up a new set of problems for the established Jewish community. Yet it was through its charitable activities that Boston's Central and Eastern European communities formed their first opinions of one another and forged their first communal links. From independent aid societies, through the formation in 1895 of the Federation of Jewish Charities (the first federated charity system in the United States) to gradual sharing of power among the German and Russian community leaders, to the Federation's restructuring as a professional social work-based organization in 1917, charitable activity pressed the full community into mutual recognition and support.[35] The tradition and power of charitable work in the Jewish community created initial alliances that would soon be mirrored in the community's religious and political life as well.

In the community's religious life, the period between 1880 and 1918 also witnessed a gradual movement toward common ground. The synagogues, too, reflected the Boston Jewish community's evolving understanding of itself as Americans and as Jews. Rabbi Solomon Schindler of Adath (Temple) Israel, for example, urged loyalty to Judaism but emphasized above it the brotherhood of all people and the commonality of ethics among all religions. Toward the end of his life he returned to a more moderate view, arguing against his successor, Rabbi Charles Fleischer, that Judaism's individuality must indeed be preserved. Fleischer was never so convinced and left the congregation in 1911 committed to the universality of religion, especially in an American environment.[36]

Rabbi Harry Levi succeeded Charles Fleischer, and his inaugural sermon seemed to resolve the tension between being an American and being a Jew that Schindler and Fleischer had addressed in such different ways. Levi testified both to the spiritual truths of Judaism and to its need to remain distinct from other religions. Judaism, he told his congregation, was not simply an ethical system but a code of ethics built upon religious beliefs that gave them "sanction and authority."[37] The function of the synagogue was to bind its members to the Jewish faith and to impress upon them the importance of bringing religious conviction to daily life. And while he supported Reform measures that included vernacular prayers, use of an organ and a choir, Levi reminded his congregation that religious services were performed not for "intellectual delight" or for "social diversion" but for "spiritual uplift."[38] At the same time, he preached a strongly patriotic Judaism, calling on all Jews to identify fully with American secular life and to sacrifice themselves, if necessary, "on the altar of the country's welfare."[39] A strong religious life was fundamental to good citizenship, Levi believed. "Between America and Judaism," he was fond of saying, "there is no incompatibility."[40] Believing that to be a good Jew was synonymous with being a good American, he used his pulpit to speak out against social injustice in Boston and the nation. A strong critic of child labor, immigration restriction, racism, materialism, and war, Levi never lost his faith in American democracy, and believed that the solution to the nation's divisions was through the ballot and by individual charity.

Conservative and Orthodox rabbis also spoke out on political issues. Some supported women's suffrage because it was in harmony with the "spirit of Judaism" and defended striking workers because of the injustice displayed by greedy bosses.[41]

They used Jewish holidays to preach social justice and political activism to their congregations. Religious services held on such American holidays as Lincoln's Birthday and Thanksgiving gave the rabbis the opportunity to urge Jews to celebrate secular holidays without losing their ties to Judaism. Their goals were to reconcile Jewish culture with American history. Through complete devotion to Judaism, they believed, Jews could become patriotic American citizens.[42]

❦

Before the mass immigration of Eastern European Jews in the late 19th century, Boston's Jewish community was not very active in city or regional secular politics. When the city's Jews voted, they did not vote any differently from their Christian neighbors. Early Jewish leaders viewed with distrust anyone who tried to convince the community to enter the political arena as a separate ethnic/religious voting block. Boston's Jews, like those in other urban centers, were sensitive to any suggestion that they were "hyphenated Americans" and rejected almost all social behavior that might label them as being different from other Americans.

The influx of Russian Jews changed the nature of the Boston Jewish community's political behavior. Russian Jews brought with them dreams of recreating a Jewish state in Palestine and organized Hebrew political clubs in Jewish neighborhoods. For the first time in the community's history, Jewish candidates for political office openly courted their fellow Jews for support based on their common ethnic bonds.[43] The rise of antisemitism in Boston also gave Jews a renewed sense of community and an urgency to unite behind politicians who would fight for Jewish interests. Pushed by outside forces to recognize the need for Jewish self-protection and pulled by the lure of political patronage and power, the city's Jews banded together to fight for candidates sympathetic to their causes—this despite traditional German Jewish warnings against mixing religion and politics.[44]

Ironically, Boston Jews' first major foray into the political area was led by a German Jew, Louis D. Brandeis. Speaking at a Thanksgiving Day celebration in 1905 which also commemorated the 250th anniversary of the Jews' arrival in America, Brandeis urged leaders of the Jewish community to support Louis Frothingham's mayoral campaign against John F. Fitzgerald—the future President's grandfather.[45] Like Boston's earlier German Jewish leaders, Brandeis was hesi-

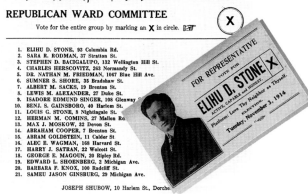

FIG. 19. Election posters in Yiddish and English promoting Elihu D. Stone and other Jewish political candidates. *American Jewish Historical Society.*

FIG. 20. Advertisement
for Menauhant Hotel,
South Shore, forbidding
"Hebrew Patronage,"
1905. *American Jewish
Historical Society.*

tant to call for a "Jewish vote" and argued that American democracy required that all other national or religious affiliations be dropped. But Judaism also required ethics and honesty in government, secure justification for the community's support of Frothingham. Other speakers echoed Brandeis's sentiments in the first important break from the older, defensive posture taken by leaders of the first generation of German Jews who had argued that support of Jewish culture, Zionism, and self-assertion as an ethnic group were antithetical to American ideals.

The summer of 1905 also saw the emergence of a Jewish voting block on ward-level issues. Mildred Kallen, a young Jewish teacher in the West End's Washington School and sister of Horace Kallen, informed Robert Silverman, a Jewish law student at Boston University, that she believed Joseph Harrington, the school's headmaster, had misappropriated funds and set a poor example for the students.[46] Because the public schools played such an important role in the Jews' socio-economic mobility, the possibility of corruption not only violated the community's faith in good government but also threatened to prevent the children from gaining admission to the city's two college preparatory high schools.

When Martin Lomasney, the political boss of the West End, and Julia Duff, Harrington's sister and a School Board member, defended Harrington's record, the case became a symbolic fight against ward boss politics. A subcommittee of the School Committee composed of Duff and four others investigated Silverman's charges against Harrington. A majority voted to exonerate Harrington while one member voted to dismiss him. In front of the entire School Committee, Julia Duff berated the man who wrote the dissenting report and accused Silverman, Kallen, and other "conspirators" of unjustly accusing her brother.[47]

Harrington's exoneration proved to be a Pyrrhic victory for Julia Duff. The Silverman affair provided the editors of the *Boston Advocate* with a sufficient cause to call for a "Jewish vote" against her reelection. It was the duty of parents to "stand up" for the children and fight against the "cheap ward politicians" who demanded that Jews vote for the ward boss's friends. Equating a vote for Duff with a vote for "grafters, self-seekers, and notoriety-hunters," the *Boston Advocate* hoped to break the hold of Martin Lomasney on the Jewish voters in the West End.[48] When Duff was soundly defeated the paper proudly labeled the election a "victory for the children."[49]

The School Committee fight marked the first time in Boston's history that the Jewish population unabashedly entered the political arena as a self-conscious voting unit. Although community leaders still deplored the "injection of sectarianism into public affairs," they argued that there were times when self-defense warranted "racial solidarity."[50] This concern over clean politics and good government spilled over into the general election of 1905. The *Advocate* now began to examine each candidate individually and endorse them not by party or philosophical position, but by municipal performance. Massive voting registration drives took place among Jewish citizens. As the numbers of Jews living in Boston increased to over 70,000 in the second decade of the 20th century, distinct "Jewish interests" emerged that included such diverse topics as immigration restriction,

FIG. 21. Hendricks Club, Democratic heaquarters, Boston's West End, from a July 1908 newspaper article. *Boston Public Library, Print Department.*

regulation of kosher food, public education, the state's "Blue Laws," and the rise of local and international antisemitism.[51] Although many of these issues had already surfaced in the 19th century, they became political touchstones in the 20th century after Jews became a sizable voting block and after Jewish leaders had accepted the idea of a "Jewish vote." In politics, Boston's Jewish community had found additional common ground.

The emergence of an outspoken Jewish political voice also helped make Zionism a more appealing movement among Boston's Jews. If Jews could remain loyal Americans when they spoke out for Jewish interests in local and national politics, then, without appearing unpatriotic, they could also support an international movement that promised to alleviate Jewish suffering in the world by establishing a separate Jewish state.[52]

Public expressions of Jewish culture grew in many other venues. The Harvard Menorah Society, founded in 1906 by Henry Hurwitz and a handful of other undergraduates, became the center of Jewish activity on campus and an important center of Zionist thought in the Boston area. The Menorah Society's faith that the

FIG. 22. Salem Street, North End, Boston, 1901. A banner commemorating the recent assassination of President McKinley in the rear. Yiddish sign in the foreground advertises Jewish books, Torah scrolls, prayer shawls, and *etrogim* (citrons) for the holiday of Sukkot. *Private collection.*

"freest functioning of democracy" would come from the "harmonization of the various cultures and traditions" was one of the first modern statements of cultural pluralism. Horace Kallen, Harvard President Charles Eliot, and others used the Menorah Society podium to articulate the possibility of people retaining their ethnic and religious individuality while remaining committed and loyal American citizens. Louis D. Brandeis, among others, was persuaded by Kallen's arguments, and many historians trace the origins of Brandeis's support for Zionism and ethnic pluralism to his relationship with Kallen.[53] Even Solomon Schindler changed his views of Zionism in his last years. Before his death in 1915, he came to see in Zionism the potential for creating a Jewish renaissance. Mary Antin, too, came to believe that full assimilation was "a confession of failure and acknowledgement of weakness." All alike argued for the compatibility of Americanism, Zionism, and strong Jewish identity.[54]

That confidence was perhaps best expressed in the summer of 1915, when eight Zionist organizations gathered for a weeklong conference in Boston. Mayor James Michael Curley offered the Zionists the key to the city, and American and Zionist flags decked the streets. In the Public Garden, a large floral display featured a Star of David at its center. At the opening ceremony in Ford Hall, Jacob De Haas told the assembled thousands that in Boston, "the essential traditions of America were nursed into life and strength," traditions in which Boston's Jews now played a role.[55] The convention's remarkable display of unity marked the high point not only for Boston's Zionists but also for the Jewish community as a whole in the period 1880–1917. For the entire week, and long afterwards, the old distinctions between Germans and Russians, Republicans and Democrats, rich and poor, Orthodox and Reform, seemed to disappear. In one of the many ironies of Jewish life, the rise of antisemitism in Boston and in the world hastened the formation of a durable, outwardly directed, and confident American Jewish spirit. The extent to which Zionism and American Judaism had lost their unpatriotic images was best expressed by the *Boston Post* when it editorialized at the end of the convention that "it was in a notable sense a popular gathering, representative not of class politics but essentially and collectively of American Citizenship."[56] The description applied not only to Zionists, but to Boston's Jewish community as a whole.

1. *Boston Advocate*, 22 January 1909.

2. Samuel Joseph, "Jewish Immigration to the United States from 1881 to 1910," in Faculty of Political Science of Columbia University, ed., *Studies in History, Economics and Public Law* 59 (1914), 62.

3. U.S. Government, *Annual Report of the Commissioner-General of Immigration* (Washington D.C.: Government Printing Office, 1899–1918). "Hebrews" were listed as a separate category beginning in 1899.

4. Baron de Hirsch Papers, box 37, American Jewish Historical Society, Waltham, Massachusetts.

5. Simon Kuznets, "Immigration of Russian Jews to the United States: Background and Structure," *Perspectives in American History* 9 (1975): 95–194, 112–15.

6. de Hirsch Papers, Outside Organizations' Correspondence, Boston-H, box 54, folder two.

7. William Alan Braverman, "The Ascent of Boston's Jews, 1630–1918," (Ph.D. diss., Harvard University, 1990), 55–58.

8. Arnold A. Wieder, *The Early Jewish Community of Boston's North End: A Sociologically Oriented Study of an Eastern European Jewish Immigrant Community in an American Big City Neighborhood Between 1870 and 1900* (Waltham, Mass.: Brandeis University, 1962), 21.

9. Kevie Carmen, "Recollections of the Early Years, 1887–1926," (typescript), 34. American Jewish Historical Society.

10. Philip Davis, *And Crown Thy Good* (New York: Philosophical Library, 1952), 118.

11. Robert A. Woods, ed., *The City Wilderness: A Settlement Study by Residents and Associates of the South End House* (Boston: Houghton Mifflin, 1898), 39.

12. Wieder, *Early Jewish Community*, 45–52; Nathan M. Kaganoff, Martha Katz-Hyman, and Michael Strassfeld, eds., "Organized Jewish Group Activity in 19th Century Massachusetts: A Check List Recording all Groups Identified, Their Purposes, Years of Existence, a Listing of Prominent Individuals Connected With the Program, as Well as Eventual Disposition When Known," [typescript], 1979. American Jewish Historical Society.

13. Walter Muir Whitehill, *Boston: A Topographical History* (Cambridge: Harvard University Press, 1978), 177–78; Robert A. Woods, ed., *Americans in Process: A Settlement Study By Residents and Associates of the South End House. North and West Ends, Boston* (Boston: Houghton Miffliny, 1902), 4–5, 41.

14. Woods, *Americans in Process*, 4–5.

15. Thomas H. O'Connor, *Bibles, Brahmins, and Bosses: A Short History of Boston* (Boston: Trustees of the Public Library of the City of Boston, 1984), 122.

16. Braverman, *Ascent of Boston's Jews*, 73–78.

17. Sam Bass Warner, Jr., *Streetcar Suburbs: The Process of Growth in Boston, 1870–1900*, 2d ed. (Cambridge: Harvard University Press, 1978); Francis Russell, "The Coming of the Jews," *Antioch Review* 15 (March 1955): 21–24.

18. Braverman, *Ascent of Boston's Jews*, 100.

19. Israel Feinberg, (unpublished and untitled memoir, typescript 55 pp.), 25–27. Private collection, Mr. Archibald Feinberg.

20. Feinberg, unpublished memoir, 28–29, 41, 54.

21. Braverman, *Ascent of Boston's Jews*, 102.

22. Braverman, *Ascent of Boston's Jews*, 103–04.

23. Braverman, *Ascent of Boston's Jews*, 105–08; Carmen, "Recollections of the Early Years," 28–32, 45–49, 54–100.

24. Braverman, *Ascent of Boston's Jews*, 106; Carmen, "Recollections of the Early Years," 37, 40–45.

25. *Boston Jewish Chronicle*, 26 August 1892.

26. Bernard Bailyn and others, *Glimpses of the Harvard Past* (Cambridge: Harvard University Press, 1986), 127.

27. *Boston Advocate*, 8 May 1908; also 10 November 1905, 22 September 1905, 22 February 1907.

28. Davis, along with other Boston leaders and Samuel Gompers of the A.F.L. started the Women's Trade Union League and served as the delegate from Boston at the International Union meeting in Cleveland, Ohio in 1903. Philip Davis, *And Crown Thy Good*, 133–72.

29. Minnie Corder, quoted in *The South End* (Boston: The Boston 200 Corporation, 1976), 5–6. For a fuller list of Boston Jewish worker organizations see footnote 66, chap. 3, in Braverman, *Ascent of Boston's Jews*.

30. Braverman, *Ascent of Boston's Jews*, 116.

31. Braverman, *Ascent of Boston's Jews*, 116.

32. Braverman, *Ascent of Boston's Jews*, 116-17.

33. See, for example, *Boston Hebrew Observer*, 5 January 1883; *Boston Jewish Advocate*, 26 September 1913, 3 October 1913, 4 July 1913, 11 July 1913; Solomon Schindler, *Israelites in Boston, A Tale Describing the Development of Judaism in Boston* (Boston: Berwick and Smith, 1889), chap. five.

34. Francis Robert Walsh, "The *Boston Pilot*: A Newspaper for the Irish Immigrant, 1829–1908" (Ph.D. diss., Boston University, 1968). The drive of the first generation for material success had some negative aspects too. Unlike in Russian Jewish life where leaders were often from the educated and religious classes, in Boston and other American cities, the leaders were often simply the wealthiest Jews.

35. For a fuller history of community and philanthropy in Boston, see Braverman, *Ascent of Boston's Jews*, 121–49, and Susan Ebert's chapter in this volume.

36. Braverman, *Ascent of Boston's Jews*, 151–94.

37. *Boston Advocate*, 22 September 1911.

38. *Boston Advocate*, 1 December 1911, 22 December 1911, 29 December 1911.

39. *Boston Advocate*, 16 February, 1912.

40. *Boston Advocate*, 23 February 1912.

41. *Boston Advocate*, 15 January 1909, 22 January 1909.

42. *Boston Advocate*, 19 April 1917. For a fuller account of the history of Boston's synagogue community in this period, see Braverman, *Ascent of Boston's Jews*, 151–200, and David Kaufman's essay in this volume.

43. For more on Jewish voting behavior in Boston, see Braverman, *Ascent of Boston's Jews,* 218–54 and "Appendix: An Analysis of Jewish Voting Patterns in Boston, 1900–1918," 270-372; and Gerald H. Gamm, *The Making of New Deal Democrats: Voting Behavior and Realignment in Boston, 1920–1940* (Chicago: University of Chicago Press, 1989).

44. Braverman, *Ascent of Boston's Jews*, chap. 6.

45. Louis D. Brandeis to Adolph Brandeis, 29 November 1905, in Melvin I. Urofsky and David W. Levy, eds., *Letters of Louis D. Brandeis, Volume I 1870–1907: Urban Reformer* (Albany: State University of New York Press, 1971), 386; Allon Gal, *Brandeis of Boston* (Cambridge: Harvard University Press, 1980), 92–93.

46. Gal, *Brandeis of Boston*, 85; *Boston Advocate*, 29 September 1905, 6 October 1905.

47. *Boston Advocate*, 29 September 1905, 13 October 1905, 17 November 1905.

48. *Boston Advocate*, 29 September 1905, 24 November 1905, 8 December 1905.

49. *Boston Advocate*, 22 December 1905.

50. *Boston Advocate*, 22 September 1905.

51. Braverman, *Ascent of Boston's Jews*, 237–44.

52. Braverman, *Ascent of Boston's Jews*, 244.

53. See Gal, *Brandeis of Boston*, for a fuller discussion of the relationship between Brandeis and Kallen.

54. *Boston Advocate*, 3 February 1916, 15 February 1917. For more on Zionism and the Boston Jewish community see Braverman, *Ascent of Boston's Jews*, 244–54, and Mark Raider's essay in this volume.

55. *Boston Advocate*, 2 July 1915.

56. *Boston Post*, 2 July 1915.

*From Margin to Mainstream,*
*1917-1967*

*Overleaf:* West End, Boston,
1950's. *Photograph by Jules Aarons.*

# LEON A. JICK

# *From Margin to Mainstream, 1917-1967*

"Enlarge the site of your tent, extend the size of your dwelling."
ISAIAH 54:2

HE HALF CENTURY between the First World War and the Six Day War saw Boston Jewry come of age. During this period, immigrants metamorphosed into ethnics, urbanites became suburbanites, and local Jews emerged as significant players on the national and international stage. Boston's Jewish population grew by about 100,000 during these years, from an estimated 75,000 in 1917 to 176,000 fifty years later. This kept the city even in terms of its rank among America's Jewish communities. The fifth largest Jewish community in 1917, on a par with Cleveland, Boston in 1967 still ranked number five, somewhat below Chicago (Cleveland, meanwhile, had dropped to tenth place).[1]

By all accounts, 1917 was a watershed year. America entered the First World War and established itself as a major power on the world scene. American Jewry emerged at about the same time as the steward of world Jewry. England, in 1917, promulgated the Balfour Declaration favoring the establishment of a "national home in Palestine" for the Jewish people. That same year, in Washington, an immigration restriction bill was passed over the veto of President Woodrow Wilson—an ominous portent of the xenophobia and even more severe restrictions to come. Meanwhile, back in Boston, the community's best-known Jew, the people's lawyer and Zionist leader Louis D. Brandeis, was in the middle of his first term as a justice of the United States Supreme Court—the first Jew ever to achieve that honor. Thanks in part to his efforts, two thousand Bostonians jammed into Tremont Temple in November 1917 to hail the Balfour Declaration and the promise of a renewed Jewish homeland.

With America's entry into the war, Boston Jews played active roles in support of the war effort. Many young Jews, immigrants and natives alike, entered the armed

FIG. 1. "United Chelsea Mothers League of Mass.," 1919. By the end of the First World War, the first waves of Eastern European immigrants and their children had settled into their new lives in America, mainly living and associating among themselves. According to the daughter of Rose Freedman Needleman (Rose is seated center, front row), the Chelsea League was organized as a choir and restructured during WWI to support the U.S. war effort. *Natalie Needleman Breitman Velleman.*

forces, an experience that furthered their Americanization and gave some their first taste of leadership experience. Among those who achieved visibility for their wartime achievements were Abraham E. Pinanski, later a prominent judge and communal leader, Harry Dexter White, later Assistant Secretary of the Treasury under President Franklin D. Roosevelt, and Ben Ulin, later one of the community's most active communal leaders. Other Boston Jews, including Louis Kirstein, Herbert Ehrmann, and Felix Frankfurter assumed administrative positions in the war effort. Eager to demonstrate both their patriotism and their successful integration into American life, Boston Jews carefully chronicled their wartime accomplishments, filling pages of *The Jewish Advocate* with details of their exploits.[2]

On the home front, similar signs of activity emerged. The Federated Jewish Charities, reorganized in 1916, embarked on its first modern fundraising campaign. Louis Kirstein, a department store executive at Filene's and a prominent civic leader, headed the effort; he soon became known as New England's most successful fundraiser. Influenced by Brandeis, Kirstein, a Zionist, appealed to a full spectrum of Boston Jews. In two months, beginning in March 1917, he managed to transform a lackluster campaign that had raised $70,000 from twelve hundred contributors into a community-wide campaign to which eight thousand Jews contributed, raising an unprecedented $250,000. The gifted new executive director of the Charities, Morris Waldman, used some of the money to expand outreach to the East European Jewish community, upgrading Federation services for immigrants and—for the first time anywhere in the country—providing Federation support for Jewish education. His plan was to rally all segments of the community to work together; his slogan was "A United Israel for Charity."[3]

The buoyant optimism of the war years was tempered in the decades that followed by an unrelenting barrage of antisemitism on both the national and local levels. The early twenties witnessed a revival of the Ku Klux Klan and the publication by Henry Ford of the infamous forgery, *The Protocols of the Elders of Zion*, in his widely circulated newspaper, *The Dearborn Independent*. Harvard's president, A. Lawrence

Lowell, introduced a quota system aimed at limiting the number of Jews at the college. Hotels, clubs, and businesses likewise erected barriers to keep Jews out. Meanwhile, young Jews in Boston suffered sporadic beatings from local toughs, and at least one synagogue was stoned.

Boston Jews disagreed as to how they should best respond to this unexpected wave of hostility. One rabbi, Samuel Abrams of Temple Ohabei Shalom, encouraged his congregants to defend themselves vigorously and unrelentingly. Sumner S. Shore, an Orthodox layman at Congregation Beth Hamidrash Hagadol, on the other hand, urged his fellow Jews "to be doubly honest and doubly good." The "best method of fighting anti-semitism," he wrote, was for Jews to "try, as far as is physically possible, to be better than the other fellow." In the aspiring, achieving, and anxious Boston Jewish community of these years, asser-tiveness and timidity coexisted.[4]

FIG. 2. East Boston Immigration Building, the direct port of entry for immigrants into Boston for almost a century, as photographed January 17, 1925. *Boston Public Library, Print Department.*

FIG. 3. Passover Seder for new Jewish arrivals at the East Boston Immigration Building, 1921. *American Jewish Historical Society.*

Antisemitism did not, however, prevent the community from developing insti-tutionally. If anything, anti-Jewish pressure from the outside world encouraged local Jews to turn inward and develop their own communal resources. In 1920, the Bureau of Jewish Education was established. A year later, Hebrew Teachers College was reorganized and acquired a home of its own in Roxbury. In 1923, the Beth Israel Hospital launched a campaign for one million dollars to move from its Rox-bury location and build a new facility near the Harvard Medical Center. Louis Kirstein, speaking at the ground-breaking, pointed to the "right of the Jews to build a hospital in a location of their own choosing, rather than in a restricted ghetto."[5] The new hospital was dedicated on August 1, 1928, by which time it had established an affiliation with Harvard and Tufts Medical Schools, the first Jewish hospital in America with such prestigious affiliations. That same year, in what would be the last great Jewish building project before the onset of the Great Depression, Temple Israel dedicated its new Meeting House on the Riverway.

As it grew institutionally, the Boston Jewish community also gained in public recognition and influence. As early as 1917, at the suggestion of local Zionists, Mayor James Michael Curley invited the nascent American Jewish Congress to meet in Boston. The meeting never took place, but the invitation, two years after the holding of the Zionist convention in Boston, helped to place the city on the national Jewish map. Four years later, when Chaim Weizmann and Albert Einstein visited America on a nationwide tour on behalf of the proposed Hebrew University in Jerusalem, Boston was on their itinerary; both the mayor and the governor turned out to welcome them. In 1922, another Zionist, Elihu Stone, achieved recognition when he was appointed Assistant United States Attorney for the district of Massachusetts. Two years therafter David Lourie was appointed judge of the Superior Criminal Court. Jews demonstrated their new power in a different way in 1929, when the Massachusetts legislature, over the governor's veto, passed a bill introduced by Representative Isidor H. Fox providing for the sale of foodstuffs on Sunday when Rosh Hashanah or Yom Kippur fell on a Monday. A year later, they demonstrated their national connections when President Herbert Hoover appointed Boston banker Abraham Ratshesky ambassador to Czechoslovakia. All of these achievements were still meager in comparison to the power wielded by Boston's Brahmin aristocracy or the Irish Catholic politicians. Nevertheless, they represented progress. Jews felt optimistic that in the political realm, as in so many others, they were gaining standing.[6]

The Depression dampened some of this optimism. Jews, like other middle class Americans, found their hopes shattered as unemployment spread and communal institutions faced unprecedented financial pressures. "Local institutions of Jewish education," Barbara M. Solomon observed, "were the hardest hit. In the early 1930's the schools could not always pay their Hebrew teachers even small salaries."[7] The arrival in Boston of penniless refugees fleeing from Nazi persecutions only exacerbated what was already a desperate situation.

In response, public and private institutions banded together to mount emergency fundraising campaigns in which a wide range of Jews and Jewish organizations participated. Through the Federation, the Jewish community organized a Vocational Bureau, offered family relief to those with children, and depleted its own resources to meet the needs of those in dire straits. The Federation also served as an important model and its director as a prime consultant for the creation, in 1935, of the Community Federation of Boston, a predecessor to the United Way. The assumption of greater responsibility for public welfare by the Federal Government under President Roosevelt did much to alleviate the problem of poor relief nationwide. Yet paradoxically, as Barbara Solomon showed, "the role of private agencies was enhanced rather than diminished." Local philanthropies remained better able to offer the individual "neighborly or professional help which the government could not give."[8]

European developments weighed heavily upon Boston Jewry during these years. Although immigration had been severely restricted by legislation in 1924, victims of persecution and others seeking a new life continued to find refuge in Boston — increasingly so as Hitlerism spread. A year before Hitler came to power, in 1932, Rabbi Joseph D. Soloveitchik, scion of a distinguished rabbinic family, settled in the city, fresh from having received his doctoral dissertation at the University of Berlin. He quickly became a central presence within the Orthodox community (see Joseph Reimer's essay in this volume), and remained for almost half a century the city's ultimate Orthodox rabbinic authority.[9]

FIG. 4. November 1, 1923, the "Carmania" brings new immigrants into Boston in the race to beat the U.S. immigration restriction laws scheduled to take effect in 1924. The laws imposed quotas on immigration based on country of origin, and were designed specifically to bar foreigners from Eastern Europe and Southern Italy. *Boston Public Library, Print Department.*

Most European Jewish immigrants to Boston during these years arrived later in the decade and under more trying circumstances. Penniless and emotionally drained, they struggled to eke out a living in the city and mourned the world that they had lost. An informal Boston Committee for Refugees, chaired by business executive Walter Bieringer, worked to assist these victims. The committee achieved national recognition and in 1938 participated in the establishment of the National Refugee Service. That same year, recent German Jewish immigrants in Boston, seeking fellowship and a means for self help, founded a *landsmanshaft*, the Immigrants Mutual Aid Society. A different form of refugee assistance was devised in 1939 by the wives of various Harvard faculty members. Known as The Window Shop, it was a small dressmaking and gift shop where textiles, hats, fashion accessories, and baked goods were sold, many of them produced by refugees themselves. Within a year, according to one account, the shop had grown "into a bakery, tea room, and restaurant" and was functioning "as a placement, referral and retraining center for refugee women." Later, The Window Shop established Friendship House, a lecture and language center to foster mutual understanding between immigrants and native-born Americans.[10]

Elsewhere, however, Jewish refugees were greeted more coldly. Surviving members of the Immigration Restriction League, the organization that had backed the nativist legislation of 1924, loudly protested their arrival. Supporters of the radio priest, Father Charles Coughlin, and other antisemitic propagandists made all Jews feel unwelcome. Meanwhile, the city's citadels of higher education, Harvard and the Massachusetts Institute of Technology, proved at best lukewarm. As a result, the

best known refugee scholars failed to settle in Boston. Even where a Jewish scholar with some influence attempted to help, as MIT's Norbert Wiener did in 1935, prejudice often won out. In that case, Wiener discovered that MIT administrators worried about "the tactical danger of having too large a proportion of the mathematical staff from the Jewish race." At Harvard, the most eminent American mathematician of the day, G. D. Birkhoff, was reportedly described (by no less an authority than Albert Einstein) as "one of the world's greatest academic antisemites."[11]

Boston Jewry pulled together in the face of such adversity. In 1940, in a bid to raise more funds for local, national and overseas needs, the city became the first Jewish community in the United States to combine its fundraising into one joint appeal—a development that did not occur in New York until 1973. A year later, on December 7, 1941, while the Japanese attack on Pearl Harbor was still in progress, the same spirit of unity was displayed at the inaugural meeting of the Associated Synagogues of Greater Boston, "the first time in the history of Greater Boston," according to *The Jewish Advocate*, "that all branches of Judaism met together."[12]

Jews also took solace from the fact that, slowly but surely, they were gaining political recognition at all levels. In 1935, Judge Jacob Kaplan was appointed by the governor to chair the Boston Finance Commission—an appointment lauded by *The Jewish Advocate* for lending "conclusive proof to the proposition that men of brilliance in this country have not suffered disabilities by reason of their being Jews . . . despite the anti-Semitic activities being fostered by so many un-American groups." That same year, David K. Niles was appointed labor assistant to Harry Hopkins, director of the Works Progress Administration. He remained in Washington, becoming assistant to President Roosevelt in 1942 and assuming greater responsibilities as assistant to President Truman, where he served as a conduit between the Jewish community and the White House and was influential in persuading the President to support the founding and recognition of the State of Israel.

In 1939, Felix Frankfurter, protégé of Louis Brandeis and at the time a professor at the Harvard Law School, became the second Jew from Boston (and the third Jew in history) to be appointed to the United States Supreme Court. He was selected over the objections of Jews like Arthur Hays Sulzberger of the *New York Times* who warned that the appointment would play into the hands of antisemites at home and abroad. The symbolic significance of the appointment was considerable, for just ten months earlier the justice's eighty-two-year-old Viennese uncle, the Jewish scholar Solomon Frankfurter, had been briefly imprisoned by the Nazis as punishment for his "unguarded remarks." Still another Boston Jewish lawyer, Charles Wyzanski, was appointed late in 1941 to be judge of the United States District Court of Mass-

FIG. 9. Scenes from postcards of the Jewish Hospitality House, 47 Mount Vernon Street, Boston, run by the Jewish Welfare Board during World War II as a nonsectarian center for the use of members of the Army and Navy.

*Background image:* Jewish Hospitality House.

*Images top to bottom:* Thanksgiving Dinner just before the attack on Pearl Harbor; Hostess Room where families and friends could gather or seek advice; Reading Room where "a well stocked library" included English, Yiddish, and Hebrew literature; Assembly Hall where "wholesome entertainments are provided"; and the Jewish Welfare Board Hut at Camp Devens, Massachusetts which sponsored religious services, social clubs, and discussion groups. *Harvey Fenton.*

achusetts, the first Jew ever to attain this position. Earlier, he had served on the staff of the United States solicitor general, defending the constitutionality of the Wagner National Labor Relations Act and the Social Security Act before the United States Supreme Court. In 1943, Wyzanski married Gisela Warburg, daughter of the exiled German-Jewish banker and communal leader Max Warburg. In later years, she became an influential communal figure in her own right, playing an active role in Zionist and interfaith activities.[13]

America's entry into the Second World War further galvanized the Jewish community. It also temporarily silenced some antisemitic elements in the city who had openly sympathized with the Nazis and accused Jews of pushing America into war. Large numbers of local Jews joined up or were conscripted into the armed forces; some became heroes. One widely distributed account of "official awards presented to servicemen of Jewish faith" listed such local area Jews as Lieutenant Donald S. Bloch, age 23, of Roxbury who won an Air Medal for distinguishing himself during the bombing of Nauru in the South Pacific; Sergeant Sidney Devers, age 24, of Boston, who won both an Air Medal and an Oak Leaf Cluster "for heroism as a top-turret gunner on a B-17 during raids in occupied Europe"; Private Barnet S. Klass, age 29, of Dorchester, who won a Purple Heart and was killed in action on Guadalcanal; and Major Jacob Shapiro, age 29, of Brookline, who won a Silver Star, Croix de Guerre, and a Purple Heart "for extraordinary heroism as leader of an American tank unit in Tunisia, and for wounds received in action there."[14]

On the home front, as the full extent of the Nazi extermination policy against Jews became known, Boston Jewry mounted a mass demonstration at Boston Garden on May 2, 1943, under the cry "Jewry's crisis calls for justice." Some 20,000 Jews filled the Garden and 10,000 more gathered outside, unable to gain entry. Governor Leverett Saltonstall and Mayor Maurice Tobin served as honorary chairmen of the demonstration, and Assistant Secretary of State Adolph Berle was scheduled to speak but was "unable to come because of illness." He sent a message declaring that the only solution was the defeat of the Nazis—the standard administration justification for its policy of inaction. The statement echoed what had been said at the Bermuda Conference on Refugees that ended just two days before. That conference, later described by one delegate as "a facade for inaction," rejected most of the proposals submitted to it. As Morris D. Waldman, now executive vice-president of the American Jewish Committee understood, nothing henceforward would stop the Nazis; "the Jews of Europe are doomed."[15]

American Jewry prepared nevertheless to convene an American Jewish Conference aimed at presenting a united platform of Jewish demands to the Allied powers.

Boston area Jews elected seventeen representatives to this conference, including two from Chelsea, one from Lynn, and one from Malden. The delegation included Judges Jennie L. Barron, Lewis Goldberg, and David Rose; Rabbis Joshua Loth Liebman, Joseph Shubow, and Sidney S. Guthman; the Rev. H. Leon Masovetsky, and the Zionist leader Elihu Stone. With their support, the Conference adopted a resolution calling for the establishment of a "Jewish Commonwealth" in Palestine and an end to "unwarranted restrictions on Jewish immigration and land settlement." The resolution resulted in the withdrawal from the Conference of the American Jewish Committee and further exacerbated tensions between Zionists and their opponents. As a result, and notwithstanding the victory of the pro-Zionist Boston delegation, the Conference as a whole was a failure, a painful demonstration of communal disunity at a time of crisis.[16]

The defeat of the Nazis, followed shortly thereafter by the full exposure of their atrocities and the creation of the State of Israel, commenced a new era in the history of Boston Jewry, one that saw the community emerge into the social mainstream. Jews, like postwar Americans generally, enjoyed a remarkable degree of prosperity and self-confidence during this era. Population movement from cities to suburbs increased from a trickle to a tidal wave. The G. I. Bill of Rights made it possible for millions of young men from lower middle class and working class backgrounds to acquire professional skills. A new class of Jewish entrepreneurs took their place in community leadership and demonstrated new levels of generosity; in just three years (1945-48) the size of the Associated Jewish Philanthropies campaign practically tripled. Family size increased. Affiliation with religious institutions mushroomed. America's love affair with the automobile became a passion and changed the living and working patterns of multitudes.[17]

Antisemitism declined in the postwar period. In Boston, anti-Jewish violence had climaxed on October 18, 1943, when a banner headline in the New York newspaper *PM* shrieked "CHRISTIAN FRONT HOODLUMS TERRORIZE BOSTON JEWS!" Now tensions relaxed. The vigorous efforts

FIG. 10. Palestine Protest Program parade and demonstration, FDR Chapter of the American Jewish Congress, April 8, 1948. *American Jewish Historical Society.*

of Boston's new archbishop, Richard Cushing, and the establishment in 1944 of the Jewish Community Council, headed by Robert Segal, who had previously distinguished himself by his pioneering work for improving community relations in Cincinnati, had much to do with this change. The fact that antisemitism had become associated in the public mind with Hitlerism, opposition to democracy, and threats to the nation certainly helped.[18]

As antisemitism declined, suburbanization increased. Jews had actually begun their great trek out to the suburbs years before, as Gerald Gamm shows in his essay in this volume. By World War II, the center of the community already lay in the "first suburbs," Roxbury and Dorchester, and many Jews had moved into the "second suburbs," Brookline, Brighton, and Newton. Now, in the postwar decades, thanks to massive new housing construction, inexpensive government subsidized mortgages, and the outlawing of "gentlemen's agreements" that promoted residential segregation, the movement of Jews out to suburbia mushroomed. New synagogues sprouted where none had been before, and in 1948 land was purchased in Brighton for a new Brookline-Brighton-Newton Jewish Community Center. By 1955, the circuit of Jewish residential areas had widened to include thirty different communities covering 700 square miles. The "Jews of Boston" had become the "Jews of Greater Boston," a change that was officially confirmed when the Associated Jewish Philanthropies revised its by-laws to bring Greater Boston Jews into its purview.[19]

In some respects, the Jews of postwar Boston gave expression to their Judaism far more publicly than Jews had in earlier eras. This may appear ironic, since by most measures Jewish observance had actually declined. But suburban Jews, now far removed from the casual Jewishness of the urban immigrant ghetto, seem to have felt, in sociologist Herbert Gans's words, a need "to provide clearly visible institutions and symbols with which to maintain and reinforce the ethnic identification of the next generation." They sought, in other words, a kind of "symbolic ethnicity."[20]

Public demonstrations met part of this need. Already in 1951, when Israel's Prime Minister, David Ben-Gurion, arrived in Boston for a rally at Boston Garden, 300,000 people jammed the downtown area to cheer him. He was greeted by the governor and mayor, addressed a joint session of the Massachusetts legislature, and visited major Jewish institutions.[21] Demonstrations for Israel, against antisemitism, and in defense of Jewish rights around the world would in the years ahead become a regular feature of Boston Jewish public life, providing local Jews with the opportunity both to identify with their people and to affect public policy.

The creation of Brandeis University likewise reflected this new public expression of Judaism. In 1946, a group headed by Rabbi Israel Goldstein of New York

announced its intention to establish a "university open to all, free from quotas, with merit the sole consideration" on the site of defunct Middlesex University in Waltham. The project was described as "an affirmative expression of the will of a group of Americans who are Jews and who want to make this offering to the culture of the nation." After numerous controversies and reorganizations, the New York trustees withdrew and the project was rescued by an "unlikely group of founding fathers." Brandeis University was opened in the fall of 1948 with Abram Sachar as president, George Alpert of Boston as chairman of the board, and a group of eight Boston trustees, four of whom were immigrants who had never gone to college themselves but were determined to give others the educational opportunity that they had been denied. They also shared the hope of Israel Goldstein that the college might stand as "a symbol of Jewish dignity and self-respect."[22]

Even the art produced by Boston Jews reflected the new mood that characterized this era. In the immediate postwar years a highly regarded school of painting emerged known as "Boston Expressionism." Its foremost representatives were the distinguished artists Hyman Bloom, Jack Levine, and David Aronson, and their sub-

ject matter dealt with "images of social and political satire, spiritual ecstacy, religious ritual and ordinary and extraordinary human events." Many of the images these expressionists produced were explicitly Jewish, notably some "passionately sympathetic depictions of Jewish worship services." In choosing these subjects, they consciously sought to demonstate the close nexus that they perceived between their "humanist vision" and their strong Jewish ethos.[23]

This same openness with respect to Judaism came to characterize many other aspects of Boston Jewish culture during these years. At Brandeis, the appointment of faculty members like Ludwig Lewisohn, Marie Syrkin, Simon Rawidowicz, Nahum Glatzer, and Alexander Altmann gave the campus a high Jewish cultural tone. These scholars, together with Professor Harry Wolfson of Harvard, Rabbi Joseph Soloveitchik, and the professors at Hebrew Teachers College made Boston into an eminent center of Jewish learning and teaching. The presence in Boston of a number of gifted and articulate rabbis strengthened this tradition. Roland Gittelsohn of Temple Israel, Albert Gordon of Temple Emanuel (Newton), Israel Kazis of Mishkan Tefila, and Judah Nadich of Kehillath Israel all were formidable preachers,

FIG. 12. Advertising poster for "When Hearts Speak," Yiddish theatre performance, Franklin Park Theatre, Roxbury, October 7, 1935. *American Jewish Historical Society.*

teachers, and writers who provided Jewish leadership both within Greater Boston and beyond.

In 1955, Julius Morse, a descendent of one of Boston's oldest Jewish families, looked back on his community and expressed contentment with its accomplishments:

> *We find the 150,000 Jews prominent in all sectors of the commercial life of the city. Sons and grandsons of the immigrants of the '90s are graduating from our colleges and technical schools to become executive heads of many old business houses while the older members of self same families begin to lay aside much of their wealth to endow schools and colleges—professorships, credit unions, homes for the underprivileged, hospitals, etc. Truly, Jews are a moving spirit in the commercial life of Boston.*[24]

What Morse could not have recognized was that this same "moving spirit" was actually driving the majority of Jews away from the city of Boston. The Jewish population of Dorchester and Mattapan was dwindling; as Boston Jews moved up economically, they moved out to the suburbs. This movement of Jews accelerated rapidly in the postwar period. Jewish institutions followed in the wake of their constituencies: Hebrew Teachers College moved in 1951, Mishkan Tefila in 1958, the Bostoner Rebbe (Grand Rabbi Levi I. Horowitz) in 1961, and Maimonides School in 1962. Other institutions (like Levine's Funeral Home) created "branches" in the suburbs; these in time became their main centers of operation, and the facility back in Dorchester was closed. Violence, "redlining" by local banks, and blockbusting by unscrupulous real estate agents hastened the movement of Jews out of their Dorchester and Mattapan neighborhoods, but they were not, as recently alleged, the cause of their migration.[25] Instead, Boston Jews moved because their socioeconomic situation improved—and because the suburbs proved so invitingly alluring.

The Jewish movement out of Dorchester and Mattapan, like all such transitions, was accompanied by hardship and heartache, particularly for those left behind who felt abandoned. A high percentage of these were elderly Jews, who found it difficult to relocate for economic as well as emotional reasons. Mistakes and misjudgments, most of them well-intentioned, were made by communal and institutional leaders alike. For the most part, however, the leadership of Boston Jewry proved responsive in addressing the problems and needs of inner city Jews. They set up a multi-service center to assist them, they provided funds to help them move, and they developed appropriate forms of housing and counseling to alleviate their hardship and distress. In the final analysis, the displaced Jews of Roxbury, Dorchester, and Mattapan fared better than those in similar circumstances in many other American cities.[26]

Otherwise, the early years of the 1960's brimmed with optimism. The nomination and subsequent election of John F. Kennedy as President of the United States was greeted with widespread enthusiasm among Boston Jews, for many Boston Jewish leaders knew him intimately and trusted him. The appointment of two Jews—Arthur Goldberg and Abraham Ribicoff—to the President's cabinet seemingly confirmed this judgment, providing new evidence of Jews' entry into the mainstream of American life.[27]

A number of Boston Jews emerged as leaders on the national Jewish scene at this time. Lewis Weinstein became, successively, president of the National Community Relations Advisory Council, president of the Council of Jewish Federations and Welfare Funds, and chairman of the Conference of Presidents of Major Jewish Organizations. Herbert Ehrmann became president of the American Jewish Committee. Moses Feuerstein was elected president of the Union of Orthodox Jewish Congregations. Dewey Stone, longtime Zionist activist and national chairman of the United Israel Appeal, took the lead in negotiating a reorganization of the Jewish Agency. No wonder that Golda Meir, visiting in 1960, declared Boston "one of my favorite cities."[28]

Boston Jews also began to take their place side by side with the Yankee Protestant elite as leaders of the city's major cultural institutions, many of which had previously kept Jews out. An important breakthrough was achieved when Sidney Rabb, prominent businessman and communal leader, became president of the Board of Trustees of the Boston Public Library. Rabb subsequently served on the boards of the Museum of Fine Arts and the Boston Symphony, the latter an institution that had long accepted Jewish musicians and conductors (including Serge Koussevitzky, Arthur Fiedler, Eric Leinsdorf, William Steinberg, Richard Burgin, and Joseph Silverstein), but had generally kept Jews off its board. Numerous Jewish philanthropists followed in Rabb's wake; indeed, as in many other cities, philanthropy and community service served as gateways to other forms of social equality.

Even as they gained entry into the cultural strongholds of the Protestant establishment, Boston Jews also reached out their hands to their African-American and

Catholic neighbors, participating actively both in the Civil Rights movement and in the movement for Catholic-Jewish reconciliation inaugurated by the Second Vatican Council. When Martin Luther King, Jr., delivered his celebrated "I Have A Dream" address at the 1963 Civil Rights march on Washington, many Boston Jews were in attendance. Boston rabbis likewise joined King at the 1965 clergy march for black voting rights in Selma, Alabama. Locally, the Rev. Virgil Wood, a close assistant to King and the regional representative of the Southern Christian Leadership Conference, had many Jewish friends; in 1965 he celebrated Passover *seder* with the Orthodox rabbi of Congregation Agudas Israel on Woodrow Avenue, Meyer Strassfeld. A few days later, King himself visited Boston and addressed Passover services at Temple Israel. A year after that, in what may have been the high-water mark in Black-Jewish cooperation in Boston, Kivie Kaplan, a Boston Jewish philanthropist and noted civil rights activist, became national president of the NAACP.[29]

Catholic-Jewish relations had been steadily improving in Boston for two decades, since the appointment of Richard Cushing as Archbishop in 1944 (he was elevated to Cardinal in 1958). In 1963, the Second Vatican Council acted to absolve Jews of complicity in Jesus's crucifixion, a move that met with mixed responses on the part of Jews, who had never regarded themselves as guilty in the first place. Ultimately, however, Vatican II proved highly significant since it paved the way for Catholic-Jewish rapprochement on a host of levels, including the battle to win freedom for Jews in the Soviet Union. Cushing himself underscored this relationship on December 15, 1966, when he spoke out movingly before a crowd of one thousand

Boston Jews convened by the Jewish Community Council of Boston to demonstrate on behalf of Soviet Jewry. Five years later, on May 28, 1971, the Boston Archdiocese's Committee on Catholic-Jewish Relations proclaimed Soviet Jewish oppression "an injustice that compels us to speak in the name of moral and religious principles."[30]

Besides Soviet Jewry, the other new cause that took its place on the communal agenda of the 1960's was the movement to commemorate the Holocaust. The word "holocaust" applied to the destruction of European Jewry was unknown before that time, but soon entered the lexicon as the standard term for a catastrophe without precedent or parallel. On April 21, 1960, a Martyrs Observance was held in Boston, commemorating the 17th anniversary of the Warsaw Ghetto uprising.[31] This marked a modest beginning to what would become a major theme in American Jewish life, and an annual public observance, leading ultimately to plans for a permanent Boston memorial to the Holocaust's victims.

All of these themes—memories of the Holocaust, efforts at improved inter-group relations, heightened Jewish activism, the emergence of Jews into positions of power and influence, and the willingness of Jews to identify religiously through public demonstrations—came together in May 1967. In a dramatic challenge to the very existence to the State of Israel, Egypt closed the Straits of Tiran to Israeli vessels, United Nations peacekeeping troops were withdrawn, the promises and guarantees given by the United States to secure Israel's withdrawal from the Sinai in 1957 were dishonored, and Arab armies massed troops on all of Israel's borders. Fearing the worst, Boston Jews, along with Jews throughout the diaspora, responded with an unprecedented outpouring of concern and support. Hundreds in Boston volunteered to go to Israel to serve in whatever capacity necessary. Thousands marched in public rallies on the Common in Boston and at the White House in Washington. Tens of thousands, "from Hebrew school children to golden-agers," contributed record sums of money to a hastily-organized Israel Emergency Fund. Calling on their friends, their neighbors, their representatives, anyone whom they thought might help, Boston area Jews used all the means and power at their disposal to keep the State of Israel alive. Never had the community been so united in support of a common aim.[32]

Just fifty years earlier, a far weaker community of Boston Jews, most of them immigrants, had publicly hailed the Balfour Declaration and the promise of a renewed Jewish homeland. Now it was a far stronger Boston Jewish community that marshalled its resources to protect that promise. And so, when Israel achieved its astounding victory in the Six Day War it represented a victory for the Jews of Boston as well. For them, as for Jews in so many other places, the Six Day War marked an historical turning point: an affirmation of Boston Jewry's emergence into the mainstream, and an experience that was itself life transforming and Jewishly affirming.

# Notes

1. *American Jewish Year Book (AJYB)* 19 (1917–18), 412; 69 (1968), 286.

2. *Jewish Advocate*, 26 July 1917; 16 August 1917.

3. Barbara M. Solomon, *Pioneers in Service: The History of the Associated Jewish Philanthropies of Boston* (Boston: Associated Jewish Philanthropies, 1956), 94–101.

4. *JA*, 14 October 1920; *Yearbook of the Men's Club of Congregation Beth Hamidrash Hagadol 1922–1923* (Boston: 1923), 11–14.

5. Arthur J. Linenthal, *First A Dream: The History of Boston's Jewish Hospitals 1896 to 1928* (Boston: Beth Israel Hospital, 1990), 494.

6. *AJYB* 20 (1918-1919), 157; *Jewish Advocate*, 17 May 1921; 16 March 1922; *AJYB* 27 (1925–1926), 144; 30 (1928–1929), 26; Isaac Fein, *Boston: Where It All Began* (Boston: Bicentennial Committee, 1976), 76.

7. Solomon, *Pioneers in Service*, 132.

8. Solomon, *Pioneers in Service*, 130–35.

9. Aaron Rakeffet-Rothkoff, "Rabbi Yosef Dov Soloveitchik: Biographical Highlights," *Jewish Action* 53 (Summer 1993): 19–22.

10. Solomon, *Pioneers in Service*, 144–45; Herbert A. Strauss, ed., *Jewish Immigrants of the Nazi Period in the U.S.A.* (New York: K.G. Saur, 1978), vol. 1, 124–25. The Window Shop closed in 1972, but its bakery survives in The Blacksmith House as part of the Cambridge Center for Adult Education.

11. Strauss, *Jewish Immigrants of the Nazi Period*, 46; Nathan Reingold, "Refugee Mathematicians in the United States, 1933–1941: Reception and Reaction," in *The Muses Flee Hitler: Cultural Transfer and Adaptation 1930–1945*, ed. Jerell C. Jackman and Carla M. Borden (Washington, D.C.: Smithsonian Institution Press, 1983), 210–13.

12. Solomon, *Pioneers in Service*, 145–46; *Jewish Advocate*, 12 December 1941.

13. *Jewish Advocate*, 4 January 1935; "David K. Niles," *Encyclopædia Judaica* (Jerusalem: Keter, 1972), vol. 12, col. 1161–62; Michael E. Parrish, *Felix Frankfurter and His Times: The Reform Years* (New York: Free Press, 1982), 273–78; Julius J. Marke, "Charles Edward Wyzanski," *Encyclopædia Judaica* (Jerusalem: Keter, 1971), col. 682; Ron Chernow, *The Warburgs* (New York: Random House, 1993), 519, 712–13.

14. Nathan C. Belth, ed., *Fighting For America* (New York: National Jewish Welfare Board, 1944), 98, 105, 111, 131, 156.

15. *Jewish Advocate*, 16 April 1943; David S. Wyman, *The Abandonment of the Jews: America and the Holocaust 1941–1945* (New York: Pantheon, 1984), 104–23, especially 122–23.

16. Alexander S. Kohanski, ed., *The American Jewish Conference: Its Organization and Proceedings of the First Session August 29 to September 2, 1943* (New York: American Jewish Conference, 1944), especially 180–81, 350.

17. Kenneth T. Jackson, *Crabgrass Frontier: The Suburbanization of the United States* (New York: Oxford University Press, 1985); Albert I. Gordon, *Jews in Suburbia* (Boston: Beacon Press, 1959); Solomon, *Pioneers in Service*, 150–51.

18. Robert Segal, *The Early Years of the Jewish Community Council of Metropolitan Boston* (Boston, 1986), 6–7; *Jewish Advocate*, 4, 18 January 1945; 3 May 1945; see also Jonathan D. Sarna's essay in this volume.

19. Solomon, *Pioneers in Service*, 150–51.

20. Herbert J. Gans, "The Origin and Growth of a Jewish Community in the Suburbs: A Study of the Jews of Park Forest," in Marshall Sklare, ed., *The Jews* (New York: Free Press, 1958), 247; Herbert J. Gans, "Symbolic Ethnicity: The Future of Ethnic Groups and Cultures in America," *Ethnic and Racial Studies* 2 (January 1979): 1–20.

21. *Jewish Advocate*, 18 March, 15 April, 17 May 1951.

22. *Jewish Advocate*, 29 April, 5 August 1948; Israel Goldstein, *Brandeis University: Chapter of its Founding* (New York: Bloch, 1951), especially 72–74, 100; Abram L. Sachar, *A Host At Last* (Boston: Little, Brown, 1976), 12–30.

23. Theodore F. Wolff, "The Persistence of the Expressionist Mode in Boston," *Expressionism in Boston: 1945–1985* (Lincoln, Mass.: 1986), 6.

24. *Jewish Advocate*, 27 January 1955.

25. Hillel Levine and Lawrence Harmon, *The Death of an American Jewish Community: A Tragedy of Good Intensions* (New York: Free Press, 1992).

26. Yona Ginsberg, *Jews in a Changing Neighborhood: The Study of Mattapan* (New York: Free Press, 1975); Levine and Harmon, *Death of an American Jewish Community*; "Responses to the Book: *The Death of an American Jewish Community*," *Jewish Advocate*, 20–26 December 1991, 11; Gerald H. Gamm, "Exploding Myths Surrounding Exodus of Boston Jewry," *Jewish Advocate*, 27 March – 2 April 1992, 11.

27. *Jewish Advocate*, 21 July, 22 December 1960.

28. *Jewish Advocate*, 25 February 1960, 25 August 1960, 4 July 1963, 5 December 1963, 19 May 1960, 7 April 1960, 26 May 1960.

29. *Jewish Advocate*, 22 August 1963; Levine and Harmon, *Death of an American Jewish Community*, 83–86, 134–136.

30. William W. Orbach, *The American Movement to Aid Soviet Jews* (Amherst: University of Massachusetts Press, 1979), 101.

31. *Jewish Advocate*, 21 April 1960.

32. See *Jewish Advocate* and other Boston newspapers, 23 May – 15 June 1967.

*Moving Apart and Growing Together,*
*1967 – 1994*

*Overleaf:* The Klezmer Conservatory Band, founded at the New England Conservatory in 1980 by Hankus Netsky (kneeling, with saxophone), has brought Yiddish and Yiddish-American music to audiences throughout the world. *Klezmer Conservatory Band.*

SHERRY ISRAEL

# Moving Apart and Growing Together, 1967-1994

ופרצת ימה וקדמה וצפנה ונגבה
"You shall spread out to the west and to the east,
to the north and to the south."
GENESIS 28:14

N JUNE 1967, in response to the enormity of the threat to Israel's existence, a spirit of unity galvanized the Jewish community of Boston, as it did every major Jewish community in the United States. A rally on June 4, convened by the Joint Israel Committee of the Jewish Community Council of Metropolitan Boston and the New England Zionist Council, drew an estimated 10,000 persons. "Hundreds of telephone calls flooded the switchboard at [the Combined Jewish Philanthropies] headquarters. They came from all segments of the community . . . Sacks of mail inundated the CJP offices bearing unsolicited contributions."[1]

Yet along with this coming together, trends of a very different kind, which would forecast the shape of the community over the next quarter century, were already visible. The themes would be those of general American life during the same period: mobility, heterogeneity, generational changes, the adaptation or disappearance of old forms of communal expression and the evolution of new ones, the impact of the "baby-boomers," the women's movement, and changing family patterns. The variations on these themes which would be played out in Boston's Jewish community would additionally reflect some of the unique features of the community's local history and culture.

In the 1960's and after, Boston's Jews—as they had been since their arrival—were on the move socially, economically, educationally, religiously and, especially, geographically. This mobility posed a major challenge to the life of the community. For in Boston, unlike most other American Jewish communities, Jews with different kinds of interests and life-styles moved in different directions. What resulted was a kind of self-segregation of the community's various elements. By the last half of the 1960's, Boston's Jewish community had become in actuality a set of subcommunities differing from one another both socially and religiously.

Where were these subcommunities, and what were they like? The 1965 CJP community survey described three kinds of subcommunities—an inner core, a transitional area, and an outer, more suburban ring.[2] Dorchester-Mattapan and Chelsea-Malden formed the inner core. Jews had lived there longer than in the other areas. The transitional areas were in Central Boston and Brookline. Here, elements of the old, cohesive, ethnic Jewry of the first and early second generation mixed with younger newcomers. The outer ring consisted of the Jews of Newton-Wellesley, the south suburbs, and Framingham-Natick. These were families with children, living in the suburban single-family homes to which Americans who could afford them flocked after World War II.

Finally, there was Cambridge-Lexington. Although no one knew it at the time, Cambridge-Lexington's Jews in 1965 were harbingers of the Jewish future, different in almost every respect from those in other areas. They were the most likely to be newcomers, not native to greater Boston. They were mostly third and fourth generation Jews, with many highly-educated professionals among them. Large numbers did not express a preference for a particular denomination, nor have mostly Jewish friends, nor oppose the intermarriage of their children. Most did not belong to synagogues or participate in other Jewish organizations. They did participate in non-Jewish ones.

The 1965 population survey results challenged Boston's Jewish community. Its social service and educational institutions had been developed to meet the needs of an immigrant community, relatively cohesive, integrated, and firmly tied to its Jewish roots. Now, a new complexity was revealed that was redefining the community. Community planners of the time noted the change, but their only advice was for all segments of the community to learn to work together.[3]

By 1965, thirty-three and a half percent of Boston's Jews were newcomers, people who had moved into the area within the previous five-year period. Living near the communities where they worked, these in-migrants had no memories of the old Jewish neighborhoods and no loyalties to old ways of doing things. They were found in large numbers in Cambridge-Lexington (sixty-four percent of whose Jews had come from outside the metropolitan area in the previous five years) and Framingham-Natick (sixty-two percent). The proportions were slightly lower but still marked in Brookline-Brighton (thirty-four percent), Newton-Wellesley (thirty-two

FIG. 1. Map of the Greater Boston metropolitan area. Based on a map in Sherry Israel, *Boston's Jewish Community: The 1985 CJP Demographic Study* (Boston: Combined Jewish Philanthropies, 1987). Dark line denotes Boston standard metropolitan statistical area.

percent) and Central Boston (forty-nine percent). By contrast, in the south suburbs, the proportion of newcomers was only eleven percent.

The same trend continued over the next twenty years. In 1975, twenty-eight percent of Boston's Jews were newcomers who had not lived in the city ten years before; in 1985 the comparable figure was thirty percent.[4] This huge new population had arrived for educational and employment opportunities. Many of them were enrolled or employed in the area's academic institutions, or working in the legal, medical, financial, professional, and rising technology fields. At the same time, Jews continued moving from the center toward the periphery in all directions—west, south, and north. The changes were mostly gradual and evolutionary. The community's challenge was thus multiplied: it had to find a cohesive center for a set of increasingly separate subcommunities, and at the same time make large numbers of newcomers feel at home.

The impact of students and young people on the Boston Jewish community has been particularly profound. The 1970's and 1980's were a time of social change throughout America, and Boston's Jewish community shared in the changes. First there were the "baby boomers," that great bulge in America's population created by the high birth rate between, roughly, 1946 and 1962. Their presence was officially noted in Boston Jewry in 1975, when 47,000 young adults between twenty-one and thirty were found to be the community's single largest age group, forming twenty-four percent of the Jewish population. The majority of them were newcomers, and there was great uncertainly as to whether or not they would stay in the Boston area, marry, and have children.[5] Initially, the organized community responded only to those in college, and even that response proved hesitant. But Boston's young Jews were about to set their own agenda.

The baby boomers came to Boston to attend college and graduate school, to engage in post-college training opportunities, and to participate in the burgeoning high tech industries. By sheer dint of their numbers and activism, they formed a subcommunity of their own in the culture of Jewish Boston: the student and young adult community. They lived primarily in Allston, Brighton, Cambridge, and parts of Brookline, with a smaller group centered around Brandeis University in Waltham. They created their own publications, and like other geographically-based subcommunities, thought of their own community as the whole community. Jewish Boston, as they conceived it, was "young, friendly, and well-educated . . . a trend setter in many areas of Jewish life, particularly . . . Jewish culture."[6]

They burst onto the national scene in 1969. That year, the General Assembly of the Council of Jewish Federations took place in Boston, and a group composed primarily of graduate students from Boston-area schools sought confrontation, protesting publicly on behalf of what they saw as the Federations' neglect of Jewish education. To their surprise, they were invited to speak to the assembled leaders of American Jewry. Their demands eventually led to national federation funding for the Institute of Jewish Life, a three-year experiment aimed at finding and funding creative Jewish ventures. The Institute's best-known offspring include CLAL (National Jewish Center for Learning and Leadership), the first *Jewish Catalog*, and the National Media Center, now the National Center for Jewish Film at Brandeis

University. The Institute also raised community consciousness on behalf of Jewish education.

Another creation of the student (counter) culture of the time was Havurat Shalom. Opened in Somerville in 1968, it had a dual purpose—providing a setting for alternate expressions of serious Jewish religious sensibilities and serving as a seminary to exempt young Jews from the draft. (The Bostoner Rebbe, Rabbi Levi I. Horowitz, opened a seminary for similar reasons at the same time.) In time, Havurat Shalom served as a training ground for numbers of individuals who went on to become influential scholars and religious leaders of American Jewish life. Along with several Hillel foundations, notably those at Brandeis and Harvard, Havurat Shalom also helped nurture a number of additional alternative religious groups—*havurot* and *minyanim*, both within congregations and free-standing— that have become a permanent feature of Boston's religious life and have inspired similar groups in other cities as well.

More broadly, the 1969 GA protest and the increased numbers of Jewish students in the Boston area turned the community into a crucible for student innovations of every kind. Campus Hillel organizations grew in strength and were banded together in 1971 in the Metropolitan Hillel Council. The Zamir Chorale, founded by students in 1969, promoted deeper appreciation of Jewish music and pioneered new audiences for Jewish choral singing. *Genesis 2*, an alternative Jewish student magazine, was published for nearly twenty years, becoming a national publication in its final years. In addition, Boston students helped launch the Student Struggle for Soviet Jewry, a significant player along with Action for Soviet Jewry in moving the American Jewish community to a more public and activist stance on behalf of Soviet Jewish emigration. Students also sent daily contingents to the last congregations in Mattapan, to help insure *minyanim* for elderly Jewish citizens. And students helped make *Simchat Torah* celebrations at Temple Beth Shalom in Cambridge (the "Tremont Street shul") and the Talner Rebbe's Congregation Beth David in Brookline into memorable community events.

Boston's young Jews innovated not only in their communal lives but also in the domestic sphere. Most notably, they put off getting married. By the end of the 1970's there was a significant new group of Boston Jews known as "young

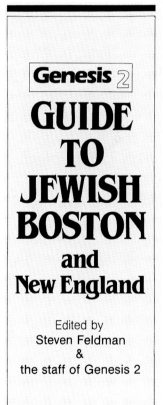

**Genesis 2**

# GUIDE TO JEWISH BOSTON and New England

Edited by
Steven Feldman
&
the staff of Genesis 2

adults," a euphemism for those approaching thirty, or in their thirties, and single. Too old for Hillel and not ready to join congregations, they felt unconnected with existing Jewish organizations. By the mid-1970's, a combination of institutional and independent initiatives attempted to integrate this group into the broader community.[7]

By 1985, Boston had the youngest Jewish community in America, and the "generation gap" was getting wider. Some 47,000 Jews in their thirties resided in greater Boston, and sixty percent of them had lived there ten years earlier. Younger adults also continued gravitating to Boston, swelling the number of area Jews in their twenties to 53,000 people. Two thirds of this younger group—over 33,000 Jews, equal to the entire population of Newton—were single, and so were 10,000 Jews in their thirties, nearly a quarter of that population. Many of them, especially in the older group, lived across the Charles River, closer to the high tech centers around Route 128 or near the colleges and universities. While Harvard and MIT Hillel served some of this population, most existing Jewish organizations did not, geared as they were to married or elderly constituencies.

The younger and single population thus represented a dramatic challenge to the Boston Jewish community. It crystallized the growing impact of newcomers and the widening gap between natives and strangers within Boston Jewry. For even as it helped to redefine the community, reducing its average age and making it more cosmopolitan and innovative, it also highlighted new distinctions, complicating efforts to unify the community around a common set of institutions and values.

The youthfulness and diversity of the contemporary Boston Jewish community has also stimulated the development of other distinctive (albeit overlapping) Jewish subcommunities, each with its own constituency and its own call on communal resources. The largest of these by far is the Jewish women's community, reflecting changing gender roles throughout the country in the 1980's. With women's expanded participation in the workforce, large numbers began to attain advanced degrees and to become managers and professionals as well as clerical workers. Increasingly, married women and women with children stayed in the workplace. One result was a need for child care. A CJP Task Force studied the issue in the 1980's and recommended that CJP fund an entirely new agency to deal with daycare, on the model of the Philadelphia Federation. The proposal was rejected as too costly, but CJP did provide seed money for grass-roots Jewish daycare in Cambridge, a parent-run daycare in Brookline-Brighton starting in 1984, and Gan Yeladim daycare center, which opened in Newton in 1988 and is now managed by the Jewish Community Centers of Greater Boston. The Leventhal-Sidman Jewish Community Center also added daycare to its programs in its Newton and Brookline locations.

Women also began moving into leadership roles in the overall Jewish community. Back when Golda Meir came to speak on behalf of the Israel Emergency Fund in June, 1967, the letter of invitation from CJP had announced that "because of limited space, this meeting is for men only."[8] (Are we permitted to wonder how they let Golda in?) By 1980, CJP had elected its first woman president, Ruth Fein, who also served as its first female Campaign Chair in 1988. Other women headed the campaign again in 1989 and 1992–1993. The Jewish Community Relations Council and the Jewish Community Center of Greater Boston had their first woman presidents in 1984. Women also became executive directors of significant Jewish community agencies in the 1980's, among them the Jewish Family and Children's Service, the Jewish Vocational Service, the American Jewish Congress regional office and the Jewish Community Housing for the Elderly. No women served as congregational rabbis in Greater Boston in 1983, but ten years later there were six in Reform, Conservative, and Reconstructionist congregations, plus other women rabbis serving as directors or associate directors at five local Hillel foundations.

Jewish women in Boston continued to support and to volunteer in Boston's traditional Jewish women's organizations. They have also organized several new ones, with agendas as diverse as women's issues in Israel, Jewish women's spirituality, and the academic discipline of Jewish women's studies. A Jewish women's networking conference held under the auspices of the Hornstein Program in Jewish Communal Service at Brandeis in 1992 drew participants from twenty-two separate women's organizations in greater Boston. These organizations defined and represented the new subcommunity of Boston Jewish women, one that, like the young adults, was

FIG. 4, *opposite.* Sephardi music ensemble Voice of the Turtle was founded in the 1970's by Judith Wachs. The group, which enjoys an international reputation, draws its repertory from the full range of Sephardi cultures. Photograph by Susan Wilson. *Voice of the Turtle.*

FIG. 5, *opposite.* The Zamir Chorale of Boston, founded and directed by Joshua Jacobson in 1969. The Zamir Chorale is now in residence at Hebrew College, Brookline. Photograph, 1991, by Joe Demb. *Zamir Chorale of Boston.*

FIG. 6. Three generations of "New American" singers, after a 1993 performance at the Leventhal-Sidman Jewish Community Center, Newton, Massachusetts. *Leventhal-Sidman Jewish Community Center.*

FIG. 7. Havdalah Service, Congregation Beth Pinchas, ca. 1979. *New England Chassidic Center, Brookline, Massachusetts.*

shaped not by neighborhood but by common interests and experiences.

Another new subcommunity of Jews that developed in Boston in recent decades consists of New Americans from the former Soviet Union. With its burgeoning high tech and academic environments, Boston undertook to absorb some 2,000 of the first wave of Jews to leave the then-Soviet Union in the 1970's. Between 1981 and 1987, as the flow out of the Soviet Union slowed to a trickle, Boston continued to receive a large share of the emigrés, but the totals for that period were only about 1,000. Then, in 1987, the gates opened again, and nearly 6,000 additional Soviet Jewish refugees flowed into the community. At the same time, Federal Refugee Resettlement grants, which had paid the major portion of basic resettlement costs for the earlier refugees, were cut back severely. CJP responded by increasing New American resettlement funds and initiating a special New Freedom Trail Campaign in 1989. Between 1989 and 1992, CJP allocated over $2.6 million to the resettlement budget. Jewish Family and Children's Service, along with the Jewish Vocational Service, continued to manage basic resettlement activities, with significant help from the Synagogue Council, Hebrew College, the day schools, community centers, and local synagogues.

By the beginning of the 1990's, Soviet Jews of the "first wave" could be found throughout the metropolitan area, taking their place alongside the rest of Boston Jewry. Newer immigrants and the elderly from the first wave remained clustered in Allston-Brighton, where the Orthodox among them are helping to maintain Congregation Kadimah-Toras Moshe. Other significant groups settled in Sharon and Malden, with a smaller group helping in the revival of an Orthodox synagogue in Newton Corner.

The final new subcommunity to impact decisively on Boston's Jewish community consists of younger Orthodox Jews. Within walking distance of their synagogues in Brookline, Brighton, Newton, and Sharon, many of the young Orthodox are highly trained professionals: doctors and dentists, computer experts,

insurance brokers, scientists. Well-educated, sophisticated, and vibrant, they transformed and revitalized Boston's Orthodoxy, which in earlier decades had largely been the preserve of locally-born Jews, many of them small businessmen and housewives who had moved west from Roxbury and Dorchester.

FIG. 8. Beth Din (Rabbinical Court of Justice) in session 1969–1970 deliberating on "questions of conscience" brought in connection with the Vietnam War. Judges seated left to right: Rabbi Hersh Tenenbaum, Rabbi Mordechai Y. Golinkin, and Rabbi Samuel I. Korff, Rabbinic Administrator. The Beth Din and Kashrus Commission are administered by the Council of Orthodox Rabbis (Vaad Harabonim) with the support of the Synagogue Council, whose affiliates include the entire spectrum of Boston-area synagogues. *Rabbi Ira A. Korff.*

The Orthodox of Boston a generation ago were "conventionally Orthodox," doing what Jews they knew had always done. The younger Jews are, by contrast, "ideologically Orthodox," observant by conviction and education as well as by tradition. The more right-wing among them maintain fairly separate institutions; the centrists participate more fully in the organizations of the wider Jewish community. All support the day schools and other local Orthodox institutions generously. Boston's Orthodox community now supports both a *kollel* and an institution to provide high-level text study for women. The community is also politically adept: the winter of 1993 saw the completion of an *eruv* encompassing the Orthodox residential sections of Brookline, Brighton, and Newton, which had been under planning and construction for nearly a decade.[9] The new Orthodox cosmopolitanism is also reflected in its restaurants. At one point in 1993 Greater Boston boasted ten kosher (not just "kosher-style") restaurants—one each in Sharon and Boston, two in Newton, and six in Brookline and Brighton, as well as two kosher pizza parlors. Only one restaurant was a deli; the others offered middle eastern, Persian, Chinese, and vegetarian fare. In their own way, the restaurants reflect the ethos of the young Orthodox: they experience the dining possibilities available within the larger community and at the same time conform to the dietary standards that keep Orthodox Jews separate and distinct.

As Boston's Jewish population has increased, dispersed, diversified, and even fragmented since the mid-1960's, Boston's Jewish institutions have struggled to respond. Initially, small Jewish community centers were developed in new areas, linked to one another in a loosely tied association—the Association of Jewish Community Centers. At the end of the 1960's, these centers included the Brookline-Brighton-Newton Jewish Community Center (BBN), located at the intersection of these three communities near Cleveland Circle; affiliated centers in Quincy, Brock-

FIG. 9. The Heritage at Cleveland Circle, a project of National Development of New England and A•D•S Senior Housing, under construction in 1994 on the site of the former Brookline-Brighton-Newton Jewish Community Center. The Heritage will provide assisted living apartments for senior citizens, and preschool and meeting rooms for the Leventhal-Sidman Jewish Community Center, Brookline campus. *Leventhal-Sidman Jewish Community Center.*

ton, Chelsea, and Revere; and allied programs in Coolidge Corner and Dorchester. In 1978, however, the association reorganized and changed its name from plural to singular: the Jewish Community Center of Greater Boston (JCCGB).[10] The change was more than symbolic. It signified two critical shifts in institutional thrust: from old neighborhood settlement houses to new suburban centers with an accent on recreation and education, and from a loose and locally-based system of governance to a more centralized one.

In the north, the community center system was contracting. The Chelsea YMHA and Revere JCC merged in the late 1970's. A third site, North Area JCC, had been opened in Malden. All three became the Metro North JCC. But in the 1980's, as the Jewish population declined and aged, the community center buildings in Chelsea and Revere closed. Programs continued under the Metro North name in Malden and Revere.

In 1979, land was purchased in South Newton along the Charles River for a new Jewish Community Campus. Located near Needham and Route 128, the site was within a short drive for very many of Boston's suburban Jewish families. On the site of the former Xaverian Brothers' Novitiate, plans were made to erect a Jewish Community Center, communal offices, and a branch of Jewish Community Housing for the Elderly. The Campus was envisaged as a focal gathering place for an increasingly scattered and divided community.

Plans for building the Campus and a new Center created a furor in the synagogue community. Rabbis and congregational leaders felt they had not been sufficiently consulted or involved in the planning. Many believed a new Center would compete with their synagogues for members. Organized in 1978 as the Coalition of West Suburban Congregations, they mobilized opposition to the use of communal funds for the project. A CJP ad hoc committee formed to address their concerns. At issue was the concept of Jewish community itself, the relationship among synagogues, Jewish Community Centers, and the CJP, and the locus of Jewish life in Boston. Should the community create a unifying "center" and if so, should that "center" be primarily spiritual or social?[11] The result was a productive compromise: the Community Center went forward; a new relationship was forged among the synagogues, the Center, and the CJP; and a new organization, the Synagogue Council, was created in 1981. Funded by CJP, the Synagogue Council was intended to be a voice for the congregational world and a locus for joint congregational activities and programs. Meanwhile, the Leventhal-Sidman Jewish Community Center was built on the Gosman Jewish Community Campus in Newton and dedicated in October 1983.

FIG. 10. Israeli dancing at Israel Independence Day celebration, one of the largest annual gatherings of the Boston-area Jewish community, June 1992, at the Leventhal-Sidman Jewish Community Center, Newton, Massachusetts. Israel Independence Day has also been celebrated on the Esplanade along the Charles River in Boston, and is planned for Brookline's Harvard Street in 1995. *Jewish Community Centers of Greater Boston.*

The lessons of this episode were not lost on the CJP or the JCCGB as they turned their attention to creating a Center for the community's other major population base in the south area. This time, local rabbis were actively involved as planning proceeded. In 1988, the Striar Jewish Community Center opened on the Fireman Campus in Stoughton with full local community support.

Even as these two new Jewish Centers sought to unify Boston area Jews and to provide a place of entry into the community for Boston's unaffiliated and secular Jews, synagogues also responded to the community's growing diversity. In 1992, there were twenty synagogues in Greater Boston that had not existed twenty years earlier, and more variety than ever before: four of them were Orthodox, two Conservative, five Independent, one Traditional, two Reconstructionist, two Sephardic, four Chabad. The most notable growth occurred in areas of Jewish population expansion, including Wayland, Cambridge, Concord, Acton, Lexington, Sharon, Needham, Sudbury, and Canton.

At the same time, other activities have successfully created community and cooperation among Boston's diverse groups. One is the Jewish Cemetery Association, formed in 1984 by the CJP, the Jewish Community Relations Council, and the Synagogue Council. It was organized initially to renovate five abandoned Jewish cemeteries in West Roxbury and subsequently assumed responsibility for the management of fifty-four cemeteries in eastern Massachusetts.[12] To complement the community's continuing relationship with the Jewish state, new forms of support for Israel were pioneered based on high tech investment. CJP began funding the CJP Interagency Volunteer Program (later to be renamed the Jewish Community Volunteer Program) in 1984, to coordinate volunteer activities across the Jewish community. CHAI House, the first Jewish-sponsored residence for developmentally-disabled Jewish adults, opened under the auspices of Jewish Family and Children's Service, but with its own governance.

The years between 1967 and 1994 saw the unprecedented physical and demographic expansion of Boston's Jewish community. From neighborhood-based groups of individuals often sharing the same European or Boston experiences, Boston's Jewish community has, over the last thirty years, taken on a new look. Like the city as a whole, it has become younger, more diverse, and more dispersed. The organic communities of the early- and mid-20th century have been supplanted. The challenge of the past thirty years has been to maintain a sense of connectedness amid this growing diversity. As the community approaches the end of the 20th century, it must continue to seek ways to engage and unify a more heterogeneous and dispersed Jewish population than it has ever known.

*Notes*

The author would like to thank the following people who were interviewed in the course of preparation of this chapter, and who offered information and insights not easily available elsewhere: Susan Ebert, Sue Anne Endelman, Robert Fein, Rabbi Arthur Green, Rabbi Abraham Halbfinger, Bernard Hyatt, Rabbi Richard J. Israel, Professor Leon Jick, Aaron Kischel, Dr. Daniel Margolis, Rabbi Paul Menitoff, Ellsworth Rosen, Rabbi Sanford Seltzer, and Alan Teperow. The author also thanks Michael Feldberg, Executive Director of the American Jewish Historical Society, for access to the Society's archives.

1. *Jewish Advocate* (Boston), 8 June 1967.

2. Morris Axelrod, Floyd J. Fowler, Jr., and Arnold Gurin, *A Community Survey for Long Range Planning* (Boston: Combined Jewish Philanthropies, 1967), 16–17, 180–91.

3. Axelrod, Fowler, and Gurin, *A Community Survey*, 206.

4. Floyd J. Fowler, Jr., *1975 Community Survey*, reanalysis of data in Table 3.5, 29 (Boston: Combined Jewish Philanthropies, 1977); Sherry Israel, *Boston's Jewish Community: The 1985 CJP Demographic Study* (Boston: Combined Jewish Philanthropies, 1987), 126.

5. Fowler, *1975 Community Survey*, 12–13.

6. Morey Schapira and Robert Brauner, eds., *Jewish Boston 1973–1974*, (Boston: Jewish Boston, Inc., 1973).

7. The Combined Jewish Philanthropies formed its Young Professionals Division. The Jewish Community Center of Greater Boston opened the Jewish Young Adult Center in Brookline for predominantly social programs in 1979. Later renamed Centerpoint, it closed in 1991. A number of Jewish dating services opened their doors, mostly private and entrepreneurial. The Hillel Council created a small dating service for college students in the 1980's, and the JCCGB's dating/matchmaking service opened in Newton. Several private groups began putting on dances and other social events for Jewish singles and young professionals; the "Matzo Ball" drew hundreds on Christmas Eve. In the mid-eighties, the Synagogue Council began sponsoring "Shabbat Shalom Boston," a monthly series of services at different congregations geared to young adults. Chabad House and Congregation Beth Pinchas (both Orthodox) each introduced Shabbat programs and retreats for college students and young adults. By 1994, CJP and many communal organizations and synagogues were reassessing their young adult programs and creating new ones to serve this important sector of the community.

8. Israel Emergency Fund "Letter of Invitation" (Boston: Combined Jewish Philanthropies) 13 June 1967.

9. Irene Sege, "The Eruv is Up," *Boston Globe*, 10 February 1993.

10. In 1994, in recognition of the expansion of the community center movement, the organization changed its name back to Jewish Community Centers of Greater Boston.

11. For a fuller discussion of the community center and synagogue-center movements in Boston, see David Kaufman's essay in this volume.

12. *Guide to Jewish Cemeteries* (Boston: Jewish Cemetery Association of Massachusetts, 1992).

# In Search of Suburbs:
## Boston's Jewish Districts, 1843-1994

GERALD H. GAMM

# *In Search of Suburbs:*
## Boston's Jewish Districts, 1843–1994

חבורה ומשפחה כך הן דומים לכיפת אבנים את נוטל ממנה אבן אחת ובלה ובלה מתרועעת

"A community and a family are similar to a pile of stones:
if you remove one stone, the pile becomes shaky."

MIDRASH BERESHIT RABBAH 100

 N JUNE 1918, members of Roxbury's Crawford Street Syna-
gogue gathered for celebration. It was an especially hopeful
spring. In the year that had just passed, the British had issued the
Balfour Declaration, President Wilson had outlined his Fourteen
Points, and the Yanks had arrived in Europe to make the world
safe for democracy. Meanwhile, the Red Sox—Baseball Champions of the World in
1915 and 1916—were on the verge of winning yet another World Series that summer, led by their star pitcher and batter Babe Ruth.

Just five years after its founding and three years after it had completed work on
the Crawford Street Synagogue, Beth Hamidrash Hagadol had emerged by 1918 as
one of Boston Jewry's leading suburban institutions. That spring, the congregation
had elected its first rabbi, Louis M. Epstein. Educated at Orthodox yeshivot as well
as at the Jewish Theological Seminary, Epstein was honored in June at a banquet
held in the synagogue. Earlier in the day, leaders of Beth Hamidrash Hagadol
marked the congregation's fifth anniversary with a flag-raising ceremony attended
by Lieutenant Governor Calvin Coolidge, Speaker Channing Cox, and Congressman James A. Gallivan. The Crawford Street Synagogue was quickly becoming "an
up-to-date Orthodox synagogue" committed to the "promotion of modern Judaism
in the community," a "unifying force between the old Jew of foreign breeding and
the young Jew of American breeding."[1]

The Crawford Street Synagogue was the center of a quickly growing Jewish
suburb: by the early 1920's, the congregation boasted a membership of five hundred
families, as well as an active Sisterhood, Men's Club, and Junior Council. The synagogue stood in Roxbury's Elm Hill district, which bordered Franklin Park. When

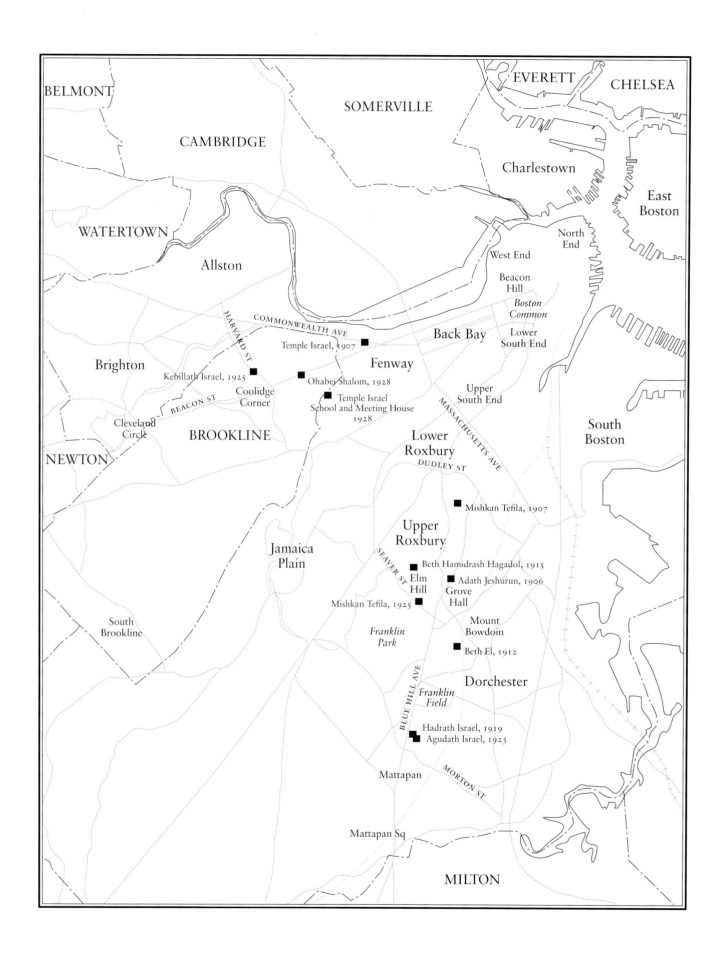

BELMONT

CAMBRIDGE

SOMERVILLE

EVERETT CHELSEA

Charlestown

East Boston

WATERTOWN

Allston

North End

West End

Beacon Hill

*Boston Common*

COMMONWEALTH AVE

Back Bay

Lower South End

HARVARD ST

Temple Israel, 1907

Fenway

Brighton

Kehillath Israel, 1925

BEACON ST

Coolidge Corner

Ohabei Shalom, 1928

Temple Israel School and Meeting House 1928

Upper South End

MASSACHUSETTS AVE

South Boston

Cleveland Circle

BROOKLINE

Lower Roxbury

NEWTON

DUDLEY ST

Mishkan Tefila, 1907

Upper Roxbury

Jamaica Plain

SEAVER ST

Beth Hamidrash Hagadol, 1915

Elm Hill

Adath Jeshurun, 1906

Grove Hall

Mishkan Tefila, 1925

South Brookline

*Franklin Park*

Mount Bowdoin

Beth El, 1912

Dorchester

BLUE HILL AVE

*Franklin Field*

Hadrath Israel, 1919

Agudath Israel, 1923

Mattapan

MORTON ST

Mattapan Sq

MILTON

Beth Hamidrash Hagadol had been organized, in 1913, Elm Hill had still been an
affluent, heavily Protestant area of large
homes on tree-lined, hilly streets, an upper-
middle-class suburban district connected to
downtown Boston by streetcar lines. By the
late 1910's, large numbers of middle-class
Jews were settling in the Elm Hill district.
Other middle-class Jewish districts were
developing at the same time in Dorchester's
Mount Bowdoin–Franklin Park district and
Dorchester's Mattapan district, while a

fourth suburban Jewish settlement was already well-established along the few
blocks of Blue Hill Avenue in Roxbury that ran north from Grove Hall to Quincy
Street.

In 1918 five major suburban synagogues served Boston Jewry. One of them, the
Reform Temple Israel, stood on Commonwealth Avenue, near Brookline. The other
four were located in Roxbury and Dorchester. As Beth Hamidrash Hagadol's Crawford Street Synagogue anchored the Elm Hill Jewish community, so Adath Jeshurun's Blue Hill Avenue Synagogue and Beth El's Fowler Street Synagogue were the
preeminent suburban congregations of the Blue Hill Avenue–Grove Hall district and
the Mount Bowdoin–Franklin Park district. Temple Mishkan Tefila, the city's only
Conservative congregation, stood in a more distant section of Roxbury, but in 1918
it had dedicated a new schoolhouse and community building in Elm Hill, the first
stage in a plan to relocate the temple; the new temple was completed in the middle
1920's.

While there were many other congregations in Dorchester and upper Roxbury,
these four were distinctive. They worshiped in large, impressive synagogue structures, the most substantial Jewish communal structures in their districts. They
served middle-class, suburban congregations. And they were sympathetic to many
of the reforms associated with the Conservative Movement. In 1918, at a time when
the branches of American Judaism were not yet well-defined, three of the congregations described themselves as "modern Orthodox"; only Mishkan Tefila had openly
embraced Conservatism. But all four congregations were (or would soon be) affiliated with the United Synagogue of America, all four were led by rabbis who had
been educated at the Jewish Theological Seminary, and all four rabbis were introducing new programs to attract young adults and children to the synagogues, in the

process modifying and abandoning traditional religious practices. Soon after assuming the pulpit at the Crawford Street Synagogue, Rabbi Epstein became the national president of the Rabbinical Assembly.

What Epstein found when he arrived in Roxbury in 1918 was a cluster of suburban settlements that had become New England's cradle of Conservative Judaism. As the religious and cultural expression of middle-class Americanized Jews, the Conservative Movement was taking root in Boston's first Jewish suburbs. Since the earliest years of Jewish settlement in Boston, Jewish women and men had yearned for a suburban environment where they could raise their children, define their place in the larger community, and build institutions for the ages. They had found their suburbs, they had built their temples, and they were embracing the effort to adapt traditional Judaism to the needs and aspirations of a new generation. For Rabbi Epstein as for many other Jews in Roxbury and Dorchester, the spring of 1918 was a time to celebrate accomplishment and it was a time full of promise.

Boston's Jewish community had begun in humble circumstances in the 1840's, as a few, poor German and Polish immigrants gathered to worship and to assist one another in adjusting to a strange new land. To most Bostonians, these early Jews were invisible. Since its founding by European settlers in 1630, Boston had been home to a population that was overwhelmingly white, Protestant, and English. In the 1840's, as tens of thousands of Irish Catholics began to crowd into the city, the small influx of Central European Jews was a trivial event. Only in retrospect, only when Boston's Jewish community grew in numbers and stature, would the affairs of those few early Jews assume a larger importance.

Those first Jews made their homes in the lower South End, where they established the city's first Jewish community. Located directly south of Boston Common, the lower South End included what is today the city's theater district. The lower South End was a nondescript neighborhood; unlike the North End, Fort Hill, Summer Street, Beacon Hill, and the upper South End, it had never been a fashionable district. In the 1840's, the lower South End still sat at the far edge of the city. Beyond it, Boston's land mass narrowed into an isthmus that connected the city's peninsula with Roxbury and the mainland. About 17,000 people lived in the lower South End in the middle 1840's. Most of them were American-born and Protestant; no more than one hundred were Jews. In February 1843, eighteen men, all of them from Central Europe, organized a synagogue in the lower South End. The men included a soap maker, a hotel keeper, a furrier, cap makers, and peddlers. Many of them had worshiped together for the High Holy Days a few months earlier; now they laid the foundations of Ohabei Shalom, the city's first Jewish congregation.

Ohabei Shalom, for a decade the only Jewish congregation in Boston, made the lower South End the center of the city's infant Jewish community. The synagogue drew new families to the district: as German and Polish Jews arrived in Boston, many of them settled in the lower South End and became members of the congregation. By 1851, there were about 125 Jewish families in Boston. Ohabei Shalom, which had been worshiping in makeshift rooms and halls, purchased land on Warren (now Warrenton) Street that year and began raising funds for a new synagogue building. The modest frame synagogue was dedicated in the spring of 1852. By the end of the decade, two other congregations had been organized in Boston. Both congregations, Adath Israel and Mishkan Israel, were founded by former members of Ohabei Shalom. Both congregations were located in the lower South End, within blocks of the Warren Street synagogue.

Boston's Jewish population grew steadily. In 1875, the rabbi serving Ohabei Shalom estimated that 3,000 Jews lived in the city. They were "occupied in trade and industry," he wrote. "Some have acquired competence and own nice homes, many are able to support themselves in reasonable comfort, but the majority work hard and earn little."[2] All three of Boston's original congregations remained in the lower South End. Ohabei Shalom had moved into a large brick church on Warrenton Street, Adath Israel was located on Pleasant Street, and Mishkan Israel worshiped in a new frame synagogue on Ash Street.

Though most of the city's Jews remained poor, some had prospered. Adath Israel and Ohabei Shalom embraced religious reforms in the middle and late 1870's, and many Jews began to move out of the lower South End, seeking homes in other residential districts. From the lower South End, which was home to a poor population of native-born and foreign-born whites as well as to several hundred blacks, a few of the city's leading German and Polish Jews moved to suburban districts like Roxbury and Brookline. But many more settled in the upper, "new" South End where— the isthmus now a wide expanse of newly made land—handsome bowfront homes had been built along elegant streets in the 1850's and 1860's. Recognizing the need for a new temple, Adath Israel announced plans to relocate to a new district of the city. In 1885 the congregation dedicated its "new and fair temple of worship."[3] The most impressive synagogue built in Boston before the 20th century, it stood at the corner of Columbus Avenue and Northampton Street; at the far edge of the upper South End, the structure stood more than a mile away from the old Pleasant Street synagogue in the lower South End. Two years later, in 1887, Ohabei Shalom also abandoned the lower South End, acquiring a church on Union Park Street, in the upper South End.

Although most respectable Yankee families had left the upper South End by the 1880's, the area continued to attract many middle-class residents seeking a fine residential neighborhood away from the city's business and tenement districts. Among those new residents were many Jewish families. Still evident in the district, William I. Cole wrote in 1898, are "many evidences of what the best of the South End was like in the days when this part of the city was a prosperous residential quarter. Several of the squares here—though almost entirely deserted by their old residents— are still outwardly as pleasant places of abode as can be found within the main city."[4] It was here that Adath Israel and Ohabei Shalom dedicated their new temples in the 1880's. And it was here, in 1898, that Mishkan Tefila—a congregation formed three years before by the merger of Mishkan Israel with Shaaray Tefila, another congregation in the lower South End—dedicated its new synagogue, on the corner of Shawmut Avenue and Madison Street. In the last two decades of the century, as they became increasingly well-established in the life of the city, Boston's Central European Jews invested their future in the upper South End.

FIG. 3. Organized in the West End about 1915, the Chassidic congregation of Grand Rabbi Pinchas D. Horowitz moved into this building at 87 Poplar Street at the end of the decade. The congregation remained in the West End until the 1940's, when it moved to Dorchester. *American Jewish Historical Society.*

❀

Two institutions established by the city's Central European Jews in the late 19th century were the Boston Young Men's Hebrew Association and the Hebrew Industrial School (which became the Hecht Neighborhood House). The Boston YMHA rented a hall in the upper South End, where the association helped young men find jobs and provided a simple gymnasium, club rooms, and a social center. Its location, far removed from the East European community emerging in the North End of the city, defined the Boston YMHA as an institution for Central European Jews. "Between the North Enders and the South Enders," Barbara Miller Solomon later wrote, "there seemed to be a solid wall of division; whether young or old they went their separate ways in synagogues, charities and social clubs." The Hebrew Industrial School represented an early breaching of that wall of division. Established by Lina Hecht, the American-born wife of a prominent German Jew, the Hebrew Industrial School was founded in the North End in 1890 to teach East European Jewish girls how to cook and sew. By the middle 1890's, having moved to the nearby West End and

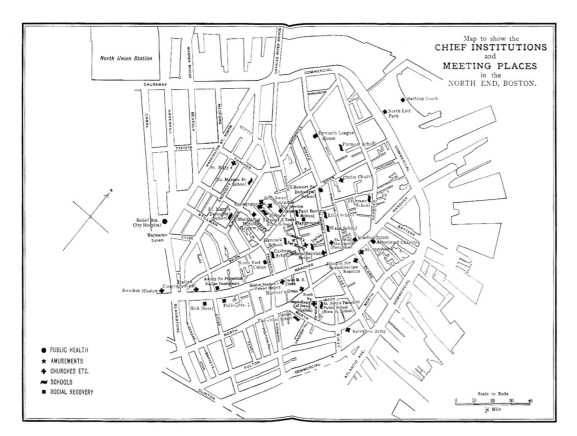

FIG. 4. "Chief Institutions and Meeting Places in the North End, Boston," as printed in Robert A. Woods, editor, *Americans in Process: A Settlement House Study*, Boston: Houghton Mifflin, 1902.

expanded in order to serve boys as well as girls, Hecht's school had already taught more than one thousand immigrant children the skills to be "wage earners, bread-winners and self-respecting intelligent citizens."[5]

That Hecht organized her school in the North End—and that she quickly moved it to the West End—reflected her desire to serve the great population centers of Boston's East European Jewish community. The North End lay at the opposite end of the city from the South End. Unlike the South End, which was a relatively new area of European settlement, the North End had been Boston's principal residential district since the 17th century. By the middle of the 19th century, the North End had become a notorious tenement district, a stronghold of the city's burgeoning Irish population. Not until the early 1880's did significant numbers of Jews and Italians begin to settle there. Between 1880 and 1895, the Italian population of the North End increased from several hundred to 7,700, while the district's Jewish population increased from a few hundred to 6,200. With its large population of Irish, Italians, and Jews, the North End in the 1890's was the most "strikingly foreign" of Boston's districts.[6]

East European immigrants made up nearly all of the North End's Jewish population. Clustered along Salem Street and its narrow, crowded side streets, these East European Jews created the first Jewish enclave in the city. While German and Polish

FIG. 5. Fruit vendor with pushcart in Boston's North End. *Boston Public Library, Print Department.*

Jews had established a Jewish community in the South End, there had been too few of them to dominate the neighborhood or any section of it. But in the North End a cohesive Jewish neighborhood took shape in the 1880's. "The great centre of the Jewish population of Boston is in the North End," an 1892 account recorded. "Less than twenty-five years ago the number of Jews in the North End was very small, the strictly Jewish district comprising but a few blocks. From this nucleus, and by immigration, they have spread till they have almost absorbed the locality." In the 1890's, when the North End's Jewish community was at its peak, Beth Israel's synagogue on Baldwin Place, near Salem Street, was "the headquarters of orthodox Judaism in Boston."[7]

Arriving poor, the Jews of the North End worked hard to support their families. "This is the first stopping-place of the immigrant," according to an 1892 description of the North End. "Here, if he has no money to start himself, he will find some one to fill his pack on credit and send him out to the country to peddle. Peddling is the chief industry of the people of this quarter." As Stephan Thernstrom later argued, "That the Jews were heavily concentrated in callings that involved risk-taking and developed business skills was . . . very significant for the economic future of the group." The North End was the densest, most congested section of the city. "While there is much that is of peculiar interest in Jewish life, there can be, where there is so much squalor, but little real beauty," Jessie Fremont Beale and Anne Withington, two settlement house workers, wrote at the turn of the century. "On the streets the commercial instinct is everywhere evident. The dangling old clothes, the pawnshop windows filled with everything that could possibly be turned into money, the baskets, barrels and carts of foul-smelling fish, do not add to the charm of the scene, and are hardly offset by the boxes of green vegetables and ripe fruits which border the sidewalk."[8]

Jews in the North End made their homes in overcrowded tenements. "Yet it is in their homes that the Jews rise to their best level. The family life is usually worthy of admiration. The parents are devoted guardians," Beale and Withington observed in 1902. "Even in the homes of the poorest, candles are always lighted for the Friday evening service, and the family assemble for the beginning of the Sabbath." In a new world, in the midst of poverty, East European immigrants attempted to reconcile their Jewish heritage with the demands and temptations of American society. "It is one of the sad and disappointing aspects of life for the older members of the Jewish community," Frederick A. Bushée noted, "that, as time goes by, the language and customs of the new country become a serious barrier between their children and themselves." Americanized immigrants and American-born Jews were not easily confined in the North End's Jewish ghetto.[9]

Having grown through the 1880's, the Jewish community of the North End was at its largest and most vital in the 1890's. By the turn of the century, the North End's Jewish population was shrinking. Jews were expanding their settlements in other districts, as the North End became heavily Italian. Bushée noted in 1902 that large numbers of Jews had already left the North End. "Although it has been a popular belief that a greater mass of Jews than of any other sub-division of humanity will collect in a given space, a longer acquaintance with the Italians has forced one to abandon this idea," he wrote. "When the North End reached the point of human saturation, the less persistent material—that is, the Jews and the Irish—found its way to neighboring places, leaving the Italians in possession."[10] The Italian population of the North End increased from 7,700 to 18,000 between 1895 and 1905, while the district's Jewish population fell from 6,200 to 4,700. By 1920, the Jewish presence in the North End was negligible.

East European Jews rapidly expanded beyond Boston's North End. Between 1880 and 1910, Boston's Jewish population grew from about 4,000 to 65,000; including Jews who lived in surrounding cities and towns, Greater Boston's Jewish population in 1910 approached 100,000. With the great influx of East European Jews, earlier Jewish settlers and their descendants became only a small fragment of Boston Jewry. Beginning in the 1880's, the history of Boston Jewry became, in large measure, a history of the Jews who came from Eastern Europe. This new wave of immigrants inundated whole residential districts in Boston as well as parts of surrounding cities. By the turn of the century, the patterns of East European immigrant life that had been established first in the North End were being replicated in many other districts.

Chelsea, an industrial city just north of Boston, became the center of a large Jewish community. "Arlington Street was inhabited by poor Jews, poor Negroes, and a sprinkling of poor Irish," Mary Antin wrote, describing the street that her immigrant family lived on in the 1890's. "My father rented a tenement with a store in the basement. He put in a few barrels of flour and of sugar, a few boxes of crackers, a few gallons of kerosene, an assortment of soap of the 'save the coupon' brands; in the cellar, a few barrels of potatoes, and a pyramid of kindling-wood; in the showcase, an alluring display of penny candy. He put out his sign, with a gilt-lettered

FIG. 6. "Palestine in Chelsea" broadside, June 4, 1924. *American Jewish Historical Society.*

FIG. 7. Avenue Bazaar, Brockton, December 20, 1899. Store owned by the Maurice Milionthaler family. *American Jewish Historical Society.*

warning of 'Strictly Cash,' and proceeded to give credit indiscriminately. That was the regular way to do business on Arlington Street."[11] Between 1890 and 1900, Chelsea's Jewish population had grown from one hundred to 3,000. By 1910, about 10,000 Jews lived in Chelsea. From the late 1910's until the early 1950's, when Chelsea's Jewish community started to fall in size, between 18,000 and 24,000 Jews lived in the city, representing half of Chelsea's population. Chelsea, home to thousands of poor immigrant families and a flourishing set of Jewish institutions, had become "Yerushalayim D'America."

Other cities near Boston attracted smaller numbers of Jews. Malden, also north of Boston, was home to 5,500 Jews in 1910. About 4,000 Jews had settled in Lynn by 1910, and 4,000 had settled in Brockton; both cities were major centers of shoe manufacturing. Smaller immigrant communities had formed in Salem, Somerville, and Everett as well as in Peabody, a center of the leather industry. Another small community was developing in Quincy. Finally, about 3,500 Jews lived in Cambridge, just across the Charles River from Boston. "Industrially the Jew continues to be a trader and keeps various kinds of small shops. Several Jewish mills and factories making clothing have been started," Albert J. Kennedy wrote early in the century, surveying Cambridge's immigrant Jewish community. "The rag and junk dealers abound, and the Cambridge Street district is dotted with barns and buildings wherein this filthy and dangerous business is carried on."[12]

While substantial Jewish communities existed outside of Boston, it was in the neighborhoods of Boston that East European Jewish life was concentrated at the turn of the century. The lower South End—where years earlier German and Polish immigrants had created the city's first Jewish community—began to attract East European Jews in the late 1880's. "It is remarkable how rapidly the Jewish population has increased within the last few years," Bushée observed in 1898. About 3,500

East European Jews lived in the lower South End in 1895; 8,000 lived there in 1910. By the turn of the century, the lower South End was a tenement and lodging house district. Harrison Avenue "is the heart of the South End ghetto," Mary Antin wrote in 1912. "Its multifarious business bursts through the narrow shop doors, and overruns the basements, the sidewalk, the street itself, in pushcarts and open-air stands. Its multitudinous population bursts through the greasy tenement doors, and floods the corridors,

the doorsteps, the gutters, the side streets, pushing in and out among the pushcarts, all day long and half the night besides." In East Boston, at the other end of the city, lived about 5,000 Jews in 1910, while 3,000 Jews lived in South Boston.[13]

Chelsea and the South End attracted large Jewish communities at the beginning of the century, but it was the West End that became Boston's principal stronghold of East European Jewry. The West End was immediately adjacent to the North End, and the West End's Jewish community had developed as an extension of North End Jewry. Already by 1895, more Jews lived in the West End than in the North End. Between 1895 and 1905, when the Jewish population of the North End fell from 6,200 to 4,700, the Jewish population of the West End increased from 6,300 to

17,000. In 1910, about 24,000 Jews lived in the West End. For two decades—from the middle 1890's through the middle 1910's, when the West End's Jewish population began steadily to decline—the West End was the largest Jewish district in Boston.

The West End extended from the North End to Beacon Hill. Beyond the West End, on the south slope of Beacon Hill, was an upper-class residential neighborhood. Except for "a colony of negroes living in extreme squalor" on the back of Beacon Hill, the West End had been "a comfortable, fairly well-to-do community" from its initial development early in the 19th century through the middle of the century. Irish immigrants settled in the West End, but through the 1880's the district's population was not "of so foreign a character as that of the North End." Beginning in the late 1880's, as large numbers of East European Jews began moving into the district, the character of the West End was transformed. "A large part of the population is huddled into old houses originally built for the

FIG. 10. "Chief Institutions and Meeting Places in the West End, Boston," as printed in Robert A. Woods, editor, *Americans in Process: A Settlement House Study*, Boston: Houghton Mifflin, 1902.

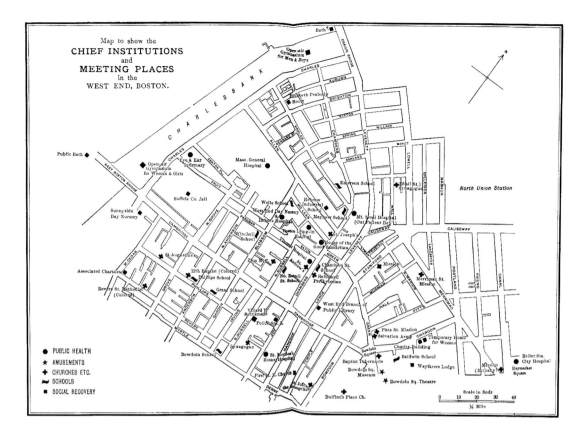

use of single families. Many of the smaller tenement houses are built in rear yards and courts," Robert A. Woods wrote in 1902. "There are many large newly built tenement blocks, in which the evil devices involved in making over old houses are perpetuated in the new." The section of the West End that lay next to the North End had become overwhelmingly Jewish by the late 1890's; the opposite section of the West End, which included "the bleak northeast slope" of Beacon Hill, still contained a large population of African-Americans, Irish, and native-stock white Americans, though Jews had begun to move into that section as well. By the middle 1900's, Jews had settled throughout the district.[14]

As the Jewish settlement was expanding, blacks were moving out of the West End, vacating streets on the back of Beacon Hill that had been heavily African-American since the early 19th century. The Jews had become "inured through long centuries to overcrowding and uncleanliness," Woods argued in 1902. "There are actually streets in the West End where, while Jews are moving in, Negro housewives are gathering up their skirts and seeking a more spotless environment." By the 1890's, large numbers of African-Americans were leaving the West End. "The Hebrew children in the district were multiplying at the rate they multiplied in Goshen when Joseph ruled Egypt," leaders of the Twelfth Baptist Church, an African-American church, concluded in 1905. The north slope of Beacon Hill, the church's home since its founding, had been "deserted" by blacks and had become "congested by a Hebrew population."[15]

The Twelfth Baptist Church sold its structure on Phillips Street to the Vilna congregation in the next year. With the sale, the Twelfth Baptist Church became the third African-American church in the West End to be acquired by a Jewish congregation. In 1902, noting that the African Meeting House had been sold to Anshe Libavitz "a year or two ago," Cole suggested that "the change in the ownership of this building within so recent a time registers the curious social displacement that is coming about in that part of the West End."[16] Within four years, the African Methodist Episcopal Zion Church, on North Russell Street, and the Twelfth Baptist Church were also synagogues.

FIG. 11. Chambers Street, West End, Boston, 1912. Note the crowded, alley-like entrance to Barton Court on the right. *Boston Public Library, Print Department.*

The A.M.E. Zion Church and the Twelfth Baptist Church both relocated to the upper South End, where they moved into two of the city's outstanding temple buildings. This exchange of churches for synagogues, synagogues for churches, was poetic. For as immigrant Jews were displacing blacks from the north slope of Beacon Hill, so blacks were settling in large numbers in the upper South End, where Central European Jews had located their temples just a few years before. By 1900, nearly 3,500 African-Americans had settled in the upper South End. Adath Israel sold its temple on Columbus Avenue to the A.M.E. Zion Church, which dedicated it in June 1903. Two years later, Mishkan Tefila agreed to sell its synagogue on Shawmut Avenue to the Twelfth Baptist Church; the church dedicated the structure in 1906.[17]

While Temple Adath Israel moved to Commonwealth Avenue, near Brookline, Mishkan Tefila moved to the Dudley Street district of upper Roxbury. In May 1907 Mishkan Tefila dedicated its temple on Moreland Street; here, the congregation embraced the Conservative Movement. "We are face to face with the risen generation of the second migration to this Commonwealth," the *Boston Advocate* declared in an editorial marking the dedication of the Moreland Street Temple. The Central European Jews who had created Mishkan Tefila no longer led it; increasingly, the congregation's membership was drawn from "the risen generation of the second migration," from the ranks of middle-class East European Jews. "The vast majority of the members, and the district in which the house of worship is situated, suggest the new congregation. The congregation of the risen generation." Adath Jeshurun's Blue Hill Avenue Synagogue, dedicated in the fall of 1906, and Mishkan Tefila's Moreland Street Temple "point almost clearly to the future paths of the faith and life of the majority of our Jewish citizens." Led by young and prospering East Europeans, committed to tradition but equally to religious reform, and located in upper Roxbury, the two congregations were the founding congregations of suburban Boston Jewry.[18]

From the turn of the century until the middle 1920's, the suburban center of Boston Jewry was in Dorchester and upper Roxbury. Many of the early Jewish residents in these suburban districts had begun coming from the North End in the late 1890's and early 1900's. "As the North End began to lose," the *Jewish Advocate* observed in the summer of 1910, "the center began to shift to Dorchester and Roxbury." The main body of leadership in these new suburbs was drawn from East European families. In 1907, a leader of the Blue Hill Avenue Synagogue referred with pride to "the present standing of their members, . . . Jewish immigrants who by faithful industry had risen so as to be able to move out into better and more healthful quarters where they now possess an excellent place of worship." The suburban expansion of Dorchester and upper Roxbury's Jewish centers depended on the increasing prosperity of East European Jews and their exodus from the North End, the West End, Chelsea, and other areas of immigrant settlement.[19]

Dorchester and Roxbury's Jewish districts are the crossroads of Boston Jewish history. The neighborhoods that followed Blue Hill Avenue for three miles—from the Elm Hill and Grove Hall sections of Roxbury, through the Franklin Park–Franklin Field–Mount Bowdoin district of Dorchester, to the Mattapan district of Dorchester—were home in the late 1920's and early 1930's to 77,000 Jews, half of the Jewish population of Greater Boston. As late as 1950, about 70,000 Jews still lived in the Roxbury-Dorchester area. From the middle 1910's until the late 1950's, Jewish life in Boston was centered on these neighborhoods. As early suburban districts, they were without rival: in 1920, when 44,000 Jews lived in Dorchester and upper Roxbury, 3,000 lived in the Brookline–Brighton–Newton area, 5,000 lived in Revere, and 1,000 lived in Winthrop. The vast belt of settlement in Roxbury and Dorchester, which was born as a set of suburbs and which evolved into a set of working-class ethnic neighborhoods, was the belt that connected Boston Jewry's immigrant past to its suburban future.

The Jewish settlement in upper Roxbury and Dorchester took shape in the 1900's and 1910's as four discrete suburban districts, each developing around its own set of institutions. The first of those suburban districts emerged at the turn of

FIG. 12. Revere, Winthrop, and Everett, early suburban Jewish districts on the North Shore. From top: Wheeler's food stand, Revere Beach, early 1920's, *Bernard Shavelson and Family*; Girls bathing at Revere Beach, early 1920's, *Bernard Shavelson and Family*; Flooding on Shirley Street, Winthrop, November 1932, *Boston Public Library, Print Department*; "Five Families Built This" brochure, Everett, Massachusetts. *Private collection*; Dr. William Shavelson, Rebecca Wheeler Shavelson, Dr. Samuel Smith, and Gertrude Wheeler Smith, on Shirley Avenue, Revere, late 1920's, *Bernard Shavelson and Family*.

FIG. 13. Blue Hill Avenue Synagogue (Adath Jeshurun), Grove Hall–Blue Hill Avenue district, Roxbury. *Photograph by Brett Miller.*

FIG. 14. Brunswick Street, Grove Hall–Blue Hill Avenue district, Roxbury. As middle-class Jews settled in this district in the first years of the twentieth century, they built substantial apartment buildings. *Photograph by Richard Heath.*

the century along a few blocks of Blue Hill Avenue. Adath Jeshurun, which had been founded in 1894 in another part of Roxbury, relocated to the Grove Hall–Blue Hill Avenue district in 1900. For the next few years, Adath Jeshurun worshiped in a three-story frame chapel. The only synagogue in Dorchester and upper Roxbury, the structure served as the Jewish "communal center of the neighborhood" and attracted increasing numbers of Jewish families to the suburban district. In the spring of 1905, the congregation broke ground for a new synagogue building. The Blue Hill Avenue Synagogue was dedicated in September 1906. It was an extraordinary achievement. According to the *Boston Journal*, the Blue Hill Avenue Synagogue was "probably the finest structure of its kind in New England." The structure, which cost between $100,000 and $150,000, was built by a congregation of 140 families. "Owing to the small number in the congregation," the *Journal* noted, "the achievement of building this magnificent edifice reflects very creditably on the efforts of the people in the little congregation."[20]

Though by the middle 1910's five other synagogues and the Boston YMHA stood within a few blocks of Adath Jeshurun's Blue Hill Avenue Synagogue, the great structure and its congregation remained the focal point of the Grove Hall–Blue Hill Avenue district. But the suburban character of the district was changing, undermined by the migration of working-class and lower-middle-class Jews into the district. As two settlement house workers warned in the early 1910's, "If the streets are to be kept clean, the houses repaired and the general air of orderliness maintained, the traditions which have made for such conditions must not be swamped by an inrush of those who still conform to West and North End or even Russian standards." Large numbers of Jews had begun moving into the district from the North End, the West End, and, especially after a major 1908 fire, Chelsea. The earlier Jews in the district had been "of a more assimilated type," Marion Booth and Ordway Tead noted, "but the Chelsea Fire marked the beginning of an immigration of Russian Jews which has yet to cease." While the district's original Jewish residents had purchased single-family homes, which were well-maintained and "kept up with attractive gardens and good lawns," an increasing number of Jews moving into the area were building multi-family structures or converting old houses into tenements. "It is here that the danger lies," Booth and Tead argued. "The Jewish property holders do not hesitate to build cheap brick blocks or poorly constructed three-deckers, and in the event of this a type of family lower in the economic scale is attracted and the richer families go farther out."[21]

By the early 1910's, three new suburban Jewish districts were emerging in Dorchester and upper Roxbury. In Dorchester's Mount Bowdoin district, a small group of Jewish families organized a congregation in the middle 1900's. In 1910 the congregation, Beth El, purchased land on Fowler Street, two blocks from Mount Bowdoin Station. "Dorchester is to have its first regular built synagogue," the *Jewish Advocate* announced on its front page. "The undertaking points directly to the spread of the community into the suburban parts of Boston." Beth El's Fowler Street Synagogue was dedicated in September 1912. One year later, Jews in Roxbury's Elm Hill district organized Beth Hamidrash Hagadol. "It must be apparent to every Jew in Roxbury and Elm Hill District, that there is dire necessity for a new house of worship in that vicinity," they wrote in an appeal for funds. "Such facilities as exist at present do not by any means meet the needs of the community." Beth Hamidrash Hagadol's Crawford Street Synagogue, the outstanding institution of Elm Hill Jewry, was completed in 1915. That December, Hadrath Israel, in Dorchester's Mattapan district, purchased land for "a new Synagogue." Organized four years earlier, Hadrath Israel was Mattapan's oldest congregation. The proposed new structure was not built: Hadrath Israel moved instead into a former Baptist church on Woodrow Avenue. By the middle 1910's, the Mattapan district—served by two congregations, Hadrath Israel and Agudath Israel, neither of which had yet erected a permanent structure—contained the most heavily Jewish neighborhood in Dorchester, and handsome new synagogue buildings stood in the growing Jewish suburbs of Elm Hill and Mount Bowdoin. When the Crawford Street Synagogue gathered in 1918 for its flag-raising ceremony and to honor Rabbi Epstein, the suburban Jewish communities

FIG. 15. Fowler Street Synagogue (Beth El), Mount Bowdoin district, Dorchester, photographed in January 1923. *The Boston Herald Library.*

FIG. 16. Rabbi Louis M. Epstein, who served Roxbury's Beth Hamidrash Hagadol from 1918 until 1925, when he moved to Brookline and became the first rabbi of Kehillath Israel. *American Jewish Historical Society.*

FIG. 17. Shavuot service at Nightingale Street Synagogue (Chai Odom), Franklin Field district, Dorchester, May 1939. *Boston Public Library, Print Department.*

of Dorchester and upper Roxbury were prospering.[22]

But the prosperous years were brief indeed. Like the Grove Hall–Blue Hill Avenue district, which already had been transformed into a working-class ethnic neighborhood, the districts in Elm Hill, Mount Bowdoin–Franklin Park, and Mattapan eroded in socio-economic status. By the early 1920's, working-class and lower-middle-class Jews were settling throughout the Jewish districts of Roxbury and Dorchester. "Store-keepers had transformed Erie Street from the quiet residential neighborhood my grandparents had sought as Jewish pioneers in the district into a semipermanent bazaar," Theodore H. White recalled, describing his childhood in Dorchester's Mount Bowdoin– Franklin Park district. "Whatever you wanted you could buy on Erie Street. Or else someone could get it for you. Herrings were stacked in barrels outside the fish stores, and flies buzzed over the herrings. Fresh-caught fish lay on slabs, and little boys were allowed to keep the fishhooks for the trouble of extracting them. All butcher shops were kosher, sawdust on the floor, chopping blocks scrubbed clean every day, unplucked chickens piled in flop heaps in the store window, from which housewives squeezed and prodded, then picked and chose. . . . But it was the peddlers who gave the street its sound and motion."[23] Middle-class families had begun moving en masse out of Dorchester and upper Roxbury by the early 1920's. The Elm Hill district alone retained a residual appeal as a suburban neighborhood, but its appeal was relative only to the other Jewish districts of Dorchester and Roxbury. It was in altogether new parts of Greater Boston, above all in the suburban town of Brookline, that most middle-class Jews were settling. The suburban era in Roxbury and Dorchester had abruptly ended.

As the streetcar suburbs became urban neighborhoods in the 1920's, middle-class suburban life receded into memory. Even memory was obliterated, as three-deckers filled parks and open fields, as old single-family houses were converted into multi-family dwellings, as suburban temples became urban synagogues. The four original areas of settlement were forgotten, as each expanded outward and as all four districts merged and became one vast, interconnected Jewish community. From Elm Hill and Grove Hall in Roxbury, through the Franklin Park and Mount Bowdoin and Franklin Field sections of Dorchester, to Dorchester's Mattapan section, Blue Hill Avenue ran through the largest Jewish community in New England. Until the early 1950's, when the area's Jewish population began to fall sharply in size,

FIG. 18. Former areas of suburban Jewish settlement in Roxbury and Dorchester became working-class and lower-middle-class neighborhoods in the 1920's and remained major centers of Boston Jewish life for decades. *From top:* G&G Delicatessen, Blue Hill Avenue, Mattapan, late 1960's, *The Boston Globe*; Boston Young Men's Hebrew Association, Seaver Street and Humboldt Avenue, Elm Hill district, Roxbury, in the converted Goldsmith mansion, *Combined Jewish Philanthropies*; Interior, G&G Delicatessen, Blue Hill Avenue, Mattapan, November 1962. *Seated, from left to right:* Harold Klingsberg, Ben Klingsberg (owner), State Representative Julius Ansel, and unidentified man. *The Boston Herald Library*; Three-deckers in Dorchester, photographed in 1980, *American Jewish Historical Society*; Taking the Torah from the ark on the last day of Passover, April 1939, at Temple Mishkan Tefila, Seaver Street and Elm Hill Avenue, Elm Hill district, Roxbury, *American Jewish Historical Society*.

bakeries and grocery stores and fruit shops and kosher butchers lined Blue Hill Avenue for three miles. Jewish children gathered at the wall at Franklin Field each year on the High Holy Days, the oldest boys and girls getting the wall's best section. Jews throughout Roxbury and Dorchester participated in clubs and classes and sporting events at the Boston YMHA and the Hecht House: both had relocated into the district and become major community centers.

But, as Mark Mirsky suggested, "Of all the fortresses only one reached the proportions, could claim palatial amenities that testify to a high culture, that immense landmark which any traveller who has passed down Blue Hill avenue will smile in recognition of, the G&G." The G&G Delicatessen stood in Dorchester's Mattapan district. "On the tables of the cafeteria talmudic jurisprudence sorted out racing results, politics, the stock market," Mirsky remembered, "and the student could look up from his 'desk' to leer at the young girls sipping cream soda under the immense wings of their mothers; watch the whole world of Blue Hill avenue revolve through the G&G's glass gate."[24] Each election year, a large wooden platform was erected outside the G&G. That platform was the routine campaign stop and election-eve gathering place of state representatives, city councillors, mayors, presidents and vice presidents of the United States. From across Dorchester and Roxbury, Jews would come to the G&G. They would come on crisp fall nights to the delicatessen at the corner of Blue Hill Avenue and Woodrow Avenue, part of the crowd gathered at this unlikely citadel of American democracy and this lasting symbol of their vital community.

Dorchester and Roxbury had proved ephemeral suburbs. In the 1920's, as middle-class Jews left in search of new suburban homes, the lower-middle-class and working-class Jews arriving in Dorchester and Roxbury secured leadership of the district's institutions. While Mishkan Tefila, which depended on the continued support of members who were moving in large numbers to Brookline and Newton, remained a Conservative temple, Dorchester and Roxbury's three other suburban synagogues severed their connections with the Conservative Movement and became traditional Orthodox synagogues. All three institutions—Adath Jeshurun's Blue Hill Avenue Synagogue, Beth El's Fowler Street Synagogue, and Beth Hamidrash Hagadol's Crawford Street Synagogue—abandoned their late Friday evening services, abandoned their choirs, abandoned their array of youth activities, abandoned their hymnals and their family pews. These congregations withdrew from the United Synagogue, and, by the early 1930's, none would again be served by a rabbi who had attended the Jewish Theological Seminary or belonged to the Rabbinical Assembly.[25]

In January 1925, Louis Epstein announced his decision to resign as rabbi of the Crawford Street Synagogue. His resignation was prompted not by the promise of another job but by the fact that he had "not been receiving the proper co-operation of his congregation." Within a few months, Rabbi Epstein became the first rabbi of Brookline's Kehillath Israel. In Brookline, Epstein could serve many of the middle-class families who had brought him to Roxbury just a few years earlier. Kehillath Israel, like the three original suburban congregations of Dorchester and Roxbury, described itself as "modern Orthodox" rather than Conservative, but Kehillath Israel served a suburban district whose middle-class Jewish community was growing in the 1920's. Support for Conservative innovation had shifted decisively, with middle-class Jewry, to suburban Brookline. That June, as Rabbi Epstein prepared to leave Roxbury, a group of prominent Boston Jews, including the past presidents of the Crawford Street Synagogue, held a banquet in his honor. "While Roxbury should lament his leaving," David M. Shohet, the rabbi of Dorchester's Temple Beth El, declared in good humor, "it should rejoice over the fact that he is only going over to Brookline 'as all progressive Jews seem to be doing.'"[26]

A few affluent, assimilated Jewish families had begun to settle in Brookline and the adjacent Boston district of Allston–Brighton at the turn of the century. Many of the first Jews settling in Brookline were of Central European descent. At the time that "the West End became the center of Jewish population," the *Jewish Advocate* noted in 1910, "one element went to the Back Bay and Brookline." Brookline was one of Boston's most prestigious suburbs. It was, according to a 1907 story in the *Boston Evening Transcript*, "the richest town in the entire world." The magnificent Temple Israel, dedicated that year on Commonwealth Avenue, was located between Boston's upper-class Back Bay and the town of Brookline. But Temple Israel was not a Brookline institution and its ritual had never been acceptable to observant Jews: it was a congregation that attracted members from all over the Boston area; its temple, located physically in Boston, stood one and one-half miles from the section of Brookline where most Jews were settling; and its ritual was Reform. In the spring of 1911, a group of ten Jews formed a small Orthodox congregation in Brookline, using their own homes for religious services. For most Jews, the organization of this group, which eventually became Kehillath Israel, marked the true beginning of the Brookline Jewish community. In 1917, having become firmly established, Kehillath Israel acquired a private dwelling on Harvard Street and converted it into a synagogue.[27]

FIG. 19. Alter Brothers Kosher Meat Market, Harvard Street, Brookline, 1980. For three decades, the synagogues, restaurants and shops around Brookline's Harvard Street have anchored a vibrant center of Boston Jewish culture. *American Jewish Historical Society.*

By 1929, three imposing synagogue-centers stood in or near Brookline. On Harvard Street, four blocks from Coolidge Corner, Kehillath Israel maintained a handsome new temple and schoolhouse. Ohabei Shalom, moving from the South End, worshiped in a new temple and congregational building on Beacon Street. And a few blocks away, on Boston's Riverway, stood the new school and meeting house of Temple Israel, which continued to worship in its white marble temple on Commonwealth Avenue. With the sole exception of Adath Israel's temple, none of these structures had yet opened five years earlier. These three synagogue-centers had all been completed in the period 1925–29. In 1930, about 8,000 Jews lived in Brookline: Jews, who had constituted less than three percent of Brookline's population in 1920, now represented seventeen percent of the town's residents.

The Brookline Jewish community developed as part of a larger suburban settlement that extended across the town line into the Boston districts of Allston and Brighton. More than 4,000 Jews had settled in the Allston-Brighton area by 1930. Through the 1920's, the Allston-Brighton Jewish community had depended on the institutions that stood in Brookline. Kehillath Israel and the commercial district on Harvard Street were easily accessible to Jews in Allston, but Jews in Brighton lived farther away from the center of the Brookline Jewish community. In 1933, a small group of Brighton Jews, frustrated by the long walk to Kehillath Israel, organized B'nai Moshe. "It was a distance to go to Harvard Street," Sam Shecter, an early member of the congregation, recalled. "Most of us wouldn't ride, and it was a hell of a walk, especially when you were wearing an $18 suit and it was raining like hell."[28] A Conservative temple, B'nai Moshe worshiped until the late 1940's in a former house on Chestnut Hill Avenue.

In November 1932, Herman H. Rubenovitz, rabbi of Temple Mishkan Tefila, observed "that the trend of the Jewish population has definitely set in toward Newton, just as fifteen years ago it was in the direction of Brookline." The peopling of Newton, like the peopling of Brookline and Brighton, rested on a sustained exodus of middle-class and upper-middle-class families from older Jewish centers, especially from Chelsea and the Roxbury-Dorchester area. No more than a few hundred

Jews lived in Newton in 1920: organized around an Orthodox synagogue, this small immigrant community had existed in Newton's Nonantum district since the late 19th century. Similar settlements had formed in many New England cities, miniature versions of the Jewish communities that had emerged simultaneously in Brockton and Lynn and Chelsea. By 1930, the Jewish population of Newton had grown to 1,400, and most of the Jews settling in Newton in the 1920's had no connection to the old settlement in Nonantum. Though still few in number in the early 1930's, these new residents formed the nucleus of Newton's suburban Jewish community.[29]

As a young child in 1933, Burton Bernstein moved with his family (including his older brother, Leonard) to a "red brick mansion" in Newton. Bernstein's father, who was vice-president of Temple Mishkan Tefila, was persuaded to move by a friend who sat on the temple's board of directors. The two families moved from Roxbury, settling near each other in new homes in Newton's Chestnut Hill district. From Newton, Bernstein's father commuted by trolley to his job in Boston. "Newton in the thirties was a country suburb—especially the undeveloped section we lived in," Bernstein wrote. Little traffic passed by his house, and, "in my early years, much of that meagre traffic was horse-drawn—Hood Milk delivery drays, sidewalk snowplows pulled by steaming ponies, even private rigs. The area was, in the main, both genteel and Gentile. Broad meadows shaded by stands of first-growth beech and oak were not uncommon. Most of the houses along the gaslit streets were old, gracious, well-landscaped, and inhabited by moderately rich Protestants. A few Jewish families had settled there in the twenties, and, as more could afford the upward move from Roxbury, their number grew to a sizable minority of the population."[30]

Bernstein's parents and their friends remained active in Roxbury's Temple Mishkan Tefila, but it was not easy for most Jews in Newton to maintain their ties to temples in Roxbury, Dorchester, Chelsea, and Brookline; by the middle 1930's, a group of Newton Jews decided to form their own synagogue. Meeting in a private home in the fall of 1935, this group organized High Holy Day services and a religious school. Temple Emanuel, a Conservative congregation, quickly prospered. That December, its members purchased land in Newton Centre "for the erection of a Temple, Educational and Community Centre." The structure was built in 1937; in the early 1950's, the congregation built an auditorium and new classrooms. "We have a congregation which has grown from 26 families to 738 families in 15 years," Albert I. Gordon, Temple Emanuel's rabbi, stated in 1950. "Our classrooms are filled to overflowing with children. Those who come to worship in the synagogue or in the chapel are crowded into areas built for far fewer numbers than we try to accommodate." By 1950, about 8,000 Jews lived in Newton. That spring, a group of Newton Jews organized Temple Shalom, a Reform congregation. Another group established Temple Reyim in West Newton in 1952; originally organized in the late 1940's as the Newton Jewish Community Center, Temple Reyim became Newton's second Conservative congregation.[31]

Nearby, in South Brookline, a new suburban Jewish community was developing by the late 1930's. Though physically in Brookline, South Brookline was detached from the main part of town, and its Jewish residents were isolated from the town's large Jewish population. Geography connected the suburban homes in South Brookline more closely to Newton's Chestnut Hill district than to northern Brookline. In 1939, about thirty families in South Brookline organized the Southern Brookline Community Center. The group acquired their own building in the early 1940's, dedicating it in 1942 as a community center and synagogue and installing a Conservative rabbi as their first rabbi. Taking the name Temple Emeth, the group built its permanent temple in the late 1940's. By then, about 2,000 Jews had settled in the district.

Brookline, Brighton, and Allston were home to a large and thriving suburban Jewish community in 1950. One-third of Brookline's population was Jewish: not including South Brookline, the Brookline Jewish community had grown to about 17,000. Nearby, in Allston and Brighton, lived another 13,000 Jews. B'nai Moshe had dedicated the basement of its new temple on Commonwealth Avenue, Kehillath Israel had become one of the most influential Conservative congregations in the United States, and new synagogues and temples—Young Israel of Brookline, Kadimah, Temple Sinai, and Temple Beth Zion—had been organized. The Brookline Jewish community continued growing in the 1950's and 1960's. Hebrew Teachers College, Maimonides School, the New England Hebrew Academy, and a few Orthodox synagogues relocated from the Dorchester-Roxbury area into the Brookline-Brighton area. By 1960, more than 22,000 Jews lived in northern Brookline. Since the middle 1960's, when at least 25,000 Jews lived in the area, northern Brookline's Jewish population has declined somewhat: about 20,000 Jews lived in northern Brookline in the early 1990's. The number of Jews in the Allston-Brighton district has fluctuated between 10,000 and 15,000 since the middle 1940's.

While the Jewish population of Brookline, Brighton, and Allston has changed relatively little in size since the 1950's, it has changed dramatically in character. Families with children have become a small minority of the area's Jewish population. Over the last few decades, the Brookline-Brighton-Allston area has become a stronghold of students, childless young adults, elderly adults, and Russian immigrants. The Jewish households in the district have grown more transient, as one cohort of immigrants and students replaces another. As a consequence of these changes, many of the institutions that once dominated the Brookline community—and whose impact, in some cases, extended across New England—have been marginalized. Except for Temple Israel, which remains strong and enjoys support throughout the Boston area, the outstanding Conservative and Reform congregations of Brookline and Brighton have grown smaller and weaker since the 1960's. Kehillath Israel, Ohabei Shalom, Sinai, Beth Zion, and B'nai Moshe have all been struggling in recent years in ways that their leaders a generation earlier could not have envisioned.

But a walk down Harvard Street in the 1990's testifies to the continued vibrancy of the Jewish community in and around Brookline. As the large temples of Brookline and Brighton have declined, the area's Orthodox congregations and Jewish day schools have flourished. Supported by young adults, immigrants, older residents, and a large Orthodox community, the Jewish shopping district on Harvard Street has remained strong. Harvard Street has been the center of Brookline Jewry since the 1910's. With the exodus of Jews from Dorchester and Roxbury and the consequent decline of the Jewish district on Blue Hill Avenue, Harvard Street emerged in the 1960's as the commercial and cultural center of the entire Boston Jewish community.

Newton's Jewish population nearly quadrupled in size in the 1950's and early 1960's. About 27,000 Jews lived in Newton in 1960; another 4,000 Jews lived in South Brookline. By the middle 1960's, Newton's Jewish population had grown to about 31,000, while South Brookline's Jewish population remained unchanged. In 1958, Temple Mishkan Tefila relocated from Roxbury to Chestnut Hill. Three years earlier, leaders of Dorchester's Temple Beth El organized an Orthodox congregation in Newton. Beth El–Atereth Israel grew quickly; dissident members organized Newton's other major Orthodox congregation, Shaarei Tefillah, in 1983. The Solomon Schechter Day School of Greater Boston, established in the early 1960's, has been located in Newton since 1962. And since the middle 1950's, when the Brookline-Brighton-Newton Jewish Community Center was built in Cleveland Circle, Newton's Jews have supported a large community center. The Leventhal-Sidman Jewish Community Center opened on the Gosman Campus in the 1980's. From the middle 1960's through the present, the Jewish populations of Newton and South Brookline have remained stable in size and the area's Jewish institutions have remained strong.

For three decades, since it surpassed Roxbury and Dorchester's Jewish population in size, Newton's Jewish community has been the largest in Greater Boston. But the ascendancy of Newton Jewry reflects the postwar splintering of Greater Boston's Jewish community. While the Roxbury-Dorchester district once housed one of every two Jews in the Boston area, Newton at its height has housed one in seven. Tightly concentrated in certain districts for more than a century—the South End, the North End, the West End, and, above all, Roxbury and Dorchester— Boston Jewry now spills out across the metropolitan area. Newton is certainly the first and most important of the Jewish suburbs in Greater Boston, but it is the first among many equals.

The same exodus that fed Newton, Brighton, and Brookline transformed the city's older Jewish districts. Life on Blue Hill Avenue was bustling in the early 1950's, but it was the life of a working-class community: the world of middle-class, suburban Jews had long since shifted elsewhere. Between the late 1920's and early 1950's, Roxbury and Dorchester's Jewish population had fallen only slightly, from 77,000 to 70,000. As middle-class Jews left the area for Brookline or Newton, working-class Jews had continued to settle in the area. But in the early 1950's, fewer Jews were moving into Roxbury and Dorchester, while increasing numbers of Jews already in the area were moving into the middle class and deciding to leave. The Jewish population in the Roxbury-Dorchester district began plummeting. Throughout the Roxbury-Dorchester area—from Grove Hall and Elm Hill in Roxbury, from Dorchester's Franklin Field and Franklin Park districts, from Mattapan—Jews began leaving in growing numbers. The Jewish population in the district fell from 70,000 in 1950, to 47,000 in 1960, to 16,000 in 1970, to several hundred by the late 1970's. First in Roxbury, then in the Franklin Park and Franklin Field sections in Dorchester, then in Mattapan, African-Americans settled in the former Jewish districts. In the early 1970's, Jewish life in the Roxbury-Dorchester area ended.

FIG. 20. Members of Congregation Chevra Shas, Mattapan, packing to move from their synagogue in 1973. *The Boston Globe.*

Journalists, scholars, politicians, and residents of these neighborhoods have attempted to explain the rapid Jewish exodus from Dorchester and Roxbury. Hillel Levine and Lawrence Harmon recently argued that the collapse of the area's Jewish community resulted from the indifference of suburban Jewish leaders, the activity of real-estate agents, and a mortgage program created in

1968 by Boston bankers. But none of those factors caused the Jewish exodus—indeed, by 1968, when the mortgage program began, the area's Jewish neighborhoods were already in their last stages of disintegration.[32] At root, the Jewish exodus was caused by socioeconomic mobility. An increasing number of Roxbury and Dorchester's Jews were attaining middle-class status in the 1950's and 1960's. Following a pattern established decades earlier, they left for the suburbs: the continuing exodus depopulated the area's Jewish community and undermined its institutions. Its institutions collapsing, the Jewish community that remained in Mattapan in the late 1960's could not sustain itself. Prejudice, rising crime, and racial fears contributed to the flight from Mattapan. But Mattapan Jewry, like the Jews of Chelsea and Lynn and Revere, ultimately suffered because of the suburban dream of the tens of thousands who had already left the old neighborhoods behind.

The suburban dream was knit deeply into the life of Roxbury and Dorchester's Jewish community: only in retrospect do most of Boston's Jews mourn for the old community on Blue Hill Avenue. "The action was no longer in Dorchester but out in Newton, Brookline, Sharon, where the girls were wealthy, their ranch houses dazzling brick after the brown wooden bunkers on the avenue," Mark Mirsky wrote, recalling the 1950's. "Jack and Marion's in Brookline was the place to take a girl, not the G&G, their sandwiches were bigger, the decor 'fabulous.' The G&G by comparison looked sad, old-fashioned," Mirsky wrote. "Dorchester was comfortable, a bit run down but not seedy. It was friendly, a community, but fashion and its silent patron, marriage, dictated that it must crumble. No girl was going to be left behind on Blue Hill avenue. No matter how high the rent or mortgage, Brookline, Ho! A flight of families with eligible girls began. It became a rout, a panic-stricken rush. In a few years my friends who had sisters were all gone. Fled. The ranks in the G&G were not yet thinned noticeably but the seed crop was gone. The loins of Israel sat in Jack & Marion's."[33]

For those who left for the suburbs through the middle 1960's, the "panic-stricken rush" was exhilarating. In city after city, new suburban districts proliferated in the years after World War II. *Commentary* published a series of articles by Sylvia Rothchild in the 1950's and early 1960's that described life in one of these new suburban Jewish communities, an unidentified town in New England. To protect the anonymity of the town, Rothchild wrote the articles under a pseudonym and called the town "Northrup." In 1949, when Rothchild and her husband discovered "Northrup," there were fewer than one hundred Jewish families in the town. That year "the Northrup Jewish Community Center" had dedicated a small temple, which stood on a site midway between the town square and the town's large lake.

Fig. 21. Temple Israel (Sharon Jewish Community Center), Sharon. Temple building dedicated in 1949. *Temple Israel, Sharon, Massachusetts.*

After seeing the temple and learning that "Northrup" was a popular summer resort for Jews, the Rothchilds decided to settle in the town. Many other Jews were also moving into the town, most of them attracted initially by the large tracts of small, low-cost homes being built in areas like "Northrup Heights." By the middle 1950's, the town's old farms were quickly disappearing. "Streets stretching like tentacles from the main thoroughfares meet each other in the woods and fields. New houses are larger and more expensive than the old ones," Rothchild wrote in 1956. "The town has attracted middle-income people for the most part, salesmen, professionals, and small businessmen." Many of those moving into "Northrup" were families with young children. Between 1946 and 1960—when the town's whole population grew from 4,000 to 10,000—the Jewish population of "Northrup" grew from 300 to 5,000.[34]

Rothchild had settled in a town, she noted in 1962, whose "Jewish community has grown from a small, struggling minority into an affluent majority":[35] she had settled in the Boston suburb of Sharon. By the late 1950's, Sharon supported three synagogues—Temple Israel, a Conservative congregation of 600 families which had emerged out of the Sharon Jewish Community Center; a new Reform temple, Temple Sinai, with 160 families; and Adath Sharon, a mixed-seating traditional congregation, with sixty families, which met in an old summer synagogue that had been built near the lake years before by Jews with permanent homes in Brookline, Newton, and Roxbury's Elm Hill. Each congregation supported its own Hebrew school, and about 500 children attended the Temple Israel Hebrew school. In the spring of 1962, Temple Israel dedicated additional classrooms as well as a large hall to accommodate High Holy Day services and social functions; for the three previous years, the temple had held High Holy Day services under a tent.

The postwar transformation of Sharon's population was the underlying cause of a controversy that catapulted the town into national prominence in December 1962, when three of the town's public school principals announced that Christmas trees would not be placed in the classrooms of their schools. While many of Sharon's Jews supported the ban, they had not sought the ban; the principals had acted on their own initiative, basing their decisions on the principle of the separation of church and state. Many residents of the town, especially long-time, non-Jewish residents, regarded Christmas trees as innocuous seasonal symbols and were puzzled that others objected to the tradition of placing the trees in classrooms. One Sharonite expressed her anger in a poem that she sent to the *Sharon Advocate*: "Christmas, Bah! humbug! said some people in town / And trampled our traditions into the ground. / Their decision—not wise, their reason—not clear / But they ruined Christmas for all this year."[36] The anger was palpable, but the ban stood. Sharon had changed permanently: most of the town's population no longer shared "our traditions."

By the early 1960's, other major suburban Jewish communities had emerged in Milton and in the North Shore towns of Swampscott and Marblehead. Sharon, Milton, and the Swampscott-Marblehead area were home to the largest of the new Jewish communities, though several other cities and towns—Medford, Lexington, Arlington, Belmont, Watertown, Framingham, Natick, Randolph, and Hull—also attracted substantial numbers of Jews in the 1950's. Many of the Jews settling in Milton as well as Sharon came from the Dorchester-Roxbury area. Temple Shalom, Milton's Conservative congregation, dedicated its basement facility in 1949. In the middle 1950's, Temple Shalom resumed work on its building, and Bnai Jacob, an Orthodox congregation, was organized. On Boston's North Shore, the towns of Swampscott and Marblehead attracted Jews from Chelsea, Malden, Revere, and Lynn. Temple Israel, a Conservative congregation organized in Swampscott in 1946, acquired its own building in the next year. In the middle 1950's, when Temple Israel broke ground for its permanent synagogue, two other congregations were organized in the Swampscott-Marblehead area: Temple Sinai, also a Conservative congregation, and Temple Emanu-El, a Reform congregation. A third Conservative congregation, Temple Beth El, relocated from Lynn to Swampscott in the 1960's.

About 5,000 Jews lived in Milton in 1960, and about 8,000 lived in Swampscott and Marblehead. As in Sharon, the development of these new suburban Jewish communities had public policy consequences. In 1957, a group of observant Jews in Milton petitioned to schedule the annual town meeting on a day other than Saturday. Many of Milton's "old-timers" were upset by the petition, concluding that "the Jews are trying to tell *us* how to run our community!" A decade later, in 1969, the Marblehead School Committee decided to end Christmas celebrations in the town's schools. Responding to those who objected to the new policy, Marblehead's school

Fig. 22. View of Swampscott, middle 1960's, indicating the future site of Temple Beth El, which was relocating to Swampscott from Lynn. Temple Israel, another Conservative temple, is visible at top, while a marsh and the ocean are visible at bottom. Reprinted from Temple Beth El, *Souvenir History and Program Commemorating the Golden Anniversary of Temple Beth El, Swampscott, Massachusetts, 1926–1976, 5686–5736. Private collection.*

Fig. 23. Children learning about Chanukah, Hertz Nursery School, Sharon, 1991. *Hertz Nursery School.*

committee chairman explained that "in communities with a significant Jewish population this is a very sensitive area and the problem must be faced."[37]

Framingham became a major Jewish center in the 1960's. Temple Beth Am, a young Reform congregation, dedicated its temple in Framingham in 1963. That same year, Temple Beth Sholom, a Conservative congregation descended from an older Orthodox synagogue, broke ground for its temple. Beth Sholom traced its lineage to the small immigrant community that had formed in Framingham in the late 19th century; with the influx of suburban families into Framingham in the 1950's and 1960's, the older congregation became a foundation of the town's new Conservative temple. By 1970, more Jews lived in Framingham than in any other postwar suburb except the Marblehead-Swampscott area.

Randolph's Jewish community developed entirely in the postwar era. As late as 1950, no more than fifteen or twenty Jewish families lived in the town. Randolph Jewry emerged in the 1950's and 1960's, as the exodus from Roxbury and Dorchester entered its final stages. From the Roxbury-Dorchester area, "everybody was going to Randolph," one woman later remembered. "We just followed the crowd."[38] By the early 1960's, Jews in Randolph had organized Temple Beth Am, a Conservative temple, and joined with Jews in nearby Canton to establish Temple Beth David, a Reform congregation. An Orthodox synagogue, formed in 1968, eventually merged with two former Dorchester congregations to become Young Israel–Kehillath Jacob of Mattapan and Randolph. The Orthodox synagogue and Jewish shops on North Main Street offered continuity to the large numbers of Jews who came to Randolph from the disintegrating Jewish neighborhoods in Dorchester and Roxbury.

Though different in many ways, the Jewish communities in Randolph and Milton both grew because of their close connections to the former Jewish district in the Roxbury-Dorchester area. Milton Jewry had developed as a suburban extension of the Roxbury-Dorchester Jewish community. Most of Milton's Jews had settled near Mattapan Square, near the synagogues and shopping district that extended down Blue Hill Avenue into Dorchester. The collapse of the Jewish community in Roxbury and Dorchester dealt a sharp blow to the Milton Jewish community. In the early 1970's, when about 7,000 Jews lived in the town, Milton's Jewish population began to decline; fewer than 2,500 Jews remained in Milton at the end of the decade. It was in Randolph, more than in any other of Boston's suburbs, that the last of Dorchester and Roxbury's working-class and lower-middle-class Jews had settled in the late 1950's and 1960's. Of the major Jewish suburbs in 1970, only Randolph contained large numbers of blue-collar workers: craftsmen, foremen, construction workers, mechanics, repairmen, operatives, laborers. The median family income, the median level of education, and the average price of a house were all substantially lower in Randolph than in Sharon, Milton, Marblehead, Swampscott, or Framingham.[39] By the middle 1980's, as increasing numbers of residents moved to higher-status suburbs, Randolph's Jewish population started to fall in size. More than 9,000 Jews lived in Randolph in 1980; in the early 1990's, about 6,000 remained.

Lexington, a town northwest of Boston that attracted many Jews in the 1950's, became one of Boston's principal Jewish suburbs in the 1970's. Temple Emunah and Temple Isaiah, Lexington's leading temples, both trace their origins to 1959, with the decision of the Arlington-Lexington-Bedford Jewish Community Center that year to hire a rabbi. The center's board chose a Reform rabbi, but the full membership of the community center reversed the decision and elected a Conservative rabbi. Dissident members resigned from the community center, hired the Reform rabbi, and organized Temple Isaiah. The remaining members of the community center, who supported the Conservative rabbi, created Temple Emunah. Attracted by Lexington's excellent public schools and the high-technology firms on Routes 2 and 128, thousands of Jews settled in the town in the 1970's and 1980's.

Needham and Stoughton, which attracted large numbers of Jews in the 1970's, and Natick and Peabody, which became major new Jewish suburbs in the 1980's, all developed in the shadows of larger, established Jewish communities. Many Jews moved into these new suburbs in part to distance themselves from the strong institutional centers nearby, while other Jews were attracted to the new communities because of their proximity to these nearby Jewish centers: for both reasons, strong and independent institutions emerged more slowly in these areas than in the earlier suburbs. Needham lies at the edge of Newton. About 5,000 Jews lived in Needham in the early 1980's, more than in any other postwar suburb except Framingham, Sharon, Randolph, and the Marblehead-Swampscott area. Yet until 1983, only one of Needham's two temples supported a full-time rabbi. Natick, near Framingham, and Stoughton—surrounded by Sharon, Randolph, and Brockton—each maintained just one temple. Unlike the three other suburbs, whose Jewish communities emerged immediately adjacent to existing Jewish suburbs, Peabody's suburban Jewish community developed in West Peabody, an area relatively distant from the existing Jewish center in Swampscott and Marblehead. While the city's tanneries had attracted immigrants to downtown Peabody at the turn of the century, it was the postwar housing development in West Peabody that brought suburban Jewish families to the city. Peabody Jews established an independent set of institutions early in the suburban influx, in the 1960's erecting both Beth Shalom, a Reform temple, and Ner Tamid, a Conservative temple, in West Peabody.

The development of large Jewish communities in Needham, Stoughton, Natick, and Peabody established a new pattern of suburban growth in the Boston area. The major suburban communities that emerged in the 1950's and 1960's—Sharon, Milton, Swampscott and Marblehead, Framingham, Randolph, and Lexington—traced their roots to Jewish neighborhoods in Boston itself and to the immigrant settlements that surrounded Boston. This first generation of postwar suburbs, though geographically dispersed around the edges of Boston, Brookline, and Newton, nevertheless retained a direct connection to the large, centrally located districts of Jewish settlement that had still existed at mid-century. All of these suburbs were founded by Jews who shared a common past in the neighborhoods of Boston and Chelsea. With the disappearance of those old neighborhoods, that common past, too, is rapidly dissipating. It is the postwar suburbs themselves that now feed the growth of new suburbs. Thus the Jewish populations of Needham, Natick, Peabody, and Stoughton developed as extensions of the Jewish centers in Newton, Framingham, the Marblehead-Swampscott area, and the Sharon-Randolph area. Since the early 1980's, large numbers of Jews have settled in Wellesley and Weston, which both border Newton and Natick. Near Framingham, also west of Boston, substantial Jewish communities have formed in Sudbury and Wayland. Smaller communities have emerged beyond Lexington in the towns of Concord and Acton by the middle 1990's, and, near Peabody, in the towns of Lynnfield and Danvers. South of Boston, radiating outward from the Sharon-Stoughton-Randolph area, many Jews have moved into Canton and Easton.

The center no longer holds. At mid-century, Roxbury and Dorchester were still home to much of Boston Jewry; secondary centers existed in the Brookline-Brighton area and Chelsea. As century's end approaches, the Jews of Roxbury and Dorchester are not part of the memory even of forty-year-old adults, and the Jews of Chelsea are scarce. The Brookline-Brighton area in the 1990's remains one of Boston's two great

Jewish strongholds, but its population has changed. Brookline-Brighton Jewry is a heavily transient population. Other large transient communities of Jewish students and young professionals exist in Cambridge, Somerville, Medford, Arlington, Belmont, Watertown, and Waltham. Indeed, in the middle 1990's more Jews live in Cambridge, where the new Harvard-Radcliffe Hillel is the city's primary Jewish institution, than in any of Boston's postwar suburbs. In Boston proper, large numbers of young Jews live in the Back Bay, the Fenway, and, fittingly, the South End.

More than 150 years have passed since the city's first Jews settled in the South End and organized a synagogue. It was in the South End, then in the North End and the West End and Chelsea, that Boston's Jews first began to dream of suburban homes. The suburban promise of Dorchester and upper Roxbury—the promise that seemed on the verge of fulfillment when members of the Crawford Street Synagogue gathered in the spring of 1918—proved illusory. Only when Jews arrived in Brookline, Brighton, and Newton did they begin to establish lasting communities.

But the price of Boston's suburban communities has been the dispersal of the city's Jews. Newton, the outstanding suburban stronghold, is a suburb and not a metropolitan center. Jews in other parts of Greater Boston cannot easily utilize Newton's institutions. Thus Sharon, in the middle 1990's the largest of the postwar suburbs, has now become the nucleus of an increasingly well-developed and self-contained suburban community. That community extends beyond Sharon's borders to include Jews in Stoughton, Randolph, Canton, Easton, and Brockton—as well as Jews who have begun settling in Foxboro, Mansfield, and Walpole. In Sharon alone live 10,000 Jews, about two-thirds of the town's population. Sharon's Jewish community supports six congregations, including three Orthodox synagogues that have been established since the middle 1970's. The town is home to the only *eruv* and the most substantial Orthodox community outside of Brookline, Brighton, and Newton. The Striar Jewish Community Center, which opened on Stoughton's Fireman

Fig. 24. Temple Israel, Sharon, January 1995, with construction of new sanctuary nearing completion. *Temple Israel, Sharon, Massachusetts.*

Campus in the late 1980's, attracts a large portion of its membership from Sharon. Sharon's Conservative Jews, working with Jews in surrounding towns in the late 1980's, played leading roles in the organization of the South Area Solomon Schechter Day School in Stoughton, the first Schechter school in the Boston area outside of Newton. And in the spring of 1994, Temple Israel, which dedicated its modest sanctuary in Sharon in 1949 and completed an expansion of the building in the early 1960's, broke ground for a large new sanctuary and additional classroom space.

The strength of Sharon's Jewish community, like the strength of Newton's— where Mishkan Tefila recently added a nursery school building to its temple, where Temple Emanuel just launched a capital campaign to improve its facility, and where the Solomon Schechter Day School of Greater Boston is raising funds to convert a large warehouse into a modern school building and to expand the school's programs—suggests the achievement of Boston's Jews. With the exceptions of Milton and Randolph, the postwar suburbs continue to sustain stable Jewish communities. Meanwhile, new suburban communities grow on the metropolitan frontier. The longevity and vigor of the Jewish communities in Newton and most of the postwar suburbs is unparalleled in the history of Boston Jewry: the old immigrant districts had never been regarded as permanent areas of settlement, and the suburban era in Roxbury and Dorchester was shorter than the life of Milton's Jewish community. The suburban Jewish presence in Newton has already existed as long as the entire period of Jewish settlement in Dorchester and Roxbury. Though the search for new suburbs continues, by now the search itself has borne fruit. The fruit is at once sweet and bitter. It is sweet because Boston's Jews have built communities that have persisted for decades and have built institutions to serve those suburban enclaves. Yet it is bitter because those same achievements, the dream of generations of Boston Jews, institutionalize the fragmentation of the city's Jewish community. Blue Hill Avenue is now gone forever.

I am grateful to Deborah Astor, Rory Austin, Judith Chyten, Constance Comins, Rabbi Bernard Eisenman, Frances Gam, Gertrude Gam, Edna Glass, Nancy Glynn, Sharon Goldstein, Sheila Halet, Fredda Hamilton, Cheryl Heitin, Irving Herbster, Bernie Hyatt, Helen Kadish, Rabbi Shamai Kanter, Andrea Kline, Marvin Lampert, Bernice Leonard, James J. Leonard, Sam Levine, Maxine Levy, Israel Mindick, Carolyn Nathan, Phyllis Osher, Sharon Parisi, Toby Pugh, Roz Rosenburg, Sylvia Rothchild, Jonathan Sarna, Ellen Smith, Sandra Spector, Rabbi Barry Starr, Merle Trilling, Rabbi Cary David Yales, and Jan Zidle for their assistance.

1. Congregation Beth Hamidrash Hagadol, *Year Book, 5683 (1922–1923)* (Boston: The Monroe Service, n.d.), 110, Congregation Beth Hamidrash Hagadol Yearbooks and Souvenir Books, American Jewish Historical Society; "Would Enroll 1000," *Jewish Advocate*, 26 May 1921, 7.

2. Albert Ehrenfried, *A Chronicle of Boston Jewry: From the Colonial Settlement to 1900* (Privately published, 1963), 430 n.2, American Jewish Historical Society.

3. "Adath Israel: Imposing Dedication of the New Temple on Columbus Avenue," *Boston Hebrew Observer*, 6 February 1885, 4.

4. William I. Cole, "Introductory," in *The City Wilderness*, ed. Robert A. Woods (Boston: Houghton Mifflin, 1898), 6.

5. Barbara Miller Solomon, "Pioneers in Service: The History of the Associated Jewish Philanthropies of Boston," *Jewish Advocate*, 27 June 1957, feature section, 6, 8.

6. Frederick A. Bushée, "Population," in *The City Wilderness*, ed. Robert A. Woods (Boston: Houghton Mifflin, 1898), 37. See also Frederick A. Bushée, "The Invading Host," in *Americans in Process*, ed. Robert A. Woods (Boston: Houghton Mifflin, 1902), 42–43.

7. "The Jews at the North End," in *History of the Jews of Boston and New England* (Boston: Jewish Chronicle Publishing Co., 1892), American Jewish Historical Society; William I. Cole, "Two Ancient Faiths," in *Americans in Process*, ed. Robert A. Woods, 276.

8. "The Jews at the North End," in *History of the Jews of Boston and New England*; Stephan Thernstrom, *The Other Bostonians* (Cambridge: Harvard University Press, 1973), 137; Jessie Fremont Beale and Anne Withington, "Life's Amenities," in *Americans in Process*, ed. Robert A. Woods, 237.

9. Beale and Withington, "Life's Amenities," 240; Bushée, "Invading Host," 54–55.

10. Bushée, "Invading Host," 44.

11. Mary Antin, *The Promised Land* (Boston: Houghton Mifflin, 1912), 195–96.

12. Albert J. Kennedy, "Cambridgeport," in *The Zone of Emergence*, ed. Robert A. Woods and Albert J. Kennedy, abr. and ed. Sam Bass Warner, Jr., 2d ed. (Cambridge: Massachusetts Institute of Technology Press, 1962), 76.

13. Bushée, "Population," 41; Antin, *Promised Land*, 287.

14. Elizabeth Y. Rutan, "Before the Invasion," in *Americans in Process*, ed. Robert A. Woods, 37; Bushée, "Invading Host," 40; Robert A. Woods, "Livelihood," in *Americans in Process*, ed. Robert A. Woods, 139; Robert A. Woods, "Metes and Bounds," in *Americans in Process*, ed. Robert A. Woods, 2.

15. Woods, "Livelihood," 139–40; Twelfth Baptist Church, *Dedicatory Programme: The New Twelfth Baptist Church, Corner Madison Street and Shawmut Ave., Boston, Massachusetts, November 11 to December 31, '06* (1906), 24, 22, Twelfth Baptist Church, Roxbury. See also John Daniels, *In Freedom's Birthplace* (Boston: Houghton Mifflin, 1914), 143–45.

16. Cole, "Two Ancient Faiths," 276.

17. Frederick A. Bushée, *Ethnic Factors in the Population of Boston*, Publications of the American Economic Association, 3d ser., vol. 4, no. 2 (New York: Macmillan, 1903), 25–26; "Former Synagogue Now a Church," *Boston Globe*, 7 June 1903, 13; "In Its New Home," *Boston Globe*, 8 June 1903, 12; Twelfth Baptist Church, *Dedicatory Programme*.

18. "Mishkan Tefila," editorial, *Boston Advocate*, probably 17 May 1907, Congregation Mishkan Tefila Archives, Newton.

19. "By the Way," *Jewish Advocate*, 26 August 1910, 4; "The Simchas Torah Celebration at Blue Hill Avenue Synagogue a Great Success," *Boston Advocate*, 27 September 1907, 7.

20. Aaron Pinkney, "Milestone in the Roxbury Jewish Community," *Jewish Advocate*, 26 October 1950, 8; "New Roxbury Synagogue To Be Dedicated Sunday Afternoon Costs Its Members $100,000," *Boston Journal*, 14 September 1906, 2.

21. Marion Booth and Ordway Tead, "Dorchester, Ward 16," in *The Zone of Emergence*, ed. Robert A. Woods and others, 157–58.

22. "Land Purchased for Synagogue for Dorchester District," *Jewish Advocate*, 2 September 1910, 1; "Beth Hamidrash Hagodel of Roxbury Asks for Assistance," *Jewish Advocate*, 3 July 1914, 1, 8; "Cong. Hadrath Israel," *Jewish Advocate*, 28 November 1918, 4.

23. Theodore H. White, *In Search of History: A Personal Adventure* (New York: Harper & Row, 1978), 26–27. See also Gerald H. Gamm, "Neighborhood Roots: Exodus and Stability in Boston, 1870–1990" (Ph.D. diss., Harvard University, 1994).

24. Mark Mirsky, "Last Bleak Echoes of a Thousand Years: The G&G on Blue Hill Ave.," *Boston Sunday Globe*, 7 March 1971, A:3.

25. Gamm, "Neighborhood Roots," 347–56.

26. "Rabbi Louis M. Epstein Resigns," *Jewish Advocate*, 8 January 1925, 3; "Present Rabbi Epstein with Automobile," *Jewish Advocate*, 2 July 1925, 2.

27. "By the Way," *Jewish Advocate*, 26 August 1910, 4; "World's Richest Town," *Boston Evening Transcript*, 15 February 1907, 1. See also Gamm, "Neighborhood Roots," 315–16.

28.  Elie Kaunfer, "Brighton's B'nai Moshe: A Temple at the Crossroads," *Jewish Advocate*, 31 July–6 August 1992, 20.

29.  Rabbi Herman H. Rubenovitz to the chairman and members of the Board of Directors, Congregation Mishkan Tefila, 8 November 1932, Temple Mishkan Tefila Minutes, American Jewish Archives. See also Gamm, "Neighborhood Roots," 319–20; Albert I. Gordon, *Jews in Suburbia* (Boston: Beacon Press, 1959), 21–29.

30.  Burton Bernstein, *Family Matters: Sam, Jennie, and the Kids* (New York: Summit Books, 1982), 72, 76, also 74–75, 79.

31.  "Complete Plans for Temple in Newton," *Jewish Advocate*, 13 December 1935, 2:6; "Temple Emanuel Plans $500,000 Building Drive," *Jewish Advocate*, 13 April 1950, 1, 7. See also Gamm, "Neighborhood Roots," 321–22.

32.  For a discussion of these issues, see Hillel Levine and Lawrence Harmon, "Profits and Prophets: Overcoming Civil Rights in Boston," *Tikkun*, July/August 1988, 45–48, 94–96; Hillel Levine and Lawrence Harmon, *The Death of an American Jewish Community: A Tragedy of Good Intentions* (New York: Free Press, 1992); Gerald H. Gamm, "Exploding Myths Surrounding Exodus of Boston Jewry," *Jewish Advocate*, 27 March–2 April 1992, 11; Lawrence Harmon and Hillel Levine, "A Response to Gerald Gamm," *Jewish Advocate*, 10–16 April 1992, 11; Gerald H. Gamm, "Facts vs. Myth About Boston Jewish Exodus," *Jewish Advocate*, 1–7 May 1992, 9; Gamm, "Neighborhood Roots."

33.  Mark Mirsky, "Last Bleak Echoes of a Thousand Years," A:3, A:8.

34.  Evelyn N. Rossman [Sylvia Rothchild], "The Community and I—Belonging: Its Satisfactions and Dissatisfactions," *Commentary* 18 (November 1954): 396; Evelyn N. Rossman [Sylvia Rothchild], "The Community and I: Two Years Later—The Wine, or the Blessing?" *Commentary* 21 (March 1956): 230. See also Gordon, *Jews in Suburbia*, 111.

35.  Evelyn N. Rossman [Sylvia Rothchild], "A Fund-Raiser Comes to Northrup," *Commentary* 33 (March 1962): 218.

36.  Catherine L. Haddad, "Sharon's Modern Day Version of Dicken's [*sic*] 'Christmas Carol,'" *Sharon Advocate*, 20 December 1962, 3.

37.  Gordon, *Jews in Suburbia*, 183; Stephen Kurkjian, "Limits to Yule Ban Up to Marblehead School Principals," *Boston Sunday Globe*, 30 November 1969, 37.

38.  Alan Lupo, "The Jews of Randolph," *Boston Globe*, 10 May 1994, 70.

39.  United States Department of Commerce, Bureau of the Census, *1970 Census of Population and Housing—Census Tracts: Boston, Mass. Standard Metropolitan Statistical Area* (Washington, D.C.: U.S. Government Printing Office, 1972). For each town, I collected data for those census tracts containing large numbers of residents whose parents were born in the U.S.S.R. These are the census tracts that I examined: in Framingham, tracts 3831, 3836, 3837, 3838, 3839, 3840; in Marblehead, tract 2031; in Milton, tract 4162; in Randolph, tracts 4201, 4202, 4203; in Sharon, tracts 4141, 4142, 4143; and in Swampscott, tracts 2021, 2022.

# Temples in the American Athens:
# A History of the Synagogues of Boston

*Overleaf*: Chambers Street Shul, West End, Boston, ark and *bimah*, built by Sam Katz in 1920. Sam Katz is standing at the far right. *American Jewish Historical Society*.

DAVID KAUFMAN

# Temples in the American Athens:
## A History of the Synagogues of Boston

ועשו לי מקדש ושבנתי בתובם
"And let them make Me a sanctuary that I may dwell among them."
EXODUS 25:8

OSTON'S FIRST SYNAGOGUE was dedicated with impressive ceremony on March 26, 1852. The building was an achievement worth celebrating since the first German and Polish Jewish settlers had arrived little more than a decade before. Those early Boston Jews first gathered for high holiday services in the fall of 1842, and as their numbers grew they established congregation *Ohabei Shalom* (Lovers of Peace). By the time of the dedication the congregation boasted "eighty male members and their families." Anticipating continued growth, they built their synagogue to accommodate over 400 worshippers.[1]

Before building their communal home, the immigrant Jews of mid-19th century Boston had formed a private community, closeted away from the glare of the out-side world. The 1852 dedication publicly asserted the new Jewish presence in Boston. Three years before, British consul Thomas C. Gratton had written, "Boston does not, I believe, contain one individual Israelite."[2] After 1852, such a statement would not have been possible. The new synagogue represented the transformation of the insular Jewish community into a more worldly religious corporation, a mem-ber of the greater citizenry, a public presence as an American "church."[3] We might justifiably claim that it was the 1852 dedication, rather than the first *minyan* (prayer quorum) of 1842, which signified the beginning of the Boston Jewish community.

In Boston as elsewhere, synagogue and community were deeply intertwined. As the central institution of the community, the synagogue linked Jews together and provided religious and cultural continuity by serving as the focal point of Jewish life: a place for worship, study, public assembly, socializing, social welfare, and cele-brations of holiday and life cycle events. At the same time, the synagogue represented

**ISRAELITISH SYNAGOGUE,**

WARREN STREET.

FIG. 1. Ohabei Shalom, 73 Warren Street, Boston, built 1852. The original synagogue of the Boston Jewish community as depicted in the *Boston Almanac* of 1854. The building no longer exists. *American Jewish Historical Society*

the Jewish community to the outside world. It reflected both self-perception and public image.

An excellent way to study a Jewish community, therefore, is to examine the succession of its synagogue buildings, marking the progress of congregations through time and space, and charting their economic attainments, social aspirations, and religious development.[4] Bostonians have always generated their built environment and religious architecture as a source of civic pride, marking each neighborhood with its own array of church steeples. The Jews of Boston erected their own "synagogue steeples" with each successive move to a new neighborhood. Upon their departure, their synagogues remained behind as a visual testament to that era of the community's history. The following survey of Boston's synagogues traces the rise of Jewish life in a given time and place, its eclipse, and then regeneration in new eras and new neighborhoods. The story of Boston's synagogue and Boston's Jewish community are, in many times and places, one.

The 1852 Ohabei Shalom synagogue was located on Warren Street, a narrow, crooked side street in the old South End, at the heart of the first Jewish neighborhood of Boston. Familiarly called the "Warren Street Shul," the small, wooden, rather inconspicuous structure bore no external symbols or signs of its Jewish affiliation. Its modest look may have reflected lingering insecurities of the immigrant community. But aspirations to a higher status also showed in the building's architecture. Ohabei Shalom was built in a subtly dignifed Italianate style by carpenter Samuel Jepson. On a smaller scale, its design reflected the Greek Revival elegance of the Universalist church across the street. (See fig. 4.) Yet it had Jewish influence as well. The Warren Street Shul was likely modelled after the only other New England synagogue of the time: the Touro Synagogue of Newport, Rhode Island.

The Touro Synagogue was designed by Peter Harrison and built for Newport's Sephardic Jewish community in 1763. During the Revolutionary era, the few Jews living in Boston often considered themselves a part of Newport's synagogue community.[5] By building their own shul in 1852, the Ashkenazic Jews of Boston declared their independence; yet at the same time, they sustained the connection to Newport and paid homage by imitating its architecture. The Warren Street Shul, like the Touro Synagogue before it, was a squat, squarish, unsteepled and uneccelesiastical "meeting house." The arrangement of windows and doors on the façade was the same as Touro's, though Ohabei Shalom had double arched windows, evoking the tablets of the ten Commandments.[6] As at Newport, the Boston synagogue was laid out in traditional fashion with a central *bimah* (Torah-reading platform), built-in

FIG. 2. Touro Synagogue, Newport, Rhode Island, built 1763. The Touro Synagogue may have served as the model for Ohabei Shalom in 1852. Today it is the oldest standing synagogue building in the United States, a national landmark. *American Jewish Historical Society.*

*aron kodesh* (holy ark), separate women's gallery, and an annex containing "rooms for a school and for business meetings of the trustees of the society, and for other purposes." In addition, there were "bathing rooms for the females of the society, after the ancient customs of the Israelites."[7] The Jews of Boston need not have looked to "ancient customs," however, for their model, the Touro Synagogue, was an *American* exemplar of traditional Judaism.

Having established its autonomous existence, Ohabei Shalom set a precedent soon to be repeated in Boston. Dissension arose within the congregation, and secessions occurred in 1854 and 1858. The first offshoot was made up of the German-Jewish founders of Ohabei Shalom who, despite the more recently arrived Polish majority, felt that they were the rightful "owners" of the synagogue and ought to be able to determine its religious and cultural tone. Leaving Warren Street in 1854, they took the rabbi, the Torah scroll, the shofar, and the name "Ohabei Shalom" with them. Later that same year, Judah Touro died in New Orleans and bequeathed a large portion of his fortune to Jewish institutions around the country, including: "to the Hebrew Congregation 'Ohabay Shalome' of Boston, Massachusetts, five thousand dollars."[8] Both Ohabei Shaloms claimed the money, and brought their case to a civil court which ruled that the name, and hence the legacy, belonged to the segment of the community that had remained within the congregational building. Ohabei Shalom was the Warren Street Shul and none other. The German and Polish Jews of Boston were thus taught the concrete importance of a church edifice.[9]

The German seceders then took the name Adath Israel (later known as Temple Israel), and settled into a renovated house on nearby Pleasant Street (today the corner of Melrose and Broadway), just a stone's throw away from the Warren Street Shul. The second synagogue in Boston was dedicated in September 1854. The building does not survive, but as built by "Messrs. Powell and McNutt" was "a long, narrow, yellow frame structure with a capacity of 250." *The Boston Traveler* continued,

> *The church sits a little back from the street and is capable of accommodating some two hundred persons. It is so constructed that the worshipper sits facing toward the East, the direction of Jerusalem. The females are seated in a gallery surrounding three sides of the church, being scrupulously separated from the males. On both sides of the only aisle are lamps which are kept burning during the service. The singers stand in front of the minister with their hats on, and neither the minister nor the congregation are uncovered during the ceremonies.*[10]

Adath Israel's sustained growth began after 1859 when it purchased land in Wakefield for use as a cemetery. At a time before the existence of independent Jewish cemeteries, the provision of a burial plot was a key inducement to prospective members of the congregation. Again serving communal needs, the earliest organization of Jewish philanthropy in Boston also took place in the Pleasant Street Synagogue. In 1861 the Hebrew Benevolent Association was formed there, and eight years later the Ladies Hebrew Sewing Circle was added. Adath Israel was rapidly

FIG. 3. Touro Synagogue, 1763. Interior view showing the central *bimah* (Torah-reading platform), built-in *aron kodesh* (holy ark), and separate women's gallery. *American Jewish Historical Society.*

conforming to the norms of American church life, though it would not take the first steps toward Reform Judaism until the 1870's. Like its parent congregation Ohabei Shalom, Adath Israel remained a traditional synagogue throughout the period of the Civil War.[11]

Mishkan Israel, the third congregation in Boston, was also traditionalist and remained so until its later emergence as the first Conservative synagogue of Boston. Following the secession of Adath Israel, the breakup of community continued when "Die Israelitische Gemeinde Mishkan Israel" was founded in 1858.[12] Mishkan Israel also came to be known as the "Krotoschiner Shul" for the large number of its members from that region of East Prussia. As was common, the congregation may have been formed originally as a *landsmanshaft*— a mutual aid society joining immigrants from the same place of origin. Like many such immigrant shuls, it began meeting in "a little room in a tenement house" on Oswego Street, moved five years later to "a small hall" on Harrison Avenue, and after four years to a "fairly commodious hall" on Orange Street.[13] All were locations in the old South End, and none of the sites survive. On Orange Street, Mishkan Israel leased the entire building. The growing congregation occupied the upper floor and rented the smaller hall on the ground floor to another immigrant *landsmanshaft*, the Dutch congregation Beth Eil.

Mishkan Israel stayed at the Orange Street location from 1867 to 1871 when the congregation at last occupied a formal synagogue structure. Like the two preceding synagogues in the South End, the new synagogue on Ash Street was described as "a modest frame structure." It was "erected at a cost of $5,600 with the ark and altar at the extreme end, and two rows of pews divided by a center aisle. There was a gallery for the women and school rooms in the vestry."[14]

Unfortunately, neither the Pleasant Street Synagogue of Adath Israel nor the Ash Street Synagogue of Mishkan Israel have come down to us in pictorial form. It is also unclear whether they were renovations or newly built structures. The lack of contemporary depictions indicates the modest nature of these structures as well as the persistence of the symbolic role of Ohabei Shalom, whose synagogue façade would remain the one and only public face of the Jewish community until 1886.

Though there were only three synagogue buildings in Boston prior to 1870, there were other congregations. As early as 1849, before the first secession from Ohabei Shalom, the Polish Jews of Boston attempted to establish a separate congregation called Beth Israel. Services were held for the high holidays of that year, and a burial society and cemetery were established in Cambridge. But the offshoot dissolved as the Polish faction soon gained the upper hand in Ohabei Shalom, which became known colloquially as the "Polish Synagogue" after 1854. The Dutch congregation Beth Eil was established in 1859. The "Hollanders," as they were called, first "established a chapel on Gloucester Place in the South End and acquired land for a cemetery in Melrose."[15] Beth Eil later moved to Orange Street and eventually to Dover Street. The congregation went into decline after the Civil War and in 1875 amalgamated with its *chevra* (auxiliary society) for the purpose of maintaining its cemetery. In that same year, Congregation Beth Eil was

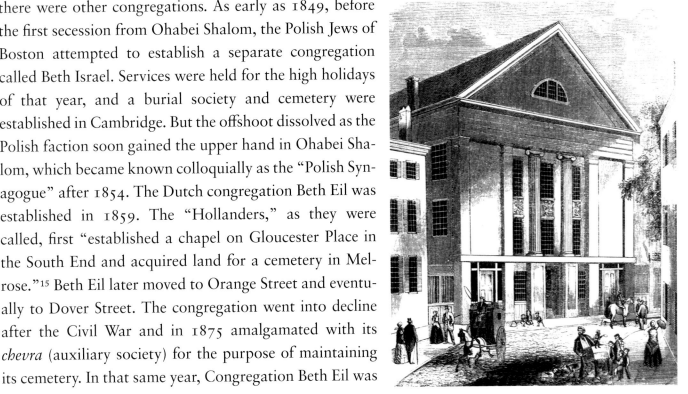

FIG. 4. Ohabei Shalom, 76 Warrenton Street, Boston, occupied 1863–86. Built as a Universalist church in 1839, the historic structure stands in today's theater district as the Charles Playhouse. Illustrated in Edmund V. Gillon, Jr., *Early Illustrations and Views of American Architecture* (New York: Dover Publications, Inc., 1971), Figure 70.

described by Rabbi Hirsch Falk Vidaver of Ohabei Shalom as follows:

> *Dutch, progressive in spirit; these Jews nevertheless have done nothing to propagate the faith. They meet on Saturdays and pray in Hebrew, though few of them understand their own prayers. They make no effort to sustain the principles of Judaism, nor do they exert themselves to transmit Jewish learning or loyalty to their children. Even if they do not devote themselves to the study of our Hebrew literature, as do the Russians, they should at least realize their responsibility for the proper religious instruction of their youth.*[16]

With such inattention to Jewish education, Beth Eil did not last as a congregation. Nor did they consider a synagogue building a priority. Neither Beth Israel, Beth Eil, nor any number of other ephemeral congregations were housed in synagogue structures of their own—together with a Hebrew school, the main guarantors of congregational continuity.

In 1863, Ohabei Shalom met its practical need for more space by purchasing the Universalist church building across the street for $15,500 and renovating the interior for an additional $2,500. (See fig. 4.) As in many other American Jewish communities, the former immigrants' eagerness to move into better and larger quarters engendered a willingness to acquire houses of worship formerly used by gentiles. In contrast to the old country, churches did not seem so foreign and forbidding in this land of equality of religion. Indeed, they were often just across the street, equal in position and stature. The move into a church building demonstrated the powerful idea that in America, Judaism was as much at home as any Christian denomination.

The move onto church premises, reflecting integration into America, would entail some internal changes in the practice of Judaism. The sanctuary of the new Ohabei Shalom synagogue now faced westward instead of the traditional eastern orientation, but the Americanizing congregation paid little heed to the transgression of Jewish custom. This was the first in a series of reforms to be enacted in the new building, and an example of the effect of a new physical environment upon religious standards.

America itself had a great impact upon the life of the synagogue. Like every other Boston church in 1865, as well as its two fellow synagogues, the Warrenton Street Synagogue was draped in black and held a special service for mourning the death of President Lincoln—both innovations for a synagogue. The fractious period of the Civil War witnessed the rise of two factions within the congregation, one desiring change, the other demanding the retention of traditional religious norms. The tension was reflected in the continual search for adequate leadership. During the 1860's alone, the congregation experienced no less than five changes of "rabbi."[17] Only the new synagogue building provided a sense of stability.

The post-Civil War period thus saw the rise of Reform Judaism in Boston, a movement spurred by a number of factors. One was the arrival of university-trained rabbis from Germany who brought with them the ideology of Reform, as when in 1868 Rabbi J. T. Nathan was invited to deliver an address on Reform Judaism to the members of Ohabei Shalom.[18] The German congregation Adath Israel acted more decisively in this regard when it hired Rabbi Solomon Schindler in 1874. Schindler promptly abolished the second day of Jewish holiday observance, adopted Adolph Huebsch's Reform liturgy, and introduced weekly German sermons.[19] Adath Israel also began calling itself "Temple." Reform in America was also a matter of "Protestantization," a case of the synagogue imitating the practices of the church.[20] Such practical—as opposed to ideological—reforms instituted during the early 1870's at both Ohabei Shalom and Adath Israel included shortening of the service, the imposition of Protestant-like decorum, and the introduction of a choir and organ.[21]

Most critically, however, reform was prompted by the Americanization of the immigrant community and its growing recognition that the future lay with the younger generation. For this reason, the principal unit of the congregation became the family. Accordingly, the first confirmation of boys and girls in a Boston congregation was celebrated in Ohabei Shalom in 1870, and five years later, mixed seating in family pews was adopted.[22] Another youth-oriented innovation of the time was the creation of the first Young Men's Hebrew Association of Boston, founded in the vestry of Ohabei Shalom in 1875. Though the YMHA served primarily as an employment bureau (occupying a room in city hall for that purpose), the idea of its serving as a youth wing of the synagogue was certainly influenced by the Warrenton Street Young Women's Christian Association located immediately next door. Thus we see the combined effect of a new physical plant, the Protestant environment, modern rabbis, generational change, and proximity to other American institutions toward the "reforming" of a Jewish congregation—all factors embodied by the adaptation of a church building for use as a synagogue.

When Ohabei Shalom moved into yet another church structure in 1887, it was no longer alone. The history of the Jewish community of Boston is replete with examples of the church-synagogue connection. In 1875, the Sunday School of Adath Israel occupied part of a Unitarian church building. The Theodore Parker Meeting-

FIG. 5. Theodore Parker Memorial Hall, 49 Berkeley Street, Boston, built 1872. Originally a Unitarian meeting house, Parker Memorial served the South End Jewish community from the 1870's through the turn of the century. *Photograph by Carl Mastandrea.*

House on Berkeley Street, built in 1872, was an institutional church, a non-sectarian community center in the midst of the growing immigrant community of the South End. In the year following Temple Israel's move into the building, another congregation formed in neighboring Paine Hall. Congregation Shaaray Tefila, whose 1876 charter committed it to "the worship of Jehovah according to the orthodox ritual of Polish Jews,"[23] occupied those quarters during 1877–78 and 1883–85, when it moved into the Pleasant Street building recently vacated by Adath Israel. During the interim, from 1879–82, Shaaray Tefila (in English referred to as "Gates of Prayer") was housed in a former church—due to the munificence of one of its more memorable members, Alfred A. Marcus.[24]

Marcus was an eccentric Jewish philanthropist and staunch traditionalist known as "der Afrikaner" from having made his fortune in the South African diamond trade. The most colorful story of a Jewish "church" in Boston is his. A founding member of Shaaray Tefila, Marcus soon established his own private congregation as well, apparently dissatisfied with the reformist tendency of the time. In 1878 he purchased the church building on Church Street, corner of Winchester—again in close proximity to the other South End congregations—and converted it into a synagogue, later described as "one of the prettiest in this city."[25] Marcus perceived it as the central Orthodox Synagogue of Boston and grandly entitled it "Zion's Holy Prophets of Israel Memorial Synagogue."

Tradition and innovation came into conflict in Marcus's shul in 1889. On the first *yahrzeit* (anniversary) of his wife's death Marcus "had a telephone erected from the synagogue, a mile distant, to his residence, so that the beloved daughter could say the responses and also the Kaddish in her darling mother's memory."[26] The action was criticized by Reform rabbi Solomon Schindler, who wrote "Orthodoxy always objected to grant such privileges to women, and here we have a so-called 'orthodox' who desires his daughter to say Kaddish by telephone ..."[27] Marcus's Church Street Shul remained in operation until 1895.

Prior to that time, three South End congregations—the private synagogue of Alfred Marcus, Shaaray Tefila, and Mishkan Israel—led an interrelated existence. Shaaray Tefila (1876) may have been an attempted offshoot of the older Mishkan Israel (1858), for two years after its founding they were listed in the press as one congregation.[28] Marcus organized Zion's Holy Prophets in 1878, just two years after he had helped found Shaaray Tefila where he was still listed as its president in 1880.[29]

Another news item of 1883 indicates that Shaaray Tefila might actually have seceded from Alfred Marcus:

> *Mr. Markus* [sic] *did not possess the confidence of his congregation, to which he liberally donated the free use of two magnificent temples* [Church Street and Pleasant Street]. *The congregation as a body rather gave up their elegant place of worship in Church Street, and removed to a hired room in Paine Hall, than to submit to the dictatorial whims of Mr. Markus.*[30]

Mishkan Israel and Shaaray Tefila finally merged in 1895, becoming "Mishkan Tefila." As a unified congregation they purchased a church building in 1897, dedicated it in 1898, and later moved into yet another church structure in 1907. (See fig. 14.) In search of stability and permanence, congregations may merge. But in the construction of community, there is nothing like a synagogue of one's own.

During the 1880's, the Jewish population was rapidly moving away from the old South End (today's theater district) and each of the major congregations began to consider relocation. Ohabei Shalom appointed a committee in 1883 "to sell the synagogue which the Congregation occupies at present, and to buy a suitable site for a new building."[31] Despite "quite extensive alterations" reportedly underway in the Warrenton Street Synagogue in 1885,[32] the congregation followed its own precedent and in 1887 purchased the former Unitarian church of the great Edward Everett Hale, located on Union Park Street in a more fashionable section of the South End (today's South End). Hale himself was present at the dedication. Few renovations were necessary, for the family pews and organ were to be used by the now fully Reformed congregation. A new ark was installed, but the more revealing installation was a new set of stained glass windows depicting figures from the Bible. Both the stained glass and the human images were innovations (or transgressions, depending on one's point of view) in a synagogue. For over a generation, from 1887 through the mid-1920's, Temple Ohabei Shalom was housed on Union Park Street, the religious and social center of the South End Jewish community.

In an item of 1888, the *Jewish Messenger* reported:

> *Since the addition of the Union Park Temple to Boston's list of Jewish houses of worship, we have two edifices, that and the Columbus Avenue Temple, which are an honor to*

FIG. 6. Ohabei Shalom, 11 Union Park Street, Boston, occupied 1887–mid 1920's. It is presently a Greek Orthodox church in today's South End. *American Jewish Historical Society.*

FIG. 7. Temple Israel, 600 Columbus Avenue, corner of Northampton, Boston, built 1885. The first architecturally significant synagogue in Boston and the source of the *Rundbogenstil* trend. The former synagogue is today the African Methodist Episcopal Zion Church. (See FIG. 15 for a contemporary view of the structure.) *American Jewish Historical Society.*

*the sense of religious obligation of our citizens. They meet every want, and it is a delight to worship within their precincts.*[33]

The "Columbus Avenue Temple" referred to was the new synagogue of Congregation Adath Israel. In the midst of the trend to convert church buildings into synagogues, Adath Israel succeeded in constructing its own sanctuary in 1885. To design Boston's first Reform temple, the congregation hired the architectural firm of Weissbein and Jones. Louis Weissbein, an assimilated German Jew, looked to modern synagogue precedents in the Bavarian homeland and adopted their round-arched style— in German, *Rundbogenstil*—originally employed to convey a sense of religious propriety.[34] In the new context, however, the Romanesque Revival style reflected the immigrant origins of an "ethnic church."[35] Its Boston parallel was not the famous Trinity Church by Henry Hobson Richardson, but the parish churches of the immigrant Catholic communities (Irish, Italian, and Polish) designed by lesser known architects such as Patrick Keeley.[36] In his design for Temple Israel, Weissbein did incorporate one element of the typical Protestant church—he capped the twin stair towers with peaked "steeples," the better to blend in with the skyline of contemporary Boston. Yet atop each steeple was a tiny Star of David. The gable was likewise crowned by the Ten Commandments, and the large star of the central rose window completed the picture. The new Temple Israel may have been intended as a New England church, but its Jewish affiliation was unmistakable.

In its new congregational home, Temple Israel surpassed Ohabei Shalom in prestige and visibility and became the leading synagogue of Boston. From its pulpit, Rabbi Solomon Schindler held forth on the common religion of humanity, attracting large audiences of Jews and non-Jews alike. Schindler's radical Reform sermons were reprinted in the local press and both he and his congregation came to represent the most progressive element of the Jewish community to the city of Boston. Temple Israel provided key leadership to the Jewish community, an elite reputation that has persisted through much of its subsequent history. The most exclusive Jewish social club in Boston, the Elysium Club, was formed by members of Temple Israel in 1880 and chartered in 1889. Its new clubhouse on Huntington Avenue was dedicated in 1891, also designed by Louis Weissbein and located a short distance from the Temple. Members of Temple Israel were also instrumental in the Federation of

Jewish Charities. In 1895 Rabbi Schindler left the pulpit to become the Federation's first superintendent, with offices in the Municipal Charities Building of the West End. Schindler still served the Jewish community, but at increasing physical and ideological distance from the Temple.

The Americanized "Germans" of Temple Israel would also maintain their distance from the "Russian" immigrant community when, less than twenty years later, they left the South End and planned a new temple on Commonwealth Avenue past Kenmore Square. For the 1906 construction, they chose one of the leading architects of Boston, Clarence Blackall. Blackall had designed Boston's first "skyscraper" as well as many of the city's theaters.[37] The new Temple Israel of Boston was intended to be nothing less than a replica of Solomon's Temple of Jerusalem, as imagined by the theatrical architect.[38] Blackall incorporated Egyptian and Byzantine motifs, capping his creation with a large cast-concrete dome surrounded by four smaller cupolas. Its most striking feature was the interior arrangement of the "Egyptian" ark and bimah (i.e., pylon and obelisk) dominated from behind by massive, trumpet-like organ pipes in the shape of a lotus blossom. As a religious statement, it heralded the "triumph" of classical Reform Judaism—the characteristic expression of the wealthiest and most assimilated members of the Jewish community. Temple Israel's rabbi, Charles Fleischer, would later leave the fold altogether, but the congregation maintained its Jewish identity in the Commonwealth Avenue temple for over a half-century to come.[39]

FIG. 8. Temple Israel, Commonwealth Avenue, built 1906. Today the building serves as the Morse Auditorium of Boston University. *Temple Israel, Boston.*

FIG. 9. Temple Israel, 1906. Interior view. The architect explained: "The trumpet is always associated . . . with victory and conquest, and . . . symbolizes the confident world-outlook of the Jewish faith." (Quoted in Obst, p. 29.) *Temple Israel, Boston.*

The two Temple Israel sanctuaries, the first dedicated on Columbus Avenue in 1885, and the second built on Commonwealth Avenue in 1906, coincided in time with the two leading synagogues of the East European immigrant community. In 1886 Congregation Shomre Beth Abraham dedicated its new synagogue premises on Hanover Street in the North End, and in 1906 Congregation Adath Jeshurun built its new home on Blue Hill Avenue in Roxbury. It might have been expected that the syna-

gogues of the immigrant community would depart dramatically from their Americanized predecessors. But as we shall see, their surprising similarities often revealed the hidden ties of community, even between the assimilated Central European Jews and the newly-arrived East Europeans.

The first East European immigrant synagogue was established by the pioneer congregation of the North End. The so-called "Russian" Jewish community (the first settlers of the North End were mostly Lithuanian Jews) had its beginnings in the early 1870's, when the first immigrant congregations were formed. They began meeting in rented rooms along Hanover Street—the main street of the North End and the center of Boston's clothing trade. Several of the *minyanim* united in 1875 to form Shomre Shabbes (Sabbath observers) in a small hall leased at 219 Hanover Street. Isaac B. Reinherz served as both *hazan* (cantor) and *shochet* (kosher butcher) until 1886.[40] Shomre Shabbes was soon joined by a second congregation, Beth Abraham, located at 193 Hanover in 1879. In 1885, part of Beth Abraham merged with Shomre Shabbes to form Shomre Beth Abraham. The remainder of the congregation moved to 231 Hanover and adopted an English name, the House of Prayer.

Even more often than their Central European predecessors, the East Europeans tended to find their religious homes in church buildings. In 1883, for the purpose of establishing a communal Talmud Torah, the immigrant Jewish community rented space in Cockerel Hall on Hanover Street, an historic colonial church rebuilt in the 19th century as a Seaman's Bethel. Three years later, in 1886, the Talmud Torah was joined by Shomre Beth Abraham, which moved into new quarters of its own on the

FIG. 10. Cockerel Hall, 287 Hanover Street, North End, Boston, housed the North End Talmud Torah from 1883–92, Congregation Shomre Beth Abraham from 1886–93, and Congregation Chevra T'hilim from 1893–99. Today it is a residential building. *Photograph by Carl Mastandrea.*

FIG. 11. Beth Israel, Baldwin Place off Salem Street, North End, Boston, occupied 1889–1920. *Society for the Preservation of New England Antiquities, Boston, Massachusetts.*

third floor of Cockerel Hall. About that time, Shomre Beth Abraham brought Rabbi Moshe Zevulun Margolies (known by the acronym RaMaZ) from Lithuania to serve as its religious leader. The black-bearded and black-garbed Ramaz would often be seen walking down Hanover Street, passing the Christian missionaries and Boston workingmen who occupied the lower floors of the same building. Though he returned to Lithuania briefly, he soon came back to become the "chief rabbi" of Boston's Orthodox community, serving the numerous immigrant congregations that were increasing yearly.[41]

In 1888 a group of younger men of Shomre Beth Abraham seceded and formed their own congregation called Beth Israel. One year later they purchased a former Baptist church located at the end of Baldwin Place, an alley off of Salem Street in the North End. They renovated the interior, installing a sanctuary on the ground floor and school and meeting rooms above, and dedicated the new synagogue in 1890. In the next year, a modern Talmud Torah, the "Baldwin Place Hebrew Free School," opened in a building on one side of the narrow alley. In 1893, the parent Shomre Beth Abraham congregation merged with its Beth Israel offshoot, and the Ramaz was installed in its pulpit. Baldwin Place, anchored by its community synagogue, thereafter became the *shulhof* (synagogue court) of the North End Jewish community, and for the next three decades the "Baldwin Place Shul" stood at the center of Boston Orthodoxy. All manner of social events took place in the shul including public lectures, Zionist forums, lodge meetings, technical school classes, American and Jewish holiday celebrations, and even a Hebrew School for girls.

FIG. 12. Anshe Libawitz, 8 Smith Court off Joy Street, Boston, occupied 1899–1972. The historic structure is presently restored as the oldest standing black church in America. *American Jewish Historical Society.*

At the same time, numerous *landsmanshaft* congregations were forming in the North End and its neighboring Jewish community of the West End. By the turn of the century, there were some 53 "synagogues" in Boston, the majority *landsmanshaftn*.[42] Very quickly, however, they began to transcend their immigrant origins and to move up the ladder of social and economic mobility. In 1899, for example, Anshe Libawitz was able to purchase its own building on Smith Court in Beacon Hill, soon joined by two other *landsmanshaft shuls*, Anshe Stonier and Anshe Zytomir. Not surprisingly, it purchased a church building. The 1806 former African Meeting House was the historic church of Boston's African-American community on the north

FIG. 13. Anshe Libawitz, 1899. Interior view, ca. 1942. *American Jewish Historical Society.*

slope of Beacon Hill, then part of Boston's West End.[43] As European immigrants moved into the neighborhood, the native blacks migrated to the South End and Roxbury.[44] They left behind their communal buildings and sold them to the new residents. In the famous African-American church on Beacon Hill, surrounded by "the grandeur of the unspoiled simplicity of classic lines of a Colonial church,"[45] immigrant Jews established a traditional Jewish communal life.

A few blocks away, yet another *landsmanshaft shul* from the West End, Anshe Vilna, moved into the former

FIG. 14. Mishkan Tefila, Moreland and Copeland Streets, occupied 1907–1924. The former Immanuel Congregational Church was dedicated as Temple Mishkan Tefila on May 12, 1907. Dignitaries attending the services included Mayor John "Honey Fitz" Fitzgerald, Reverend Edward Everett Hale, and Rabbis Charles Fleischer (Reform), Moshe Z. Margolies (Orthodox), and Phineas Israeli (Conservative). A playground occupies the site today. *Society for the Preservation of New England Antiquities, Boston, Massachusetts.*

Twelfth (Colored) Baptist Church on Phillips Street.[46] Anshe Sfard, the first Jewish congregation of the North Shore community of Lynn (founded in 1889) occupied two successive church buildings: in 1919 the congregation moved into a church structure on Commercial Street, built by the Puritan settlers of Lynn in 1682, and in 1950 followed their Protestant predecessors into the former First Congregational Church on Vine Street.[47] In 1907, Mishkan Tefila purchased the second of its two church buildings, a Gothic Revival structure on Moreland Street in Roxbury. Though the steepled building was immediately recognizable as a church, the congregants celebrated the dedication of their new temple. While they welcomed the added space of the church vestry, the organ posed a challenge. Some members wanted nothing to do with the Christian apparatus, while others favored its use. A compromise was achieved whereby the organ was retained, but only used "during the Sunday night lectures and any entertainment which may be held in the Synagogue."[48] The solution lasted until 1914 when the young Rabbi Herman Rubenovitz convinced the congregation that organ music in Sabbath and holiday services was both permissible and desirable.[49] Once again, we see the indirect effect of an American church building on the religious life of the Jewish community. Like Ohabei Shalom, Beth Israel, and Anshe Libawitz before it, Mishkan Tefila had begun its transition into a modern American synagogue on church premises.

Following the turn of the century, the immigrant community began to erect synagogue buildings of its own. One of the first was Shaarei Jerusalem of the North End, a congregation founded in 1889. In 1903 it erected a new synagogue adjacent to the Baldwin Place Shul on neighboring Carroll Place. The street was officially renamed "Jerusalem Place" following the dedication of the Shaarei Jerusalem synagogue. Though the synagogue building was demolished in 1945, the street name remains to this day.[50]

Most often, however, new synagogue buildings were built in new areas of settlement. The Jewish pioneers of these areas were so eager to build that their synagogues often preceded the community. The synagogue then became a magnet for Jewish population movement and an incentive for community development, trends encouraged by real estate agents and rabbis alike. For example, Rabbi Louis Epstein of Roxbury's Beth Hamidrash Hagadol recalled that congregation's genesis as follows:

*One foolish plan called for another, this time the most daring one, namely to erect a modern up-to-the-moment house of worship that shall be a credit to Boston Jewry. Little did the small group of men then think that that most daring undertaking shall leave room for regret that it was not even more daring. Little did they think that in a measure Roxbury Jewry would build itself around the Crawford Street Synagogue, that its seating capacity of eleven to twelve hundred would only meet half of that need. It was beyond human powers to look ahead ten years and to see what the synagogue would mean to the community. . . . The Crawford Street Synagogue is an illustration of the fact that not always is a synagogue built where the Jewish community is, but that sometimes the community is built where the synagogue is. Our Synagogue has in a great measure been the making of the Roxbury Jewish community.*[51]

Sometimes the strategy did not work, so that immigrant synagogues were established in areas which never attracted a major Jewish population. Jewish congregations in mainly Irish neighborhoods such as Jamaica Plain, Hyde Park, and South Boston did not endure.[52] Other synagogues in would-be Jewish settlements included Mishkan Tefila in Roxbury Crossing (1898), Ahavath Sholom in East Saugus (1911), and Agudas Achim Anshei Sfard in Newtonville (1912).

Other neighborhoods attracted a more significant immigrant Jewish presence. In 1893, for example, Congregation Ohel Jacob pioneered the Jewish community of East Boston, and Anshe Poland was founded in the North End, soon moving to become the first East European immigrant shul of the South End. After more than a decade of existence, the shuls built their own synagogue buildings: Ohel Jacob on the corner of Paris and Gove (1907), and Anshe Poland on Oswego Street in the South End (1906 and 1920). Similar synagogues were constructed in Cambridge (1901), Lynn (1905), Malden (1905), and Everett (1911), all enclaves of immigrant Jewish life in the period prior to World War I.

Still unsure of themselves, the Orthodox immigrant congregations sought an established role model for their transformation into American houses of worship. The Reform Temple Israel's 1885 building on Columbus Avenue, built in a German Romanesque style to express the congregation's cultural and religious ties to the European homeland, met this need. For very different reasons, the design was copied by a number of East European immigrant congregations and thereby became the dominant synagogue style of the Boston area. The imitative shuls included Beth Israel on Columbia Street in Cambridge (1901), Ahabat Sholom on Church Street in

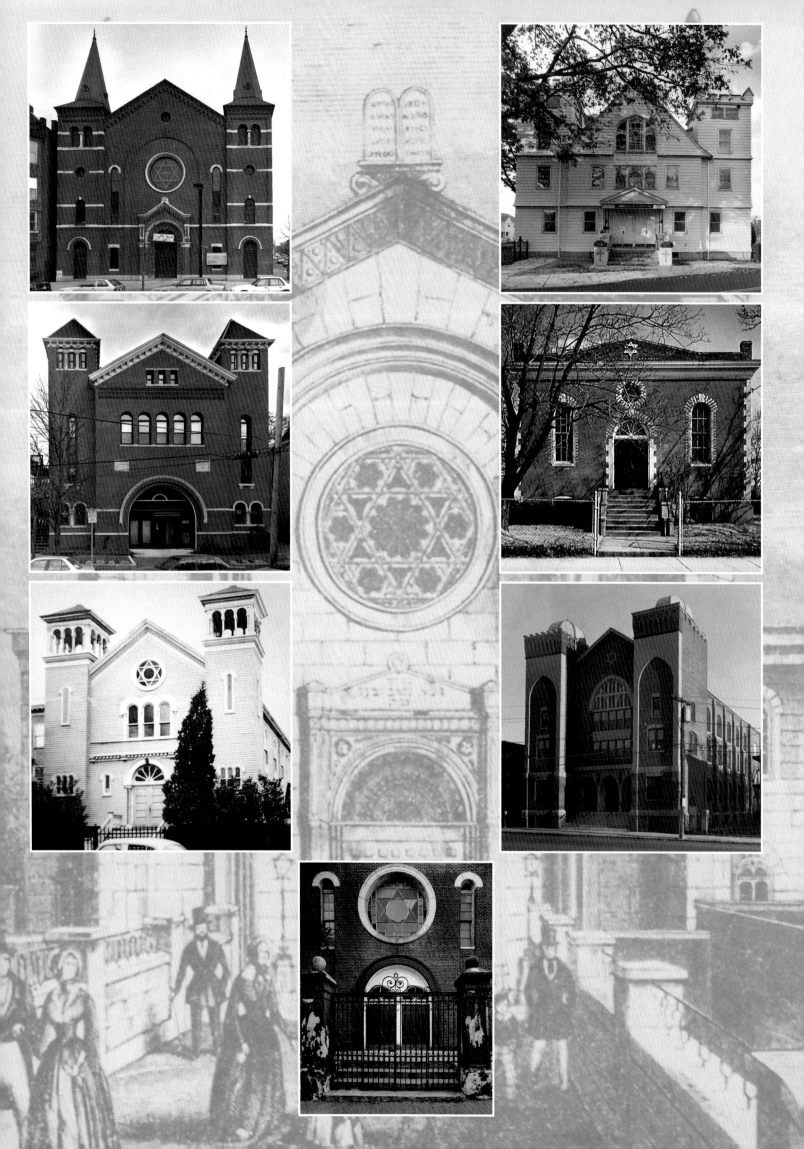

Lynn (1905), Adath Jeshurun on Blue Hill Avenue in Roxbury (1906), Agudas Sholom on Walnut Street in Chelsea (1908), Agudas Achim Anshei Sfard on Adams Street in Newtonville (1912), Beth Hamidrash Hagadol on Crawford Street in Roxbury (1915), and the new Vilna Synagogue on Phillips Street in the Beacon Hill section of the West End (1919). All were pioneering congregations in new areas of Jewish settlement and all aspired to leadership status in their respective communities. Such ambition entailed the construction of an impressive synagogue, inspired in both concept and form by the leading Jewish congregation of Boston, the radical Reform Temple Israel.

Architectural imitation was but one indicator of communal solidarity. Another was the name chosen by the new congregation. The 1888 choice of "Beth Israel" by the Baldwin Place Shul may have been influenced by the established Temple Israel, and Beth Israel of Cambridge was very possibly named after its North End predecessor. More certainly, both Ahabat Sholom of Lynn and Agudas Sholom (originally chartered as "Ohabei Shalom of Chelsea") were named in imitation of Ohabei Shalom of Boston. Yet no one actually called their shul "Beth Israel" or "Ohabei Shalom." Unconsciously influenced by the Reform institutions, the Orthodox Jewish immigrants of Boston would often lapse into calling their shul, "temple."[53]

Most often, however, the colloquial name for any particular congregation was the "*Streetname* Shul." Members of such synagogues often did not even know the real name of their congregation, so common was the popular usage. In America, this practice began in the immigrant district and reached its zenith in the area of second settlement. It was used to distinguish the various synagogues of a neighborhood or of a city from one another and by extension reflected the role of these institutions as communal signposts, each defining its own "turf," or sub-community. For example, former residents of Chelsea will nostalgically enumerate its synagogues as: the "Walnut Street Shul," the "Elm Street Shul," the "Third Street Shul," the "Orange Street Shul," the "Chestnut Street Shul," the "Shurtleff Street Shul," and so forth. Communal identification of this sort typified the immigrant era.

A common feature shared by many of these shuls was a beautiful, hand-carved wooden ark, which in the Boston area was often the work of cabinetmaker Samuel Katz. Katz was a Russian Jewish immigrant who applied his woodworking skills to the furnishing of synagogue sanctuaries, first in upstate New York and later in the Boston area. Settling in Chelsea, he was responsible for the ark and bimah construction in several of its thirteen synagogues. Subsequently, synagogues all over the Boston region ordered arks "Built By Sam Katz." In 1920, the Chambers Street Shul in the West End installed one of Katz's creations and soon other congregations fol-

FIG. 15. The *Rundbogenstil* synagogues of Boston. Dates indicate year built.

*Background illustration: Hamburg Synagogue, Germany, 1855.*

*Inset photographs from top left, counterclockwise:* Temple Israel of Boston (Northampton at Columbus Avenue, 1885), *Photograph by Carl Mastandrea*; Beth Israel of Cambridge (Columbia Street, 1901), *Photograph by Carl Mastandrea*; Ahabat Sholom of Lynn (Church Street, 1905), *North Shore Jewish Historical Society, Lynn, Massachusetts*; Anshe Vilna of Boston (Phillips Street, 1919), *Photograph by A. Samuel Laundon*; Agudas Sholom of Chelsea (Walnut Street, 1909), *Photograph by Carl Mastandrea*; Agudas Achim Anshei Sfard (Adams Street, Newton, 1912), *Agudas Achim Anshei Sfard*; Hadrath Israel of Mattapan, Boston (Walnut Street, 1919; towers added 1929), *Photograph by Carl Mastandrea.*

FIG. 16. Arks and *bimoth* built by Sam Katz in the 1920's. (Dates indicate year synagogue was built.)

*Background photograph:* Anshe Poland, Oswego Street, South End (1920), *The Kates and Katz Families.*

*Inset photographs from top left, counterclockwise:* Agudath Israel Anshe Sfard, Woodrow Avenue, Dorchester (1923); Agudas Sholom, Walnut Street, Chelsea (1909); Linas Hazedek Bet Israel, Chestnut Street, Chelsea (1924); Shaare Zion, Orange Street, Chelsea (1912). *Photographs by Carl Mastandrea;*

lowed suit. In 1923, the Woodrow Avenue Shul of Dorchester was dedicated with a Sam Katz ark, and in 1924, the Adams Street Shul of Newton installed one in its twelve-year-old building.[54] In both interior furnishings and exterior architecture, the synagogues of Boston linked Jews together as part of one Jewish culture and one community.

During the first quarter of the 20th century, the three major areas of Jewish settlement in the Boston area were the West End, Chelsea, and Roxbury. Each district saw the establishment of numerous synagogues. One observer noted that "Not counting synagogues over stores and private home chapels, some fifteen congregations flourished in the West End."[55] Although the founding shuls of these areas were initially just as tenuous as those in such areas as South Boston and Cambridge, the West End, Chelsea, and Roxbury soon proved far more popular as Jewish neighborhoods. The history of their synagogues testifies to their communal success.

Roxbury serves as a prime example. The earliest forays into Roxbury were extensions of the 19th-century Jewish community of the South End. Congregation Har Moriah (which later became a mutual benefit society) was established on Westminster Street in the "Boston Highlands" (Roxbury) as early as 1878. Several blocks away, in 1891, a congregation named Adath Jeshurun was established at Naures Hall on Tremont Street (north of Ruggles) and moved to Dudley Street three years later. In 1898, Mishkan Tefila moved from the South End to a church building on Shawmut Avenue in the South End/Roxbury Crossing district and in 1907 moved further into Roxbury when it occupied yet another church on Moreland Street. At the turn of the century, Adath Jeshurun (or perhaps a congregation of the same name) was reestablished on Blue Hill Avenue, the main artery of the future Jewish neighborhood.[56]

Even as Adath Jeshurun was building its new synagogue in 1906, the first breakaway congregation appeared, founded by Simon Cabelinsky and called Shaare Tefila. Its synagogue and school complex on Otisfield Street were completed in 1923. Beth Hamidrash Hagadol, the main competitor to Adath Jeshurun, was founded in 1913, and its synagogue on Crawford Street was built two years later. (See fig. 18.) Two more congregations, Sons of Abraham on Wayland Street and Toras Moshe on Harold Street, were each established in 1915. All of these pre–World War I congregations were located within a mile radius, clearly establishing the parameters of the Jewish community of Roxbury.

The case of Roxbury congregation Adath Jeshurun—famous in Boston Jewish

lore as the "Blue Hill Avenue Shul"—provides an example of the transitional synagogue of the immigrant generation and the tensions between old-style Orthodoxy and the new American Judaism. In the decade following the dedication of the Baldwin Place Shul in the North End, some of its better-off members began to migrate to the suburb of Roxbury. There, in 1900, several former members regrouped to form a daughter congregation of the North End Shul, and considered the Ramaz to be their rabbi.[57] Of the founders of the "new" Adath Jeshurun, Davis Krokyn, Nathan Pinanski, Joseph Rudnick, and Myer Dana were all in the real estate business; in the Jewish parlance of their day they were "real-estateniks." At first they leased a wooden church on Blue Hill Avenue, corner of Lawrence Avenue, and one year later bought the building. The construction of a new synagogue, while expressing sincere religious sentiments, would also reflect their interest in property development and the affluence that had started to come their way.

Building the synagogue was a community effort.[58] The building campaign was launched in 1904, initiated by Nathan Pinanski's pledge of $1,000. Acting as contractor, Davis Krokyn hired builder Fred Norcross and had his own son draw up the plans. Young Jacob Krokyn graduated from the Harvard School of Architecture in 1905; it is possible that the design for Adath Jeshurun had been a student project.[59] In the same year, construction commenced at the corner of Blue Hill Avenue and Brunswick Street, and the new synagogue building was dedicated in time for *Rosh Hashana* of 1906.[60] Reporting upon the dedication to the greater Jewish community, the *Boston Advocate* described this latest addition to Boston's synagogues:

> *The edifice now dedicated is a splendid and imposing structure which will be for all time a monument to the self-sacrifice and religious fervor of this congregation. It is of brick, with stone trimmings, and cost more than $100,000. It is finished in new oak and marble. The seating capacity is estimated at 1200. Besides the synagogue proper there are Sabbath school rooms and a large hall. The building is heated by steam and lighted by electricity . . .*[61]

The architectural design of the Blue Hill Avenue synagogue was striking and revealed much about the young congregation. In their new building, the pioneers of Jewish settlement in Roxbury associated themselves with their prestigious former chief rabbi, the Ramaz, who had recently been installed in the pulpit of Kehilath Jeshurun, the leading Orthodox synagogue of New York City. Kehilath Jeshurun served as the design inspiration for the new synagogue's stoop and arcaded entryway.[62] Jacob Krokyn also made reference to the Reform temple of Boston, again applying the *Rundbogenstil* to a Boston synagogue. By incorporating aspects of both a Reform temple and an Orthodox shul into his design, he hinted at the possibilities of a new synagogue synthesis for the future.

In interior arrangement, "the synagogue of Adath Jeshurun was planned to include not only a chapel, but club rooms, a banquet and public hall, Kosher kitchen, classrooms and a library."[63] In this, the precedent was not just Kehilath Jeshurun in New York, but also the former shul of the Ramaz, the Baldwin Place Shul of Boston. The Blue Hill Avenue Shul would likewise provide a community space and banquet facility, advertised as "Brunswick Hall" (its entrance was on Brunswick Street). The Jews of Roxbury had arrived.

With the departure of the Ramaz from Boston, Adath Jeshurun sought to engage a congregational rabbi of its own. In early 1908, it hired a young English-speaking rabbi named Phineas (Pinchas) Israeli.[64] In 1910, Rabbi Israeli set forth a vision of the synagogue of the future in an address entitled, "The American Congregation, the Center of Religious Activities," likely influenced by his brother-in-law Mordecai Kaplan, later the founder of Reconstructionist Judaism.[65] Kaplan came to the Blue Hill Avenue Shul in 1914 and observed the first of Israeli's innovations, a "Junior Congregation," said to be the first ever within an Orthodox synagogue in America. After the Friday night service—also an innovation in Orthodoxy—Kaplan spoke to the congregants, observing that "the main auditorium of the synagogue was filled with young and middle-aged people, men and women sitting together." At Shabbat services the next day, he was shocked by the contrast: "In the morning the auditorium was half filled with middle-aged and old men and a few women of the old fashioned type in the gallery."[66] Apparently, Israeli had organized his congregation into two separate entities, split between old and young, separate seating and mixed, Sabbath morning and Friday evening services. Such a compromise between tradition and modernity was tenable for a time, but would not last for long.

Phineas Israeli left Adath Jeshurun in 1918 for an educational post in Chelsea. The leadership of Adath Jeshurun had resisted his progressive ideas for a family- and community-oriented institution, and rather than changing with the times, they let their rabbi go. Founded with great promise, the Blue Hill Avenue Synagogue now began to decline, returning in a sense to being a *landsmanshaft shul* of former North

Enders in Roxbury. In the early 1920's, the congregation erected a separate building several blocks away, effectively cutting off the school from the synagogue. The new Menorah Institute became successful as an independent communal institution, but the child-centered synagogue which Rabbi Israeli had envisioned for Adath Jeshurun was gone. At the same time, a group of younger members who were "dissatisfied with the conventional services" and who no longer had the option of a Junior Congregation, began meeting on their own and soon established a separate congregation, Young Israel of Greater Boston.[67] They met at first in a room at the Blue Hill Avenue Shul, then moved into the Menorah Institute for five years, and ultimately acquired their own building in 1930. Changes in the location and demography of the Roxbury Jewish community were also clearly evident by the mid-1920's, with the establishment of the new Kehillath Israel synagogue in Brookline in 1924 and the new Mishkan Tefila synagogue in Roxbury in 1925. Both were founded by ex-members and children of Adath Jeshurun. All of these youth-oriented offshoots reveal Adath Jeshurun on Blue Hill Avenue as a precursor of the "synagogue-center"—a new type of synagogue created to serve the community as a center for worship, education, and social life.[68]

The synagogue-center experiment, designed to serve the rising generation of American Jews, grew into a national movement during the 1920's. Some of its more important precedents emerged in the Boston Jewish community. For example, on August 31, 1908, the "Yavne Congregation" was chartered in the Commonwealth of Massachusetts and commenced its activities at 4 Milton Street in the West End. The new venture was described as "the only Zionist congregation in this country," and in 1910, its rabbi was listed as Aaron Gorowitz.[69] Zionism was attractive as a synagogue ideology for its potential to unify the Jewish community—being neither Reform nor Orthodox it was trans-denominational, relating to the Jewish people as a whole. Furthermore, it could be employed to win back the disaffected

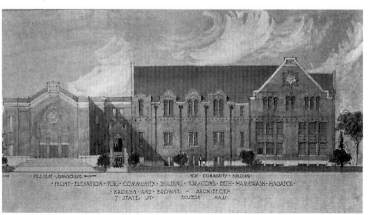

young—the modern Zionist movement was conceived as an activist, updated version of Judaism and had strong appeal to second generation Jews.

Other solutions to the problem of the young were offered in the January 1909 issues of the *Boston Advocate* in a symposium entitled, "Can the Synagogue Do Anything to Attract the Younger Generation? If So, What?" The youth surveyed offered a variety of suggestions. One advised "a single method of ventilation for the synagogue." Another suggested that "the synagogue be made as beautiful as possible in physical appearance . . . Then only could the young Jew be made to feel the inner meaning and beauty . . ." Saul Shore wrote, "Our rabbis should get at us, organize us into national clubs, religious clubs . . . Large vestries, nay, even the smallest chamber of the synagogue should be converted to meeting rooms, gamerooms, Sunday Schools, religious classes, and public libraries." Daniel Bloomfield added, "clubs for social purposes, and to study Jewish questions and ideals as well as clubs for Bible study should be organized by every synagogue . . ."[70]

In the second installment of the symposium, the editor of the paper (probably Jacob De Haas, the Zionist leader and director of the Boston YMHA) reiterated the recommendation to expand the scope of synagogue activity:

> *Up to our own times the synagogue was the congregational pivot . . .*
> *because the life of the congregation was conducted within its four walls . . .*
> *It was a house of learning, house of worship, meeting house, all rolled in*
> *one, with a court of justice in an ante-room and a school in another. It was*
> *not a place to which a Jew went on occasion, it was the place in which*
> *every Jew passed quite a large portion of his life. It was the headquarters*
> *of a tiny Jewish municipality. The break begun by Reform, was widened*
> *by the lodge movement, but there is nothing repugnant historically to such*
> *development within the synagogue structure as the housing of a social*
> *settlement, library, gymnasium . . .*[71]

In response to the needs of the new generation, the post-WWI period would see a mini-boom of synagogue construction. Just to the south of Roxbury, for example, the younger Jewish community of Dorchester was growing rapidly, as evidenced by its new synagogue buildings. The pioneer congregation of Dorchester was Beth El, founded on Fowler Street in 1908. In the same year, Congregation Hadrath Israel was founded in Roxbury, where it occupied the Elm Hill Baptist Church on Crawford Street (the building which later became the Hebrew Teacher's College of Boston). Hadrath Israel moved to Dorchester in 1914 and five years later acquired a building on Woodrow Avenue off of Blue Hill Avenue. The well-known "Woodrow Avenue

FIG. 20. Agudath Israel
Anshei Sfard, 220
Woodrow Avenue, built
1923. The building is
now Temple Salem, a
Haitian Seventh Day
Adventist Church.
*Photograph by Carl
Mastandrea.*

Shul" was not Hadrath Israel, however, but its first offshoot, Agudath Israel Anshei Sfard, founded in 1915. It completed its impressive new synagogue in 1923, located just across the street from its predecessor. A third synagogue joined the Woodrow Avenue group in 1928 with the construction of Chevra Shas next to Hadrath Israel, later to be joined by the G&G delicatessen. Together, these religious and culinary institutions made up the social center of the Jewish community. Continuing south along Blue Hill Avenue, other significant synagogues of Dorchester included Chai Odom on Nightingale Street (1922), Temple Beth Hillel on Morton Street (incorporated into the Dorchester-Mattapan Hebrew School building of 1930), and moving into Mattapan, Kehillath Jacob on Fessendon Street (1939). Fulfilling the early vision of the Blue Hill Avenue Shul, the Dorchester synagogues served the community as true synagogue-centers.

In the 1920's, Boston became a leader of the nationwide synagogue-center movement. During that prosperous decade, four major synagogue-center projects were undertaken, thus determining and helping to identify the four leading synagogues of Boston: Ohabei Shalom, Temple Israel, Mishkan Tefila, and Kehillath Israel. The first three were the original congregations of Jewish Boston. Brookline-born Kehillath Israel laid claim to no less impressive roots, since it traced its lineage back through the Blue Hill Avenue Shul of Roxbury to the Baldwin Place Shul of the North End. Of the four, Temple Israel was ultra-Reform, Ohabei Shalom moderate Reform, Mishkan Tefila Conservative, and Kehillath Israel modern Orthodox (later shifting to Conservative). Mishkan Tefila was located in the middle class community of Roxbury/Dorchester. The other three were located in the somewhat more upscale Brookline.[72] All four undertook their synagogue-center projects with some awareness of the others' plans and were clearly motivated by a sense of competition.

Kehillath Israel, or "K.I." as it came to be known, was established in 1911 as the original congregation of Brookline. Created as a private minyan of thirty-six members, it "began to realize that in order to fulfill its purpose, it would have to accommodate the social and educational demands of the Jewish neighborhood also."[73] Land was purchased in May 1921, and the cornerstone for a new synagogue was laid in October 1923. Originally defined as "A Modern Orthodox Congregation,"

K.I. adopted mixed seating only after the dedication of its new building in January 1925.[74] In August of the same year, the noted scholar Louis M. Epstein was called to the Brookline pulpit from the Crawford Street Shul of Roxbury. Many of the early members of K.I. had also moved from Roxbury where they had belonged to either the Crawford Street or the Blue Hill Avenue Shul.

Epstein had arrived in Boston in 1918 to become rabbi of Beth Hamidrash Hagadol on Crawford Street. Under his leadership, the congregation thrived, soon developing into both a congregational and a communal center. By 1923, Epstein could boast, "We have thirteen hundred souls permanently organized into our congregational system and we serve on the average—some more, some less—approximately ten thousand Jewish souls in our community."[75] The congregation had the architectural firm of Krokyn, Browne, & Rosenstein draw up plans for a new community building to be added to the original structure—complete with banquet hall, classrooms, clubrooms, and gymnasium. (See fig. 19.) Like its contemporary congregation on Blue Hill Avenue, Beth Hamidrash Hagadol never succeeded in creating a synagogue-center on Crawford Street. However, both its rabbi and Jewish architect would later realize the vision elsewhere.[76]

Rabbi Epstein moved to Kehillath Israel in 1925, the year the synagogue building was dedicated. Designed by the firm of MacNaughton & Robinson, its pre-cast concrete façade was called "Byzantine in character"[77] but seemed more like a combination of the traditional Boston *Rundbogenstil*, the 1907 "Solomonic" Temple Israel on Commonwealth Avenue, and the contemporary style of Art Deco. In its eclectic structure and under its scholarly rabbi, K.I. continued to grow. In 1929 it added a new school building and social hall, and in 1948 a new community house and auditorium building were added next door—designed by none other than Jacob Krokyn. At its central location on Harvard Street—which thereafter became a main Jewish shopping thoroughfare—K.I. became the most active congregation in Brookline and a leading synagogue-center of the Boston Jewish community.[78]

The campaign to build a new "Jewish Center" for the rapidly growing Roxbury-Dorchester Jewish community was launched at Mishkan

FIG. 21. Kehillath Israel, 384 Harvard Street, Brookline, built 1925. The original Jewish institution on Harvard Street, the synagogue today anchors a lively shopping street of Kosher restaurants and Jewish bookstores. The original structure of 1925 stands to the right and the 1948 addition flanks it to the left. *Photograph by Carl Mastandrea.*

Tefila's anniversary banquet on December 21, 1919. The site at the corner of Seaver Street and Elm Hill Avenue, facing Franklin Park, was purchased in 1920, and the architectural firm chosen was Krokyn, Browne & Rosenstein. Sometime in 1920–22, just as a nationwide synagogue-center movement was underway, the architects joined the building committee on an inspection tour of potential models for the new project.[79] In a letter to the *Jewish Advocate* signed, "J. Frederick Krokyn," the Harvard-educated architect from the Jewish North End set forth his personal vision:

> *The new building represents an event in the progress of the faith and is evidence of the Jewish renaissance here. Its location, in the heart of the largest Jewish population in New England, is unsurpassed in beauty and accessibility and lends itself perfectly for the purpose. The building will be an expression of modern American architecture, a striking symbol to the world of our harmony with American culture and traditions. . . The architects are thus planning a building to express the ideals and aspirations of a great Jewish community.*[80]

In the 1920's, Mishkan Tefila represented the left wing of the Conservative movement. Conservative Judaism was still in an early stage of development, and congregations such as Mishkan Tefila provided the setting for its maturation into a independent movement on the American Jewish scene. As a new type of synagogue—a Conservative synagogue-center—Mishkan Tefila introduced a new form of American Judaism.[81]

But incipient Conservatism was not the only impetus for the new construction. In March of 1923, Alexander Brin, the editor of the *Jewish Advocate*, ran a special issue in which he appealed for funds for the Mishkan Tefila "Victory Drive" and personally advocated the "realization of the Model Temple Mishkan Tefila." In a public editorial he insisted,

> *The new Temple Mishkan Tefila is not a luxury; it is a necessity. It is impossible to develop Jewish life if our buildings handicap rather than encourage us. A weakened spiritual condition makes it easier for the anti-Semites to attack us. This community could do more work—NECESSARY WORK—if we had proper facilities. Ours is a job of education. That is why we need modern temples and centres.*[82]

Other articles by members of the congregation cited "the fact that the majority of our members are under thirty-five years of age" and required new facilities to meet their needs. Rabbi Rubenovitz wrote of "The Synagogue As A Community Center," suggesting,

> *The problem of the synagogue cannot be satisfactorily solved until it is prepared to serve the community, not only through its religious schools and divine service, but also by offering facilities for wholesome diversion and refined entertainment. It must offer to our people, both young and old, meeting rooms, assembly halls, reading rooms, a well equipped gymnasium, a swimming pool and athletic field. Whatever makes for the physical, moral, and social development of our people, whatever tends to enlarge, sweeten and refine human life, must be included within the scope of the synagogue.*[83]

The final construction did not include the proposed athletic facilities, for in the same year and just one block away on Seaver Street, the Boston YMHA Gymnasium Building was constructed with those very amenities. Rubenovitz served as Director of Religious Education for the YMHA, and the architect for the new YMHA building was Jacob Krokyn. The YMHA and its neighboring synagogue-center were not competing but complementary institutions.

The monumental Mishkan Tefila was dedicated on September 13, 1925, having cost approximately $750,000. As at Kehillath Israel in Brookline, a schoolhouse building was added to the rear of the main structure in 1929, at a further cost of $300,000, bringing the total outlay to over $1 million dollars. Rubenovitz later recalled the significance of the new complex: "The dedication of our temple on Seaver Street marked the beginning of a new epoch in the evolution of Jewish life in New England. Here was finally realized the old idea of a *Stadt Shul*, a great central synagogue which could serve as a place of assembly for the entire community whenever some special occasion demanded it."[84] Indeed, throughout the interwar heyday of the second generation Jewish community, Mishkan Tefila was the dominant institutional presence in Roxbury, due in no small part to the imposing synagogue-center edifice of 1925.

FIG. 22. Early architectural scheme for Mishkan Tefila, Seaver Street, Roxbury, Boston. *American Jewish Historical Society.*

FIG. 23. Mishkan Tefila, Seaver Street, built 1925. It was sold to the Lubavitcher Hasidim in 1958, and then to a school of performing arts in 1968. It stands today as an abandoned ruin. *American Jewish Historical Society.*

A third major synagogue-center was erected by Ohabei Shalom at its new location on Beacon Street, the main avenue of Brookline. Ohabei Shalom had remained in the South End until the end of WWI, by which time most of its membership had left that district, many moving to Brookline. In late 1920, land was purchased for the construction of a new congregational home. At its new site on Beacon Street, Temple Ohabei Shalom would be geographically located between Kehillath Israel on Harvard Street and Temple Israel on Commonwealth Avenue—its two historic offshoots. Religiously as well, Ohabei Shalom was situated midway between them; while K.I. was moderate Orthodox and Temple Israel was classical Reform, Ohabei Shalom wavered between moderate Reform and classical Conservatism. More to the point, it directly competed with the other two congregations for prestige and influence: as opposed to Temple Israel, it saw itself as the rightful "leading congregation" of Boston; and as opposed to Kehillath Israel, it aspired to be the "central synagogue" of Brookline. Ohabei Shalom therefore hired the architect of the 1907 Temple Israel and planned a magnificent new temple to overshadow both its competitors.

In April 1922, the congregation held a banquet to raise funds for their building project. Rabbi Samuel J. Abrams spoke of "A Possession Forever."

> *What is this New Temple Ohabei Shalom? Let me tell you at least what we shall strive to make it—a monument of the standing of the Jews of this metropolis of the 20th century! More than that; it is to be a witness to the fact that though we have risen in wealth and power, and though we yield to none of our fellow-citizens in love of country, we have not forgotten the rock whence we were hewn. In its artistic completeness, it is to be an offering recording for years, or—may God grant—for centuries to come, at once the prosperity and the gratitude which are ours in being privileged to be counted among those who served this holy cause.*[85]

The architect made his statement in stone and brick. Clarence Blackall's commission to design the new Ohabei Shalom was an opportunity to expand upon his earlier scheme for Temple Israel, both literally and figuratively. The 1920's design was much larger in scale, far more intricate in its polychromatic detail, and in the end, a much more expensive undertaking. It too was topped by a massive dome. The original scheme also called for a towering minaret on the corner of the building, which, though never built, was described as follows:

> *The dome is about ninety feet high and the tower is one hundred and seventy to the top of its Menorah. The tower, which has a lantern top, will*

*provide a most distinguishing landmark on the long perspective of Beacon Street. The lantern has a gilded patterned top surmounted by the Menorah and will have a large light source to stream from its arcaded windows.*[86]

"A Beacon unto the Nations," the new Beacon Street temple would be anything but inconspicuous. Where Temple Israel had been a modernized Solomonic temple, the new Ohabei Shalom would be Boston's version of the Hagia Sophia, the greatest architectural monument of ancient Byzantium. The Byzantine revival had become the reigning style of synagogue architecture in America, adapted for contemporary synagogue-centers in San Francisco, Chicago, Cleveland, Newark, New York, Providence, and now, Boston.[87] The style was thought to refer to recent excavations of Byzantine synagogues in Palestine, and evoked associations of an oriental Mediterranean civilization not far removed from the sources of Judaism.

FIG. 24. Early architectural rendering of Ohabei Shalom on Beacon Street, Brookline, showing unbuilt minaret. *Congregation Ohabei Shalom.*

The rabbi, congregation, and architect of Ohabei Shalom envisioned the planned edifice as a monument to the arrival of the Jews in Brookline and the presence of Judaism in Boston. In 1925, the same year as the dedications of Kehillath Israel and Mishkan Tefila, Ohabei Shalom dedicated its new "Temple Center" school and administration building. Its "cultural purposes" would be served by an auditorium, a supper and play room (to be used as a gymnasium or recreation room), dressing rooms, class and meeting rooms, music rooms, a museum, library and reading

FIG. 25. Ohabei Shalom, 1187 Beacon Street, Brookline, built in 1928, as it appears today. *Photograph by Carl Mastandrea.*

room.[88] Three years later, in 1928, the adjacent temple edifice was dedicated, minus the minaret but impressive nonetheless.

Not to be outdone by its fellow congregations, Temple Israel began planning for its new synagogue-center complex in 1923. In 1917 the congregational historian had written, "Adath Israel is now unquestionably the strongest individual Jewish institution, the most influential Congregation in New England."[89] But that image would soon be threatened, as Mishkan Tefila, Kehillath Israel, and Ohabei Shalom all announced plans for insti-

FIG. 26. Temple Israel, Riverway and Long-wood Avenue, Boston, proposed design, 1926. Though never built in its entirety, the grandiose complex reveals the high aspirations of Temple Israel in the 1920's. *Temple Israel, Boston.*

FIG. 27. Temple Israel Meeting House, River-way and Longwood Avenue, Boston, built 1928. The 1974 addition on the left was designed by The Architects Collaborative, in stark contrast to the original building. *Photograph by Carl Mastandrea.*

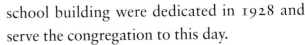

tutional expansion during the next few years. Felix Vorenberg, president of Temple Israel, also observed that Boston was "far behind the Jews of other cities" in building synagogue-centers.[90]

In April 1924 Temple Israel purchased land on the Riverway, along the border between Brookline and Boston, and the process of planning the new Temple was begun. The architectural firm of McLaughlin & Burr—designers of the nearby Harvard Medical School —was chosen.[91] Plans were developed with congregational input, and in February 1926, the new design was publicized in the local press. The architects planned "a beautiful structure of classic design facing on the Riverway, with the great Temple as the central dominating building flanked on either side by the less important entrances of the Social and Administrative units. . . [and] At the rear of the group and fronting on Plymouth Street is the Educational building of the group. Here are rooms where approximately 1000 pupils will be given religious instruction."[92] The west wing, called the "Meeting House," and the connected school building were dedicated in 1928 and serve the congregation to this day.

The remainder of the monumental project was never completed. The stock market crash of 1929 and the ensuing depression put the construction on hold. Even so, the vision of the magnificent temple lived on. The congregational bulletin continued to carry the depiction of the planned edifice on its masthead throughout the next decade. The image was dropped only in November 1938—a date coincident with *Kristallnacht*, the terrible night during which hundreds of synagogue buildings were destroyed throughout Germany. Harry Levi, the rabbi of Temple Israel, was deeply affected by the Nazi threat, and it was likely he who removed the grandiose image from the bulletin.[93] Jewish life would be forever changed by the events of World War II, and synagogue architecture would reflect that change. While synagogue builders of the earlier period faced the outside world boldly, erecting monumental structures on grand boulevards, after the War the synagogue turned inward, seeking a secure and viable communal life behind the ivy-covered brick walls of suburbia.

FIG. 28. Temple Emanuel, 385 Ward Street, Newton, built 1937. Boston's first suburban synagogue, its modest scale reflects the diminished expectations of the Jewish communities in the 1930's. The congregation grew to over 1,000 families after World War II, and its adjoining center building was added in 1952. *Photograph by David Kaufman.*

The first suburban synagogue of the Boston Jewish community was Temple Emanuel of Newton, founded in 1935. Though parallel congregations were founded in Brighton (Bnai Moshe, 1933), Belmont-Watertown (Beth El Temple Center, ca. 1935), Chelsea (Temple Emmanuel, 1938), and in Mattapan (Kehillath Jacob, 1938 and Temple Beth Hillel, 1944), it was Newton that became, after Brookline, the principal Jewish suburb of Boston. Temple Emanuel's first structure was built in 1937 on Ward Street, in a sedate neo-Georgian style and on a rather modest scale. Like most other pioneer suburban congregations, it affiliated with the Conservative movement and was conceived as a synagogue-center, a full-service Jewish institution.

FIG. 29. Temple Emeth, 194 Grove Street, South Brookline, built 1949. Note the tree in the forecourt, representing *etz ha-chayim* (the tree of life) and symbolizing the centrality of the Torah in Jewish life. *Photograph by David Kaufman.*

Temple Emanuel was soon joined by Temple Emeth of South Brookline, which was originally formed as a Jewish community center in 1939. Its award-winning modernist structure was designed by Carney Goldberg and built in 1949. At the same time, the new synagogue of Temple Beth Zion was completed on Beacon Street in Brookline. Like the Newton synagogue, it was of Georgian Revival design. A fourth new Conservative congregation, Temple Reyim of Newton, was also first organized as a Jewish center in 1949 and erected its own building some nine years later. Like Temple Emeth, it was in the modern style, designed by The Architects Collaborative, the firm founded by Walter Gropius of the *Bauhaus* movement. Apparently, Conservative congregations of

FIG. 30. Temple Sinai,
Charles Street and Se-
wall Avenue, Brookline.
This Colonial Revival
structure was built in
1916 for the Second Uni-
tarian Society of Brook-
line and acquired by
Temple Sinai in 1944.
*Photograph by David
Kaufman.*

FIG. 31. Mishkan Tefila,
300 Hammond Pond
Parkway, Chestnut Hill,
Brookline, built 1957.
The congregation has
remained at this loca-
tion, its fifth synagogue
building, for the longest
period in its history.
*Congregation Mishkan
Tefila.*

the 1940's were faced with the dilemma of whether to lean toward the modern or the traditional, as neatly expressed by their choice of architect and architectural style.

The Reform community of Boston began to expand with the formation of Temple Sinai in the summer of 1939. An offshoot from Temple Israel, it followed precedent by purchasing a former church building in 1943. The first Reform incursion into suburbia took place in 1950 with the formation of Temple Shalom in Newton. After meeting in church buildings for its first five years, Temple Shalom dedicated a modern temple and school building in 1956, described as "contemporary in design, though traditionally Jewish in content."[94] In 1955, Temple Tifereth Israel of Malden built its new building, and at the same time, "converted" from Conservative to Reform. In keeping with the conservativism of New England, however, most Boston-area congregations remained Conservative. Those who desired Reform often commuted back into the city to the ever-prestigious Temple Israel—a reversal of the general pattern of traditional city versus progressive suburb.

The best known suburban synagogue of the 1950's was the new Mishkan Tefila in Chestnut Hill. Determined to transplant the grandeur of the Roxbury temple to its new location, the congregation selected the leading synagogue architect of the time, Percival Goodman. A devoted modernist, Goodman designed an integrated complex of buildings surrounded by a large parking lot, a synagogue-center for the suburbs. Also concerned with the æsthetics of spirituality, the Jewish architect set the project back into its wooded site to incorporate a sense of nature and to encourage contemplation of God's creation. Securely situated on Hammond Pond Parkway since 1957, Mishkan Tefila has not forgotten its earlier roots. When a Nursery Youth Center was added in 1993, the congregation salvaged and reconstructed a fragment of the original Roxbury building—the Ten Commandments—to evoke a sense of congregational history.[95]

Perhaps the most celebrated new synagogue of the Boston suburbs was the Berlin Chapel at Brandeis University in Waltham. Brandeis was founded in 1948 and dedicated its religious complex in October 1955. Three chapels—Protestant, Catholic, and Jewish—appear the same in size and carry the same general abstract design but exhibit individual details and variations. They are sited so as never to cast shadows on one another. Here in architectonic terms was a dramatic evocation of religious pluralism, paralleling Will Herberg's 1955 bestseller, *Protestant-Catholic-Jew*. In the postwar context, the Jewish chapel at Brandeis represented a proud synthesis of Jewish and American ideals.[96]

Ironically, the most significant developments of the following decade were those which rejected the synthesis. Orthodoxy in Boston experienced a revival in the 1960's as prominent rabbinic leaders reestablished themselves in Brookline. Earlier, during the 1930's

FIG. 32. Chai Odom, 77 Englewood Avenue, Brookline. The congregation moved from its Nightingale Avenue location in Dorchester to this renovated Brookline house in 1968. *Photograph by David Kaufman.*

and 1940's, Hasidic rabbis such as the Bostoner Rebbe (Levi I. Horowitz) and modern Orthodox rabbis such as Joseph D. Soloveitchik had been attracted to the thriving Jewish communities of Roxbury and Dorchester.[97] As the Jewish communities relocated to the Brookline area during the following decades, the Orthodox leaders followed suit and brought their institutions with them. The new Brookline congregations included the Beth Pinchas congregation of the Bostoner Rebbe, Beth David of the Talner Rebbe (M. Z. Twersky), Chai Odom of Shloma Margolis (and later Mordecai Savitsky), and the Maimonides School which functioned as a quasi-congregation under Rabbi Soloveitchik. The Young Israel of Brookline was established during the 1940's as an outgrowth of Congregation Sons of Israel, founded in Brookline in 1926. Other suburban Orthodox congregations included Beth-El Atereth Israel, which moved from Dorchester to Newton and erected a new complex in 1965. Kadimah Toras-Moshe, founded as a Conservative congregation in the mid-1940's, converted to Orthodoxy during the 1960's in a renovated nursing home on Washington Street in Brighton.

FIG. 33. Beth Pinchas, 1710 Beacon Street, Brookline. Founded in 1919 in Boston's West End, the Chassidic Center moved to 61 Columbia Road, Dorchester in 1944, and to Brookline in 1961. *Photograph by David Kaufman.*

Many of these suburban Orthodox congregations preserved a feature of synagogue architecture pioneered in the older neighborhoods—the renovated house. Roxbury and Dorchester congregations such as Toras Moshe on Harold Street, Beth Jacob on Norfolk Street, Young Israel on Blue Hill Avenue, and Anshe Sheptovka on Lawrence Avenue were all housed in former private residences. Besides the economic motive for such a renovation, Orthodox Jews of the era treated their shul like a second home, and so the conversion of a house

FIG. 34. Havurat Shalom, 113 College Avenue, Somerville. *Photograph by Carl Mastandrea.*

FIG. 35. Havurat Shalom, interior. *Photograph by Carl Mastandrea.*

into a synagogue made symbolic as well as financial sense.[98] Orthodox congregations remain far more likely to turn a house into a *shtibl* (small synagogue) than to construct a new synagogue building. Thus Beth Pinchas, Beth David, and Chai Odom all occupy former private homes in Brookline, renovated to meet the needs of a congregation and to provide space for the domicile of their rabbis. Young Israel of Brookline occupied two successive houses, first on Fuller Street and then on Green Street, where it added a new wing in 1957 and constructed a new synagogue building in 1964.[99] Other examples of the suburban-home turned synagogue include Bnai Jacob on Blue Hills Parkway in Milton and Shaarei Tefilla on Morseland Avenue in Newton, down the block from its parent congregation, Beth-El Atereth Israel.

The intimacy of the house/synagogue also appealed to the Havurah movement of the 1960's Jewish counterculture.[100] A "havurah" (literally, "fellowship") is an informal synagogue-community that has no rabbi, no congregational bureaucracy, and no permanent structure. The most famous Havurah in America was founded in "an old rambling yellow house in Somerville, Mass." in 1968.[101] Called the Havurat Shalom Community Seminary, it gained immortality of a sort with the 1973 publication of its homegrown guide for the perplexed, *the Jewish Catalog*. Havurat Shalom remains today in its original home, an apt metaphor for its emphasis upon experiential Judaism and intimate Jewish community. Now over a quarter century old, the "Hav" also represents continuity—the current prayer room has not

changed since first depicted in *the Jewish Catalog*, with pillows on the floor and a wicker ark with a macrame cover on the wall.

Havurat Shalom spearheaded the Havurah movement in the United States, and Boston has remained a center of Havurah activity. The *Guide to Jewish Boston* for 1986 listed over a dozen "Havurot and Minyanim."[102] Most of them do not have permanent homes, and often use church vestries for their services—a further gloss on the Boston church-synagogue tradition. More recently formed Havurot in Boston include the Reconstructionist Congregations Dorshei Tzedek and Shir Hadash, whose creative names—"seekers of justice" and "new song" respectively—reflect a new trend in Jewish life.

The same search for intimacy and community that inspired both the Orthodox *shtibls* and the countercultural havurot also influenced some mainstream congregations. In 1968 Temple Israel sold its Commonwealth Avenue Temple to Boston University, and commissioned The Architects Collaborative to design a new sanctuary to join its 1928 Meeting House on the Riverway. (See fig. 27.) The new structure, dedicated in 1973 and best known for its sculptural ornament by Louise Nevelson, is a prime example of the contemporary trend toward internalization. Whereas the original design was a grand neo-classical temple oriented to the avenue, the modern scheme turns in upon itself, emphasizing the interior functions of synagogue life. Similarly, the Boston Synagogue of 1974, the designated heir to the West End synagogues destroyed by urban renewal, is the very picture of "safe space."[103] Both structures are walled, windowless shelters lit within by skylights. The synagogue was no longer aspiring to be a "light unto the nations," but rather, a place of interior illumination and spiritual sanctuary for Jews.

Other recent synagogue structures extend these themes of light and shelter. Congregation Kerem Shalom of Concord dedicated its synagogue in 1989, more than a decade after its founding as the Concord Area Jewish Group. Designed by Michael Rosenfeld, the synagogue displays two public faces. The rear of the synagogue, facing Route 2, is intended to deflect the noise of the highway and presents the appearance of a bunkered hill, an architectural "*tel*." In contrast, the front of the synagogue is open and welcoming, a picture window upon the Jewish activities inside. The interior is both flexible in plan and skylit for effect, creating an intimate, spiritual environment. Another synagogue in this mode is the expansion of Shir Tikva of Wayland, designed by

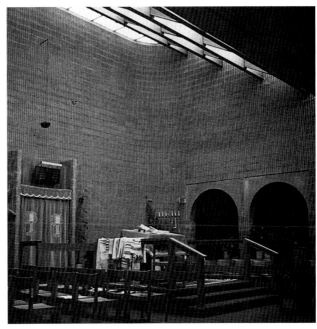

FIG. 36. Boston Synagogue, 55 Martha Road, Boston, built 1974. Formerly called the Charles River Park Synagogue. *Photograph by David Kaufman.*
FIG. 37. Kerem Shalom, Route 2, Concord, built 1989. An example of an informal havurah—the Concord Area Jewish Group, in a building of light and community. *Nick Wheeler, Wheeler Photographics.*

Crissman & Solomon Architects and dedicated in 1992.

Finally, two projects of the early 1990's looked to the future and the past of synagogue design in the Boston Jewish community. Israeli architect Moshe Safdie's 1994 Harvard University Hillel complex aimed to address the diversity of American Judaism in a building designed to serve Reform, Orthodox, Egalitarian and Conservative *minyanim*. The lone remaining synagogue structure in the first area of Boston's East European immigrant settlement, the West End's Vilna Shul of 1919, was purchased by the Vilna Center for Jewish Heritage in 1994 with the stated mission of restoring the building and creating a cultural center and museum of Boston Jewish history on its premises.[104]

Since the 1850's when Boston's earliest synagogues arose, the city's houses of Jewish worship have embodied central themes of Jewish life in Boston: how immigrants banded together in small informal congregations and ensured their communal continuity by acquiring a synagogue structure; how the acquisition of church structures and acculturation into the greater community encouraged the reforming of the synagogue; how the various Jewish subcommunities which began their existence in the South, North, and West Ends moved to nearby locales such as Roxbury, Chelsea, and Brookline, and eventually relocated to the southern, northern, and western suburbs; how the greater Jewish community maintained a sense of unity despite its geographic dispersal in part through its synagogue architecture; how the tension between traditional Judaism and modern American life led to the creation of new forms of Jewish community such as the synagogue-center and Conservative Judaism; how the architecture of the synagogue revealed the social and economic status of the Jewish community as well as its religious aspirations; and how Jews have responded to America through creative religious expression, as exemplified by modern Orthodoxy and the Havurah movement—both premised upon the formation of intimate community. All of these transformations represent efforts to recreate the synagogue to accommodate changing circumstances and fresh needs. By building and rebuilding their synagogues, Boston Jews have indeed preserved the structure of their community.

I wish to acknowledge two individuals who inspired my journey of discovery into the synagogues of Boston: Gerald Bernstein, professor of architectural history at Brandeis, who first suggested the project and guided its early stages; and Steve Kellerman, whose love for the subject and eagerness to explore Jewish Boston animated my own enthusiasm. I thank them as well as the many fellow enthusiasts I have met along the way.

1. Lee M. Friedman, "The Dedication of Massachusetts' First Synagogue," chap. 10 in *Jewish Pioneers and Patriots* (Philadelphia: The Jewish Publication Society of America, 1942), 116–29. The membership of 80 families represented two-thirds of the total Jewish population. For early population estimates, see Stephen G. Mostov, "A Sociological Portrait of German Jewish Immigrants in Boston," *AJS Review* 3 (1978).

2. As quoted in Arthur Mann, *Growth and Achievement: Temple Israel, 1854–1954* (Cambridge: Riverside Press, 1954), 20.

3. See for example the 1854 depiction of Ohabei Shalom as one of the "new churches in Boston" [fig. 1]. Furthermore, the transition from immigrant shul to American synagogue may be expressed in sociological terms as the transition from "sect" to "church."

4. To trace religious development alone, we might do better to trace the history of the rabbinate. For example, Arthur Mann's *Growth and Achievement* is a noteworthy congregational history which focuses upon each successive rabbi of Temple Israel. This study of the synagogue encompasses both the religious and the social history of Boston Jewry. Hence, individuals who are primarily religious figures (e.g., rabbis), individuals whose roles were primarily sociopolitical (Jewish secularists, radicals, cultural figures), or men and women unaffiliated with Jewish life per se will not be featured in this survey.

5. For example, in 1816 "Mr. Abraham Touro applied to the Town Clerk [of Boston] & requested that his religious profession might be recorded on the Town's books—& that he belonged to a Synagogue of the Jews." As quoted in Lee M. Friedman, "Medford's Jewish Street," chap. 21 in *Jewish Pioneers*, 247. Despite the fact that there was no longer a Jewish population in Newport, its synagogue and Jewish cemetery remained the only ones in New England. Abraham Touro lived and died in Boston, but was buried in Newport in 1822. The term "synagogue-community" is commonly used to describe the all-encompassing institution characteristic of colonial Jewry. Its post-1825 disintegration into a "community of synagogues" was a turning point in the history of American Judaism, giving rise to intracommunal competition and pluralism. The history of Ohabei Shalom may be seen in this light—yielding to the exigencies of the time, its attempt to create a unified synagogue-community in Boston ended with the secessions of 1849, 1854, and 1858.

6. The symbolism was probably unintentional, for had it been intended there likely would have been some comment upon this unusual use of architectural ornament. On the other hand, the ark inside was topped by an engraved "white marble slab" symbolizing the Ten Commandments. See Friedman, *Jewish Pioneers,* 126, for a description of the synagogue interior.

7. From the *Boston Almanac* description of 1854 (see frontispiece to "Israelites in Boston" in this volume). Prior to the 19th century, all synagogues—both Sephardic and Ashkenazic—had separate bimot, separate seating for women, and separate spaces for auxiliary functions.

8. "Will of the Late Judah Touro," Publications of the American Jewish Historical Society [*PAJHS*] 13 (1905), 107.

9. On the court case, see Jeanette S. and Abraham E. Nizel, *Congregation Ohabei Shalom: Pioneers of the Boston Jewish Community—An Historical Perspective of the First One Hundred and Forty Years, 1842–1982* (Boston: By the Congregation, 1982), 12.

10. As quoted in Mann, *Growth and Achievement,* 27.

11. Stella D. Obst, *The Story of Adath Israel* (Boston: By the Congregation, 1917).

12. According to A. G. Daniels' 1910 congregational history, "From Ghetto to Temple," reprinted in *Temple Mishkan Tefila: A History, 1858–1958* (Newton, Mass.: By the Congregation, 1958), 15–17. As Gerald Gamm points out, the date of incorporation is open to question.

13. Daniels, "From Ghetto to Temple," 15.

14. Daniels, "From Ghetto to Temple," 16.

15. Albert Ehrenfried, *A Chronicle of Boston Jewry: From the Colonial Settlement to 1900* (Boston: Privately printed, 1963), 427–28.

16. From a letter to the Hebrew periodical *Ha-Shachar* 7:32 (1875), as quoted in Ehrenfried, *Boston Jewry,* 430.

17. Jewish religious leadership in 19th-century America was often invested in men who did not possess rabbinic ordination. In one case at Ohabei Shalom, that of "Reverend" Benjamin E. Jacobs, the complaint against him seems to have been his lack of proper credentials. Ehrenfried, *Boston Jewry,* 356, n. 7.

18. Z. Broches, "A Chapter in the History of the Jews of Boston," *YIVO Annual* 9 (New York: YIVO Institute, 1954), 208. Broches continues: "The Orthodox majority of the membership felt that it was an act of desecration to speak about reforms in the synagogue itself and they served notice that the rabbi would not be permitted to speak in the synagogue. The pro-Reform faction then rented a hall in which Rabbi Nathan delivered three lectures." Two years later, the congregation found a less controversial candidate for rabbi in Hirsh Falk Vidaver who held both traditional ordination and a Ph.D.; he was a modern rabbi though by no means a reformer.

19. Ehrenfried relates Schindler's hiring to the rising generation: "By 1874 a number of younger people had joined and brought with them an insistence upon alterations in conformity with the modern spirit, which by now was asserting itself across the nation." Ehrenfried, *Boston Jewry,* 388–89. For more on Schindler, see Mann, *Growth and Achievement,* 45–62.

20. For example, see Michael Meyer, "Christian Influence on Early German Reform Judaism," in *Studies in Jewish Bibliography History and Literature,* ed. Charles Berlin (New York: Ktav, 1971), 289–303; and on the American context, Lance Sussman, "Isaac Leeser and the Protestantization of American Judaism," *American Jewish Archives* 38:1 (1986). On the adoption of the term "temple," see Rachel Wischnitzer, *Synagogue Architecture in the United States: History and Interpretation* (Philadelphia: Jewish Publication Society of America, 1955), 48.

21. On the reforming of Ohabei Shalom, see Ehrenfried, *Boston Jewry,* 359–65. On Temple Israel, see Susan Abramson, "The Social History of the Changes within Temple Adath Israel" (unpublished manuscript, Temple Israel Library, 1973).

22. But not without heated controversy. See Broches, "A Chapter in the History of the Jews of Boston," 208–210. See also Jonathan D. Sarna, "The Debate Over Mixed Seating in the American Synagogue," in *The American Synagogue: A Sanctuary Transformed,* ed. Jack Wertheimer (New York: Cambridge University Press, 1987), 363–94.

23. As quoted in a listing of all Jewish organizations and institutions in Massachusetts prior to 1900 (American Jewish Historical Society), 310.

24. The dates of occupancy are derived from listings in the Boston City Directory, courtesy of Gerald Gamm.

25. Solomon Schindler, *Israelites in Boston* (1889), as quoted in Ehrenfried, *Boston Jewry,* 441, n. 5.

26. From an account in the *Hebrew Standard* as quoted in Ehrenfried, *Boston Jewry,* 440, n. 4. See also "Sermon Preached at the Orthodox Jewish Synagogue, Boston, Nissan 11. 5648 [1887–1888]," American Jewish Historical Society, Waltham, Massachusetts.

27. As quoted in Ehrenfried, *Boston Jewry,* 441.

28. "Congregation *Mishkan Israel Shaare Tefiloh,* Ash street, I. B. Reinherz, *chassan,* or reader. This is the third largest in the city, is composed of two congregations merged and has about 50 families. It owns the property which it occupies as a synagogue. . . it belongs to the orthodox wing of the sect." *Boston Hebrew Observer,* 3 January 1878.

29. *American Israelite* (1880), as reprinted in *Temple Mishkan Tefila: A History,* 14: "Rev. H. Phillips of New York, has been elected minister of the Congregation Shaaray Tefila, of this city, of which Mr. A. A. Marcus is the founder and President." In his 1932 memoir, Philip Cowen adds: "At his own expense [Marcus] purchased and maintained a synagogue—Shaarai Tefilah—and provided for daily service therein. He was very generous toward another orthodox synagogue in Boston, providing it with a Scroll of the Law and its appurtenances." Cowen, *Memories of an American Jew* (New York: International Press, 1932), 48.

30. *Boston Hebrew Observer,* 9 March 1883, 73.

31. *Boston Hebrew Observer,* 25 May 1883, 164.

32. *Boston Hebrew Observer,* 4 September 1885, 4.

33. *Jewish Messenger,* 7 December 1888, 5.

34. Carol H. Krinsky, *Synagogues of Europe: Architecture, History, Meaning* (New York: Architectural History Foundation, 1985), 78–79. Also see Rachel Wischnitzer, *Synagogue Architecture in the United States,* 42–57.

35. A term commonly employed in the sociology of religion. Marshall Sklare defines the ethnic church as "a fellowship whose members are differentiated from those belonging to other denominations by virtue of their special *descent* as well as by their doctrines or practices." Sklare, *Conservative Judaism: An American Religious Movement,* 2nd ed. (New York: University Press of America, 1985), 35.

36. New York architect Patrick C. Keeley was responsible for two important South End churches: the 1875 Cathedral of the Holy Cross on Washington Street and the 1860 Immaculate Conception Church on Harrison Avenue, commissioned by the Jesuit order. Louis Weissbein was hired by the Jesuits also, for the adjoining rectory building, the site of the founding of Boston College. All three structures stand today.

37. The "skyscraper" was the ten-storied Winthrop Building of 1893, still located at 276–278 Washington Street. Blackall's extant theater buildings include Tremont Temple (1896), the Colonial Theatre (1900), the Modern Theatre (1913), the Wilbur Theatre (1914), and the Metropolitan Theater (1925; now the Wang Center). Michael and Susan Southworth, *The Boston Society of Architects' A.I.A. Guide to Boston* (Chester, Conn.: Globe Pequot Press, 1984).

38. Regarding the architect's intentions, see Clarence H. Blackall, "The Symbolism of Temple Israel," as quoted in Obst, *Adath Israel,* 28–31.

39. For the full story of Fleischer's rabbinate and eventual "apostacy," see Mann, *Growth and Achievement,* 63–83.

40. Maurice Milonthaler, "The North End of Boston: Gateway to the Goldener Land" (Milonthaler papers, American Jewish Historical Society), 27–28. See also Arnold Wieder, *The Early Jewish Community of Boston's North End* (Waltham: Brandeis University, 1962). Reinherz was also associated briefly with Mishkan Israel Shaare Tefiloh. Responding to the 1875 letter of Rabbi Vidaver (see above n. 16), he defended Orthodoxy and insisted that "no good American ridicules the customs and prayers of his ancestors." As quoted in Ehrenfried, *Boston Jewry,* 431.

41. S. N. Behrman ironically relates that the Ramaz left America because he found it too modern and secular, yet upon returning to Lithuania he was rejected for being an "American" rabbi. Behrman, *The Worcester Account* (New York: Random House, 1954), 138.

42. Listing of all Jewish organizations and institutions in Massachusetts prior to 1900 (American Jewish Historical Society), 2.

43. Designed, it is believed, by Asher Benjamin in 1806, the historic structure is the oldest standing African-American church in America. Together with its neighboring schoolhouse on Joy Street, it is now the Museum of Afro-

American History. On the building's former use as a synagogue, see Lee M. Friedman, "A Beacon Hill Synagogue," in *Old Time New England* 33:1 (1942).

44. This is a reversal of the more familiar pattern of synagogues converted into African-American churches. Anshe Libawitz is not alone in this respect. B'nai Jeshurun, the second Jewish congregation of New York City, dedicated a former African-American church as its synagogue in 1826.

45. Friedman, "A Beacon Hill Synagogue," 1.

46. For a description of the procession and dedication ceremonies, see the *Boston Advocate*, 14 September 1906, 3.

47. Harry Cushing, "A History of the Religious Institutions of Greater Boston," *Jewish Advocate—Fiftieth Anniversary Issue*, 26 June 1952, sec. 3, 4. For examples of other churches converted into synagogues in the Boston area in the early 20th century, see Albert Ehrenfried, "A Chapter in the Evolution of the Boston Synagogue," in *Jewish Advocate*, 30 September 1943.

48. *Jewish Advocate*, 28 May 1909, 1.

49. In a journal entry of November 1915, Mordecai Kaplan described a visit to Mishkan Tefila and criticized the decision to employ the organ as misguided and ineffective. See Kaplan, private journal, vol. 1, 204–05, Rare Book Room of the Jewish Theological Seminary of America; cf., Rabbi Herman H. Rubenovitz and Mignon L. Rubenovitz, *The Waking Heart* (Cambridge: Nathaniel Dame., 1967), 34. Rubenovitz disagreed with Kaplan, having witnessed the effective use of organ music in synagogue ritual on a trip to Europe.

50. Ehrenfried, *Boston Jewry*, 446, notes the significance of the synagogue's demise: "Shaari Jerusalem . . . was the last synagogue to disappear from this once teeming area. The demolition of its formerly notable building in 1945 wrote the finis for North End Jewry."

51. Louis M. Epstein, "The Crawford Street Synagogue," in *Tenth Anniversary Souvenir Book—Crawford Street Synagogue* (Boston: By the Congregation, 1923), 10–11.

52. See the essay by Gerald Gamm in this volume for further discussion of this phenomenon, and Ehrenfried, "A Chapter in the Evolution of the Boston Synagogue" for a partial list of such synagogues.

53. Isaac M. Fein, *Boston—Where It All Began: An Historical Perspective of the Boston Jewish Community* (Boston Jewish Bicenteniial Committee, 1976), 52. In the Boston area, a Conservative congregation is just as likely to be named "Temple" as a Reform congregation. Thus, in the early 1920's, the summer residents of Nantasket Beach named their traditional synagogue, "Temple Israel," and in the 1930's, two new Conservative congregations of the Boston suburbs were named "Temple Emanuel," in apparent imitation of the leading Reform temple of New York.

54. Thelma Fleishman, *Agudas Achim Anshei Sfard: The Adams Street Synagogue, Newton, Massachusetts* (Newton: The Jackson Homestead, 1986), 44–45. The full story of Sam Katz is being further researched by this author. At last count, there are over twenty extant Katz arks in the Boston area.

55. Cushing, "A History of the Religious Institutions."

56. Sam B. Warner, Jr., *Streetcar Suburbs: The Process of Growth in Boston, 1870–1900* (Cambridge: Harvard University Press, 1962).

57. Evidence of the relationship between the congregations abounds. For example, David Krokyn, a founder (in 1887) and the first vice-president of Beth Israel (which moved to Baldwin Place in 1889), was also one of the builders of the Blue Hill Avenue Shul; the cantor at the Baldwin Place Shul, Morton Halpern, was "imported" from the North End to Roxbury; and in 1923, the two congregations were officially merged, the child absorbing the parent (repeating the same process that had occurred in the North End when Beth Israel absorbed Shomrei Beth Abraham).

58. *Boston Morning Journal*, 14 September 1906: "The edifice which now adorns that part of Roxbury is probably the finest structure of its kind in New England. There are only 140 members in this congregation and only 100 who are in a position to contribute anything substantial toward the cost of building the synagogue . . . owing to the small number in the congregation the achievement of building this magnificent edifice reflects very credibly on the efforts of the people in the little congregation."

59. Obituary of J. Frederick Krokyn (1881-1960), *Jewish Advocate*, 8 December 1960, 15-A. The attribution of Adath Jeshurun's design to Krokyn is made by Aaron Pinkney, "Pioneer Congregations of the North End," *Jewish Advocate*, 14 April 1949, 10-B.

60. One honored guest attending the ceremony was the mayor of Boston, John "Honey Fitz" Fitzgerald (grandfather of John F. Kennedy). The colorful Irish politician noted in his speech that he too was a from the North End.

61. *Boston Advocate*, 21 September 1906.

62. Similarly, Shaarai Torah of Worcester, Massachusetts, also built a synagogue after the design of Kehilath Jeshurun in the same year the Blue Hill Avenue Shul was built. Behrman, *The Worcester Account*, 106; Norma Feingold, *Shaarai Torah: Life Cycle of a Synagogue* (Worcester Historical Museum, 1991), 24.

63. Richard Heath, "The House of the Flock of the Righteous: The Song of Adath Jeshurun" (unpublished manuscript, American Jewish Historical Society), 4.

64. Phineas Israeli graduated from the Jewish Theological Seminary in 1902 in the same class as Mordecai M. Kaplan, whose sister Sophie he married. For Israeli's involvement in a controversy concerning the seating of a uniformed sailor during 1908 that eventually involved the President of the United States, see the *Boston Advocate*, 2–23 October 1908; and Esther Panitz, *Simon Wolf* (Rutherford N.J.: Fairleigh Dickinson University Press, 1987), 95–96.

65. On Israeli's address see *Temple Mishkan Tefila*, 14, and the *Jewish Advocate*, 30 December 1910, 1. On Kaplan see Mel Scult, *Judaism Faces the Twentieth Century: A Biography of Mordecai M. Kaplan* (Detroit: Wayne State University Press, 1993).

66. Kaplan, private journal, vol. 1, 127 (29 December 1914).

67. *WPA Historical Records Survey-Federal Writer's Project,* Jewish Congregations of Massachusetts, 1942.

68. David Kaufman, *"Shul with a Pool": The Synagogue-Center in American Jewish Life, 1875–1925* (Ph.D. diss., Brandeis University, 1993).

69. *American Jewish Yearbook 5671* (Philadelphia: The Jewish Publication Society of America, 1910) 258. See also *Jewish Advocate,* 6 October 1911, 5.

70. *Boston Advocate,* 1 January 1909, 5; 8 January 1909, 5.

71. *Boston Advocate,* 8 January 1909, 8.

72. Even Mishkan Tefila considered locating in Brookline following World War I. Temple Israel was not in Brookline proper, but just over the border in Boston. Its selection of a site on the Riverway was clearly intended to serve the growing Jewish population of Brookline, a short walk or drive away.

73. D. Margolis, "Purposes of Kehillath Israel" (unpublished manuscript, Kehillath Israel archives.)

74. As late as 1942 Kehillath Israel could still claim: "Some people call us Progressive Orthodox; others call us Right Wing Conservative. We should like to rise above appelations [sic] and confine ourselves within no party lines but to be humble and worthy servants of *Klal Yisroel.*" *Congregation Kehillath Israel—Jubilee Banquet,* 20 December 1942, Kehillath Israel archives.

75. *Tenth Anniversary Souvenir Book—Crawford Street Synagogue,* 12.

76. Jacob Krokyn had earlier designed the 1906 building of Adath Jeshurun on Blue Hill Avenue, and his firm would later design synagogue-centers for Mishkan Tefila in 1925 and B'nai Moshe in 1954, as well as the "community house" additions for Kehillath Israel in 1947 and for Temple Emanuel in 1952.

77. "Kehillath Israel — 380 Harvard Street," Kehillath Israel archives.

78. In 1934, K.I. was described as follows: "As an institution, Kehillath Israel is the religious center for nearly a thousand families that comprise the membership in the Congregation, the Brotherhood and the Sisterhood. To them there is a ceaseless flow of religious inspiration, education and activity out of their sanctuary on Harvard Street by means of the daily, Sabbath and Holy Day services, the daily Hebrew School, the lectures and courses and classes, the Brotherhood's and Sisterhood's rich activities and interesting meetings. But it is not only an institution for members; it is a community institution in the full sense of the word. . . . Whether it is of any material benefit to the institution or not, it is always a source of pride to us to see our synagogue thronged day after day with hundreds and thousands of men and women and children; every one finding some spiritual service there." "Kehillath Israel—An Institution and an Ideal," published on the 10th anniversary of the synagogue building, 1934. Kehillath Israel archives.

79. Morris Bronstein, chairman of the committee, later recalled: "We visited nearly every modern temple in New York City, Brooklyn and New Jersey. From there we gained wonderful ideas of designs in architecture which have been of help to us in our plans." *Jewish Advocate,* 12 March 1923.

80. *Jewish Advocate,* 12 March 1923.

81. Prior to the 1922 groundbreaking, Mishkan Tefila's press releases acknowledged its pathbreaking vision, describing the architecture of "The Jewish Temple and Community Center" as "American Renaissance."

82. *Jewish Advocate,* 12 March 1923.

83. *Jewish Advocate,* 12 March 1923.

84. Herman H. Rubenovitz, "My Rabbinate at Temple Mishkan Tefila: A History from 1910 to 1946," in *Temple Mishkan Tefila,* 24.

85. *Brotherhood T.O.S. Banquet and Hall Program,* 4 April 1922, Ohabei Shalom archives. President F. Wingersky added the following: "Our Brotherhood must continue to play its important part in the building of the New Temple. Majestically our new edifice will stand, a monument for all time, and a sacred memory to the men and women whose time and money made the project possible. The erection of this Temple is a public answer to the arguments that the Jew is a rank materialist, a Godless people."

86. "The Temple Center and The Temple," ca. 1925, Ohabei Shalom archives.

87. Wischnitzer, *Synagogue Architecture,* 106–117. Temple Emanu-El of Providence was designed by Krokyn, Browne, & Rosenstein. The Temple (Tifereth Israel) of Cleveland was designed by Charles Greco, who served as consulting architect for Ohabei Shalom.

88. "The Temple Center and The Temple."

89. Obst, *Adath Israel,* 27.

90. Message of President Felix Vorenberg to the 69th Annual Meeting of Congregation Adath Israel, 8 April 1923, Temple Israel archives.

91. McLaughlin & Burr offered the advantage of using leftover building materials from the Harvard Medical School site. The Temple Israel Meeting House and School building are thus constructed from the same Indiana limestone as their neighbor.

92. Press release describing "Temple Israel," 31 January 1926, Temple Israel archives.

93. Mann, *Growth and Achievement,* 97.

94. As quoted in Albert Gordon, *Jews in Suburbia* (Boston: Beacon Press, 1959), 108.

95. Concerning the move of Mishkan Tefila from Roxbury to Chestnut Hill, see Paula Hyman, "From City to Suburb: Temple Mishkan Tefila of Boston," in *The American Synagogue,* ed. Jack Wertheimer (New York: Cambridge University Press, 1987), 185–205; Hillel Levine and Lawrence Harmon, *The Death of an American Jewish Community: A Tragedy of Good Intentions* (New York: The Free Press, 1992), 58–65; see also Gerald Gamm's critique of

Levine and Harmon, "Exploding Myths Surrounding Exodus of Boston Jewry," in *Jewish Advocate* 27 March–2 April 1992, 11. On the 1957 construction, see articles by the rabbi, congregational president, architect, and contractor in *Temple Mishkan Tefila*, 31–63; and on the 1993 additions, Roslyn Singer, "Pieces of the Past Inspire Mishkan Tefila," *Jewish Advocate*, 28 May–3 June 1993.

96. Abram L. Sachar, "The Three Chapels," chap. 7 in *A Host at Last* (Boston: Little, Brown, 1976).

97. See Hanoch Teller, *The Bostoner* (New York: Feldheim Publishers, 1990) on the Bostoner Rebbe. Joseph Dov Soloveitchik (1903–1993) settled in Roxbury in 1932. Following the war, "the Rav" emerged as the preeminent Talmudic scholar in America and the "unchallenged leader of mainstream Orthodoxy." Obituary, *New York Times*, 10 April 1993. See also David Singer and Moshe Sokol, "Joseph Soloveitchik: Lonely Man of Faith," *Modern Judaism* 2:3 (October 1982), 227–72.

98. For a fuller treatment of this phenomenon see Samuel Heilman, *Synagogue Life: A Study in Symbolic Interaction* (Chicago: University of Chicago Press, 1976).

99. "History of the Young Israel of Brookline," in *Young Israel of Brookline—Dedication,* 14 June 1964. The Green Street structure was destroyed by fire in 1994. After an exhaustive search, the congregation hired the firm of Graham Gund to design a new synagogue complex on the same site.

100. On the Havurah movement see Riv-Ellen Prell, *Prayer & Community: The Havurah in American Judaism* (Detroit: Wayne State University Press, 1989).

101. As quoted in the *Jewish Catalog,* ed. Richard Siegel, Michael Strassfeld, and Sharon Strassfeld (Philadelphia: The Jewish Publication Society of America, 1973), 6. Michael Strassfeld grew up in Dorchester, the son of the rabbi of the Woodrow Avenue Shul.

102. *Guide to Jewish Boston and New England,* ed. Steven Feldman (Cambridge: Genesis 2, 1986), 59–62. The listed Havurot include Am Tikva, B'nai Or of Boston, Brookline Egalitarian Minyan, Minyan Shaleym, and the Newton Centre Shabbat Minyan.

103. The Boston Synagogue, formerly called the Charles River Park Synagogue, is the direct descendant of the two leading congregations of the West End. In 1888, Beth Jacob was established in a school building on Wall Street. Beth Hamidrash Hagodol was founded in 1904 and built its synagogue-center on North Russell Street in 1923. In 1941 the two formed a united congregation called Beth Hamidrash Hagodol Beth Jacob. On the history of the neighborhood, see *The Last Tenement: Confronting Community and Urban Renewal in Boston's West End,* ed. Sean Fisher and Carolyn Hughes (Boston: The Bostonian Society, 1992).

104. Barbara Kaplan, Hallie Pinta, Stanley M. Smith, and The Architectural Team, Michael Liu principal, *Study on the Feasibility of Preserving the Interior of the Vilna Shul* (Boston: Historic Boston Incorporated, 1989); Michael Sinert, "Group Buys Vilna Shul, Plans Cultural Center," *Jewish Advocate,* 28 January–3 February 1994.

# Community and Philanthropy

*Overleaf*: Passover Seder for new arrivals at the East Boston Immigration Building, 1921. *American Jewish Historical Society.*

SUSAN EBERT

# *Community and Philanthropy*

אין צדקה משתלמת אלא לפי חסד שבה
"Charity is only really fulfilled to the extent that it is motivated by lovingkindness."
TALMUD BAVLI SUKKAH 49b

OMMUNITY AND PHILANTHROPY are inextricably linked. From ancient through modern times, Jewish communities have forged their identities through philanthropy. The imperative to care for all of their members has helped Jewish communities establish structure, refining and reinventing systems of charitable enterprise until the forms of charity themselves become the framework of community.

A pioneering commitment to service and change characterize Boston's approach to philanthropy. Since its inception the Boston Jewish community has fulfilled the obligations of tradition while innovating its forms. Starting with the familiar forms, charitable institutions have been modified, shaped, and reshaped to respond to new circumstances and concerns, contemporary social thinking, and the collective American experience. The unifying factor over time has been a consistent responsiveness to the needs of the disadvantaged, the sick, the poor, and the weak.

There are many aspects to Jewish philanthropy and community in Boston. This essay focuses primarily on the organizations that eventually amalgamated into federated charities in Boston, and how their history reflects the problems and process of forging a community among Jewish Boston's disparate ethnic and social groups.

The Jewish impulse to charity is defined in terms of human value and dignity. The writers of the Talmud and early rabbinic texts taught that preserving the human spirit is as important as relieving immediate need. In Jewish tradition, the highest forms of charity are anonymous and constructive, intended not only to ameliorate problems, but also to promote self-sufficiency. Jews are enjoined to remember that *tzedakah*, the Hebrew word for charity, means righteousness and justice.

Until the middle of the 19th century there was no significant Jewish community in Boston. In its infancy it established the institutions that are the basis of communal life: a cemetery, synagogues, and then the first organizations that demonstrated at once its problems and its benevolence.

In its earliest years, Boston's tiny Jewish community provided for its indigent, its widows, orphans, and elderly in traditional ways. The Jews in Boston belonged primarily to three synagogues; each congregation took care of its own. Those in need called on the more prosperous to petition for assistance.

> *The self-sustaining and the poor members of every congregation under-stood their roles as givers and recipients in a static system of mutual benefits. The poor were an accepted part of a pattern in which the more fortunate members performed their* mitzvah, *an act of piety, by the execution of charitable duties.*[1]

The Jewish community grew quickly in the decades of the 1840's and 1850's. New arrivals created new needs and strained its capacities. On January 10, 1864, Nathan Strauss convened a meeting of "26 responsible men," all members of either Congregation Adath Israel (now Temple Israel) or Ohabei Shalom, and the United Hebrew Benevolent Society was established. The founders were manufacturers and retailers who had prospered during the Civil War. They turned to models developed by secular benevolent societies which appealed across the community for support.

By the end of its first year, the Benevolent Society had collected $800 from the 1,500 Jews who then lived in Boston, though in fact most of the support came from Adath Israel and Ohabei Shalom congregants. Those in need of aid applied to the president, who evaluated their circumstances and recommended action to the rest of the membership at monthly meetings. No records were kept.

Soon thereafter, the Benevolent adopted another Yankee custom and began to link social events and benevolence: its first charity ball was held on December 4, 1869, at Horticultural Hall and raised $2,000. The following year saw the first of its annual picnics, and 1875 inaugurated its tradition of annual banquets.

Even as the community became more Americanized in the 1870's, refugees continued to arrive, increasing the demands on charitable resources and injecting a new tension into the growing community. By now there was a clear distinction between the original "German" settlers and the new "Russians." Many new arrivals were helped by the Benevolent, but they also found assistance through lodges and *landsmanshaftn*, mutual assistance associations, that proliferated throughout the community.

Those safely past the threshold quickly evidenced broader concerns. The Young Men's Hebrew Association (YMHA), founded in 1875, staked a claim both to the intellectual improvement of the community and to the relief of the poor. Holding office hours each day from noon to 2:00 p.m., Board members received applications for assistance in rooms provided by the city. "This . . . association opened an Employment Bureau and found 'situations' for many jobless immigrants, issued peddlers licenses and stands and supplied food."[2]

FIG. 1. Lina Hecht, as illustrated in Solomon Schindler, *Israelites in Boston: A Tale Describing the Development of Judaism in Boston* (Boston: Beckwith & Smith, 1889).

Young men were not alone in serving struggling immigrants. Women established pioneering efforts to assist the new poor. In 1878, "Aunt Lina" Hecht, as she was affectionately known to two generations of young Boston Jewish women, revived the Hebrew Ladies Sewing Society, first organized in 1869. Newly defined as an auxiliary to the Benevolent, the Sewing Society distributed blankets and clothing to new arrivals. Combining its members' social and charitable impulses, the society held Chanukah parties for the poor and Calico Balls for the wealthy—which were attended by hundreds of young Bostonians.

Jacob and Lina Hecht set a model for Jewish philanthropy in Boston. Jacob, who emigrated to the United States in 1849 at the age of fourteen, had achieved success in a series of wholesale enterprises before he married the Baltimore-born Lina Frank and moved to Boston in 1867. Childless, the Hechts devoted themselves to their community.

Jacob Hecht led a group of young and progressive members of Congregation Adath Israel who brought Rabbi Solomon Schindler to the pulpit in 1873. Committed both to Reform Judaism and social innovation, Schindler was determined to address urban poverty with the most modern techniques. When he became president of the Benevolent in 1881, Hecht installed Schindler and Rabbi Raphael Lasker of Ohabei Shalom as its professional directors. Their tenure ushered in the beginnings of modern casework in the Jewish community. They maintained office hours at the Benevolent and received applications for assistance three afternoons a week. They divided the city into two districts, investigated each application for assistance, and kept records of the case history, payments, and final disposition.

Innovative as it was, even this system was overwhelmed by the massive emigration from Eastern Europe in the 1880's. Economic privation and government sanctioned pogroms in 1881, followed the next year by an edict from the Czar which barred them from the Pale of Settlement, forced thousands of Jews to leave. The pattern was to be repeated over and over again until the outbreak of the First World War. In three decades, two million Jews scraped and borrowed funds for passage, bundled their possessions, and made their way across Europe to the New World.

By the early 1880's, most Boston Jews were well established and comfortably Americanized. Many felt little kinship to the new East European refugees and even opposed their admission into the United States. In June of 1882, the British Mansion House Fund sent 415 "Russian" refugees at once and the Hebrew Emigrant Aid Society was overwhelmed.[4] Some returned to New York, but hundreds more were left without resources.

> In the cold winter of 1882–3 eighteen "Russian" families comprising 75 individuals who were refused help by Boston Jews declared that they were "disillusioned with the promised land and want to return to Russia." The Emigrant Aid Society could not expect a better decision. However, it lacked the necessary funds for transportation. With no choice left, the refugees appealed for help to the general charitable society, the Provident Association, which, in turn, placed them in the Commonwealth Alms House at Tewksbury. The Massachusetts Board of Charities, also pleased with the refugees' decision, undertook to send back to Russia all those who would be recommended by Jacob Hecht, President of the United Hebrew Benevolent Association. This was too much for the "Germans." The whole affair became a public scandal.[4]

Ultimately, the force of public opinion reawakened the community's dormant compassion. Hecht secured the agreement of the Provident Society that all Jewish immigrants applying for aid would be referred to the Benevolent, which would assume full responsibility for them. The Jews of Boston wanted none of their own on public charity.

The Benevolent became an official component of Boston's growing social service community, and in 1883 moved its offices to the municipal charity building on the corner of Chardon and Hawkins streets. Seizing this as the impetus for change, Rabbi Schindler proposed a planned and coordinated system as the only way to deal with the growing numbers of needy, and to avoid duplication and fraud. At the Benevolent's annual meeting on February 11, 1883, he proposed "a union. . . . of the Benevolent, the Ladies' Sewing Society, and the different lodges . . . If their alliance gives satisfaction, we have not the least doubt that the other societies will also join in the course of time."[5]

Schindler's proposal respected the autonomy of individual organizations and emphasized cooperative planning. At the same time, he recommended the addition of "one or two lady directors" to the Board of the Benevolent. It would take another twelve years and another crisis to persuade the community to adopt his idea. In the meantime, the pace of arrivals and problems quickened.

Over the years, both the Benevolent and the Ladies Sewing Society had collected funds to benefit those "who had grown old in our midst, who had not been successful, and who in their declining years had neither friend nor child to take care of them."[6] Despite these good intentions, their efforts produced no tangible outcome. Impatient at the pace, members of the growing "Russian" Jewish community organized as the Montefiore Society to raise funds for a home for the elderly.

FIG. 2. Leopold Morse Home for Aged and Infirm Hebrews and Orphanage, Milton, Massachusetts, 1889–1911. Photo, early 20th century. The thirty-two room mansion just outside Mattapan Square housed over sixty residents. *Combined Jewish Philanthropies.*

Leopold Morse, the community's first Jewish member of the United States House of Representatives, ended the impasse by donating funds to buy a large house near Mattapan Square for the use of both the elderly and the growing number of orphaned and abandoned Jewish children. The Leopold Morse Home for Aged and Infirm Hebrews and Orphanage opened in 1889 with a sixty-bed capacity. This improbable pairing met several communal needs, including bringing to an end the practice of placing Jewish children in non-Jewish foster homes. Additionally, it trained young orphans in a variety of trades, enabling them to be successful once they left the Home.

The reform-minded respected the practical benefits of vocational training, as both an early inculcation to the work ethic and a step to Americanization. Lina Hecht, aware of other contemporary models, engaged a dynamic young teacher named Golde Bamber in 1890 to organize the Hebrew Industrial School for girls in the North End. The school taught sewing and tailoring, millinery and cooking to hundreds of young immigrant girls. A parallel school for boys was opened in the West End in 1892.

At the end of five years, twelve hundred children had been taught to be "wage earners, breadwinners, and self-respecting intelligent citizens" at the Hebrew Industrial School. In addition, the school had stood by the motto, "a good Israelite

FIG. 3. "Program of Clubs and Class," "Pledge of the Soap and Water Club," and cover of the "Report for 1901–1902," Hebrew Industrial School, North End, Boston. Founded by Lina Hecht, the HIS was a pioneering Jewish settlement house teaching languages, job skills, and customs deemed necessary for adjustment to life in America. *American Jewish Historical Society.*

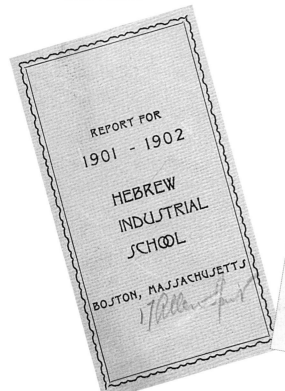

## Program of Clubs and Class.

### MONDAY
4 to 6 P. M. Dressmaking, Machine work, Three grades hand sewing, Once a month Home Improvement Club meeting and Exhibit.
6.30 to 8.30 Millinery.
7.30 to 9.00 Dressmaking.

### TUESDAY
4 to 6 Drafting, Cooking, Machine work, Three grades hand sewing.
7 to 9 P. M. Una Musa Club.
7.30 to 9.30 Drafting.

### WEDNESDAY
4 to 6 P. M. Underwear, Machine, Two grades hand sewing, Embroidery, Darning, Mending.
7 to 9 Underwear.
7.30 to 9.30 Jacob H. Hecht Club Lectures.

### THURSDAY
4 to 6 P. M. Dressmaking, Machine, Three grades hand sewing Cooking, Housekeeping.
7 to 9 Dressmaking, Orchestral Club, First Division Boot Blacks' League.

### FRIDAY
Library and Reading room open.

### SATURDAY
10.30 to 12 A. M. Sabbath School.
2 P. M. Good Manners Club, Soap and Water Club.
7.30 to 9.30 Jacob H. Hecht Club, Civics, Debates, etc.
7 to 9 Millinery, Embroidery.

### SUNDAY
10.30 A. M. Cooking Club (to open April)
2 P. M. Jacob H. Hecht Club Reading Room, Hecht Junior Workers, Civics, Debates, Entertainments.
7.30 to 9.30 Business meeting Jacob H. Hecht Club.

## One Week's Activities.

Promenade Concert and Dance given by THE JACOB H. HECHT CLUB.

Visit of a hundred children to the Sportsmen's Show, kindness of MR. B. HYNEMAN.

Talk on "Debate" by MR. MURRAY L. SEASONGOOD of Harvard University.

Talk on "Food Supplies" by MRS. LEWIS KEIFFER.

Sermon to pupils by RABBI CHARLES FLEISCHER.

REPORT FOR 1901 - 1902 HEBREW INDUSTRIAL SCHOOL BOSTON, MASSACHUSETTS

### HEBREW INDUSTRIAL SCHOOL, 17 ALLEN STREET.

LINA F. HECHT, Founder.

JACOB H. HECHT, Treasurer.

## PLEDGE OF THE Soap and Water Club.

*I hereby pledge myself to try my best to keep the following rules:*

1. To take a bath once a week.
2. To wash my head once in two weeks.
3. To keep my hair neatly combed always.
4. To have my head and hair carefully examined, once a week, by mother or older sister.
5. To wash my face, neck, ears, hands and arms every morning.
6. To brush my teeth at least once a day.
7. To wear an apron whenever possible.
8. To keep my dress free from spots.
9. To have a place for everything and everything in its place.
10. To look and behave so that I may set a good example to my little brothers and sisters and in so doing please my parents and teachers, and above all, my Heavenly Father.

Signed,........................................

GOLDE BAMBER, Supt.

will make a better citizen," by encouraging Jewish education and by respecting the hygienic and dietary laws of the Orthodox members.[7] Golde Bamber remained a singular force in Boston, ultimately heading the Hecht Neighborhood House and implementing innovative programs throughout her career. The first Boston Jewish nursery schools were established at her impetus in the 1920's.

Women continued to play a generative role in the emerging social service system. The history of the Benoth Israel (Daughters of Israel) Sheltering Home illuminates both the influence of women and the realities of the social structure of the period. It began as a group of North End mothers who, after years of sheltering immigrants in their own homes, began to collect funds for a permanent institution. When it incorporated in 1891, the Benoth Israel Home had a male president in Louis Mazor, and a ladies Board of Directors chaired by Mrs. Etta Shalitz. When the forty-bed facility opened in 1896, men had taken over its control.[8]

The Sheltering Home evoked extraordinary loyalty from those it served. Recent immigrants, once settled, became members and contributors, encouraging newer arrivals by example and deed. More religiously oriented than any of the other established institutions, in 1891 it organized the Charitable Burial Association to assure ritually correct funerals for the poor or for strangers.

In Europe the last decade of the century was marked by renewed antisemitic violence that brought new waves of refugees to the United States and sparked new efforts to assist them. A National Conference of American Jewish Organizations held in New York in 1891 established the American Committee for Ameliorating the Condition of the Russian Refugees. The Boston branch of that committee met in 1892, and with the support of the Baron De Hirsch Society opened a Free Employment Bureau under the direction of Jacob Hecht, A. C. Ratshesky and Abraham P. Spitz. In its first office at 100 Chauncy Street, the Free Employment Bureau installed a long distance telephone line to receive work orders from all parts of New England. The agency handled the employment requests of 6,500 applicants between 1892 and 1895.

There were times of genuine crisis: unprecedented immigration combined with a severe economic depression throughout the nation. As businesses failed, the tide of the needy increased. The Benevolent's Annual Report for 1894 listed extraordinary expenditures of $10,464.58 for cash, groceries, coal, dispensary, and other

FIG. 4. Benoth Israel Sheltering Home, 15 Cooper Street, North End, Boston. The approximately fifty-bed facility gave "temporary shelter to deserving Israelites, aiding them in obtaining employment, and instructing them in the customs and usages of this country, thereby enabling them to become worthy citizens." (Benoth Israel Sheltering Home Charter). *Combined Jewish Philanthropies.*

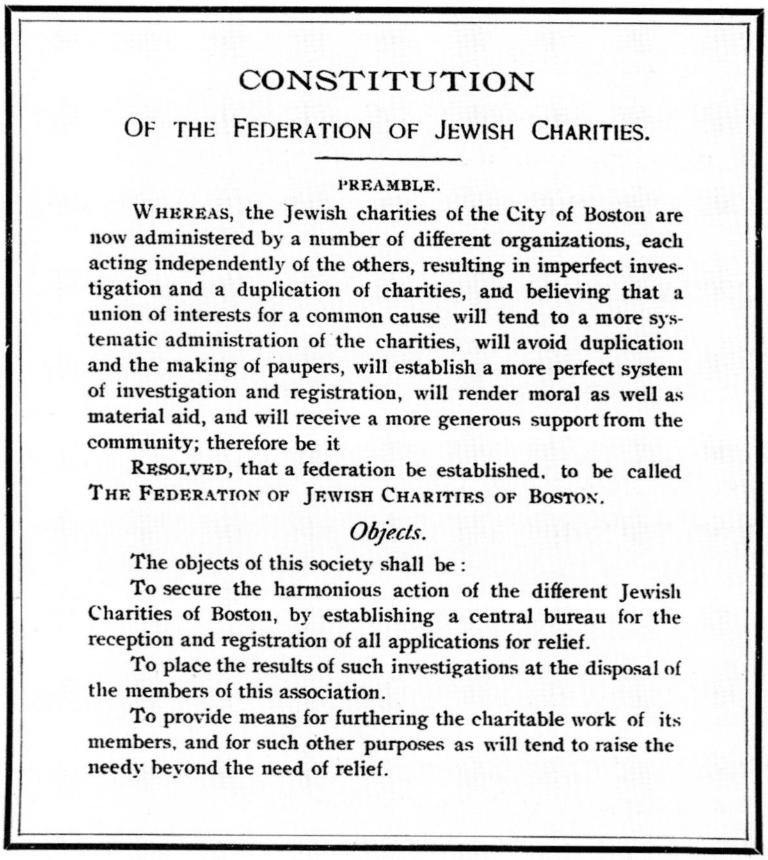

**CONSTITUTION**

OF THE FEDERATION OF JEWISH CHARITIES.

PREAMBLE.

WHEREAS, the Jewish charities of the City of Boston are now administered by a number of different organizations, each acting independently of the others, resulting in imperfect investigation and a duplication of charities, and believing that a union of interests for a common cause will tend to a more systematic administration of the charities, will avoid duplication and the making of paupers, will establish a more perfect system of investigation and registration, will render moral as well as material aid, and will receive a more generous support from the community; therefore be it

RESOLVED, that a federation be established, to be called THE FEDERATION OF JEWISH CHARITIES OF BOSTON.

*Objects.*

The objects of this society shall be :

To secure the harmonious action of the different Jewish Charities of Boston, by establishing a central bureau for the reception and registration of all applications for relief.

To place the results of such investigations at the disposal of the members of this association.

To provide means for furthering the charitable work of its members, and for such other purposes as will tend to raise the needy beyond the need of relief.

FIG. 5. Federation of Jewish Charities Constitution, 1895. *Combined Jewish Philanthropies.*

costs in aid of "1150 families, composed of 2145 adults and 3135 children."[9]

An example of the plight of just one of these immigrant families is found in the case of the family of Jael Aber. Residing with his wife and family in a tenement at 139 Leverett Street in the West End, his case fell to the sixth district case workers of the United Hebrew Benevolent Society. The case was opened on March 8, 1898. The family was recorded as consisting of Jael Aber, aged 52 yrs.; his wife Hannah, age 50 yrs.; and their children Samuel (married and living on Brighton Place); Mrs. Fannie Goldstein (another UHBA case); Morris 14 yrs.; Dora 12 yrs.; Jacob 8 yrs.; Laura 19 yrs.; and Ida 18 yrs. Jael was listed as a "smith" who had been in Boston for four years.

The case worker followed the family for two weeks.

*"Mar 8/98—They ask for aid saying that Morris who was the chief support of the family, & who earned 6.50 per week, is now out of work. Husband is consumptive & not able to leave his bed. Mr. Schindler will investigate case.*

*"Mar 9/98—Mr. Schindler calls & finds misery—some aid given.*

*"Mar 12/98—There are two grown up daughters who work & another son who is engaged to be married; but it is claimed that these children do not help the parents at all. Woman who came with Mrs. Aber is landlady of house & she wanted to be assured of her rent in the future.*

*"Mar 17/98 sent case to Mr. Danziger for further investigation.*

*March 21/98—Man died last Sunday, March 20th."*[10]

By 1895, the city's Jewish population was estimated at 20,000, including 14,000 new immigrants. Demands on the Benevolent's resources far exceeded its income. Decisive action was needed. On April 25, 1895, five organizations, the United Hebrew Benevolent Society, the Hebrew Ladies Sewing Society, the Leopold

Morse Home for the Aged and Infirm Hebrews and Orphanage, the Free Employment Bureau, and the Charitable Burial Association signed the agreement that created the Federation of Jewish Charities of Boston, the first federated charity in the United States. Jacob Hecht was elected president, and Rabbi Solomon Schindler retired from his pulpit at Temple Israel to become the Federation's first professional director.

Circumstances had forced organizational interdependence; personal connections closely tied the leadership. There was one inherent weakness: with few exceptions, the Federation represented German Jewish Boston and its leaders traced their roots to the earliest Jewish settlers. To thrive, it would need to embrace all of the growing Jewish community. But it would take the passage of decades and the organization's near disintegration before this was accomplished.

By the mid-1890's, the Jewish community was both substantial and diverse. From baseball teams to burial societies, over 400 . . . groups flourished in Jewish Boston before 1900 . . ."[10] Social and intellectual clubs, young men's and young women's groups, exclusive bachelor's and debutante societies, and early Zionist organizations all flourished, but not at the expense of charitable concerns.

Country Week, a camping program, had been organized, as had the Roxbury Ladies Aid and Fuel Society. The Ladies Helping Hand Society to aid destitute Jewish children was formed by more recent arrivals, as well as numerous settlement houses, among them the Louisa May Alcott Club funded by Godfrey M. Hyams and directed by his sisters Isabel and Sarah. All of these independent organizations underscored the vigor of the community, but also its persistent divisions along ethnic lines and the consequent weakness of the Federation.

Throughout the peak years of immigration before 1914, Boston remained a choice destination. Forty thousand Jews lived in the city in 1902; by 1907, in the aftermath of the Kishinev pogroms, the Jewish population had increased to 60,000. There were more synagogues, more *landsmanshaftn,* and more lodges. Distinctions between old and new prevailed, though by now many of the once new had been supplanted by the newer still.

FIG. 6. Photograph of Kishinev, Russia shortly after the pogrom of April 6–7, 1903. *American Jewish Historical Society.*

The Federation of Jewish Charities, still a membership organization, had secured the support of only 700 people among this now enormous population. Coordinated fundraising had been one of its original mandates, yet its most ambitious efforts failed to raise enough money to meet the requirements of its constituent agencies. The agencies continued to seek members, sponsor their own fundraising activities and hold independent events.

Moreover, the environment they confronted had changed. America was becoming increasingly complex, its problems deeper and more difficult to resolve. Growing numbers of children required temporary care while their parents struggled to achieve economic security. Increasing numbers of refugees, despairing of ever succeeding, deserted their families. Other families arrived to rejoin long-absent husbands and fathers only to discover that the husbands had made new attachments in the New World. Family, as well as community stability, underwent disruption.

Health care for the poor had become a dominant community concern. One of the earliest initiatives was The Ladies Bikur Cholim Society, which evolved in the 1880's to serve the sick. Between 1892 and 1899, the Benevolent sponsored a Jewish Dispensary for Women and Children in the North End, which offered free care and free medicines, and the Baron de Hirsch Dispensary provided care for men across the street.

FIG. 7. Mount Sinai Hospital, 130 Chambers Street, West End, Boston, 1902–1903. In five storefront rooms, Boston's only Jewish hospital provided virtually free out-patient treatment to over 5,000 Jewish and non-Jewish immigrants in its first year. *Beth Israel Hospital Archives, Boston.*

Refugees in need of in-patient care struggled to make their needs known in Boston's hospitals, where Jewish doctors were often not allowed to practice as house staff, where no staff spoke Yiddish, and where no kosher food was available to patients and no provisions were made for Sabbath observance or other Jewish rituals. Under these conditions, immigrants only reluctantly sought medical attention at Boston's hospitals, and those admitted did less well than the general patient population.[12] Several other cities with sizeable Jewish populations had already established Jewish hospitals, but Boston's Jewish community leaders rebuffed such proposals. Boston's first Jewish hospital was still decades away.

At the turn of the century, Jewish physicians took the initiative in organizing health care delivery for refugees. Their efforts culminated in the opening of two Mt. Sinai Hospital Association dispensaries in 1902 in the North and South Ends. Both offered only outpatient services, but these were generally free. Importantly, both provided information on health care and prescriptions in Yiddish and English.

The traditional Jewish concern for education and learning had been demonstrated through synagogue schools and then in the Hebrew Industrial School. In 1897, several prominent Boston women established The Boston Council for Jewish Women, a division of the National Council of Jewish Women, and made Jewish education a priority.[13] The Council established Bible study groups and then formal religious schools throughout the city.

New and old Jewish Boston were now meeting on more fronts and the sharp distinctions between the two were slowly beginning to erode. Mindful of the need to conserve and concentrate their resources, a number of groups briefly coalesced in 1906 to form the Federation of Jewish Organizations of Massachusetts. This movement paved the way to a broader-based federation, which incorporated on January 8, 1908, as the Federated Jewish Charities. To the five original members, there were now added the Helping Hand for Destitute Jewish Children, the Mt. Sinai Dispensary and the Hebrew Immigrant Aid Society.

The new member organizations shared a single important bond; they had been established by East European immigrants. But the inclusion of two orphanages in an eight-agency organization only emphasized the distinctions that remained in the community. The Federation was the creation of the original Central European settlers; the sense that Federation power remained in the hands of a select few was intensified by the practice of holding Board meetings at the exclusive Elysium Club, noted to have nearly the same membership as the Federation Board itself, as well as the Boards of Temple Israel and Ohabei Shalom.

The issue of the two orphanages framed the dilemma. The Federation had been an early advocate of foster care, but now this policy was overwhelmed by the need to balance the concerns of these two

FIG. 8. Mount Sinai Hospital, 17 Staniford Street, West End, Boston, 1903–1916. General Waiting Room, ca. 1905. In its relocated, rented four-story quarters, Mount Sinai Hospital provided "care and treatment of that portion of the sick poor, which through ignorance of the language and institutions of this country, can be more effectively treated by our organization than any other." (Mount Sinai Hospital Association Charter). *Beth Israel Hospital Archives, Boston.*

FIG. 9. Chelsea Fire as seen from Klaxine Hill, April 12, 1908. *Boston Public Library, Print Department.*

FIG. 10. The Federated Jewish Charities helped coordinate regional relief efforts for all victims of the great Chelsea Fire of 1908. Boston's West End served as a central collection and distribution point for food and clothing. *Boston Public Library, Print Department.*

constituents. The younger institution, the Home for Jewish Children, benefitted from its energetic Helping Hand Auxiliary which raised funds to build a new facility that opened on Canterbury Street in 1911. Scant weeks later, the Home for Jewish Children, and the Leopold Morse Home, which no longer served the elderly, merged.

The consolidation eliminated an obvious redundancy but reinforced the model of residential care and thus delayed the implementation of the more modern foster care service model, which in most communities was fast replacing the orphanage as a response to the needs of poor or abandoned children. The merger committed the Jewish community to the orphanage system, and "because of the judicious act of amalgamation, the Federated's child-placing program would for another two decades remain a minor experiment."[14]

It took the disaster of the Chelsea Fire on April 12, 1908, to demonstrate that the Federation could unify a community in crisis. Just a week before Passover, a destructive fire raced through Chelsea, burning 360 acres of land, destroying $12 million worth of property, and leaving 15,000 people homeless, among them 5,000 Orthodox Jews. Jewish groups from every part of the community came to the aid of the victims. The Federation coordinated relief efforts and itself provided the major funds and material aid, going into significant debt to provide necessary relief to the victims of the fire. Temporary housing was established all over the city, and Passover *seders* were provided for all those in need. It was the first time that the Federation had provided services outside of Boston.[15]

The Chelsea fire brought Boston's Jewish community together as never before in common cause and increased appreciation for the value of coordinating charitable services. But the financial aftermath of the fire was overwhelming. Relief efforts had

FIG. 11. Displaced Chelsea Fire victims receiving Passover supplies distributed by the Young Men's Hebrew Association, April 1908. *Boston Public Library, Print Department.*

left the Federation virtually bankrupt. Its members considered disbanding, but finally taxed themselves to make up a $15,000 deficit. New pressure was applied to old contributors and fundraising strategies were revised, including an innovative scheme to organize fundraising teams for trades and professions. Still, the Federation was unable to raise the $100,000 that it needed to support its agencies.

The underlying problem had been imposed by history. Boston's Jewish community was one of the youngest in America, and while many of

FIG. 12. East Boston Ladies' Auxiliary Members in Support of Beth Israel Hospital, ca. 1915. "To the great credit of Jewish women, it must here be admitted that it was they who were the first to realize the urgent need of the Hospital for the Jewish poor of this city." (*Annual Report*, Beth Israel Hospital Association, 1918– 1919.) *American Jewish Historical Society.*

its members had prospered, its underlying financial basis was neither as deep nor established as that of other Jewish communities of similar size.

In other ways, however, Boston's Jewish community was more like its urban counterparts and continued to emulate models it found in the mainstream. Community priorities and practice began to change in response to early 20th-century social thinking. Social work was by now an established profession, with the first formal training schools founded in several United States cities in the early years of the century. Child and family welfare and medical care were the pressing issues.

Into this new situation stepped Martha Michaels Silverman, who in 1911 replaced Max Mitchell to become the first (and only) woman professional to lead the Federation. Like her predecessors, she served also as the superintendent of the Benevolent. In her five-year term, she brought the principles of modern social work to both organizations and defined the Benevolent as the Federation's family service agency. She favored cash allocations over the provision of groceries and insisted that clients accepted by the agency be potentially self-sufficient and not candidates for perpetual support.

The growing professionalization of Federation agencies did not diminish the role of volunteers, who continued to broaden the spectrum of services to the poor. Alert to the possibilities of breaking the cycle of immigrant poverty, volunteers encouraged teaching the use of electric sewing machines to women at the Industrial School, enabling them to join the ranks of skilled and better paid workers. They recognized the need for recreation and sponsored summer kindergartens and outings for mothers and children.

Still, the problems spawned by modern society continued to outstrip the capacity of existing services, and volunteer leaders took the lead in trying to address them. Caring for the sick and the elderly remained prime concerns, as did young delinquent Jews, Jews in prison, unwed mothers, and abused or retarded children. The Boston Council of Jewish Women, led by Mrs. Edward S. Goulston, established a prison aid committee which in 1913 became the Jewish Prisoner's Aid Society. The Roxbury Ladies Bikur Cholim Society evolved over several decades into the Jewish

Memorial Hospital. The Hebrew Ladies Moshav Zekainim Association opened a Home for the Aged which served the community until 1957.

Grass-roots efforts by volunteer women also solved the Jewish hospital problem in Boston. Beginning in 1909,

> *"a group of mothers in the poorer section of the South End and the adjoining section of Roxbury, gathering spontaneously in the Three and Nine Cent store of Hyman Danzig, discussed the need* [for a Jewish hospital] *.... Late in 1909, their committee, through a novel fund-raising scheme, sold miniature bricks at fifty cents a piece to pay for the building of an entire hospital ... They made the most of nickels, dimes and quarters. By September, 1911, the little group of women had grown into a fund-raising society known as the Beth Israel Hospital Association."*[16]

In 1912, the North End Bikur Cholim Society joined the Association, and with leaders and financial support from the doctors and supporters of the Mt. Sinai Dispensary, $8,000 was finally raised. The Association, incorporated in 1915, purchased the old Dennison estate on Townsend Street in Roxbury, and on February 4, 1917, the first patient was admitted to the forty-five bed Beth Israel Hospital.[17]

This period also saw the formation of other organizations which would in time become Federation constituents. The Moeth Chittim Society assumed responsibility for Passover distributions to the poor. The Hebrew Free Loan Society, underwritten by personal contributions of $25,000 each from Nathan Pinanski, Albert Ginzberg, Oscar Grosberg, and Lassor Agoos, made 192 interest-free loans in 1912, the year of its inception.

The "Y" movement for both men and women was revitalized in the second decade of the 20th century. Boston delegates were active in the formation of the national council of "Y's", itself the predecessor of the National Jewish Welfare Board. Jewish education became the concern of the Central Jewish Organization which established schools and standard curricula and organized High Holy Day services for young adults.

Despite the apparent energy of the community and the increasing resources of many of its members, the financial problems of the Federation continued. In 1914, Federation president, Abraham C. Ratshesky constituted a Welfare Committee to assess the needs

FIG. 13. Beth Israel Hospital, 45 Townsend Street, Roxbury, 1916–1928. Boston's first in-patient Jewish Hospital, Beth Israel opened in a converted house with forty-five patient beds, and an allied Training School for Nurses. Since 1929, the site has been occupied by Boston's Jewish Memorial Hospital. *Beth Israel Hospital Archives, Boston.*

## To the Jews of Boston:

THE DISTRICT SERVICE comprises five welfare centres or neighborhood houses in the South End, Roxbury, Dorchester, West End and East Boston (the latter two now being established).

They serve as agencies for affording material relief to needy families; as bureaus of information and advice; and as meeting places and centres for neighborhood welfare movements and activities.

On the one hand, the District Service is a merger of nearly all Jewish organizations serving families in their homes. On the other, it is a democratic movement to encourage self-help and self-expression on the part of the people of each neighborhood.

Expenditures on behalf of needy families during the
  past seven months, 1918 ...................... $35,449.45
  Same period, 1917 ............................ 18,762.70

    Increase 1918 over 1917 ................... $16,686.75

This approximate doubling of relief expenditures is due not only to the increased cost of living but to improved standards of relief.

Yet the money granted to the needy was not nearly so helpful as the personal service rendered them by the workers—restoring them to health, giving them renewed hope and making many of them self-supporting.

### FEDERATED JEWISH CHARITIES

MORRIS D WALDMAN,
Executive Director

A. C. RATSHESKY,
President

FIG. 14. "To the Jews of Boston," *Boston Jewish Advocate*, September 11, 1918.

and the capabilities of the Federation. The Committee returned with a report that shaped the modern Federation. Deeming the Mount Sinai Dispensary inadequate, it called for its closing. Additionally, the report recommended a more centralized structure, hiring trained professional leadership, and employing social workers to deal with clients. The Federation Board ratified the report in March 1916 and promptly began its implementation.

The full restructuring, as well as most other local events, were overshadowed by the war. The outbreak of hostilities in Europe brought immigration to a standstill. Concern for those Jews who remained in Europe was expressed through the American Jewish Joint Distribution Committee which combined the efforts of the diverse religious and labor groups to aid ravaged communities.

At the same time, the anti-immigration forces which had been gathering strength over decades were on their way to a different victory. The passage of restrictive legislation in 1924 effectively ended the immense waves of immigration that had changed and shaped America in the second half of the 19th century.

Other dreams, however, won realization during the war years. The passage of the Balfour Declaration in England in 1917 fueled Zionist fervor everywhere, particularly in Boston, a stronghold of Zionist activity. The new Keren Hayesod now supplemented the fundraising efforts of the Jewish National Fund.

Reorganized and renamed the Federated Jewish Charities of Boston, Federation now had to face the challenge of reinvigorating its campaign. During the war, Americans had rallied to buy bonds. Louis Kirstein, an executive at William Filene and Sons Department Store, proposed to raise funds for the Federation by adopting Liberty Bond methods. His plan to divide the city into districts and create new committee structures met with astonishing success—the 1917 annual campaign shot up in one year from $70,000 to $250,000.

A radical redesign of social services by Morris Waldman, the new executive director, established "District Service" and created five centers in distinctively Jewish neighborhoods which provided both recreational and public welfare services. Each was headed by an experienced professional social worker, and each drew on the resources of many agencies to serve the entire community. The multi-service concept behind District Service combined the functions of community and social service centers. Outside groups—everything from art classes to Zionist clubs—met at District Service.

Jewish education remained an abiding concern, and the years after the war saw the establishment of cooperative planning for both the Hebrew schools and Sunday schools. With the supply of immigrant teachers declining, the Hebrew Teachers Training School, the antecedent of the Hebrew College, was organized in April 1918. Two years later, organizations representing religious and Hebrew schools merged to create the Bureau of Jewish Education.

Volunteers remained at the center of Federation life, bringing concerns about family and child welfare and the linkages between poverty and crime to the fore. The Jewish Big Brother Association, which joined the Federation in 1920, was a daring experiment in using volunteers to address the problems of disadvantaged boys.

By the end of the 1920's, the Beth Israel Hospital, which had moved to Brookline Avenue, and the Greater Boston Bikur Cholim (now the Jewish Memorial Hospital), which had moved into the old Beth Israel site on Townsend Street, had both become agencies of the Federation. Other member agencies included the Jewish Maternity Clinic, the Jewish Children's Aid Society, and the Benoth Israel Sheltering Home.

In the boom years of the 1920's, community and Federation both expanded facilities and services. The addition of agencies increased Federation expenses; the community threw energy and resources into building temples, schools, and hospitals. Dr. Benjamin Selekman succeeded Maurice Hexter as executive director in 1929, arriving in Boston on the eve of the stock market crash.

The decade of the Great Depression placed enormous pressures and financial obligations on philanthropic services.

FIG. 15. Beth Israel Hospital, Brookline Avenue, Boston, 1928–present. Photo, 1952. Affiliating with Harvard Medical School in 1928, Beth Israel became the first Jewish-sponsored hospital in the country to ally with a university. *Beth Israel Hospital Archives, Boston.*

FIG. 16. Associated
Jewish Philanthropies
1931–32 campaign liter-
ature. *Combined Jewish
Philanthropies.*

The Federation, renamed the Associated Jewish Philanthropies in 1930, undertook
a second long-range planning study to streamline its agencies and services. A team
of evaluators from the Bureau of Jewish Social Research in New York determined
that the centers of Jewish population had moved from the South and West Ends and
East Boston and was concentrated in Dorchester and Mattapan. They deemed District Service outmoded and suggested separated and specialized services, specific
agencies to deal with family and child welfare, and the organization of recreational
and cultural programs through the Hecht Neighborhood House and the Boston
YMHA.

The Jewish Family Welfare Association was established in 1931 to respond to
family issues, which were particularly acute during the Depression. It soon incorporated into its functions extant services on behalf of young girls, unwed mothers, and
prisoners. The Jewish Child Welfare Association, established in 1934, oversaw the

dissolution of the Home for Jewish Children, finally replacing the orphanage system with foster care or adoption.

In 1936, the Hecht Neighborhood House moved out of the West End into the old quarters of the Home for Jewish Children on American Legion Highway in Dorchester. The Federation opened a Vocational Bureau which attempted to place unemployed workers, though the number of jobless invariably exceeded the number of positions available.

The Depression also took its toll on fundraising—the 1935 campaign raised only two-thirds as much as had been raised five years before. Agency programs and personnel were sharply reduced, while the need for services increased. By the end of the decade there was some improvement, but by then there was another challenge.

For the first time in many decades, a new stream of refugees began to arrive in the United States. Fleeing Nazi Germany, they arrived to a community intent on assisting them. The Greater Boston United Jewish Campaign was organized in 1937 to meet refugee, Palestine, and national needs. The Boston Committee for Refugees, which became a Federation agency in 1938, assumed full responsibility for the arrivals, assuring financial support, health and social services, and coordinating its efforts with the Vocational and Family Service agencies.

FIG. 17. 1939 Greater Boston United Jewish Campaign logo, appeal for European refugees. *American Jewish Historical Society.*

The community continued to mount two campaigns, the Federation's fall effort for local needs and the United's spring appeal for overseas. The practice proved to be redundant and counterproductive, exhausting for workers who solicited for both and irritating to donors asked to respond to two appeals. In 1940, Boston Jews planned a single Combined Jewish Appeal, the first major community in the country to do so. The combined appeal consolidated community interests, linking those whose primary concerns were local with others who focused on overseas. Yet despite the consolidation of campaigns, the Associated Jewish Philanthropies and the Combined Jewish Appeal were to exist as separate entities for two more decades.

Like all other Americans, during the war years Boston Jews were consumed by multiple concerns. With millions of men and women in uniform, the Jewish Welfare Board, with substantial support from the Combined Jewish Appeal, opened an Army and Navy Club at 17 Commonwealth Avenue in January 1943 to meet the needs of servicemen and women. The Club was later sold to Zionist House.

The Nazi scourge and the tensions of the Great Depression had rekindled the flames of intolerance throughout the United States. Father Charles Coughlin's radio broadcasts, and the resurgence of the Ku Klux Klan and similar groups, fanned

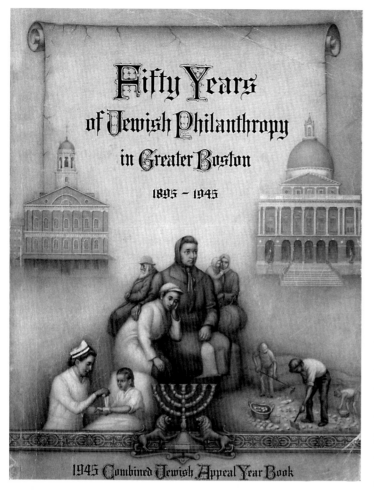

Fifty Years
of Jewish Philanthropy
in Greater Boston

1895 ~ 1945

1945 Combined Jewish Appeal Year Book

racism and antisemitism. Youngsters on the way to Hecht House in Dorchester were attacked by street gangs.[18] To raise the level of community consciousness on all sides of the issue, the Jewish Community Relations Council of Metropolitan Boston was organized in 1944 with twenty-two member organizations. In that same year, a Federation study of Jewish youth resulted in the formation of the Jewish Centers Association of Greater Boston, to unify planning and services for young people.

Post war, as the realities of the Nazi horror and the murder of six million Jews became known, Boston Jews focused on the problems of the survivors in Europe. The community mobilized for a memorable twenty-four hour SOS (Supplies for our Survivors) Campaign, collecting more than two and a half million pounds of food, clothing, and medicine which were sent to displaced persons camps. The Combined Jewish Appeal campaign for 1946 totalled nearly seven million dollars.

Two years later in 1948, a dream of centuries was realized with the founding of the State of Israel. Sixty thousand Boston Jews responded to their own sense of obligation and promise and raised $8.5 million, an unprecedented total that signaled the community's commitment to two great concerns—refugee rescue and the rebuilding of the State of Israel.

The years after the Second World War were a time of rapid growth and change for Boston's Jewish community. The anniversary of its first hundred years in 1945 had been obscured by world events, but the community had grown remarkably from a tiny enclave to one of substantial size and resources.

Its problems had changed, as had its modes of response. When the Jewish Family and Children's Service was established in 1946, it amalgamated a sequence of agencies which could be traced back to the United Hebrew Benevolent Society. The new agency's mandate differed from its predecessors; its task was to address psychological and not economic problems. Incorporating the concerns once addressed by the Home for Jewish Children, it attended also to the needs of troubled young people, as the need for most foster placement had disappeared.

Increasingly, the Boston Jewish community, once tightly settled in distinct geographic enclaves, was dispersing. From the earliest years of the century, Jews had moved to outlying parts of the city, and then to the suburbs, migrating from the North and West Ends, the East Boston and Chelsea areas, to Roxbury and Dorchester, Brookline, and Newton. The growth of the suburban communities continued after the war, as the young generation settled outside the city of Boston to raise their families. There they became increasingly educated, more affluent, and more visible and accepted in mainstream society.

To better serve the growing suburban population, the Brookline-Brighton-Newton Jewish Community Center opened in rented quarters on Harvard Street in Brookline in 1946. In 1952 it moved farther west to a larger new facility at Cleveland Circle. Hecht House also continued to grow in the 1940's, adding services for the large Jewish community in Dorchester and Mattapan.

Community energies and resources focused on building the State of Israel, and contributing to its efforts to resettle European and then North African Jews. American Jews were inspired by the success of the Israelis. "They responded with a surge of support for the creation of the State of Israel, and in the process, planted the seeds for a new kind of self-image never before seen in the Jew's long history as an alienated and victimized people."[18] The pride in Israel was reflected in vigorous and successful annual Federation campaigns.

The campaign and planning arms of the federated community remained officially separate, but so tightly intertwined that the amalgamation

FIG. 18, *upper left. Fifty Years of Jewish Philanthropy in Greater Boston 1895–1945.* (Boston: Combined Jewish Appeal, 1946). Cover illustration by Irving Bookstein.

FIG. 19, *lower left.* Banner for Combined Jewish Appeal campaign, Washington Street, Boston, 1950's.

FIG. 20, *above.* Combined Jewish Appeal campaign poster, 1950's. *American Jewish Historical Society.*

FIG. 21, *below.* Brookline-Brighton-Newton Jewish Community Center, 50 Sutherland Road, Brookline, 1952–1992. *Combined Jewish Philanthropies.*

of the Combined Jewish Appeal and the Associated Jewish Philanthropies into the Combined Jewish Philanthropies in 1960 was nearly a formality. The step asserted the Federation's position as the Jewish community's central address for fundraising and for social planning.

Here, the Federation had come full circle. Where it had once embodied ethnic distinctions in the community, it had become the umbrella under which many divergent groups and interests could meet and work together. Now, Federation called for a broadscale study of a visibly changed community that would assess the changes and their implications and enable an orderly planning process.

In 1963, the Combined Jewish Philanthropies undertook a Long Range Planning Project under the leadership of Irving Rabb, a large scale descriptive survey "to examine the needs of the Greater Boston Jewish population and to project the general direction of Jewish community services for the future."[21]

The 1965 CJP survey was based on 1,567 interviews of Boston Jewish households representative of the total population. Results set the Jewish population in the CJP area at 176,000. (The Jewish population of the larger geographic area that includes the North Shore and several outlying western suburbs was estimated at 208,000.) Data confirmed what observers had suggested. Dorchester and Mattapan no longer contained the greatest concentration of Jews. Of the 14,000 remaining (from a pre-war high of 77,000), most were over fifty. Younger Jews were now living in the south suburbs, Brookline and Brighton, Newton and Wellesley, and Framingham and Natick. Students and young singles predominated in the Back Bay and Cambridge.[21] The report continued:

> "In a single generation, we have witnessed tremendous changes in the population which are continuing. We have seen the American-born Jew supplant the immigrant, a working class population shift to a white-collar population. We have seen the Jewish population break out from the 'ghetto' and central city into the suburbs, and a rise from little or moderate education to high education."[22]

But concerns were raised by the declining levels of Jewish education within the population and the beginning trend of intermarriage among Jews under the age of thirty.[23]

The 1965 survey provided a new profile of Boston's Jewish community and pointed toward the community's changing needs. With the assurance provided by this comprehensive study, it was possible to define broad new areas that demanded action. "The data point to . . . . the need to strengthen services that are widely used

. . . . such as Jewish education, community centers, and the synagogues themselves."[24]

The needs of Boston's aging Jewish population were addressed as Jewish Community Housing for the Elderly was established with seed money from CJP. Accessing Federal housing funds, it opened its first building in Brighton to 200 elderly tenants in 1971. Ulin House was soon complemented by another 200-unit facility named Leventhal House. By the late 1980's, JCHE had added three more buildings for a total of 900 apartments.

The CJP 1975 demographic study tracked further significant changes in Boston's Jewish population. Jewish Boston had contracted—there were only 195,000 Jews in the overall geographic area and 165,000 in CJP communities. There were more, smaller households, including an extraordinary number of single young adults (47,000 aged 21–30), many of whom had come to Boston to attend college and never left. A low marriage rate also resulted in fewer young children. As a whole, the community continued to migrate south and west, leaving significant numbers in Boston, Brookline and Newton, but creating substantial new population clusters in the south, north and west. Synagogue membership had dropped and intermarriage among those under thirty had increased.[25]

In 1976 CJP leaders under President Leonard Kaplan made a crucial and controversial decision to build facilities that would serve the community where it lived, beginning in the western suburbs. The decision sparked heated debate, proponents holding that an appealing physical facility would be a magnet for Jews dispersed throughout the suburbs. Serious concerns were voiced by those who feared that a new community center would swell the ranks of those who no longer joined synagogues. The agreement to accept the large new project was accompanied by a commitment to create a Synagogue Program Fund to provide Federation support for innovative programs in synagogues throughout the community.

Land and a building were purchased from the Xaverian Brothers in Newton. The site had first been an orphanage and then a seminary. Transformed by extensive renovation and construction, CJP's Gosman Campus and Leventhal-Sidman Jewish Community Center opened in 1983.

The creation of the campus underscored a fundamental change in the role of Federation.

FIG. 22. Entrance to Ulin House, the first building built by the Jewish Community Housing for the Elderly, which opened in 1971. Today more than 1100 low-income elderly men and women live in their own apartments in JCHE's five buildings in Brighton and Newton. *Jewish Community Housing for the Elderly.*

FIG. 23. Leventhal-Sidman Jewish Community Center on the Gosman Jewish Community Campus, Newton, Massachusetts. *Leventhal-Sidman Jewish Community Center.*

Nearing its ninetieth anniversary, it had refashioned and redirected its mission to become a community-building as well as a community-service organization. To be sure, Federation agencies still focused on their unique mandates and served the real and pressing needs of their constituents. But additionally, the Federation developed its capacities to identify priorities throughout the community and begin new projects and initiatives to address them.

Community needs were formally articulated and clarified by the 1983 Communal Needs Survey. In a series of town meetings, Boston Jewry communicated its concerns: Jewish education, the needs of the frail elderly, day care, and a gathering place for the growing Jewish community in the South Area.

From the task forces established in each of these areas, concrete steps and recommendations soon emerged: $300,000 to be spent each year in supplementary Jewish education, the startup of programs to provide full-time principals to afternoon Hebrew schools, mentors for young professionals entering the field of Jewish education, and stipends for teacher training and enrichment programs. The South Area Development Fund led to the expansion of agency services in Canton and Randolph. The south area counterpart to the Newton JCC, the Striar Jewish Community Center on the Fireman Campus, broke ground in Stoughton in 1986 and was dedicated in 1988. With growing numbers of women in the work force, day care under Jewish auspices had become a pressing concern of young families. Gan Yeladim, originally cosponsored by the Jewish Community Center and Jewish Family and Children's Service opened in 1988, joining the JCCs in providing early

FIG. 24. Striar Jewish Community Center on the Fireman Campus, Stoughton, Massachusetts. *Striar Jewish Community Center.*

childhood services. Jewish Community Housing for the Elderly continued to expand its services and facilities.

New risks to the Jewish community were revealed in CJP's 1985 Demographic Study. Boston Jews were more affluent, more highly educated, more geographically dispersed than before. They were younger, more mobile, and more were native-born. Fewer remembered the Holocaust, or felt tightly attached to Israel. And more were intermarrying.[26]

The alarm sounded by the 1985 study rang even louder five years later. A national survey of the Jewish community indicated that over half of all Jews were marrying non-Jewish partners.[27] Simple arithmetic yielded sobering results. Of every four young Jews, two would marry out of the faith. Only one in three marriages would consist of two Jewish partners.

More than any previous study, this news shocked and galvanized the Jewish community. Still, by the time it was made public, Boston's Commission on Jewish Continuity, organized by the Federation and including representatives of synagogues and Jewish organizations throughout the community, was close to completing its work. The Commission's recommendations, ratified by the Federation Board in June 1993, paved the way for bold new directions in Jewish education and underlined the new spirit of cooperation that characterized Federation-synagogue relationships.

Eight synagogues and community institutions were selected as "gateways" where Jewish family educators work with parents and children, joining home and school in an unprecedented effort to engage every member of the family in Jewish learning. Jewish camping programs were broadened; Boston's Passport to Israel program to send high school students to Israel grew each year. Intensive programming for young Jewish adults, both on and off the college campus, was added to the community's priorities.

At the same time, the Federation focused on reshaping the community's relationship to Israel. Beginning in the late 1970's, Boston became involved in the reha-

FIG. 25. Governor William Weld and Mayor Eli Landau in Shaviv, Herzliya, Israel, during a 1993 Massachusetts trade mission. *Combined Jewish Philanthropies.*

bilitation of some of Israel's poorest neighborhoods through Project Renewal. Its "sister city" relationship with the Herzliya suburbs of Neve Israel and Shaviv resulted in the restoration of housing and the development of community centers and libraries in both communities.

Recognizing the eagerness of American entrepreneurs to do more than contribute funds to Israel, as well as the potential benefits to the Israeli economy, Boston's Federation has worked closely with the New England Israel Chamber of Commerce, cooperatively developing projects in Israel, providing both funding and business acumen for developing Israeli industries. The vision and energy for these new projects emanated from Barry Shrage,

the dynamic executive brought to Boston in 1987 to steer the Federation on a new course.

And still the Federation has maintained its traditional services and supports. Refugee resettlement, nearly forgotten after the end of the Second World War, again became a focus of community concern when Jews began to emigrate from the Soviet Union in the 1970's. In the aftermath of the Soviet invasion of Afghanistan, the doors slammed shut, only to reopen in the late 1980's in the spirit of glasnost. Starting in 1987, more than one thousand Jews from the former Soviet Union have arrived in Boston each year, a total of 7,500 through 1993. The family of agencies that has effected their resettlement are the descendants of those organized more than a century ago for virtually the same purposes: the Jewish Family and Children's Service, Jewish Family Service of Metrowest, Jewish Vocational Service, and the Jewish Community Center of Greater Boston. They are abetted by many other formal agency efforts, energetic synagogue programs, and hundreds of volunteers throughout the community.

As CJP celebrates its 100th anniversary, this contemporary replay of its original concerns is a forceful reminder of the power of an organized community to influence and shape the lives of its citizens. Within and outside the Federation, Boston Jews continue to demonstrate their concern for each other, for the community in which they live, and for the continuity of the Jewish people in America and in Israel. Community and philanthropy form and are formed by one another. Community and philanthropy are inextricably linked.

*Notes*

1. Barbara Miller Solomon, *Pioneers in Service* (Boston: Combined Jewish Philanthropies, 1956), 4.

2. Solomon, *Pioneers*, 10.

3. Jacob Neusner, "The Impact of Immigration and Philanthropy Upon the Boston Jewish Community (1880–1914)," *Publications of the American Jewish Historical Society* 46 (1956): 73.

4. Isaac M. Fein, *Boston—Where It All Began* (Boston: Boston Jewish Bicentennial Committee, 1976), 39–40.

5. Solomon, *Pioneers*, 15.

6. Solomon Schindler, *Israelites in Boston* (Boston: Beckwith and Smith, 1889), no pagination.

7. Solomon, *Pioneers*, 15.

8. Albert Ehrenfried, *A Chronicle of Boston Jewry, From the Colonial Settlement to 1900* (Boston: Privately printed, 1963), 544–45.

9. *Annual Report of the United Hebrew Benevolent Association, 1894* (Boston: United Hebrew Benevolent Society, 1895), 4–5.

10. "I–223, United Hebrew Benevolent Association, 1864–. Case Histories, 1888–1893," Jael Aber case file. Archives of the American Jewish Historical Society, Waltham, Massachusetts. Quoted with permission. My thanks to Ellen Smith for bringing this case to my attention.

11. *On Common Ground: The Boston Jewish Experience, 1620–1980.* (Waltham: The American Jewish Historical Society, 1980), no pagination. For a comprehensive listing of Jewish voluntary organizations in Boston before 1900, see Nathan Kaganoff, Martha Katz-Hyman, and Michael Strassfeld, eds. "Organized Jewish Group Activity in 19th Century Massachusetts: A Check List Recording All Groups Identified, Their Purposes, Years of Existence, a Listing of Prominent Individuals Connected with the Program, as Well as Eventual Disposition When Known." Typescript manuscript, American Jewish Historical Society, Waltham, Massachusetts, 1979.

12. On the early efforts of Boston's Jewish community to provide organized health care to its members see Arthur J. Linenthal, *First a Dream: The History of Boston's Jewish Hospitals 1896–1928* (Boston: Beth Israel Hospital in association with The Francis A. Countway Library of Medicine, 1990). The reluctance to use existing hospitals is discussed on pp. 19ff.

13. Solomon, *Pioneers*, 54.

14. Solomon, *Pioneers*, 76.

15. Solomon, *Pioneers*, 73–74.

16. Solomon, *Pioneers*, 84; Linenthal, *First a Dream*, chap. 8.

17. For an overview of the early Beth Israel Hospital movement, see Arthur J. Linenthal, "From Townsend Street to Brookline Avenue," *Harvard Medical Alumni Bulletin* (March/April 1978): 23–27.

18. See, for example, the "Anti-semitic Incidents at Hecht House" file in the Hecht House Archives, I–74, American Jewish Historical Society, Waltham, Massachusetts.

19. *Boston Globe* (Boston), 11 February 1985, Metro Section, 1.

20. Morris Axelrod, Floyd J. Fowler, Jr., and Arnold Gurin, *A Community Survey for Long Range Planning: A Study of the Jewish Population of Greater Boston* (Boston: The Combined Jewish Philanthropies of Greater Boston, 1967), 1.

21. Axelrod *et al., Survey*, 20.

22. Axelrod *et al., Survey*, 57.

23. Axelrod *et al., Survey*, 179.

24. Axelrod *et al., Survey*, 206.

25. Floyd J. Fowler, Jr., *1975 Community Survey: A Study of the Jewish Population of Greater Boston* (Boston: Combined Jewish Philanthropies of Greater Boston, 1977).

26. Sherry Israel, *Boston's Jewish Community: The 1985 Demographic Study* (Boston: Combined Jewish Philanthropies of Greater Boston, 1987).

27. Israel, *1985 Study*.

*Pioneers and Pacesetters:*
*Boston Jews and American Zionism*

*Overleaf:* Chaim Weizmann with his wife Vera Weizmann and Dewey Stone (far right) arriving in New York City from Israel, April, 1949, after Weizmann became President of the State of Israel. This was Weizmann's last trip to the United States. *American Jewish Historical Society.*

MARK A. RAIDER

# *Pioneers and Pacesetters:*
## Boston Jews and American Zionism

זכרו מרחוק את־יהוה וירושלם תעלה על־לבבכם
"Remember the Lord from afar, and call Jerusalem to mind."
JEREMIAH 51:50

EXT YEAR—IN AMERICA!"[1] With these words, the family of Mary Antin, the well-known Boston Jewish writer, concluded its Passover *seder* in the Russian town of Polotzk. The year was 1891 and Mary Antin's father, like thousands of East European Jews, had already emigrated to the New World, hoping to attain an economic foothold in Boston and send for the rest of his family. Acutely aware of life's fragility in the Pale of Settlement, the area to which the tsarist regime confined the Jews, the Antins were captivated by the winds of change that swept across the European continent in the late 19th century. It was an era that witnessed the *pogroms* (anti-Jewish riots) and the cruel expulsion of 20,000 Jews from Moscow, large numbers of whom flooded towns like Polotzk and whose misery was felt in practically every Jewish household. Meanwhile, the Turkish ban on immigration and settlement in Palestine reinforced the popular notion that America was the new "promised land." Mary Antin herself compared Russian Jewry under the tsars to the pharaonic slavery of the ancient Hebrews. She likened the threatening journey to America, particularly the passage by ship which could take between two to six weeks, to the parting of the Red Sea: "And if the waters of the Atlantic did not part for them, the wanderers rode its bitter flood by a miracle as great as any rod of Moses ever wrought."[2]

Mary Antin's image of America was not unique. Two centuries earlier, the Puritans of Massachusetts Bay also viewed themselves as latter-day Children of Israel passing over the vast sea to possess "the good Land."[3] Until 1760, Boston was the most populous city on the eastern seaboard. Its leaders, mostly divines and scriptural authorities, dominated colonial American society in the 17th and 18th centuries. Their collective "mind," as Daniel J. Boorstin describes it, "looked across the water"

to Europe, and colonial Bostonians viewed their nascent society as a "city upon the hill."[4] Their Biblical perspective spawned the principle of "covenant theology" and gave rise to the democratic political tradition that distinguished early New England.[5] This bipolar existence was subject to the practical exigencies of life in the New World. Gradually, there emerged a highly cosmopolitan American outlook, one in which the eschatological concept of the "return to Zion" was central but which nevertheless sought ways of making emergent American society a fully Christian nation through voluntary and persuasive means.[6]

Against this background, Boston provided fertile terrain for successive waves of European immigrants as well as the ideas and movements they transplanted to American soil. By the 19th century, Boston emerged as a center of liberal politics and religious liberal trends. It also proved to be a relatively congenial atmosphere for Jewish immigrants from Central and Eastern Europe. The Jewish immigrants brought with them their Old World *mentalité*, a mixture of rational, spiritual, and cultural attributes: secularizing tendencies, language preferences, forms of religious observance, traditional gender roles, generational discord, and variegated political ideologies. As in other urban centers, the admixture of different Jewish immigrant groups led to communal friction. An extraordinary instance in this regard occurred in 1882 when 415 Russian Jewish refugees were shipped back to New York by Boston Jewish leaders who feared the new immigrants would become a burden.[7] On the whole, however, Boston Jewish history was not accentuated by the deep-seated rivalry that elsewhere divided uptown *yahudim* ("German" Jews) and downtown *yidn* (East European Jews). As Abraham P. Spitz remarked at the 1892 dedication of Boston's Hebrew Sheltering Home: "We who live in this great country, God's most favored land . . . can hardly realize the persecutions to which our coreligionists in Russia have been subjected ... We must and shall receive them with open arms . . . We must teach them the manners and customs of an enlightened community . . . thus enabling them to become useful and desirable citizens."[8] Jewish immigrants arriving in Boston at the end of the 19th century were greeted by a relatively stable communal infrastructure, one for the most part prepared to care for the newcomers.

The rapid acculturation of Jewish immigrants in Boston was accompanied by the proliferation of local Zionist societies. Boston Zionist clubs, like other immigrant associations, were not large and their membership rosters were far from constant. But their presence *was* felt in the wider community. Viewed historically, the strength of Boston Zionism was never contingent upon its size nor, at a later stage, its fundraising ability. Instead, Boston Zionists were most influential as leaders who helped to inculcate in American Jewry a sense of kinship and responsibility for the

*Yishuv* (the Jewish community in Palestine prior to the creation of the State of Israel in 1948), and who helped to build bridges between the two emergent societies.

*Hovevei-Zion* (Lovers of Zion), the earliest Boston Zionist groups, were East European transplants which sprang up throughout the city beginning in 1889. Initially, Boston Hovevei-Zion considered themselves part of the European mother organization. This is apparent in a "special notice" issued by the Lovers of Zion Society of East Boston:

> *Dear Member:*
>
> *You are hereby given Notice that this Society will meet here after on every Sunday at 11 a.m., in Ohel Jacob Hall, Cor. Grove and Paris Sts., and* no notices or Postal Cards *will be send* [sic] *to this affect hereafter, except* on Special Meetings.
>
> *You are also requested to be present at the meeting which will be held next Sunday, as there is very Important Business to be Transacted such, as to send the (Scheckel) 25c. for each* good standing Member *to the Central Federation of Zionists in Wiena (Austria.)*
>
> *You are also notified that Mr. A. Fin has been dully* [sic] *selected as a Collector for this Society and is authorized to Collect Dues and other fees, until further notice.*
>
> *With greeting for Zion,*
> *Per order of LOUIS B. MAGID President*
> *Nathan Bloch Sec'y*[9]

There followed a plethora of Hebrew-speaking clubs and fundraising associations organized for land purchases in Palestine, so that by the turn of the century Boston was home to ten different Zionist groups: the Lovers of Zion of East Boston; the Sons and Daughters of Zion; the Hebrew National Association; the Israel K. Poznansky Lodge; the Dorshei Zion Clubs 1, 3, and 4; the Dorshath Zion Association; the Boston Daughters of Zion; and the Young People's Aid Association.[10] As the colorful club names reveal, early Boston Zionism included a multiplicity of cultural, religious, and political interests. Later, this pluralistic environment also encouraged the emergence of local branches of *Mizrahi* (an acronym for *merkaz ruhani* or "spiritual center"), a religious Zionist movement dedicated to the establishment of the Jewish people in Eretz-Israel according to the precepts of the Torah, and *Poalei-Zion* (Workers of Zion), a socialist Zionist movement that interpreted the cause of Jewish national liberation in Marxist terms. In fact, there were even a few Zionist synagogues. This array of Zionist immigrant creations augmented the existing communal infrastructure of native-born Boston Jews.

Though numerically smaller than the Zionist movement in other urban centers, Boston Zionists swiftly assumed a position of significance in the wider American movement. An early example of such influence—albeit a neglected historical episode—was the creation of the Jewish national flag in 1891 by Jacob Askowith and his son, Charles.[11] Originally prepared for use by the local Bnai Zion Educational Society, the flag consisted of a white background, two horizontal blue stripes, and a *magen David* (shield of David) inscribed with the Hebrew word "Maccabee" (later replaced by "Zion"). In 1892, a group of Bnai Zion members carried the flag (deemed the "flag of Judah" by the *Boston Globe*) in a Columbus Day parade marking the 400th anniversary of the discovery of the New World.[12]

The design for the Zionist flag was later brought to the attention of the world Zionist movement by Isaac Harris, a Bostonian who attended the First Zionist Congress in Basle, Switzerland in 1897. It is plausible that Rev. Dr. J. Shepsel Schaffer, a delegate to the First Zionist Congress representing Baltimore and Boston, also played a role in this regard. In the event, it was only at the Second Zionist Congress that the Zionist flag was officially displayed for the first time. A detailed report in London's *Jewish Chronicle* observed:

> *Every international train at Basle is met by representatives of the* [Zionist] *Bureau, bearing either the prosaic notice* [Zionist Congress] *or the Zionist flag, blue and white with the Magen David . . . It is almost impossible for anyone promenading the streets of Basle to forget that this city is again to be the scene of a Zionist Congress . . . From the balcony of the casino itself* [the site of the Congress] *may be seen proudly floating the Zionist flag in company with the National flag, and even the drivers of the fiacres engaged by the Bureau wear the emblem on their coat sleeves.*[13]

The news report also noted: "Instead of the comparatively small hall in which the sittings were held in 1897, we are assembled in the magnificent large hall of the Stadt Casino."[14] The latter statement supports the theory that a Congress postcard preserved in the Central Zionist Archives in Jerusalem, which bears a photograph of two Zionist flags adorning the entrance to the casino, is in actuality from the time of the Second Zionist Congress. Moreover, in a detailed description of the First Zionist Congress, the *Jewish Chronicle* correspondents failed to mention the pres-

Basel, Zionisten-Congress-Casino.

FIG. 1. Postcard of the Stadtcasino at the time of the Second Zionist Congress, Basel, Switzerland ca. 1898. Note the two Zionist flags (designed in Boston in 1891 by Jacob and Charles Askowith) flanking the entrance. *Central Zionist Archives, Jerusalem.*

ence of any banners whatsoever. The absence of a Zionist flag at the First Zionist Congress was also verified by Zionist leader Jacob De Haas.[15] Thus, despite assertions to the contrary—for which there is no convincing proof—the weight of historical evidence suggests that the Zionist flag originated in Boston.[16]

The year 1905, which marks a turning point in Jewish history generally, was also a watershed for American Jewry. In particular, the tide of East European Jewish immigration surged in the aftermath of the Kishinev *pogrom* and the failed Russian Revolution. The Jewish immigrants who subsequently arrived in Massachusetts swelled the ranks of local Jewish mutual aid societies, *landsmanshaftn* (self-help associations based on country of origin), trade union groups, settlement houses, and Zionist associations. In Boston, the new wave of immigrants came face to face with an earlier generation of Russian Jewish ex-patriots, large numbers of whom were already on their way to becoming acculturated into American society. Unlike the Central European Jews who preceded them, these Russian Jews were neither assimilationists nor were they inclined toward Reform conceptions of American Judaism. Instead, they embraced a mélange of radical populist and traditional values. This is well illustrated by the ethical will of Abraham Isaac Saklad, a native of Slonim, Russia, who emigrated to Boston in the early 1880's. Saklad, a staunch Hebraist, founded a Boston school in which Hebrew was the language of instruction. His will, which he composed during a 1906 visit to Turkish-ruled Palestine, admonished his family to:

> *Be good Jews, and let all that is Jewish be close to your hearts.*
> *For the Jew is distinct among the nations wherever he may dwell*
> *upon this globe . . .*
> *Should you, by chance, be employed in menial work, it matters not, for*
> *as long as the work is honest your soul will be clean and at peace.*
> *Do not forever strive to be a doctor or a lawyer, for therein is trouble*
> *and travail everywhere . . .*
> *Love the land of your forefathers, and come, like myself, to visit the*
> *Wailing Wall.*
> *Dear Children, pay heed to these words.*
> *Keep them impressed in your hearts.*
> *Children you are building a better world.*[17]

Saklad's ethical will bears the unmistakable imprint of the East European Jewish immigrant milieu. Devoted to *Yiddishkeit* and the promulgation of Diaspora Jewish life, Saklad was a passionate nationalist who viewed Eretz-Israel in personal and existential terms. His wariness of bourgeois professions and his glorification of physical toil also reflects, at least implicitly, the radical tendencies of his generation which were enunciated by the *Am Olam* (Eternal People) movement in America and the *halutzim* (pioneers) in Palestine. Such a *mentalité*, which stood in opposition to the prevailing American Jewish veneration of "the learned professions," i.e., the legal and medical spheres, was rebellious and in many instances even revolutionary.[18]

Saklad's statement is also an excellent example of American Jewry's budding attraction to the concept of "upbuilding" the Yishuv, including the promise of this-worldly Jewish redemption. Symbolized by the rural lifestyle of Jewish agricultural colonies in Palestine, this vision, rooted in Tolstoyan romanticism and prophetic Judaism, tapped an idealistic vein in the psyche of East European Jewish immigrants. The Zionist pioneering ethic was crystallized in the phrase "*kibbush haavodah*" (the conquest of labor). The very terminology, with its layers of unfolding meaning— "*avodah*," the Hebrew word for labor, is also the classical term for worship— forged a compelling synthesis. Thus, for Zionist enthusiasts like Saklad, "menial" and "honest" labor symbolized the transformation of Jewish life in toto, both in its traditional and modern forms. It offered a blueprint for the physical and spiritual regeneration of the Jewish people. Saklad, aware that American reality propelled Jews in professional and industrial directions, emphasized the centrality of Eretz-Israel in the Jewish spiritual and temporal worlds.

A very different example of Boston Zionism's early adherents can be found in the halls of New England academe. Ironically, Boston University Law School, Tufts University, and Harvard University—at which Zionist societies sprang up in 1905—were preeminent staging grounds for the very professions of which Saklad was most suspicious.[19] In fact, Harvard Law School served as a point of entry and later a center of gravity for many leading American Zionists including Louis D. Brandeis, Felix Frankfurter, Robert Szold, Julian W. Mack, Alexander Sachs, and Benjamin V. Cohen. At Harvard, notes the historian Ben Halpern, "a few Jewish students, intent on absorbing America . . . defended their distinctiveness in the citadel of Wasp culture. . . . They were encouraged by some Judeophile Yankee professors who were not otherwise partial to Jews."[20] The three most influential Harvard scholars who favored Jewish cultural activity were Nathaniel S. Shaler, whose study of ethnicity and nations led him to conclude that diversity was both unavoidable and a spur to human progress, the philosopher William James, who viewed American society as a composite of many ethnic groups, and the historian George Santayana, who posited that New England's cultural distinctiveness was rooted in its pluralistic tradition.

Among the most promising young Jewish minds first attracted to Zionism at Harvard were Horace Kallen, Harry A. Wolfson, and Henry Hurwitz. (Hurwitz eventually left the Zionist fold.) Each provides an intriguing example of Zionism's formative impact on the 20th century's first generation of Americanized, highly educated, Boston-bred Jews. At the time, American Jewish society, including nascent American Zionism, was dominated by an elite coterie of German Jewish patricians. Kallen, Wolfson, and Hurwitz, disenchanted with this situation and encouraged by the "new humanism" then being propounded in Cambridge, banded together to form the Intercollegiate Menorah Association (later known as the Menorah Society) in 1913. The Menorah Society, though it provided a congenial atmosphere for adherents of the Zionist ideal, was in actuality devoted to a wide range of Jewish cultural issues. On the basis of its moderate Zionist orientation, however, the society attracted a group of Herzlian enthusiasts and even received a subsidy from the Federation of American Zionists (FAZ), the forerunner of the Zionist Organization of America (ZOA).

The Menorah Society's rapid growth was matched by an increasingly universalist tone. After a few years, when it became clear that the society's interest in Jewish humanism would all but eclipse its original nationalist premise, an internal faction of political Zionists broke away to create the Intercollegiate Zionist Association of America (IZA). The new organization's very name was intended to distinguish it from the Menorah Society. Like their European Zionist counterparts, the Menorah and IZA sharpened their self-ascribed identities on the basis of competing cultural strategies and opposing political objectives.[21] We obtain an insider's view of this state of affairs from an essay in *Kadimah*, an IZA volume named in honor of the first important Zionist students' society in Western Europe:

> [The Menorah Society] *did not die of old age, but, instead, committed suicide. It camouflaged its Zionism by reorganizing itself as a purely non-partisan body so as to obtain a larger membership. It called itself the "menorah" . . . with a great deal of noise and a sprinkling of such decorative terms as "Jewish Culture" and "Hebraic Aroma."*
>
> *It is strange, but nevertheless true, that practically all the leaders and active workers in the Menorah organization are Zionists. They have accepted a compromise because they thought that they could reach groups whom a Zionist society could not touch. Indeed, the thing of which the Menorah boasts now, when it talks to Zionists, is its little lists of prize conversions to Zionism. As a matter of fact, though, Zionism is quite as respectable as the Menorah brand of Jewish Culture—and perhaps a little more inspiring . . . The Menorah, cautious about offending anyone by doing anything, often is about as interesting as a mid-Victorian debating society. If the Zionists had put their energies into Zionist societies, we should be better off.* [This is not] *to say that there is no virtue in the Menorah, but that what virtue there is is not of the Menorah.*[22]

The Menorah Society's openness to American culture forced the political Zionists of the IZA to evaluate their own attitude toward Diaspora Jewish life and the Zionist program known as "*Gegenwartsarbeit*" (Zionist work in the Diaspora). To be sure, this process of self-reflection did not originate with the Menorah-IZA dispute. Early Zionists like Harry Wolfson and Horace Kallen made their debut in American Jewish life as a direct result of such questioning. For example, Wolfson's poem, "The Spirit of Hebraism," which he composed in Hebrew and recited at a gathering of the Menorah Society, typifies the social idealism of many of his youthful contemporaries:

*. . . Oh, my spirit awaits but my seeking*
*To burst like a spring from the soil.*
*And if once it be free from confinement*
*It will vest in all fruit of my toil.*
*. . . It will speak from the lips of new Prophets.*
*And their truth from the heights will be hurled,*
*From a model city of Justice*
*Where its flag will blazon unfurled.*[23]

FIG. 2. Cover of *Kadimah*, a publication of the Intercollegiate Zionist Association of America, David S. Blondheim, ed. (New York: Federation of American Zionists, 1918). *American Jewish Historical Society.*

Although Wolfson alluded to the reawakening of Jewish ethnic pride and even cultural-national revival, he clearly stopped short of espousing a forthright commitment to the full-bodied nationalism of the Jewish immigrant milieu.

At this ideational juncture Kallen diverged from Wolfson, forging a new synthesis of political progressivism, cultural humanism, and the notion of Jewish auto-emancipation. Consequently, it is not surprising to find that in 1913 Kallen created a semi-secret fellowship called the *Parushim* (Pharisees or "separate"). The Parushim was a short-lived society, "an elite Zionist cadre, a vanguard for the Zionist army to come," composed of promising young American Zionists including Harvardians Israel Thurman, Henry Hurwitz, Alexander Sachs, and Benjamin V. Cohen.[24] The members regularly reported to Kallen and were totally dedicated to the Zionist cause.[25] When the Parushim disbanded, Kallen helped to found *Zeirei-Zion Hitahdut* (United Young Zionists) of America, an offshoot of the non-Marxist Labor Zionist party popular in educated European circles.[26] Soon after Zeirei-Zion's establishment in the United States, Kallen depicted the *halutzim* as "ask[ing] for nothing . . . all of a high sensibility and delicate nature . . . To reach Palestine they will endure everything, they will stop at nothing."[27] To Kallen, the *halutzim* epitomized the ongoing Jewish struggle for social equality, dignity, and autonomy as well as the Jewish people's profound disappointment with the broken promises of the European enlightenment. These young men and women also supplied tangible evidence of a specifically Jewish *mentalité,* secular and humanist in orientation, whose larger goal was the elevation of humanity's universal condition.

Of course, in characterizing the *halutzim*, Kallen was speaking figuratively about himself and Zionism as it was emerging in America's progressive period. His Zionism consisted of two chief components: the philosophy of cultural Zionism as articulated by Israel Friedlaender, or what the historian Evyatar Friesel calls "Ahad

Haamism," and the utopian voluntarist strand of Labor Zionism as it developed under the ideological guidance of Nahman Syrkin, the socialist Zionist mentor of Zeirei-Zion.[28] The former philosophy affirmed the contributions of Diaspora Jews to their lands of residence and the importance of Eretz-Israel in Jewish life. The latter sought to integrate this commitment with the struggle for a viable and socially just national home in Palestine.

Kallen's brand of Zionism held particular sway in the Jewish immigrant community. A glimpse of this situation is discerned in an unusually frank letter from Benjamin Rabalsky, head of the Boston FAZ branch, to Jacob De Haas, then secretary of the Provisional Executive Committee for General Zionist Affairs:

FIG. 3. Provisional Executive Committee for General Zionist Affairs, c. 1918. Left to right: (seated) Henrietta Szold, Rabbi Stephen S. Wise, Jacob De Haas, Robert Kesselman, Louis Lipsky, Charles Cowen, Dr. Shmaryahu Levin, Rabbi Meir Berlin; (standing) Blanche Jacobson, Adolph Hubbard, A.H. Fromenson. *American Jewish Historical Society.*

*There are candidates and prospects* [in Boston] *that would be made good Zionists but cannot afford to pay* [dues] *in advance . . . There are others who would like to become organized Zionists but prefer to belong to a Jewish* [read: Yiddish] *speaking Zionist society . . . I will repeat again that it is my opinion that Dorchester, Mattapan, Roxbury, Brighton, Newton, Watertown, Waltham, Lawrence, Fall River, and other places near Boston should have strong organized societies . . . Unless the Federation* [of American Zionists] *. . . take*[s] *such steps as is necessary to organize the masses, the Poalei-Zion will do it.*[29]

It was only after Louis D. Brandeis's emergence on the scene that Kallen's theoretical approach and Rabalsky's structural agenda were translated into popular, effective, and thoroughly American terms.

The literature about Louis D. Brandeis's relationship to Zionism is vast. In large measure, Brandeis was inducted into American Zionism as a result of his personal association with idealists like Kallen. His nationalist sentiments were further strengthened by a sense of kinship with and admiration for the East European Jewish immigrant masses. Brandeis first came into sustained contact with the immigrant community when he mediated the New York garment workers' strike at the behest of Louis E. Kirstein, the influential Boston Jewish philanthropist and vice-president of William Filene's Sons Company. Captivated by the seemingly authentic Jewishness of the Lower East Side, Brandeis emerged from this experience a profoundly changed man. Though he himself had never rejected his Jewish identity, neither had he previously given it much stock. His newfound "deep solicitude for the spiritual and moral welfare of the Jews"[30] parallels the fascination with the so-called "*Ostjuden*" (East European Jewish immigrants) that characterized German Zionism of that time.

Though the precise combination of factors that led to Brandeis's "Zionist conversion" remains a matter of scholarly debate, it is clear that the liberal Boston environment played a substantial role in his philosophical development. Boston was a seminal—if not the preeminent—intellectual center of progressive American politics in the turbulent decades that bridged the 19th and 20th centuries. Additionally, the solidarity of Boston's local ethnic groups, particularly the Irish, did much to enhance the cosmopolitan character of New England's flagship community. In those years, the Boston Irish, including no less a figure than the city's mayor Patrick Collins, were outspoken in their devotion to Eire and the campaign for an Irish Free State. Similarly, explained Jacob De Haas, editor of the Boston *Jewish Advocate* and a close adviser of Brandeis, Boston Jews sought a haven for their oppressed coreligionists overseas. For the Irish and the Jews alike, De Haas posited, working for such a cause was neither a source of conflict nor an act of disloyalty.[31] Brandeis himself, although highly sympathetic to the plight of East European Jewry, moved beyond the notion of Palestine as a refuge. His first public expression of support for constructive Zionist efforts in Palestine, in which he stressed that Zionism was the most effective Jewish program for improving society as a whole, took place at a meeting of Chelsea's Young Men's Hebrew Association in May 1913. Zionism, he exclaimed, was not strictly a matter of *noblesse oblige* but a prerequisite for the larger social and moral mission of American Jews. Later, in an address before the Eastern Council of Reform Rabbis, he fully articulated this view:

*Multiple loyalties are objectionable only if they are inconsistent. A man is a better citizen of the United States for being also a loyal citizen of his state, and of his city; for being loyal to his family, and to his profession or trade; for being loyal to his college or lodge . . . Every American Jew who aids in advancing the Jewish settlement in Palestine, though he feels that neither he nor his descendants will ever live there, will be a better man and a better American for doing so.*[32]

Brandeis' message resonated with local Zionists of all shades. This is illustrated by a leaflet advertising "Zion Flag Week," a community-wide campaign organized by the Jewish National Fund during the week of Hanukkah in December 1915. In true Brandeisian fashion, the leaflet urged that the goal of the campaign was to "provide work for laborers" in the Jewish National Fund's Palestine colonies. "When you help the National Fund, you help thereby to ameliorate Jewish need in a noble and practical way," it declared. "At the same time you help also to build the Jewish future. Buy this flag of Zion, and wear this emblem of Jewish nationality on the holiday of the Hasmoneans, giving generously at the same time to uphold the great Cause the Flag represents."[33]

FIG. 4. Louis D. Brandeis. *American Jewish Historical Society.*

When Brandeis assumed the mantle of Zionist leadership in 1914, he was 58 years old. An accomplished lawyer, respected national figure, and, after 1916, an Associate Justice of the Supreme Court, he endowed American Zionism with hitherto unknown prestige and legitimacy. De Haas saw in Brandeis a successor to Herzl; student groups like the Menorah Society and IZA viewed him as a role model; Jewish immigrants venerated him as a champion of the working class; even Presidents Woodrow Wilson and Franklin D. Roosevelt (who referred to Brandeis as "Isaiah") considered him an important confidant.[34] Brandeis's signal accomplishment was his capacity to energize a highly influential and politically effective group of Zionist leaders, especially the cadre of Harvard Law School alumni mentioned earlier. With Brandeis, Mack, and Frankfurter at its center, this innovative and powerful group provided American Zionism with a network of contacts and resources which, when fully marshalled, transformed the movement from a fledgling operation to a formidable political-economic enterprise.

With the onset of World War I, the political division of Europe, and the ensuing predicament of the World Zionist Organization, America—and above all, Brandeis himself—assumed a preeminent role in international Zionist affairs. As the only neutral base from which the World Zionist Organization could freely operate, the "Brandeis group" was elevated to the status of titular leaders and spokesmen for the world movement. Brandeis's own so-called "lieutenants" carried out major international assignments for the World Zionist Organization. On the domestic front, too, the Brandeis group's support of American Zionist interests proved to be of considerable importance. For example, the successful campaign to elect a democratic American Jewish Congress, which was advanced by three articulate spokesmen of Poalei-Zion—Nahman Syrkin, Ber Borochov, and Chaim Zhitlowski—and opposed by the powerful American Jewish Committee, brought the Brandeis group into close association with leaders of the Jewish immigrant community.[35] Consequently, a strong bond developed between the Brandeis circle and the Zionist immigrant rank-and-file. Such demonstrations of political fealty and the dramatic success of the American Jewish Congress played a crucial role in persuading subsequent American administrations and the Allies, especially the British, of the Zionists' dominant importance in American Jewish affairs.[36]

The announcement of the Balfour Declaration in 1917—in which Brandeis played a significant albeit inconspicuous role—infused Boston Zionism with an unprecedented level of optimism and energy. Local adherents of Zionism, many of whom were sympathetic to the cause but previously unenrolled in the movement, now joined by the thousands. Meanwhile, hundreds of young Boston Jews enlisted in the 39th Battalion of Royal Fusiliers, an American regiment of the British-sponsored Jewish Legion. Members of the battalion travelled along the eastern seaboard en route to the British military training camp in Windsor, Ontario. As one enthusiastic witness observed:

> At every town in New England where the train stops on the way to Canada crowds come out to wish God-speed to the men who are going to fight for the Jewish people, for them . . . Hatikvah [the Jewish national anthem] takes on a new sound and a new meaning in gatherings such as [these]. It is not the wail of a people which protests that its hope is not yet dead. It is the triumphant battle-cry of a people whose hope is to be realized.[37]

Together with their British coreligionists in the 38th "Judean" Battalion, the 39th Battalion was stationed in Palestine near Jericho. On September 22, 1918, the Jewish Legion routed the Turks from a strategic ford of the Jordan River, north of

FIG. 5. Official emblem of the Jewish Legion, reprinted in David S. Blondheim, ed., Kadimah (New York: Federation of American Zionists, 1918), p.29. American Jewish Historical Society.

the lake of Galilee, and opened the way to Damascus for the Australian and New Zealand cavalry.

In the United States, the Jewish Legion was organized by David Ben-Gurion and Yitzhak Ben-Zvi, Palestinian ex-patriots who sought to create a reservoir from which to recruit future members of the pioneering Hechalutz organization. In fact, as a result of its *halutz* core, the regiment became imbued with a strong Labor Zionist character, and after the war a group of American legionnaires provided the nucleus for the establishment of Avihayil, a *moshav ovdim* (collective settlement) near the oceanside town of Natanya.

In all, close to 8,000 American Jewish men enlisted in the Jewish Legion, of which 2,700 served in the 39th Battalion, including a sizable contingent from Boston.[38] American Jewry relished the image of a Jewish military force, particularly Zionists for whom the Jewish Legion served as a symbol of romantic patriotism. "The voluntary enlistment of Jewish boys," the chronicler Hyman L. Meites wrote, "impressed the world in striking fashion that the Jews not only wanted to regain Palestine but were willing to give their lives for it . . . Theirs were deeds of imperishable splendor."[39] Despite its exaggerated and self-congratulatory nature, Meites' assessment, like the one prior to it, sheds light on Zionism's steady penetration of American Jewish life. Beginning with the Balfour Declaration, but especially after the war, the demise of European empires and the rise of new nation-states engen-

FIG. 6. Golda Meir (far left, second row) in Boston, 1921. *The Golda Meir Memorial Association, Tel Aviv.*

נאָר אַ זעלטען בילד פֿון ציוניסטישע טרויער אַיידער דער טרויים, אין פֿארווירקליכט געווארען. — אויף דעם בילד איז זעט מען גאָלדע מייערסאָן
וערישע פֿון יינקם אין דער צווייטער ריי). מיט אַ גרופע חלוצים פאַר'ן אָפפאָרען קיין ארץ ישראל אין יאָר 1921. די פאָטאָגראפיע איז
געניימע געווארען אין פֿרענקלין פּאַרק. באָסטאָן. דאָס איז געווען, ווי איינזאָ־דרייסיג יאָר צוריק. איצט איז גאָלדע מייערסאָן
די אַרבייטס־מיניסטאָרישע פֿון מדינת ישראל.

ISRAEL'S LABOR SECRETARY, Golda Myerson, as a young lady with a group of Halutzim (Zionist pioneer workers). Mrs. Myerson is shown first from left in the 2nd row. The rare photo was made at Boston's Franklin Park shortly before Mrs. Meyerson left for the Promised Land in 1921.

dered hope that Jewish independence would soon follow. Against this background, Boston Zionist activity, previously the purview of small, select groups, attracted community-wide interest. In 1921, for example, a group of American *halutzim* — including Goldie Meyerson (later Golda Meir)—were greeted by a crowd of well-wishers at a mass celebration in Boston's Franklin Park.

Despite the groundswell of popular support for Zionism which emerged during World War I, actual membership in the ZOA plummeted during the interwar period. Indeed, in the same year as the Franklin Park celebration, Chaim Weizmann was advised to cancel a proposed tour of the United States: "The [Zionist] Organization is literally shot to pieces . . . [your trip] will not be able to give you any political assistance . . . [and] will for that reason prove a failure."[40] Moreover, the Brandeis group was ousted from its position of leadership by a Weizmann-backed faction, led by Louis Lipsky, who charged that Brandeis, Mack, and Frankfurter lacked true Jewish nationalist convictions and were primarily concerned with investment strategies and management of the Yishuv's financial interests. Though this line of attack maligned and distorted the intentions of the Brandeis group, it did touch on a raw nerve in the Zionist organization.[41]

After being deposed from the leadership of the Zionist Organization of America, the Brandeis group's Boston-based Zionist brain trust quietly and diligently pursued its agenda through a range of capital investment schemes such as the Palestine Economic Corporation, the American Zion Commonwealth, and the Palestine Land Development Company. Circumventing official American and world Zionist policy, it raised funds crucial to the operation of concessions like the Palestine Potash Company (later known as the Dead Sea Works) and hotels in Jerusalem and Tiberias, or, as in the case of a special project sponsored by Boston philanthropist Benjamin Rabalsky, in order to create a Jewish settlement in the Afula region.[42]

Lipsky differed from Brandeis in much the same way that the IZA did from the Menorah; they all differed from the legionnaires of the 39th Battalion, and certainly from the group of *halutzim* who established Avihayil and from Golda Meir's young comrades. In short, the core imperative of East European Zionism—an unwavering commitment to the notion of Eretz-Israel as the only authentic home of the Jewish people—was a litmus test that distinguished American variants of Zionism. On one side of the divide stood those sympathetic to the Herzlian program because it resolved a personal philosophical dilemma and provided a positive form of American Jewish self-identification. On the other stood Zionist adherents for whom Jewish nationalist convictions were not only central to their self-conception, but who sought to actualize such beliefs in their own lives and felt estranged, in varying degrees, from American society. Both perspectives existed (and still exist today) in a dynamic tension; the former providing a reservoir of support for the latter, the latter challenging and stimulating the Jewish commitment and content of the former. American Zionism's ideological quotient of "exile" survived from one generation to the next among the tenacious religious and socialist Zionist parties along with the tacit support of independent groups of Hebraists and certain Zionist youth organizations.

Quiescent during periods of relative social tranquility, American Zionism was activated primarily during times of stress and upheaval such as the critical years 1881–82 and 1903–05, World War I, the Depression, the rise of the Hitler regime, and the onset of World War II. Between the World Wars, Boston Zionism, like American Zionism generally, was driven by largely conservative rather than expansionist tendencies. On both the elite and popular levels, emphasis shifted away from membership campaigns and toward the consolidation of Zionist political, economic, and cultural gains.

The most dramatic singular action of this kind was Boston Zionist leader Elihu D. Stone's stewardship of the 1922 joint Congressional resolution (known as the Lodge-Fish resolution) that endorsed the creation of a Jewish national home. The bill commended the "building up of new and beneficent life in Palestine" as an act of "historic justice" and an "undertaking which will do honor to Christendom and give to the House of Israel its long-denied opportunity to reestablish a fruitful Jewish life and culture in the ancient land."[43] The Lodge-Fish resolution was essentially an effort to solidify the diplomatic advances of the Balfour Declaration in an American context. Couched in the Puritan rhetoric of its New England framers, the resolution was a timely effort to "writ[e] Zionist policy into the foreign policy of the United States." Adding to the fanfare of the occasion, Stone persuaded Senator Henry Cabot Lodge to present the resolution to Congress on the eve of the 1922 Passover holiday. For as Stone maintained, "this too was to be an act of freedom for the Jewish people and Eretz-Israel."[44]

The historian Melvin I. Urofsky persuasively argues that Lodge-Fish, though clearly a moment of high drama, was not a turning point in American Zionist history. Instead, it was a shrewd tactical maneuver aimed at mollifying American Jews in the aftermath of the 1921 nativist legislation that drastically limited the influx of so-called "new" immigrants from Southern and Eastern Europe.[45] In short, members of Congress had nothing to lose—and perhaps some political capital to gain—by supporting the bill. In the event, the joint resolution endorsed the establishment of a Jewish national home in Palestine, and although it had no impact on

Britain's foreign policy, the bill proved to be a fleeting propaganda victory for the Zionists.[46]

Of lasting importance was Boston's Zionist cultural agenda which crystallized in this period due to the city's developing Jewish educational institutions. In particular, the Hebrew Teachers College flourished under the supervision of Dr. Nissan Touroff, a noted educator whose successful tenure as director of the Yishuv's nascent school system attracted a cadre of talented young adults. In 1927, the Massachusetts legislature authorized the college to grant bachelor's, master's, and doctoral degrees in the fields of "Hebrew Literature, Hebrew Laws, and Hebrew Education." By 1930, the college boasted an enrollment of 150 students.[47] Many of these pupils went on to become leading figures in Jewish communal life and academia. By producing teachers and administrators, the college also nurtured Boston's emerging network of Hebrew classes offered by local secular and religious schools. These schools, as historian Walter Ackerman notes, were taught by staunch Hebraists and "the best teachers . . . made their pupils feel that the mastery of Hebrew was as important to the national rebirth as reclaiming a *dunam* (roughly a quarter of an acre) of land" in Palestine. One student described the intense atmosphere of the schools:

> *The Beth-El Hebrew School captured me . . . Most of our teachers were then newly arrived young immigrant scholars, who had come from post-World War I Europe to seek a secular education in Boston's universities; they taught Hebrew in the evenings to earn their living. They despised Yiddish, a language I knew from home, for to despise Yiddish was their form of snobbery; and as a matter of principle they would speak no English in class, for their cardinal political principle was Zionism. They were about to revive the Hebrew language and make it a living tongue . . .* [48]

The Hebraist Zionist milieu which animated Boston's Hebrew school network also spurred the growth of local Zionist youth organizations.[49] The late 1920's and early 1930's witnessed the coalescence of chapters of Hashomer Hatzair, the Young Poalei-Zion Alliance, Avukah, Hechalutz, Mizrachi Hatzair, Young Judea, Junior Hadassah, and Betar. As a whole these groups represented every shade of the Zionist spectrum—left, center, religious-based, and right—and they considered themselves the vanguard of the local Zionist movement. Most were initially comprised of the children of East European immigrants, but by the middle 1930's an increasing number of native-born American Jews entered the ranks of the Zionist youth orga-

FIG. 7. Avukah emblem. *Avukah Bulletin*, December 1934. *American Jewish Historical Society*.

nizations. As was elsewhere the case, a strong correlation existed between the success and level of Boston's Hebrew schools and the size and sophistication of its youth groups.[50]

The *Avukah* (Torchbearers) organization, which not only succeeded the IZA but continued to spar with the Menorah Society,[51] had an especially strong New England component and prided itself on being American Zionism's elite "intellectual element".[52] The Boston Avukah leaders venerated the Bnai Moshe society, the defunct secret Zionist order of Ahad Haam.[53] Like Kallen's society of Parushim, they viewed their agenda in national-cultural (or what might be called quasi-Ahad Haamist) terms. The original group of twelve—led by the young Joseph Shubow, an ardent Zionist who would later become a prominent Boston rabbi—selectively recruited "fellow intellectuals" with "actual and potential interests in Palestine, Zionism, [and] Hebrew culture."[54] "If our organization has any task in the future," one leader declared, "it is to add to the ranks of Zionists a number, however small, of young men who will . . . raise [Jewish] morale and strengthen faith in [Jewish] national ideals."[55] This challenge was taken up through a network of Zionist study groups, seminars, summer conferences, educational literature, monthly bulletins, and annual publications. Thus, on the one hand, the organization manifested its concern for "the problem of future Zionist leadership" and the "training of leaders through Jewish intellectual pursuits." On the other, it remained wary of "the raccoon-coated Babbit [read: Menorah Society], whose parasitic habits (economic and intellectual) prevent[ed] him from independent thinking or action."[56]

Such criticism was also a reflection, at least implicitly, of Avukah's strategy for avoiding the financial and political pitfalls of the IZA. Following the ascendance of the Lipsky group in 1921, the ZOA withdrew the IZA's subsidy and the latter "suffered, languished, then died."[57] Consequently, the Avukah leaders reasoned, their organizational success depended on the creation of a broad-based, independent framework capable of responding to the spiritual needs of alert college-age Jewish youth and promoting the Zionist agenda in relevant American terms. As one observer argued:

> *Zionism as a national movement cannot subsist only on leaders in the field of intellectual gymnastics and dialectics. Zionism needs spokesmen in every field of creative endeavor. We need our financiers as well as our educators, our medical men and legal experts as well as our craftsmen and engineers. These creative elements of tomorrow should command*

*our attention today. It is not for us to play the game of "selectivity" or "intellectualism."*[58] *Neither ought we to lull ourselves into the belief that we can make Avukah a student mass movement. Our basic task is the study and practice of Zionism among the creative elements of the Jewish student youth, and we must not dilute our program for the sake of the "feinschmecker"* [gourmet] *or the palate of the vulgar college man.*[59]

As for Avukah's political agenda, though officially apolitical, the majority of members' "sympathies [lay] with Palestine labor."[60] Even before Labor Zionism's rise to power in the Yishuv and the World Zionist Organization, this was forcefully expressed in the images of Palestinian pioneers venerated by Avukah's membership: "a common woman . . . longing for the companionship of the tillers of the soil in the *kvutzah*" (workers' cooperative); Yitzhak Ben-Zvi, who despite "his ill-fitting clothes, his disheveled hair, [and] his altogether unkempt appearance" is a "scholar," "gentleman," and "universally loved and respected" labor leader; and finally the "young, knickered figures with brown ecstatic faces sing[ing] Bialik's *nigun* (melody) and danc[ing] the *hora*."[61] Such views reflect not only a growing appreciation for Labor Zionism, but also the Palestine-based movement's resonance with particular American ideals—the nobility of labor, the glorification of pioneering, and the transformational possibilities of a youthful society.

By the middle 1930's, with the formation of several American *kibbutzei hakhsharah* (training farms) supervised by the Hechalutz Organization, Avukah, whose leadership included a core of talented New England Labor Zionist youth leaders, became overtly partisan in its orientation. In 1934, the organization officially endorsed the Histadrut program and adopted a new mandate to work closely with the League for Labor Palestine.[62] Its attitude toward Labor Zionism and changing perception of the *halutz* is captured in the April 1936 *Avukah Bulletin*. The feature article "Cap, Gown, and Shovel" touts the notion of *hakhsharah madait* (scientific training) as a step toward "enabling science and society to aid each other in Palestine" and reconciling American student Zionists' "desire for intellectual advancement with the pioneers' work of producing as a home for the Jewish people a sound collective society."[63] The article is accompanied by the vivid image of a college Zionist, pick in hand, preparing to break new ground.

Another significant expression of Boston Jewry's growing affinity for Labor Zionism came from the pulpit of Temple Israel, the city's leading Reform congregation. In 1930, Rabbi Harry Levi declared his unqualified support for the Yishuv:

*Since the Balfour Declaration . . . [the Zionist pioneers] have built roads and new factories. They have introduced scientific agriculture. They have improved health conditions . . . They have brought to the land thousands of young, sturdy, enthusiastic, ambitious young men and women, the finest possible type of immigration.*

Levi also clarified his support for Jewish nationalism, emphasizing that "Jews alone understand Jews and their problems":

*We American Jews of course will not go to live in Palestine. Nor will Jews of any land, where they are decently and humanly treated. But thousands in various parts of the world, living hopeless lives . . . will go if they can find the way to do so. We must help them find the way. We must stand with them during their pioneer days in a new land . . . This means joining the larger Zionist cause, contributing generously to it, supporting the Jewish Agency . . .* [64]

In January 1935, Levi was one of 241 Reform rabbis out of 350 members of the Central Conference of American Rabbis who broke with the movement's previously negative stance toward Zionism. On the Boston front, he was joined by his Reform colleagues Samuel Abrams, Israel Harburg, and Leo Shubow in endorsing the principles and practices of the Labor movement and the Histadrut: "We believe that the prophetic ideals espoused by Liberal Judaism are especially compatible with those of the Labor movement in Palestine . . . Liberal Judaism, in addition to its general sympathy with the rehabilitation of Palestine as the Jewish homeland, should feel an especial enthusiasm for labor Palestine."[65] In July, the Conservative movement announced its unanimous support: "We express our hearty appreciation of the contributions of the Labor movement, led by the Histadrut, to the rebuilding of the Jewish National Home in Palestine . . . We agree with the Histadrut that only through a cooperative commonwealth can such a society be established and [Jewish] religious ideals be achieved."[66]

These declarations are noteworthy for several reasons. First, they signalled an unprecedented endorsement of a particular Zionist agenda by important Boston Jewish leaders. This is significant in light of the Reform religious establishment's prior antipathy toward Zionism, which in its most extreme guise was represented by the unequivocal formula, "America is our Zion."[67] Second, it demonstrates a strong American Jewish predilection for Labor Zionism as the most viable—albeit a vicarious—program for building the Yishuv. In a manner similar to Brandeis's dictum that "there is no inconsistency between loyalty to America and loyalty to Jewry," the rabbis adopted the notion that American Zionism was essentially Labor Zionism.[68] Third, the endorsement indirectly indicates the rabbis' negative view of Revisionism and Revisionist Zionist attempts to establish an American base in the latter 1930's.[69] In pointed reference to Revisionist claims, the Conservative leaders publicly denied the charge that Labor Zionists provoked class strife, calling such accusations "a cloak behind which reactionaries have taken refuge to attack those who strive to defend the rights of the oppressed."[70] *The Jewish Advocate* of Boston went so far as to label the Revisionists as "Revisionist Fascists."[71] This sentiment, quietly shared by Boston Zionism's old guard, is illustrated in a letter Felix Frankfurter wrote to Robert Szold, president of the ZOA, about the impending 19th Zionist Congress: "Yes, I should vote as a General Zionist . . . *But*—the Histadrut is fundamentally right and the Revisionists are fundamentally wrong. Go out and see for *yourself*."[72]

Local Zionist enthusiasm for the Yishuv did not arise *ex nihilo*. It stemmed from a confluence of external societal pressures as well as profound internal changes in American Jewish life after World War I. During the interwar years, however, Boston Jews were gradually won over by a distinct Labor Zionist sensibility—even though they themselves were unaware of this development. A 1935 editorial published in *The Jewish Advocate* is typical of this general trend. Entitled "Palestine—The Land of the Future," the statement occupied nearly an entire page of the newspaper and compared the *halutzim* to the American pioneers, especially their "intelligence and industry," "enthusiasm and hope," and "generous and neighborly spirit." Set against the background of the rise of Nazism in Europe, the *Advocate* invoked the images of the American Revolution and the Hasmonean revolt. It portrayed the Yishuv as an outpost of Western and prophetic tradition, "nothing less than a miracle of miracles . . . a barren wilderness and forbidding mountainous region . . . so transformed by the genius, energy, and persistence of the Jewish pioneers as to make this small land one of the most picturesque, productive, and a bright spot in this darkened era."[73] This romantic treatment was reinforced by photographs and illustrations of the *halutzim*. In another instance, Leo Shubow contributed a six-part series to *The Boston Traveler* that lauded the revolutionary character of the Yishuv and emphasized the colonization efforts of the Jewish pioneers.[74]

Despite local enthusiasm and the valuable output of ideas and leadership, Boston Zionism, unlike its counterparts in other regions of the country, never

# Palestine Today

(AP Photo)

There is health and contentment in the face of this young Jewish colonist in Palestine, as he goes about his work. His work at the moment happens to be carrying barbed wire to build fences and protection around new land being reclaimed from the desert for his colony.

*Herewith is the fifth of the series of articles written for the Boston Traveler by Rabbi Leo Shubow, telling of Palestine and conditions he found in that country on a recent tour.*

## By RABBI LEO SHUBOW
### Temple Emanuel, Newton

The historic land of Galilee, in the region of the sea which figures so largely in both Christian and Jewish history, has many colonies, thriving at the price of hard work, cheerfully done, by groups of pioneers, many of whom are refugees from unhappy lands of central Europe.

FIG. 9, right. *The Boston Traveler* (April 15, 1938). *Papers of Leo Shubow, American Jewish Historical Society.*

FIG. 10, below. *The Jewish Advocate* (February 5, 1935), p.3.

reached the threshold of becoming a mass organization. In fact, membership in the local movement was erratic. On the eve of Hitler's rise in Germany, the period which marks the resurgence of the American Zionist agenda, Boston Zionism reached its lowest statistical ebb. In 1933, the national administration submitted "a summary of the New England situation from the point of membership" to Elihu D. Stone, then president of the local Zionist organization:

| | | |
|---|---|---|
| BEVERLY | *not a single member.* | *A few years ago they had 100.* |
| BROCKTON | *8 members* | *they had 53 members.* |
| CHELSEA | *not a member* | *they had 204 members.* |
| FALL RIVER | *4 members* | *they had 103.* |
| HOLYOKE | *not a member* | *they had 102.* |
| HAVERHILL | *not a member* | *they had 52.* |
| LAWRENCE | *3 members* | *they had 57.* |
| LOWELL | *3 members* | *they had 50.* |
| LYNN | *4 members* | *they had 117.* |
| MALDEN | *not a member* | *they had 84.* |
| NEW BEDFORD | *not a member* | *they had 28.* |
| NEWBURYPORT | *not a member* | *they had 42.* |
| NORTH ADAMS | *2 members* | *they had 42.* |
| PITTSFIELD | *2 members* | *they had 62.* |
| SPRINGFIELD | *13 members* | *they had 272.* |
| TAUNTON | *3 members* | *they had 49.* |
| WALTHAM | *not a member* | *they had 64.* |
| WORCESTER | *34 members* | *they had 57.* |

*In* BOSTON *they have 306, which is better than last year, but a few years ago you had 482. With regard to Boston, I would like to make the following points: that the Daughters of Zion has 27 members. They used to have 52. The Kadimah Club we have credited with only 3 members. They used to have 76.*[75]

Nevertheless, as this study contends, Boston Zionism's strength and importance were not solely reflected in such statistics. Rather, Boston Zionists were most influential as community leaders and spokespersons for the new American Jewish *mentalité* that evolved after World War I. This role conformed to the larger pattern of American Jewish acculturation and adjustment between the world wars, a period when American Jews placed a premium on the values of social justice, the nobility of labor, and pluralism. It also illumines why Boston Zionist leaders and intellectuals were propelled to the forefront of American Zionist leadership.

The rise of American antisemitism in the 1930's lit a fire in Boston Jewry's own backyard. The most menacing antisemitic threat on American soil in this period was Father Charles E. Coughlin, the notorious radio priest of Royal Oak, Michigan. Preaching a hateful mixture of antisemitism and anti-Communism, Coughlin explained and justified the Nazi persecution of the Jews as a legitimate reaction to so-called "Jewish Bolshevism."[76] He found an especially receptive audience among New England's working-class Irish and German Catholic communities.[77]

That Boston Jews were long the objects of genteel Brahmin antisemitism was commonly known. However, the Jewish community was shocked and greatly anguished when Harvard University invited the Nazi officer Ernst Hanfstaengl to be a marshal in its commencement parade. In response, Ben Halpern (at the time one of Harvard Professor Harry Wolfson's Ph.D. students) led a successful protest against Hanfstaengl's inclusion:

> I was "fed up" with Harvard in the 1930s, not because I was hostile to its "values" but because I cherished them and was disillusioned by Harvard's failure to live up to them . . . In 1934, the 25th anniversary class . . . decided to honor one of its members, Ernst Hanfstaengl, by naming him a marshal of the Commencement parade. Hanfstaengl's claim to distinction was his membership in the Nazi elite and in particular his personal relation to Adolf Hitler for whom, it was reported, he used to play the piano in relaxed moments. Some of us who regarded this choice as a blatant affront to the most fundamental values Harvard stood for, raised an outcry in which of course Jewish students were particularly vocal.
>
> We won, in a way, because Hanfstaengl joined the Commencement parade as a simple member of his class, not as a marshal. But our intransigent stand on values, against the interests of a Harvardian who had belonged to all the right clubs, did not make us popular. For me the drops of acid in the victory were not the cold looks of proper Harvardians but the fact that Hanfstaengl . . . was paired in the Commencement parade by a well-known Boston Jewish magistrate, who brought his innocent little grandson to walk alongside the Nazi.[78]

The virulent strains of local antisemitism prompted Boston Zionists to assess their political options. Three different examples, one an elite response and two others in a popular vein, illustrate the nature of the Boston Zionism on the eve of America's entry into World War II. In 1938, Felix Frankfurter convened a meeting of American Jewish intellectuals to analyze the results of a secret survey of "the range, intensity and direction of antisemitic sentiment in the United States." The protocol of the meeting records Frankfurter's insistence that "assimilation ceases to be a relevant solution" to the problem of antisemitism when the Nazi concept of a pure Aryan race becomes dominant in society. The solution to this dilemma, Frankfurter posited, was to create a "parallel" to the generally positive "pattern of relationships existing in Boston between the Old Protestant Yankee and the Irish, and that between the Jewish and non-Jewish groups generally." He proposed that all "Jews should take themselves for granted as Americans who were born Jews." Pointing to himself as an example, Frankfurter stressed that he went "through life without any of the usual 'Jewish' conflicts or difficulties." As a matter of policy, he recommended a broadly conceived educational program designed to "destroy the illusions and myths now surrounding the Jews, and to bring out the affirmative aspects of the contributions made by Jews, as well as other groups, to American democracy."[79]

The "New England Programme," proposed by Laurence M. Ring, a Boston Zionist activist, illustrates a different conceptual approach. Ring's views bear repeating at length:

> *Zionist aims today coincide identically with the average American Jew's feeling on the subject of Palestine . . . The average American Jew feels . . . that Palestine should be kept open as a home for Jews, particularly the Hitler-oppressed ones. BUT, your average American Jew also has the idea that Zionism involves something else. He has seen Zionists. They are fanatical. They are nationalists. They are somehow not like other Americans. They sing peculiar songs, talk their own lingo—are somehow different . . . World events have proved . . . that this Palestine project is something which Jews must have and must push. That is a conclusion your average American Jew calmly assimilates . . . He thinks like a Zionist, he gives freely to Zionist funds; he is a Zionist but he has no realization that he is. The Zionists to him are still certain other Jews. That mental quirk—that psychological barrier—must be brought to light and neatly and compellingly removed. It calls for a sort of advertising campaign—for a job in the field of public relations. It will not do merely for our leaders to say, as they do, that Zionism cannot be the monopoly of the few . . . I strongly recommend that the ZOA secure*

*expert public relations counsel and launch a real campaign . . . I am convinced* [of the urgency] *. . . of impressing the stamp of Zionist membership upon the great mass of the American Jewish public . . .* [American Jewry] *must organize itself into an articulate and visible unit. . . .* [Our] *task, as defined by the necessary and awful logic of the facts, both of Jewish existence in Europe today and of Jewish historical experience, lies ever more surely toward the land of Israel.*[80]

In comparing the views of Frankfurter and Ring, we revisit the ideological schism at the heart of the Boston Zionist experience. In the protocol of the conference called by Frankfurter, there is not a single mention of Zionism. This conspicuous omission highlights Frankfurter's perception of Zionism and the development of Palestine as a solution to the problems of some Jews—or, to paraphrase Ring, "other" Jews—but certainly not American Jewry as a whole. For activists like Ring, however, a Zionist wanted to settle Palestine for the Jewish people of which he was a living part. The urgency of this task was only exacerbated by antisemitism. Unlike Frankfurter, Ring's Jewish identity was central to his self-conception and Zionism provided a systematic response to the dilemmas of modern Jewish existence. Meanwhile, both Frankfurter's and Ring's views differed fundamentally from the radical alternative presented by Boston's Hechalutz movement. (After the Hanfstaengl affair, Ben Halpern was elected secretary general of the national organization at the urging of Enzo Sereni and Golda Meir, both of whom were Histadrut emissaries in the US.) The youth organization, which locally numbered one hundred active members in 1940, professed the ultimate aim of sending American *halutzim* to settle in Palestine.[81]

Years later, Benjamin Ulin, another local Zionist activist, illustrated this spiritual crossroads when he recalled:

I [had] *been a Zionist ever since I was in college . . . I wanted my people to survive! When I came in, the "Old Guard" was there and they wanted to control us. In the 1930s there were a number of us . . . who were vitally interested in fighting for a* [Jewish] *state. During the late '30s and '40s, we made the Brookline-Brighton-Newton district one of the largest Zionist units in America. We made it a point to enroll the leaders of our Jewish community . . .* [even] *the leaders of the philanthropies came in. Overwhelmingly, the Federation leadership was both a part of our membership and supportive of what we were trying to do . . .* [82]

Ulin's portrayal, exaggerated though it is, points out the extent to which Zionism penetrated Boston Jewish consciousness by the height of World War II. In 1943 Ulin himself appealed to the congregants of Brighton's Temple Bnai Moshe to join the local Zionist movement. As a result, a decision was taken to enroll all the congregation's members in the Brookline-Brighton-Newton Zionist district.[83] Needless to say, the mass recruitment of Temple Bnai Moshe dramatically inflated the size of the local Zionist group. Thus Ulin's remarks reveal that Boston Jewry's support for Zionism—even before the full magnitude of the Holocaust was known—rose with the tide of communal alarm that accompanied World War II. Indeed, at the height of the war a Gallup Poll indicated that "Greater Boston and New England Jewry was the most [pro-Zionist] section of the country with over 90% [of the Jewish population] favoring the creation of a Jewish state."[84]

Boston Jewry's communal strength, which stemmed from a long tradition of awareness of and commitment to general Jewish concerns, equipped local Zionist leaders with the moral and material resources to mobilize public opinion. In Ring's words, the wartime crisis facing American, European, and Palestinian Jewry required a total plan of action—"financial, political, strategic, theoretical, and practical."[85] Boston Zionist leaders responded to this challenge by actively supporting the embattled Yishuv, particularly the Labor enterprise. Harry Levine and Dewey D. Stone, two premier Boston Jewish leaders in this period, were especially supportive

FIG. 11. At Zionist dinner in honor of Dr. Abba Hillel Silver. Seated, left to right: Bernard Garber, Harry Levine, Dr. Silver, Benjamin Ulin, Abraham S. Karff, Julius Stone, president of New England Zionist Region, 1952–54, and Dewey D. Stone. Standing, left to right: Fred Monosson, president of the Jewish National Fund of New England, Henry Berlin, Joseph Rabinovitz, Rabbi Joseph S. Shubow, Max Kabatznick, Rabbi Albert I. Gordon, Dr. Morton J. Robbins, Judge Joseph Goldberg, Dr. Alexander Brin, Frank Brezniak, and Jacob Rabinovitz, president of New England Zionist Region, 1954. *Temple Bnai Moshe Dedication Book,* 1954. *American Jewish Historical Society.*

FIG. 12. Zionist rabbis and brothers: Joseph S. Shubow (left) and Leo Shubow (right). *Temple Bnai Moshe Dedication Book,* 1954. *American Jewish Historical Society.*

of the *Haganah,* the military arm of the Jewish agency, and its efforts to procure munitions.[86] David Ben-Gurion, then chairman of the Jewish Agency executive, also asked Stone to personally coordinate the purchase and transport of weapons for the Yishuv's clandestine defense force, the *Palmach (plugot mahatz,* "shock companies") as well as ships for the transport of so-called "illegal" immigrants.[87] Among the ships was the Exodus-1947, a decommissioned United Fruit vessel. The Exodus attracted world attention when a British blockade denied its 4,200 refugee passengers entry to Palestine and forcibly returned the ship to Hamburg, where those who refused to disembark were beaten with clubs and hoses. Stone also played a crucial role in persuading President Harry S. Truman to back the partition of Palestine in 1948, and again when he later "made [freshman Senator John F. Kennedy] kosher with the Jews" despite his father's pro-German sympathies as ambassador to Britain during World War II.[88]

The State of Israel and Brandeis University were both created in 1948. Ironically, the main critic of the founding of Brandeis was Chaim Weizmann, the primary architect of The Hebrew University of Jerusalem: "I raise my voice in warning: Do not waste the strength of the Jewish people. There is no substitute for Zion . . . The entire Yishuv and the young generation *must make a great concerted effort so that again only from Zion shall go forth Torah.*"[89] Simon Rawidowicz, the well-known Hebraist philosopher, defended the decision to establish a Jewish-sponsored non-sectarian institution of higher learning. He lamented Weizmann's "limiting and painful addition" of the term "only" which, he reminded the Zionist leader, was neither a faithful rendition of the Biblical phrase nor historically accurate. Rawidowicz contended that American Jews were rightfully and legitimately concerned with their "physical and spiritual future."

> *Every negative "thou shalt not" commandment in the spiritual sphere of Jewry is destructive also for Zion. This "thou shalt not" of the leader of the Zionists in our generation to the Jews of America greatly emphasizes the heavy curse hidden in that deficient Zionist ideology called the negation of the Diaspora, our greatest enemy . . . Rise and do; rise and build—that is the command of the day.*[90]

In 1950, Rawidowicz was invited to join Brandeis University by founding president Abram L. Sachar. He came in 1951, serving as Philip Lown Professor of Jewish Philosophy and Hebrew Literature as well as the first chairman of the Department of Near Eastern and Judaic Studies, America's premier department in the field.

Max Lerner, the well-known writer-critic and author of *America as a Civilization*, was one of Rawidowicz's colleagues in these years. However, Lerner, who became actively engaged in the Zionist cause after World War II, was avowedly sympathetic to the Zionist left. He explained why "being a Zionist, I am a Labor Zionist." Zionism, he affirmed, was the only viable strategy for Jewish survival, and the Labor enterprise in Israel was one of humanity's brightest hopes. The Jews in Israel, he pointed out, "brought with them the best elements of Marxism, of European democracy and liberalism, of American industrialism

FIG. 13. At a rally for Jewish statehood, from left: Harry Levine, Chaim Weizmann, and Dewey D. Stone. Boston, October 11, 1947. *Temple Bnai Moshe Dedication Book*, 1954. *American Jewish Historical Society.*

and technology, of the thinking of Tolstoy and . . . the Hebrew prophets." On this foundation, he proudly noted, Israeli Jews were building "a new vision and a new system."[91] Like Kallen before him, Lerner viewed the *halutzim* as the vanguard of both Western liberalism and Jewish humanist tradition. In the aftermath of the Holocaust, he also saw Zionism and the Labor enterprise as an opportunity for Jews to succeed where gentiles had failed.

Another celebrated figure attracted to the Brandeis University orbit was Ludwig Lewisohn, the accomplished literary critic and author best known for *The Island Within* as well as his contributions to the *New Palestine*, the *Jewish Frontier*, the *Menorah Journal*, and the *Reconstructionist*, the major Anglo-Jewish periodicals of the period. Lewisohn's political orientation was moderately left of center, but in contrast to Lerner his Zionism was deeply rooted in the quest for "acceptance of the Jewish past as a moral imperative for the intellectual Jewish conscience."[92] In a revealing piece of autobiography, Lewisohn wrote:

> *To me in my own person, the land of Palestine had a deeper and subtler message. Here, at last, was my earth. I felt it at once. I knew. Never, I*

*dare say, shall I be able to dwell upon that earth. It does not matter. At last I knew, no longer as a theory but as a living fact, the ultimate meaning of galut, of exile, and the element which constitutes that exile for us by our lack of it . . . Even the pure unhistoried earth of America is not wholly mine. Deeply as I have loved it, I am an alien there too.*[93]

Marie Syrkin, daughter of Nahman Syrkin and, in her own right, one of American Zionism's most eloquent polemicists, was a professor of English literature at Brandeis University. In 1945, Syrkin first gained attention with the publication of *Blessed Is The Match*, a remarkable portrayal of Jewish resistance during World War II. Thereafter, she continued to publish a mixture of historical and fictional works, including an authorized biography of Golda Meir, *Nahman Syrkin: Socialist Zionist*, poetry and prose, and an edited volume of writings by the Labor Zionist leader Hayim Greenberg. For much of her adult life, Syrkin stood in the vanguard of lengthy debates with such critics of Zionism as Arnold Toynbee, I. F. Stone, and Hannah Arendt. Known for her wry wit and keen insight, Syrkin was an acknowledged and formidable Zionist mind. For example, she offered this provocative analysis of Hannah Arendt's *Eichmann in Jerusalem*:

> *What is at the root of the shortcomings of Miss Arendt's trial of the trial is her view of Jewish history . . . In [her] view every affirmation of Jewish national awareness is culpable and to be strictured as either multiple loyalty or treason to a larger international ideal . . . Her much acclaimed formulation, "the banality of evil," is the corollary of her contention that the Nazi executioners were small ordinary men. However, in one respect they were extraordinary. In their single-minded dedication to the extermination of the Jews, Hitler and his accomplices were anything but banal; they were zealots. Their historic distinction is that they succeeded in making unprecedented evil banal—a different matter . . . The tenacity and special character of the Nazi purpose cannot be glossed over by the partial extenuation implicit in Arendt's facile phrase.*[94]

The concept of "Jewish national awareness" articulated by Syrkin, especially its socio-historical dimensions, was most fully developed by Ben Halpern, a native Bostonian who began his career as an American *halutz* and later turned to Jewish scholarship. Halpern, professor of modern Jewish history at Brandeis University and arguably the preeminent historian of American Zionism, was initially accorded widespread recognition as a result of his study *The American Jew: A Zionist Analysis* in which he argued that "America is different" from other Diaspora communities because of its distinctive post-feudal history.

> *What is characteristic of American Jewry, and what makes us different from [other Jewries] . . . is that we began our real history as a post-Emancipation Jewry. Emancipation was never an issue among us: we never argued the problems it presented in America, nor did we ever develop rival ideologies about it and build our institutions with reference to them.*[95]

In another scholarly work, *The Idea of the Jewish State*, Halpern analyzed "the development of the modern notion of Jewish sovereignty from the stage of a myth, with no more than emotional definition, to a rationally elaborated ideology, and from that stage to an institutional reality."[96] His third major work, *A Clash of Heroes: Brandeis, Weizmann and American Zionism*, is an attempt to unravel one of the dilemmas touched upon in this study, the impact and role of the leaders of an era—"Brandeis to that of American Jewry; Weizmann to that of prenatal Israel. They are said to have embodied the crucial experiences and offered a personal resolution of a generational crisis."[97]

Rawidowicz, Lerner, Lewisohn, Syrkin, and Halpern all gravitated to Brandeis University—where each sustained the rich tradition of Boston's Jewish intellectual commitment. Each was also a standard bearer of American Zionism: Rawidowicz, the profound thinker who viewed the only meaningful spiritual relationship between Eretz-Israel and the Diaspora as one of equal partnership; Lerner, the American progressive proudly brandishing his ethnic-national identity; Lewisohn, the secular writer-critic who celebrated the riches of the Jewish heritage; Syrkin, the penetrating and articulate polemicist; Halpern, the scholar-intellectual who transcended ideological partisanship. "Loyalty to a dogma is a tyranny which suffers only slaves in its realm," Halpern once wrote to Daniel Bell, "but loyalty to one's fellow men . . . can be a compact of love and freedom, preserving the independence of the individual and the spirit."[98] With these words, Halpern captured the meaning of American Jewish intellectual commitment and the essence of American Zionism; a sensibility neither at home in the world of dogma nor completely satisfied with the upbuilding of the Land of Israel.

To sum up, as this study illustrates on the micro-level, the decades prior to World War II witnessed Boston Zionism's gradual evolution in ideological and structural terms. Neither a complete rejection of the Old World inheritance nor an unqualified acceptance of New World surroundings, Boston Zionism developed a philosophical rhythm attuned to changes in American Jewish life and the Yishuv. During the interwar period, the ethos of the *halutzim*—the rapture of pioneering, the nobility of labor, and the attempt to elevate humanity's social condition—won the hearts and minds of diverse spheres of Boston Jewry. In the early 1930's, after Labor became the dominant force in the Yishuv and the World Zionist Organization, Boston Zionism—like American Zionism as a whole—increasingly reflected the romantic proclivities and political priorities of the Palestine-based movement. Rather than as an object of pious devotion or American Jewish largesse, Boston Zionists placed a premium on Palestine as a progressive Jewish society-in-the-making. They were especially captivated by the Yishuv's pioneers, cooperative spirit, and renascent Hebrew language. Their adulation was, in part, the product of disenchantment with the *goldene medine* (golden land) as well as horror at the rise of Nazism in Europe and antisemitism in America. For many Boston Jews, especially Zionist youth who believed they could only gaze at America's "city upon a hill" from afar, Palestine represented the opportunity to create their own "light unto the nations." At the same time, as this study posits, Boston Jewry, though numerically smaller than other American Jewish communities, played a pioneering role in the relationship between Zionism and American Jewry as a whole.

After World War II, Boston Zionism changed in the sense that its original premise and relative strength were dramatically modified. The major centers of Jewish life shifted to Israel and the United States virtually overnight, and this change ushered in a host of new challenges and problems for Zionism and Diaspora Jewry. Against this background, Boston Zionist intellectuals helped to define the terms of the ongoing debate that has since preoccupied generations of American Jews: What is the basis of Jewish culture in America? What role does Israel play in the lives of American Jews? What is the content of an American Jew's identity? Indeed, American Zionism—more than a century after the movement's inception—is still the only Jewish movement in the United States to deal with such questions in their totality. Boston Zionism—a wellspring of wealth, power, and, above all, intellect—not only produced a unique coterie of Jewish leaders in the years preceding the creation of the Jewish state, but continues to contribute to American Jewry's vitality in its wake.

1. Mary Antin, *The Promised Land,* reprint (Princeton: Princeton University Press, 2d ed., 1969), 141.

2. Antin, *The Promised Land,* 141. See also Mary Antin, *From Plotzk to Boston,* reprint (New York: Markus Wiener, 1986).

3. John Winthrop, "A Model of Christian Charity," in *American Ground: Vistas, Visions & Revisions,* ed. Robert H. Fossum and John K. Roth (New York: Paragon House, 1988), 21–22.

4. Daniel J. Boorstin, *The Americans: The Colonial Experience* (New York: Random House, 1958), 295.

5. Moshe Davis, "The Holy Land Idea in American Spiritual History," in *With Eyes Toward Zion: Scholars Colloquium on American-Holy Land Studies,* ed. Moshe Davis (New York: Arno Press, 1977), 5.

6. Robert T. Handy, "Sources for Understanding American Christian Attitudes toward the Holy Land, 1800–1950" in *With Eyes Toward Zion,* ed. Moshe Davis, 34–35.

7. Henry L. Feingold, general ed., *The Jewish People in America* (Baltimore and London: Johns Hopkins University Press, 1993), vol. 3, *A Time for Building: The Third Migration, 1880-1920,* by Gerald Sorin, 50–51.

8. "Abraham P. Spitz" in *History of the Jews of Boston and New England, Their Financial, Professional, and Commercial Enterprises From the Earliest Settlement of Hebrews in Boston to the Present Day: Containing a Historical and Statistical Record of Every Jewish Congregation, Fraternal Order, Benevolent Society, and Social Club Together With Biographies of Noted Men and Other Matters of Interest* (Boston: Jewish Chronicle Publishing Company, 1892), not paginated; Sorin, *A Time for Building,* 55, 151–52.

9. F25/383. Papers of Hovevei-Zion in America, Central Zionist Archives, Jerusalem.

10. *American Jewish Yearbook 5661, September 24, 1900 to September 13, 1901,* (Philadelphia: Jewish Publication Society of America, 1900), 173–74.

11. For verification of the Boston design's early appearance see *The American Hebrew* (24 July 1891).

12. *Boston Globe,* 22 October 1892, 2.

13. "The Second Basle Congress," supplement to *The Jewish Chronicle* (Boston), 2 September 1898, ii.

14. "The Second Basle Congress," iii.

15. Dora Askowith, "Miscellany: The First Zionist Flag," *Jewish Social Studies* 6 (January 1944):57.

16. Zionist historiography mistakenly attributes the flag's invention to David Wolffsohn. For example, see Mordecai Eliav, "*Lekorotav shel hadegel hazioni,*" *Kivunim* 3 (1979): 49–59; Michael Berkowitz, *Zionist Culture and West European Jewry before the First World War* (Cambridge: Cambridge University Press, 1993), 23–42; and Alexander Mishory, "*Lekorotav shel degel medinat Israel,*" *Cathedra* 62. (December 1991): 155–71.

17. Jacob Rader Marcus, *This I Believe: Documents of American Jewish Life* (Northvale and London: Jason Aronson, 1990), 151.

18. *The Jewish Encyclopedia,* (1) s.v. "America," 504.

19. *The Maccabaen* (July 1905), 49.

20. Ben Halpern, "Introduction" in *Boston Jewry and Its Relationship to Palestine and Israel—A History,* ed. Dorothy Spector (Boston: Combined Jewish Philanthropies of Greater Boston, 1974), 4.

21. Jehuda Reinharz, "On Defining Jewish National Autonomy: Demarcating Ideological Boundaries" in *Israel Heilprin Memorial Volume,* ed. Israel Bartal (Jerusalem: Merkaz Zalman Shazar, 1995).

22. Jonas S. Friedenwald, "The Intercollegiate: A Retrospect," in *Kadimah,* ed. David S. Blondheim (New York: Federation of American Zionists, 1918), 196–97.

23. Harry A. Wolfson, "The Spirit of Hebraism," trans. H.B. Ehrmann in *The Standard Book of Jewish Verse,* ed. George Kohut (New York: Dodd, Mead, 1917), 539.

24. Sarah Schmidt, "The *Parushim*: A Secret Episode in American Zionist History," *American Jewish Historical Quarterly* 65 (December 1975), 123.

25. See especially Henry Hurwitz's letter to Horace Kallen regarding Boston in Schmidt, "The *Parushim,*" 127–28.

26. Maier Bryan Fox, "Labor Zionism in America: The Challenge of the 1920s," *American Jewish Archives* 35 (April 1983), 55; Emanuel Neumann, *In the Arena: An Autobiographical Memoir* (New York: Herzl Press, 1976), 48–49.

27. Horace M. Kallen, *Zionism and World Politics: A Study in History and Social Psychology* (Garden City and Toronto: Doubleday, Page, 1921), 3.

28. See Evyatar Friesel, "Ahad Haamism in American Zionist Thought," in *At the Crossroads: Essays on Ahad Haam,* ed. Jacques Kornberg (Albany: State University of New York Press, 1983), 133–41. On utopianism and Zionism see Jonathan Frankel, *Prophecy and Politics: Socialism, Nationalism and the Russian Jews, 1862–1917* (Cambridge: Cambridge University Press, 1984), 288-328; Yosef Gorny, "*Hirhurim al hayesodot hautopiim hamahshavah hazionit,*" *Hazionot* (1984): 45–54.

29. Letter of Benjamin Rabalsky to Jacob De Haas, ca. 1916. Papers of Benjamin Rabalsky, American Jewish Historical Society, Waltham, Massachusetts.

30. Quoted in Allon Gal, *Brandeis of Boston* (Cambridge, Mass. and London: Harvard University Press, 1980), 187.

31. Leo Shubow, "Jacob DeHaas and the Boston *Jewish Advocate,*" in *Herzl Year Book,* vol. 5, ed. Raphael Patai (New York: Herzl Press, 1963), 286–87.

32. Louis D. Brandeis, "Zionism Is Consistent with American Patriotism," in *The Jew in the Modern World: A Documentary History,* eds. Paul Mendes-Flohr and Jehuda Reinharz (New York: Oxford University Press, 1980), 393.

33. "Zion Flag Week," December 1915. Papers of Benjamin Rabalsky, American Jewish Historical Society.

34. Jonathan D. Sarna, "'The Greatest Jew in the World Since Jesus Christ': The Jewish Legacy of Louis D. Brandeis," *American Jewish History* 81 (Spring/Summer 1994): 346–64.

35. Jonathan Frankel, *Prophecy and Politics*, chap. 9.

36. Jehuda Reinharz, "Zionism in the USA on the Eve of the Balfour Declaration," *Studies in Zionism* 9 (1988): 144–45.

37. Samuel Rodman, "*Ha-Gedud Ha-Ibri*," in *Kadimah*, ed. David S. Blondheim, 29.

38. Rufus Learsi, *Fulfillment: The Epic Story of Zionism* (Cleveland and New York: World, 1951), 205.

39. Hyman L. Meites, *A History of the Jews of Chicago*, reprint (Chicago: Chicago Jewish Historical Society and Wellington Publishing, Inc., 1990), 269–70.

40. Quoted in Evyatar Friesel, "Brandeis' Role in Zionism Reconsidered," *American Jewish History* 69 (September 1979), 51.

41. Ben Halpern, *A Clash of Heroes: Brandeis, Weizmann, and American Zionism* (New York and Oxford: Oxford University Press, 1987), chap. 4.

42. See Joseph B. Glass, "Balfouria: An American Zionist Colony," *Studies in Zionism* 14 (1993): 53–72.

43. Raphael Patai, ed., *Encyclopedia of Zionism and Israel*, vol. 2 (New York: Herzl Press and McGraw-Hill, 1971), 731.

44. Unpublished mss. (no title), 7–8, box 3. Papers of Elihu D. Stone, American Jewish Historical Society.

45. Maldwyn Allen Jones, *American Immigration* (Chicago and London: The University of Chicago Press, 1960), 276; John Higham, *Strangers in the Land: Patterns of American Nativism, 1860–1925* (New York: Atheneum, 1973), 277–86.

46. Melvin I. Urofsky, *American Zionism from Herzl to the Holocaust* (Garden City, New York: Anchor Press/Doubleday, 1975), 307–11.

47. Harry Levi, "Judaism," in *Fifty Years of Boston: A Memorial Volume Issued in Commemoration of the Tercentenary of 1930*, ed. Elisabeth M. Herlihy (Boston: Boston Tercentenary Committee, 1932), 624; Louis Hurwich, "Origin and Development of Jewish Teacher-training Schools in the United States: A Brief Historical Survey" in *The Education of American Jewish Teachers*, ed. Oscar I. Janowsky (Boston: Beacon Press, 1967), 5–6.

48. Quoted in Walter Ackerman, "A Land in Search of a People," paper delivered at an international conference, Ben-Gurion University, June 1993.

49. Harry Levi, "Judaism," 623–24; Leonard Finder, "The Open Door," in *The Brandeis Avukah Annual of 1932: A Collection of Essays on Contemporary Zionist Thought Dedicated to Louis D. Brandeis*, ed. Joseph Shalom Shubow (Boston: Avukah, American Student Zionist Federation, 1932), 643.

50. Mark A. Raider, "From *Yugnt* to *Halutzim*: The American Labor Zionist Youth Movement Between the First and Second World Wars," in *Zionism and Eastern Europe: New Perspectives*, ed. Allan Nadler (New York: YIVO Institute for Jewish Research, 1995).

51. Norman Salit, "The IZA and Its Significance," in *The Brandeis Avukah Annual of 1932*, 601–02.

52. *The Brandeis Avukah Annual of 1932*, iv.

53. See the emphasis on Ahad Haam in *The Brandeis Avukah Annual of 1932*, 117–45.

54. F25/56. Letter of the Provisional Executive Committee of Boston Avukah, 20 October 1925. Central Zionist Archives, Jerusalem.

55. Solomon Abramov, "Problems of Avukah Cultural Work," *The Avukah Bulletin* 4 (Adar 5692/February 1932), 2.

56. Samuel M. Blumenfield, "Whither Avukah?" *The Avukah Bulletin* 4 (Kislev 5692/December 1931), 1, 5.

57. Salit, "The IZA and Its Significance," 602.

58. A reference to the debate over Zionist criticism of Avukah including: Maurice Samuel, "The Nature of Avukah," in *The Avukah Annual of 1928*, ed. Herbert I. Bloom (New York: Avukah, American Student Zionist Federation, 1928), 9–10; S. L. Halkin, "What Ails Our Jewish American Youth," in *The Avukah Annual of 1928*, 3–4, 23–25; Samuel Saretsky, "Avukah vs. Intellectualism," in *The Avukah Annual of 1929*, ed. Leo Schwartz (New York: New York Chapter, 1929), 23–25.

59. Blumenfield, "Whither Avukah?", 5.

60. Blumenfield, "Whither Avukah?", 5.

61. John J. Tepfer, "Palestinian Personalities," in *Avukah Annual, Fifth Anniversary Edition, 1925–1930*, ed. Leo W. Schwartz, John J. Tepfer, James Waterman (New York: Avukah, American Student Zionist Federation, 1930), 117, 119, 121.

62. "Avukah on Labor in Palestine," *Jewish Frontier* 4 (February 1935): 34; Sol Geffner, "Avukah—LLP," *The Avukah Bulletin* (April 1936): 6.

63. Sholom Kaas, "Cap, Gown, and Shovel," *The Avukah Bulletin* (April 1936): 1.

64. Harry Levi, *A Rabbi Speaks* (Boston: Chapple, 1930), 27–28, 31.

65. "Statement of the 241 Reform Rabbis" in *The Rabbis of America to Labor Palestine* (New York: League for Labor Palestine, 1935), 7–8. Palestine collection, American Jewish Archives, Cincinnati, Ohio.

66. "Statement of the 241 Reform Rabbis," 12–13.

67. Michael A. Meyer, "A Centennial History," in *Hebrew Union College—Jewish Institute of Religion At One Hundred Years*, ed. Samuel E. Karff (Cincinnati: Hebrew Union College Press, 1976), 45.

68. Louis D. Brandeis, "Zionism Is Consistent with American Patriotism," 393.

69. Chanoch Rosenblum, "The New Zionist Organization's American Campaign, 1936–1939," *Studies in Zionism* 12 (1991): 169–85; Rafael Medoff, "Communication: The Influence of Revisionist Zionism in America during the Early Year of World War II," *Studies in Zionism* 13 (1992): 187–90.

70. *The Rabbis of America to Labor Palestine*, 12.

71. "Immigration for Labor Palestine!" editorial, *The Jewish Advocate* (Boston) 5 February 1935, 2.

72. A406/132. Papers of Robert Szold, Central Zionist Archives, Jerusalem.

73. "Palestine—The Land of the Future" editorial, *Jewish Advocate*, 18 January 1935, 4.

74. See the April 1938 series by Leo Shubow published in *The Boston Traveler*, especially 11 April 1938, 6; 13 April 1938, 1–2; 14 April 1938, 3–4; 15 April 1938, 2. Papers of Leo Shubow, American Jewish Historical Society.

75. Letter of Morris Margulies to Elihu D. Stone, 1933. Papers of Elihu D. Stone, American Jewish Historical Society.

76. See the following issues of Coughlin's *Social Justice*: 9 January 1939, 9; 20 February 1939, 7; 28 August 1939, 6; 4 September 1939, 10; 15 January 1940, 3, 6.

77. Gary T. Marx, *The Social Basis of the Support of a Depression Era Extremist: Father Coughlin*, monograph 7 (Berkeley: Survey Research Center, University of California, 1962), 60; David J. O'Brien, *American Catholics and Social Reform: The New Deal Years* (New York: Oxford University Press, 1968), 180.

78. Quoted in Frances Malino and Phyllis Cohen Albert, eds., *Essays in Modern Jewish History: A Tribute to Ben Halpern* (London and Toronto: Associated University Presses, 1982), 11–12.

79. A264/48. "Memorandum of Discussion at a Conference Called by Mr. Felix Frankfurter," unpublished mss., December 22–23, 1938, 28–38. Papers of Felix Frankfurter, Central Zionist Archives, Jerusalem.

80. A406/117. Laurence M. Ring, "The New England Programme," unpublished mss., April 10, 1941, 5–6, 10–11, emphasis in original. Papers of Robert Szold, Central Zionist Archives, Jerusalem.

81. IV–104–61. "Hechalutz Membership," 1 January 1940. Hechalutz in America Papers, Archives of the Labor Movement/ Lavon Institute, Tel Aviv.

82. Quoted in Bernard Wax, "1939–1948: The Years of Crisis and Fulfillment" in *Boston Jewry and Its Relationship to Palestine and Israel*, 6.

83. "The Development of Bnai Moshe, 1941–1951" in *Temple Bnai Moshe Dedication Book* (Brighton, Mass.: Published by Congregation Bnai Moshe, 1954), 171–72.

84. Cited in Bernard Wax, "1939–1948: The Years of Crisis and Fulfillment," 14.

85. A406/117. Laurence M. Ring, "The New England Programme," 1.

86. Transcribed interview with Harry Levine conducted by Leonard Slater, unpublished mss., 1969, 7–14, 27, 32–33, 49–52. Papers of Harry Levine, American Jewish Historical Society.

87. Abba Eban, "Dewey David Stone: Prototype of an American Zionist," *American Jewish History* 69 (September 1979), 11–12.

88. Eban, "Dewey David Stone," 8–9, 12–14.

89. Quoted in Simon Rawidowicz, "Only from Zion: A Chapter in the Prehistory of Brandeis University," in *Israel: The Ever-Dying People and Other Essays*, ed. Benjamin C. I. Ravid (London and Toronto: Associated University Presses, 1986), 241, emphasis in original.

90. Rawidowicz, "Only from Zion," 242, 244.

91. Max Lerner, *What Labor Zionism Means to Me* (New York: Shulsinger Bros., 1949), 16, 20–21.

92. Howard M. Sachar, *A History of the Jews in America* (New York: Knopf, 1992), 424.

93. Ludwig Lewisohn, *A Jew Speaks* (New York and London: Harper & Brothers, 1931), 120–21.

94. Marie Syrkin, *The State of the Jews* (Washington, D.C.: New Republic Books and Herzl Press, 1980), 196–97, emphasis in original.

95. Ben Halpern, *The American Jew: A Zionist Analysis*, 2d ed. (New York: Schocken, 1983), 13.

96. Ben Halpern, *The Idea of the Jewish State*, 2d ed. (Cambridge.: Harvard University Press, 1969), ix.

97. Ben Halpern, *A Clash of Heroes*, 8.

98. Ben Halpern, "Letter to an Intellectual," *Jewish Frontier Anthology, 1945–1967*. (New York: Jewish Frontier Association, 1967), 75.

Passionate Visions in Contest: On the
History of Jewish Education in Boston

JOSEPH REIMER

# *Passionate Visions in Contest:*
## On the History of Jewish Education in Boston

אי אפשר לבית המדרש בלא חידוש

"There is no house of study without some novel teaching."
TALMUD HAGIGAH 3a

HEN A PROFESSOR OF JEWISH EDUCATION, trained in
the social sciences, turns to writing a history, there had best be
some explanation of what he is up to. One thing is clear: this is *not*
an objective history of Jewish education in the Boston area.
Rather, this is a reflective essay on certain aspects of that history,
an attempt to address a broad theme of this volume, the question of what is distinctive about the Boston Jewish experience.

I am locating that distinctiveness in the passionate visions that have come to
expression in the creating and maintaining of the institutions of Jewish education in
the Boston area. Looked at from a dispassionate perspective, the history of Jewish
education in the Boston area is quite similar to parallel histories in other major areas
of American Jewish settlement. But seen as historical drama, as a play of dominant
Jewish personalities articulating vivid, but contrasting visions of American Judaism
and expressing those visions in the creation of Jewish educational institutions, the
story of Jewish education in the Boston area appears both colorful and distinctive.

This claim for distinctive coloring is not mine alone, but that of my predecessors
as well. In reviewing the few scholarly accounts of this history, I discovered that the
history we have available has been written by educators who have made and lived
that history. Their accounts are crafted as much to defend their visions as to recount
the major episodes of this story.

Nor can I claim to be outside this loop. Here again a Jewish educator who has
worked for most of his career in the Boston area is reflecting on the history of educational institutions of which he has been a part. I have struggled to represent positions other than my own in ways that show their power and inner logic, but I hardly
can claim to be objective. What I hope this account does convey is that while this

history is characterized by sharply contesting visions of education, it is also marked in more recent years by a blending of visions into programs that draw from many sources. From a contemporary perspective it as important to understand how we are heirs to the many educational visions as it is to see how distinctive each vision is.

If Jews were relatively late in settling in Boston, once they arrived in any numbers they began synagogues. Ohabei Shalom was the first in 1843 and Temple Adath Israel, a German breakaway, was the second in 1854. Both synagogues were sites to Jewish schools. In 1852 Ohabei Shalom moved into its own building and opened a school for thirty students. Several years later the congregation conducted a free day school in which English and Hebrew were taught to students of both elementary and secondary grades. In 1863 Adath Israel, opened a three-day school in which both languages were taught. We know little about these schools except that they operated before public school education was widely available.[1]

In the 1870's, as the membership of Adath Israel—later to be known as Temple Israel—became more economically and socially established, they hired Boston's first Reform rabbi. Rabbi Solomon Schindler introduced a number of controversial innovations into what had been a traditional congregation: family pews, organ and choir, and vernacular prayerbooks. Along with these came the first Reform Jewish Sunday school. Its classes met on Sunday mornings and Saturday afternoons and all religious instruction was conducted in English. This format proved popular and by 1891 the school had attracted ninety students. Ohabei Shalom and a third congregation, Mishkan Israel, also opened Sunday schools which lasted for decades. The teachers in these schools were volunteers; it is unclear if the schools had any formalized, graded curriculum.[2]

With the mass immigration of Eastern European Jews that began in the 1880's came the infamous *cheder*. This one-room, ungraded Jewish schoolhouse was run privately by a *melamed* (teacher) who taught primarily in Yiddish and in too many cases showed neither much Jewish erudition nor any feel for children. Parents would bring their sons for religious instruction prior to bar mitzvah and pay the *melamed* minimally for his services. These *chederim* would come and go, provisional providers of an instructional service for impoverished immigrant families.

The more highly organized Jewish school for immigrant children was known as a Talmud Torah. This too was an importation from Eastern Europe and was of varied quality. But some were a cut above in several ways. First, the teachers had some educational training. Second, there was more emphasis on studying Hebrew. Third, there was more of a graded structure than in the *chederim*. But the Talmud Torah schools were independently run and dependent upon tuitions. In an immigrant community some opened and scraped by while others closed for lack of funds.[3]

A new development in the world of Talmud Torah education began in 1904 when two Russian Jewish educators came to Boston and opened the first Hebrew school to teach *Ivrit B'Ivrit*. Literally, "Hebrew in Hebrew," this pedagogic technique emphasized the importance of studying not only the classical Hebrew texts of Jewish tradition but also the newly developing spoken Hebrew of the Zionist movement. While this first school aroused little interest, it may have paved the way for the opening in 1907 of *Evrio* by the Jewish People's Institute, a Zionist clubhouse. *Evrio* was the first Hebrew-speaking school to flourish in Boston. By 1915, the year of its first graduating class, *Evrio* had a co-educational student body of almost 400 students.[4]

By World War I, the Boston Jewish community had developed two separate strands of Jewish schooling. In the immigrant neighborhoods there were the *chederim* and Talmud Torah schools, transplants of Eastern European Jewish culture. Among Americanized, second-generation Jews there were the synagogue-based Sunday schools which taught Judaism in English as a liberal religion for cultured Americans of this persuasion. The teachers of these two types of schools would literally not have been able to understand one another had they met to discuss Jewish education. The grounds for visions in contest had been laid.

FIG. 1. Evrio Hebrew School, 31 North Russell Street, West End, Boston, ca. 1920, in the building that also housed the "Boston Rabbinical School." *American Jewish Historical Society.*

The *chederim,* Talmud Torah schools, and Sunday schools were individual institutions developing on their own. In 1917, this picture changed with the entry into the Jewish educational field of the Federated Jewish Charities and Louis Hurwich, the man of the hour.

In 1916 Morris D. Waldman came from New York City to become the superintendent of the Boston Federated Jewish Charities. He introduced the idea of the Federation's supporting Jewish education in the community. When in 1917 a surplus of funds unexpectedly appeared in the budget, Waldman invited Louis Hurwich, an educator from Indianapolis, to conduct a survey of Jewish schools in Boston. Hurwich

FIG. 2. Yeshiva, 87 Poplar Street, West End, Boston, ca. 1920. *American Jewish Historical Society.*

found that there were 1,529 students enrolled in the Talmudei Torah schools, or Hebrew schools, and 1,800 students enrolled in the Sunday schools. But the Hebrew schools were in particularly difficult straits, with very poor facilities, a lack of funds, and a shortage of qualified teachers and principals. Hurwich recommended that the Federation allot $20,000 to the improvement of the Hebrew schools and $10,000 to the Sunday schools. His recommendations were approved by the Federation for 1918.

Such communal funding for Jewish education was quite unprecedented, but Hurwich went much further. He helped to bring together the heads of the twelve Hebrew schools and persuaded them to unite under the banner of the Associated Boston Hebrew Schools. They then elected him as superintendent of the association to implement the results of the survey. Hurwich began by tackling the shortage of qualified teachers. In 1918 the Hebrew Teachers Training School was opened to train American students to become Hebrew teachers for the schools. As a strong Zionist and advocate of the *Ivrit B'Ivrit* method of teaching, Hurwich established the training in Hebrew. The students would learn in Hebrew the subjects they would one day teach—Tanach, Hebrew language, and Jewish History—as well as receive training in pedagogy.

In parallel fashion the Sunday schools united under separate auspices and appointed Rabbi Hyman Solomon to head their Bureau of Jewish Religious Schools. In 1919 a training program in English for training Sunday school teachers was opened with a registration of one hundred students. When in 1920 Rabbi Solomon returned to the rabbinate, the two separate associations were merged into one central agency, called the Bureau of Jewish Education (BJE), with Hurwich appointed as superintendent.[5] Though this was not the first central agency of Jewish education to be established in the United States, "it was the first truly communal agency... [which] from its inception received its support from the local Federation."[6] By 1920 Jewish education had rapidly expanded: twenty-four Hebrew and thirteen Sunday schools as well as the two training programs were placed under the auspices of the BJE.

Though Hurwich was now in charge of developing both strands of Jewish education, he unapologetically brought his Hebraic agenda to the BJE. As historian

Walter Ackerman notes, Hurwich clearly insisted that "not all forms of Jewish schooling were of equal worth." Ackerman contends that the incorporation of the Reform Sunday schools into the BJE was only a tactical measure to gain the support of Federation leaders for funding Jewish education. For Hurwich had "a clear and uncomplicated notion of what constituted a Jewish education. His ambition was to create in Boston 'a miniature Volozhin' and to educate generations of American Jewish children to be the 'spiritual heirs of the traditional Ben Torah.'"[7]

FIG. 3. Reading Room, Kadima Hebrew School, Dorchester, Boston, ca. 1925. *American Jewish Historical Society.*

If Volozhin, the site of the famous 19th-century Lithuanian Yeshiva, was Hurwich's model, it is clear that the Sunday schools of the classical Reform movement could not be part of his plan. Their whole religious and educational approach was antithetical to all that Volozhin represented. Yet it was also a long way from Volozhin to the Hebrew schools of Boston. Ackerman explains how Hurwich expected to span the gap.

> *When translated into practice that vision required first of all, a significant commitment of time—a 6 year 5 day-a-week* Talmud Torah *which met for 7 ½ hours for the first two years and 10 hours-a-week thereafter. That was the framework for a curriculum which was designed to provide the linguistic base which permitted the subsequent study of the whole Torah . . . and Early Prophets . . . The course of study was rounded out by Hebrew grammar,* Dinim U'Minhagim *and History, the only subject taught in English.*[8]

Ackerman is describing Hurwich's devotion to creating an educated American Jew who would have access in the original language to the sources of Jewish tradition. This ideal found expression in the BJE curriculum that by 1923 was adopted uniformly by all the Hebrew schools affiliated with the BJE. All these schools agreed to hold classes for five days a week and teach in Hebrew the same subjects on the same schedule. This amazing degree of standardization would not have been possible had there not been a solid consensus among the school educators that this curriculum embodied the principles and methods of Jewish education in which they believed. This consensus was achieved by the Bureau working with two institutions, the Hebrew Teachers College and the Hebrew Teachers and Principals Association.

FIG. 4. Bar Mitzvah class, Malden, Massachusetts, ca. 1920. *American Jewish Historical Society.*

FIG. 5. First graduating class of Hebrew Teachers College, Roxbury, Boston, 1925. *Hebrew College, Brookline, Massachusetts.*

In 1921 Hurwich reorganized the Hebrew Teacher Training Program into the Hebrew Teachers College (HTC), a four-year degree-granting institution, with the mandate of training teachers to meet the philosophy and needs of the Hebrew schools. Two years later, Dr. Nisson Touroff,[9] the first dean of HTC, added a Hebrew high school course, called the Prozdor, to the college. In Hurwich's words, "Hebrew schools vied with each other in preparing qualified graduates for the Hebrew high school."[10] Touroff approached the principals of the Hebrew schools to request that they standardize their curriculum so their graduates could start off on equal footing in the Prozdor. By Hurwich's testimony, that argument proved persuasive and the standardized curriculum of the BJE was uniformly adopted.

Of course the schools would not have agreed had not an ideological consensus already been formed. In fact, Boston had by 1912 one of the earliest Hebrew Teachers Organizations in the country. In 1922 a parallel Principals Association was formed. These organizations, which would merge in 1948, were "both a union and a fellowship. Educators bearing the proper credentials and willing to comply with stipulated practices could belong to the organization which offered social and professional activities as well as some economic protection."[11]

The BJE worked closely with these professionals to create a mutually reinforcing system of Hebrew education. The BJE hired the staff for the schools but would only hire members of these organizations. In turn the organizations helped set the criteria of professionalization required for joining and being hired. The BJE set the salary scales by which the teachers and principals were paid, but that scale insured that no school could hire less qualified teachers for less money. Working together, the BJE and the professionals created a system of schools in Boston that shared a common vision of education and supported full-time employment for Jewish educators who had the training and commitment to make Hebrew education their life's calling.[12]

The next step in creating this mutually reinforcing system came in 1929 when the BJE introduced uniform achievement testing into all the Hebrew schools. Since the curriculum was uniform and the teachers were teaching the same material on the same schedule, the BJE could introduce content-based examinations in grades two through five to determine the achievement levels of all those students. The exams were scored at the BJE and the results for each school and class were published. Hurwich believed this was an important step in ensuring the quality of instruction in the system. He also made sure that the results of the examinations had real consequences. For the students, admission to the Prozdor depended on their level of achievement. For the teachers, advancements and salary increases were recommended in part on the basis of their students' performances on these standardized examinations.[13]

By the end of the 1920's Hurwich had put in place all the elements of the system of Hebrew education that would remain the dominant paradigm in Jewish education until the 1960's. In retrospect Ackerman believes Hurwich's achievements were monumental. "The fact remains that the 5-day-a-week Talmud Torah schools at the height of their development raised their graduates to a level of knowledge and skill only rarely matched in supplementary Jewish education in the United States."[14] Yet Ackerman and Hurwich have admitted that these schools, even at their height, had trouble retaining students. Hurwich wrote in 1929 that "the Hebrew school in its present form imposes a selection on all who enter it, and that all who are below normal intelligence drop out very early."[15] What he calls "normal intelligence" may have had much to do with children's facility with language and capacity to sit still for long hours.

FIG. 6. Mattapan Religious School, Woodrow Avenue, Mattapan, Boston. *American Jewish Historical Society.*

While Hurwich expresses regrets about these students' dropping out, the Boston system was "unashamedly elitist"—a posture Ackerman believes was influenced by Boston's ethos, by "a city which boasted of the Public Latin school . . . and such prestigious universities as Harvard and M.I.T."[16] Hurwich and his supporters could justify a very high dropout rate because they believed that the value of an educational system was to be judged by what its elite had learned and not by the fate of the "weaker" students. In Boston, from the years of World War I through World War II, when the Jewish neighborhoods had thriving ethnic cultures, that judgment may have made sense. Children dropping out of Hebrew school still lived in

# Jewish School Buildings, Past and Present, and Jewish Educational Leaders

**Menorah Institute**

24 Elm Hill Avenue, Roxbury. Erected by Congregation Adath Jeshurun in 1925. Consists of seven class-rooms, an office, a library, play rooms and an auditorium. Cost $125,000.

DR. SAMUEL PERLMAN
Dean, Hebrew Teachers' College

**Typical Jewish School Building Only a Few Years Ago**

PROFESSOR NATHAN ISAACS
President, Bureau of Jewish Education

**Beth El Hebrew School**

6 Bradshaw Street, Dorchester. Erected in 1924 by Congregation Beth El. Contains 12 class-rooms, offices, an auditorium seating 800, assembly and dining room facilities. Cost $180,000.

**Temple Center**

1187 Beacon Street, Brookline. Erected 1926 by Congregation Ohabei Shalom. Contains 13 class-rooms, offices, club-rooms and auditorium, gymnasium facilities. Cost $250,000.

**Hebrew Teachers' College**

14 Crawford Street, Roxbury. Erected 1925. Contains eight class-rooms, office, gymnasium, library and study hall, dining and medical examination rooms. Cost $80,000.

**Temple Israel School-House**

Longwood Avenue and Riverway, Boston. Erected 1928 by Congregation Adath Israel. Consists of 20 class-rooms, library, club-rooms and auditorium. Cost $1,000,000.

**Mishkan Tefila School-House**

122 Elm Hill Avenue, Roxbury. To be erected during current school year by Congregation Mishkan Tefila, at an estimated cost of $225,000. Will contain 14 class-rooms, an auditorium seating 800, a library, club-rooms, offices and meeting rooms.

**Bostoh Y. M. H. A.**

108 Seaver Street, Roxbury. Quarters of the Jehuda Halevi Sunday School.

**Metropolitan Theatre**

The above picture shows the beautiful lobby of the Metropolitan Theatre where 5,000 Jewish children will assemble on Sunday morning, October 21, to celebrate the beginning of the Jewish school year. Facilities of the Metropolitan Theatre are given free for the occasion.

DR. LOUIS HURWICH
Superintendent, Bureau of Jewish Education

**Second Year High School Class of Beth El Hebrew School**

Left to right: Upper row—R. Ruben, H. Marcus, S. Chase, M. Mundlick, M. Goldman B. Kravetz, B. Schoolman, E. Weiner. Middle row—Esther Shyken, C. Goldberg, H. H. Waldman, Mr. M. Shore, teacher of class; Mr. C. H. Waldman, principal; L. Barron, B. Linshitz, M. Leader. Last row—N. Ratefsky, R. Goldman, D. Furman, E. Tarutz.

Above pictures show a section of the pedagogical exhibit held in connection with the last year's Jewish Education Week.

DR. LEON S. MEDALIA
President, Hebrew Teachers' College

MAX SHOOLMAN
Prominent Boston Business man and philanthropist, who secured the facilities of the Metropolitan Theatre for the children's celebrations last year and also this year.

intensely Jewish environments.[17] But once those neighborhoods changed, and the Jews spread out into the more Americanized suburbs, the educational system's elitism would become too great a burden to bear.

For all the intensive focus on Hebrew education, the Talmud Torah schools were still supplementary schools whose students attended public schools as their primary form of education. Hurwich in Boston, as Samson Benderly in New York, assumed that American Jews were wedded to the practice of sending their children to the public schools.[18]

The first in Boston to challenge that assumption was Rabbi Joseph B. Soloveitchik. The scion of a famous line of Lithuanian rabbis—his grandfather was a pre-eminent *rosh yeshiva* at Volozhin—Soloveitchik emigrated to Boston in 1932, a year after completing his Ph.D. at the University of Berlin. He and his wife, Tonya, settled in Roxbury where he assumed a rabbinic post. There they found that Orthodox families, as their Conservative counterparts, were sending their children to the public schools and the Hebrew schools run by the BJE.

We do not know what Soloveitchik thought of the Talmud Torah education, but he could not abide Orthodox families sending their children to public schools. What he proposed instead, and what he and his wife became very involved in establishing, was the first 20th-century Jewish day school in New England. In 1937 the Soloveitchiks, together with a few other families, founded the Maimonides School.[19]

Pioneers in Boston, the founders of the Maimonides School were working in parallel with a handful of other Orthodox Jews who between 1935 and 1939 founded twelve other new day schools in the United States and Canada. Alvin Schiff describes a pattern of struggle that these day schools went through before establishing themselves that also is descriptive of the early days of Boston's first Orthodox day school.[20]

The Maimonides School opened with six children and one teacher and was shortly evicted from its first home in a Dorchester Hebrew school. The school relocated to the Young Israel of Roxbury in a very modest facility. The Soloveitchiks were heavily invested in keeping the school afloat but with much communal criticism for their efforts. They were accused of breaking the accepted American Jewish norm of sending children to the public and Hebrew school and of trying to recreate the Jewish ghetto of Europe. Yet despite the criticism, a small group of families formed a web of support around Rabbi Soloveitchik and remained faithful to the school

FIG. 9. Jewish education in Boston took place in a variety of locations, from individual homes, to storefront classrooms, to independent Hebrew schools, to impressive facilities attached to synagogues. *Top to bottom:* Hebrew Kindergarten, 1919, location unknown. Hashachar Hebrew School, 1006 Blue Hill Avenue, Dorchester, Boston, 1920's. Hashachar Hebrew School, interior. The curtained stage likely covers a *bimah* and *aron kodesh*. All photographs *American Jewish Historical Society*.

through its hard beginning. He, too, remained faithful to the school even after being appointed professor at the Yeshiva University in New York.

During the early years, the Maimonides School was submerged in debt. The man who would become "the Rav," the spiritual leader of modern Orthodoxy, invested much of his time fundraising for the school. In 1941 the founders managed to buy their first site in Dorchester, and by 1945 the school reached six grades and received accreditation from the Boston School Department. Yet there simply was not much support for the school, certainly not from Federation, and even a majority of Orthodox families continued to send their children to public and Hebrew schools.[21]

In the face of such indifference and hostility, why did the Soloveitchiks persist? First there was the fear that Orthodoxy was disappearing from Boston. Perhaps they realized that while the combination of public and Hebrew school education was creating a literate elite of Jewish youth, the system Hurwich established did not have a strong religious base and was not designed to protect and nurture the growth of religiosity among the young.

But beyond the fear there was also a positive alternative vision of Jewish education. Soloveitchik strongly believed in the need to create a synthesis of modernity and tradition, a Jewish educational system that took charge of both secular and religious education and taught the students to find the inner compatibility between these seemingly conflicting ways of knowing the world. Soloveitchik had no interest in recreating the ghetto but believed that by ceding the secular studies to the public schools, the Jewish community was missing an all-important opportunity to demonstrate how the synthesis is built, how each modern Jew internalizes both domains of knowledge and builds for him/herself the bridges between science and

FIG. 10. Maimonides School students and faculty, Dorchester, Boston, 1947. *Maimonides School, Brookline, Massachusetts.*

religion. That lesson could only be taught in an all-day school in which both types of learning were synthesized into an integrated curriculum.[22]

Hurwich was not critical of Rabbi Soloveitchik's efforts as he was of the Reform movement.[23] In fact there were interesting parallels between their visions. Both were Zionists who believed in the importance of teaching Hebrew. Both believed in and practiced coeducation. Both were elitists who took their models of excellence from Volozhin and Harvard. But they did part philo-

FIG. 11. Kadimah Hebrew School, 147 Canterbury Street, Dorchester, classroom with photograph of Theodore Herzl on the wall, ca. 1925. *American Jewish Historical Society.*

sophic company on the question of what is essential to Judaism and Jewish knowledge. Hurwich was definitely respectful of traditional religious practice, but for him Hebrew cultural continuity was of the essence. Soloveitchik was a supporter of the Hebrew renaissance, but for him the study of Talmud and the practice of *halacha* (Jewish law) were of the essence.

Even given the considerable overlap between these visions, Soloveitchik stood for a trend in American Judaism that Hurwich would miss. The Rav seemed to understand that for all its secular character, American culture was deeply religious, and that American Jews would follow that norm. While few Jews would become observers of *halacha*, many would seek a certain spirituality in their lives and a Jewish education for their children which had more of a religious base than the Talmud Torah offered. Hurwich's cultural Zionism would begin to seem dated after World War II.

As Rabbi Soloveitchik was struggling to establish day school education, another young and dynamic rabbi, who was soon to become famous, came to Boston with a considerable educational agenda of his own. In 1939 Temple Israel, by then the largest and most prominent Reform congregation in the Boston area, brought Joshua Loth Liebman to be its rabbi.

Under the direction of its previous leader, Rabbi Harry Levi, Temple Israel had been staunchly classical Reform in its religious philosophy and practice. While Rabbi Levi took great pride in the congregation's Sunday school and spearheaded the drive to build a magnificent building in which to house the school and many adult educational activities, he also had insisted on maintaining the educational focus on the ethical teachings of Judaism, a curriculum that could be taught once-a-week entirely in English. During the 1920's this approach was highly attractive and the Temple Israel religious school opened three branches in neighborhoods distant from the school building. But in the 1930's, when economic times turned much harder and the rise of Nazism in Europe dealt a blow to classical Reform, the Temple and its religious school lost some of its attractiveness and much of its clientele.[24]

Liebman came to Temple Israel with an ambitious program to redirect its religious outlook. He abolished Sunday services, reinstated Friday night services, reintroduced Bar Mitzvah and, with his staunchly pro-Zionist stance, brought the Hebrew language back into the gates of the temple. More broadly he taught that Judaism was more than an expression of ethical monotheism; it was the rallying point of the Jewish people, a bedrock of spiritual comfort at a time when the very survival of this people was being radically called into question.

During the 1940's Liebman introduced sweeping changes in Temple Israel's religious school. The school had been run primarily by Jewish public school teachers who taught at the school as a second job. Liebman brought a second Reform rabbi, Sylvan Schwartzman, to be the school's educational director. Together they introduced into the curriculum more traditional holiday observances, a Jewish liberal arts program, some Hebrew, and a more complete curriculum of Bible and Jewish history. Then in 1945 they took the largest step: opening a twice-weekly Hebrew program. Although voluntary, the Hebrew program was a clear statement that Sunday school was not sufficient for Reform Jews; that knowing Hebrew was not a thing of the past, a relic of Eastern European Jewish culture, but a wave of the Jewish future in America. As bar and bat mitzvah would become normative for Reform Jewish families, so would learning at least enough Hebrew to read from *Neviim*. Prophetic Judaism was soon to recover the tongue of its prophets.[25]

FIG. 12. Rabbi Joshua Loth Liebman. *Temple Israel, Boston.*

Liebman published *Peace of Mind* in 1946, and through this best-selling synthesis of religion and psychology became, almost overnight, a famous author. Unfortunately he did not live long thereafter, dying suddenly in the spring of 1948. But the religious and educational innovations that he brought to Temple Israel would remain after his death, a harbinger of the changes that would sweep in the postwar era through Reform Judaism and Reform Jewish education. Yet these changes did not bring an immediate rapprochement between the Reform community and the BJE. They had started too far apart and each was moving in accordance with its own internal ideological rhythms rather than in concert with one another.[26]

The Boston Jewish community went into the years of World War II living in concentrated neighborhoods within the city of Boston and the suburbs immediately to the west of the city. But in the years following the war the community began to move and settle in the many suburbs ringing the city. This migration did not take place at once and was not always voluntarily undertaken. But this gradual migration had enormous consequences for the institutions of Jewish education.

In 1947 Louis Hurwich retired from his dual positions as the head of the Bureau and as Dean of the Hebrew Teachers College (a position he had held since 1932). Leadership of the BJE passed to Dr. Benjamin J. Shevach who had worked for Hurwich and shared the founding vision of the BJE. Dr. Eisig Silberschlag was appointed Dean of HTC, and the College became autonomous, separating itself from the Bureau, and appointed its own Board of Trustees. At this point both institutions were located within the city and receiving their entire funding from the Federation.[27]

By 1950, large numbers of Jews had begun moving from Roxbury and Dorchester to suburbs like Brookline and Newton. Many Jewish institutions followed the population shifts. Hebrew Teachers College voted to move to Brookline in 1951. Otto and Muriel Snowden, leaders in the effort to sustain an integrated community in Roxbury, purchased the HTC property for the Freedom House.[28]

Mishkan Tefila, the oldest and largest Conservative congregation in Boston, was also located in Roxbury. The congregation concluded in the middle 1950's that its future lay in the suburbs. By 1958 the congregation moved to Newton and sold its magnificent temple and school buildings to Lubavitcher Jews.[29]

Dorchester and Mattapan, whose Jewish communities remained large in the 1950's, emerged as the home base for the five-day-a-week Hebrew schools that Shevach and the BJE championed. These schools were still thriving in the city and were also established in some of the near suburbs, notably at Kehillath Israel in Brookline. Yet even in 1950 only a third of the children attending Jewish schools were enrolled in these schools. A newer type of Hebrew school, the three-day-a-week school, which was favored in suburban areas, accounted for fourteen percent of the total enrollment. But the predominant form of Jewish schooling was the Sunday school in which almost half the children were enrolled. The 1950's saw the

FIG. 13. Dr. Benjamin J. Shevach. *Hebrew College, Brookline, Massachusetts.*

Sunday school's peak of popularity. In Temple Israel, for example, enrollment in the religious school rose from 412 in 1942 to 1,156 students in 1954.[30]

Nevertheless the banner story of the 1950's was population movement. While many new schools had opened during the 1940's—twenty in the suburbs and eight in the city—the 1950's saw more school openings and closings. Thirty-four new schools opened and nineteen existing schools closed. The direction of population movement was towards the suburbs. Only four new schools opened within the city, and ten closed. The suburbs saw the opening of thirty new schools, while nine closed.

There was also movement toward synagogue affiliation. Of

the thirty-four new schools to open in the 1950's, thirty were synagogue-affiliated. That contrasts vividly with the 1940's in which less than half of the twenty-eight new schools were synagogue-affiliated. Of course the trends toward the suburbs and synagogue affiliation overlap. Jews moving to the suburbs tended to start new synagogues in which they would open new schools. Depending on the educational outlook of the synagogue leadership, the synagogue school might be a Sunday school or a three- or five-day Hebrew school.[31]

As the Jews moved outward, the role of the BJE expanded. By 1954, twenty-one new (suburban) towns were added to the list of locations that it serviced. Dr. Shevach at the BJE and the lay leaders of the United Hebrew Schools (UHS)— an organization begun in 1945 to provide a lay voice in support of intensive Jewish education —were clearly in favor of maintaining the five-day Hebrew school as the paradigm for synagogue education. They saw no inherent difference between what Jewish education should be in the city or suburb, in a community-based Talmud Torah or a synagogue-affiliated Hebrew school.[32]

FIG. 14. Freedom House, Roxbury, the former site of the Hebrew Teachers College. *Brochure in a private collection.*

The BJE may have opposed the suburban trend towards three-day Hebrew schools, but they did accommodate to the new reality. In 1950 the Bureau issued a standardized curriculum for the three-day schools. When new three-day Hebrew schools opened, they could affiliate with the BJE and enter into the established system as a three-day school. The school would agree to follow the BJE's standardized curriculum and hire only certified teachers approved by the BJE. Yet Shevach kept certain privileges for the five-day schools. For example, entry into the Prozdor was predicated on having completed the five-day curriculum. Graduates from three-day schools were required to come up to the standards of the five-day paradigm through special preparatory classes if they wished to gain admission.[33]

Still, the three-day Hebrew schools, whose enrollments during this decade increased from fourteen to thirty-six percent of the total, put great pressure on the BJE system, particularly in terms of employment patterns. The arrangement of Hebrew schools' hiring only BJE-certified teachers became harder to maintain as the number of teaching positions kept increasing, while the positions offered were increasingly part-time. The decrease in full-time positions and the increase in part-time teaching positions would prove the hardest new development for the BJE system to handle.[34]

If the rapid expansion of the 1950's challenged the adaptive qualities of the BJE system, the 1960's, with its bewildering cultural and demographic changes, would prove overwhelming. Yet the 1960's and early 1970's were also the period when much of what was to replace the old BJE system was taking shape. As Professor Susan Shevitz of Brandeis University observed,

> *Though we tend to associate "the challenge of the sixties" with the changing cultural mores, the primary challenge to Jewish education in the Boston area was demographic. Enrollments of children in Jewish schools almost doubled between 1948 and 1960. But 1960 was the peak year, with enrollments consistently decreasing for the next 25 years. This pattern is not unique to the Boston area, but is quite consistent with national trends in Jewish education and with the maturation of the post-war baby boom.*[35]

In Boston the late fifties and sixties was the time when the remaining, vibrant urban Jewish enclaves in Dorchester and Mattapan moved out of the city.[36] Nine urban Jewish schools closed in the sixties, bringing to a virtual end the sixty-year history of Hebrew schools in the city of Boston. In 1962 the Maimonides School also moved out of Boston. But, as we will see, their move to Brookline was not seen so much as the closing of an era as the start of a new era.

The sixties, then, was the decade of the suburbs. Seventeen new schools opened in the suburbs, and by 1970 only four Jewish schools would remain in the city. It was also the decade when the three-day Hebrew school became the predominant form of schooling, with great fall-offs in enrollments in both the five-day Hebrew schools and the Sunday schools. Also for the first time enrollments in Jewish day schools began to climb.

The day school story is of interest. By 1950 there were already five day schools in Boston, all of them under Orthodox auspices, but they were small and poorly funded. Yet by 1962 Maimonides had raised the money to dedicate a million dollar new campus in Brookline for their expanded K–12 school. By then the first Conservative-sponsored Solomon Schechter Day School had opened in the Boston area, a harbinger of the growth of non-Orthodox day schools during the following decades. By 1970 day school enrollment had expanded from four percent in 1960 to nine percent of total school enrollments.[37]

But the main story of the sixties was the increasing strain between the BJE's Dr. Shevach and the Reform and Conservative congregations in the suburbs. As we saw first with Temple Israel, the Reform movement was undergoing internal changes which greatly affected its educational practice. As more Reform congregations adopted traditional ritual practices, and especially the practice of bar and bat mitzvah, the demand grew for knowledge of Hebrew. The decline in Sunday school enrollments corresponded with increasing enrollments in three-day programs sponsored by Reform congregations. In 1960 the BJE appointed a special consultant to work with Reform congregations, but the effort remained peripheral to BJE concerns.[38]

FIG. 15. Hebrew College, 43 Hawes Street (rear view), Brookline, Massachusetts. *Hebrew College.*

The main BJE concern was how to keep its now predominantly Conservative-sponsored Hebrew schools faithful to the traditional standardized curriculum. Tensions flared mainly around two issues: ideology and teacher shortages.

In synagogue-sponsored schools there is a concern, often expressed by the rabbi, to present Jewish sources in ways consistent with the movement's understanding of Judaism. During the sixties the Conservative movement on a national level invested great time and energy in creating a curriculum that reflected the movement's understanding of how Bible ought to be taught. But as that approach, known as the Melton curriculum, was quite out of line with the Bureau's traditional emphasis on textual mastery in Hebrew, the BJE fought to keep it out of the Boston-area schools. The BJE prevailed in this battle during the sixties, but was perceived by some Conservative rabbis and educators as increasingly out of step with the times.

Teaching of the Hebrew-based curriculum had always depended on the availability of trained teachers with the requisite skills to convey *Ivrit-B'Ivrit* lessons. As the numbers of both full-time teaching positions and students training at HTC began to fall precipitously, the availability of trained teachers declined. The Board-affiliated Hebrew schools were not supposed to hire other teachers who did not have proper certification. But when the shortage became acute, some schools took matters into their own hands, hiring whomever they could to fill their classrooms. The BJE saw this practice as undermining its whole system, but given the shortage of available teachers, all it could do was complain; it had little to offer in the way of trained teachers.[39]

Tensions came to a boil in the late sixties, when the Federation entered the picture and asked for changes in the BJE system. Shevach responded with a resounding defense of the traditional curriculum. But ideological defense could not produce the needed teachers. Nor was the alliance between the BJE and the educators intact as it had been. By the late sixties there were new educators in place who had not come

FIG. 16. Hebrew College reading room around 1977. *Hebrew College.*

through the HTC training and whose loyalties to the standardized curriculum were minimal. The tensions continued until Federation mandated a comprehensive study of the BJE and its functions. Perhaps not coincidently, the issuing in 1973 of that report, known as the Report of the Study Committee, corresponded with Benjamin Shevach's retirement as head of the Bureau. By the early seventies, the Hurwich-Shevach era, which had begun in 1917, had come to its end.[40]

Ackerman describes the Report of the Study Committee as calling for a basic paradigm shift: asking the BJE to move from being a supervisory body to becoming a service agency. In particular, the report recommended that "the Bureau place its emphasis on serving the needs of the schools in such areas as curriculum development, in-depth consultation and evaluation and teacher recruitment and training." Those services should be offered not only to "elementary afternoon schools but also Day Schools, Secondary Schools and programs of informal Jewish education."[41] The call was for the BJE to broaden its definition of Jewish education and work with schools and agencies on achieving *their* goals rather than see itself as setting the Jewish educational goals for the whole community.

By the seventies Jewish education in the Boston area had become a very diverse enterprise. The diversity grew out of the spread of the community to the many corners of suburbia, the influx of many Jews from other geographic areas, and the vitality of the denominational movements. The number of denominational day schools expanded and included Maimonides School (founded 1937 in Roxbury, moved to Brookline in 1962 and 1964; Orthodox), the New England Hebrew Academy (founded 1944 in Dorchester, moved to Brookline in 1967; Orthodox), Shaloh House (founded 1960 in Mattapan; moved to Milton in 1975, with schools also in Stoughton, Andover, and Brighton; Orthodox), the Solomon Schechter Day School of Greater Boston (founded 1961 in Brookline, moved to Newton in 1962; Conservative), Torah Academy (founded 1982 in Brookline; Orthodox), The Rashi School (founded 1986 in Newton, now of Needham; Reform), Striar Hebrew Academy (founded 1986 in Sharon; Orthodox), and South Area Solomon Schechter Day School (founded 1989 in Stoughton; Conservative).

There was also the burgeoning presence of Judaica on many university campuses in the Boston area. When Hurwich founded the Hebrew Teachers College in 1921 he was introducing Judaica (as taught by Jews) to higher education in the area. By the 1970's most of the major universities had professors of Judaica and some, as in the case of Brandeis University, had full departments of Judaic studies. Jewish education, or at least the teaching of Judaism, was now taking place in many contexts; no one institution could hope to define or control all these contexts.

With the end of the period of standardization came a period of diversification. There was now an open market for ideas in Jewish education. To take one example, in 1968 two rabbis on the Brandeis campus—Arthur Green and Albert Axelrad—decided to establish a new type of educational institution, the *havurah*. Their initial idea was to begin an alternative seminary that would attract college graduates who wished to pursue advanced Jewish studies, but in the context of living in an intense religious communal arrangement. Havurat Shalom Community Seminary opened its doors in Somerville in September 1968 and caused quite a stir. The Havurah was meant to be a paradigm of a new type of Jewish community in which Jewish study, practice and spirituality were to infuse the lives of the members. The language of the Havurah was heavily influenced by the counter-culture of the day and, as its critics were fast to point out, the community that it claimed to model had only limited relevance to most Jews.[42] Yet two outcomes of the *havurah* experience would have considerable influence on the course of Jewish education in this period of diversification.

In 1973 three members of Havurat Shalom published the *Jewish Catalog* which to their amazement proved to be a huge publishing success. There followed in succession the second and third *Catalogs*.[43] The idea animating the *Jewish Catalog* was simple: make available to people in a language they could understand some of the

FIG. 17. Maimonides School, Philbrick Road, Brookline, Massachusetts. *Maimonides School.*

more culturally appealing aspects of Jewish life and they would respond with interest. In a sense these volumes represent the antithesis of Hurwich's elitist vision. They were designed to make Judaism available to the masses without asking them to pass through the rigorous training of a Hebraic curriculum. Their use as curricular materials in some schools and adult education courses represented for some educators the downfall of Jewish education and for others a reaching out to new audiences.

As the *Jewish Catalog* was becoming successful, Brandeis Professor Bernard Reisman, among others, had the idea of taking the *havurah* model and applying it to synagogue life. Reisman argued that the large suburban synagogue that had developed in the 1950's was no longer meeting people's needs for community and intimacy, and that by encouraging their interested members to form *havurot*, synagogues would help to revitalize the sense of community within the congregation. A number of synagogues within the Boston area responded to Reisman's challenge and began to encourage the formation of *havurot* within their congregations. These *havurot* largely appealed to families with younger children, helping them join together to celebrate Jewish occasions.[44]

A decade later in the mid-1980's when a movement began to introduce Jewish family education into the synagogue context, it was not surprising that the Boston area would become one of the movement's active centers. There was only a small step from the formation of *havurot* in the congregation to introducing more formalized instruction and experiences for Jewish families.[45] But in contrast to the experience with *havurot* in the seventies, the introduction of family education would heavily involve the communal institutions as well as the synagogues. It would occasion the re-emergence of an institutional alliance from a past era.

The Federation—now called the Combined Jewish Philanthropies of Greater Boston—had already begun a new involvement in Jewish education by offering annual financial support to the growing number of day schools. In seeking ways to aid synagogues' work in Jewish education, CJP created a Task Force on Supplementary Jewish Education. One avenue of support included small grants to synagogues for programs in Jewish family education. The Federation turned to the BJE to help administer the grants, consult with the synagogue and schools, and evaluate the programs.[46]

As the programs in Jewish family education took hold, CJP, the synagogues, and the Jewish community centers took a further step in 1993 with the creation of Sh'arim/Gateways to Jewish Living: The Jewish Family Educator Initiative. The first goal of this initiative was to help synagogues and JCC's that had family educational programs to hire full-time Jewish family educators to coordinate these programs. The BJE continued its role of consulting with the congregations, but now the community turned to Hebrew College (which had changed its name to acknowledge that teacher training was no longer its primary mission) to develop the Family Educator Training Program. This two-year program was to help professionalize family educators by offering them courses in Jewish family life, in Judaica, and in working educationally with families.[47]

In a sense the wheel has come full circle. In pursuing the goals of Jewish family education, the CJP, the Bureau, and the College are working together, this time with the synagogues and community centers, in setting up educational programs and training educators to run them. The vision guiding Jewish family education stems more from the Havurah movement than from cultural Zionism, and the founders might wonder what courses in English on the Jewish life cycle are doing in Hebrew College. But these are how the times have changed. The BJE is servicing family educators rather than dictating practice to Hebrew teachers. But from an historical perspective, we might point out that for all of the changes in particulars, many of the elements of the system that Hurwich established are still in evidence seventy-five years after his coming to Boston.

In this historical account of Jewish education in the Boston area, it is hard to contend that what has happened in Boston has not taken place in other American Jewish communities. From Hebraism to Jewish family education, the elements are present in many other communal histories. But I would argue that Boston has its own distinctive way of pursuing this common history.

There are three inter-related elements that can be seen as distinctive to the Boston experience: (1) strongly-articulated ideologies of Jewish education that are (2) elitist in nature and (3) articulated by charismatic personalities.

Louis Hurwich remains the paradigmatic example. He was hardly alone in his generation of leading Jewish educators to hold the educational views that he espoused. But few were as dogged as he in putting those ideological convictions into practice. Few were as openly elitist as he, and few as persuasive in getting many of the other elements in the community to go along with his vision and institutional arrangements.

Rabbi Joseph Soloveitchik was not the first in the American Orthodox community to advocate the establishing of day school education. Nor is Maimonides School much different in practice from other Hebrew day schools of its kind. Yet who was as eloquent as the Rav in articulating an educational rationale for integrating secular and religious studies? Who could match his particular charisma or embody as he did that elite vision of religious experience in a secular culture?

Similarly, Rabbi Josh Loth Liebman was not the pioneer of the move in Reform Jewish education away from the classical model. Yet his particular impact on Temple Israel, itself an elitist institution in his times, was distinctive and lasting, and his ability to formulate the leading religious questions for a generation remain an impressive testimony to his charismatic leadership.

Finally when we turn to Rabbi Arthur Green, the founding leader of Havurat Shalom, we find again the qualities of a strongly-held ideological position articulated by a charismatic figure. Paradoxically, for all the popularism of Havurah ideology, Havurat Shalom itself was criticized for being an elitist institution. Perhaps its location in the Boston area contributed to that perception.

Distinctive elements represent both the strengths and weaknesses of an educational system. Walter Ackerman is concerned that "we have shied away from conscious efforts geared to the development of an elite," for "societies which ignore and neglect the formation of elites seriously mortgage their futures."[48]

But with thriving Jewish day schools and university-level programs of Judaica, Boston still tends to do well with its elite populations. Perhaps the other side also needs consideration.

For all its impressive achievements, has Jewish education in the Boston area succeeded in reaching and touching the majority of Jews who live in the area? Perhaps the future need not repeat the past and excellence need not come at the price of exclusivity.

1. Louis Hurwich, "Jewish Education in Boston (1843–1955)," *Jewish Education* 26 (Spring 1956): 22.

2. Hurwich, "Jewish Education," 23; Arthur Mann, ed., *Growth and Achievement: Temple Israel 1854–1954* (Cambridge: Riverside Press, 1954), 48–50.

3. Hurwich, "Jewish Education"; Meir Ben-Horin, "From Turn of the Century to the Late '30's," in *A History of Jewish Education*, ed. Judah Pilch (New York: American Association of Jewish Education, 1969), 56–57.

4. Hurwich, "Jewish Education."

5. Hurwich, "Jewish Education," 23–24.

6. Walter Ackerman, "From Past to Present: Notes on the History of Jewish Education in Boston," *Jewish Education* 51 (Fall 1983): 17.

7. Ackerman, "From Past to Present," 18–19.

8. Ackerman, "From Past to Present."

9. For more on noted Russian-born Hebrew writer and educator Nisson Touroff see "Nisson Touroff," in *The Universal Jewish Encyclopedia*, ed. Isaac Landman (New York: Universal Jewish Encyclopedia, 1943), vol. 10, 286.

10. Hurwich, "Jewish Education," 25.

11. Susan L. R. Shevitz, "Supplementary School Consolidation in the Jewish Community: A Symbolic Approach to Communal Decisions" (Ph.D. diss., Harvard Graduate School of Education, 1987), 76.

12. Daniel J. Margolis, "The Evolution and Uniqueness of the Jewish Educational Structure of Greater Boston," in *Studies in Judaica and Jewish Education in Honor of Louis Newman*, ed. Alexander Shapiro and Burton Cohen (New York: Ktav, 1984), 89–91.

13. Shevitz, "Supplementary School," 76; Hurwich, "Jewish Education," 26; Louis Hurwich, "Standard Examinations in Greater Boston Hebrew Schools," *Jewish Education* 1 (May 1929): 118.

14. Ackerman, "From Past to Present," 23.

15. Hurwich, "Standard Examinations," 117.

16. Ackerman, "From Past to Present," 23.

17. Hillel Levine and Lawrence Harmon, *The Death of an American Jewish Community: A Tragedy of Good Intentions.* (New York: Free Press, 1992), 33–43.

18. Walter Ackerman, "The Americanization of Jewish Education," *Judaism* 24 (Fall 1975): 416–35.

19. "Legacy: Rabbi Dr. Joseph Soloveitchik and the Maimonides School," *Kol Rambam* (October 1993): 4; "Maimonides School Dedication Commemorative Edition," *Jewish Advocate*, 13 September 1962, 2.

20. Alvin I. Schiff, *The Jewish Day School in America* (New York: Jewish Education Committee Press, 1966), 38–41.

21. "Legacy," *Kol Rambam*, 4–8; Levine and Harmon, *Death of an American Jewish Community*, 39–40.

22. "Maimonides School," *Jewish Advocate*, 2–4. For a broader philosophic statement see Joseph B. Soloveitchik, *Halakhic Man* (Philadelphia: Jewish Publication Society, 1983), 10–11.

23. Hurwich, "Jewish Education," 31.

24. Mann, *Growth and Achievement*, 38–39, 85–86.

25. Mann, *Growth and Achievement*, 102–14.

26. Ackerman, "From Past to Present," 23.

27. Hurwich, "Jewish Education," 34.

28. Levine and Harmon, *Death of an American Jewish Community*, 44–57. See also Gerald Gamm's essay in this volume.

29. Levine and Harmon, *Death of an American Jewish Community*, 58–63.

30. Shevitz, "Supplementary Schools," 75, 86; Mann, *Growth and Achievement*, 25–45.

31. Shevitz, "Supplementary Schools," 80–81.

32. Hurwich, "Jewish Education," 29; Ackerman, "From Past to Present," 22–23.

33. Ackerman, "From Past to Present," 21; Shevitz, "Supplementary Schools," 83–84.

34. Susan L. Shevitz, "The Deterioration of the Profession of Jewish Supplementary School Teaching" (Qualifying paper, Harvard Graduate School of Education, 1983).

35. Shevitz, "Supplementary Schools," 85.

36. Harmon and Levine, *Death of an American Jewish Community*. See also Gerald H. Gamm, "Neighborhood Roots: Exodus and Stability in Boston, 1870–1990" (Ph.D. diss., Harvard University, 1994).

37. Shevitz, "Supplementary Schools," 84–86; "Maimonides School," *Jewish Advocate*, 2.

38. Shevitz, "Supplementary Schools," 86–88. For changes in the Reform movement in the post-war period see Michael A. Meyer, *Response to Modernity: A History of the Reform Movement in Judaism* (New York: Oxford University Press, 1988), 354–378.

39. Shevitz, "Supplementary Schools," 89–91.

40. Shevitz, "Supplementary Schools," 93–94.

41. Ackerman, "From Past to Present," 17.

42. Stephen C. Lerner, "The Havurot," *Conservative Judaism* (Spring 1970): 2–15.

43. Richard Siegel, Michael Strassfeld, and Sharon Strassfeld, eds., *The Jewish Catalog* (Philadelphia: Jewish Publication Society, 1973); Sharon Strassfeld and Michael Strassfeld, eds., *The Second Jewish Catalog* (Philadelphia: Jewish Publication Society, 1976); *Sharon Strassfeld and Michael Strassfeld, eds.,* The Third Jewish Catalog (Philadelphia: Jewish Publication Society, 1980).

44. Bernard Reisman, *The Chavurah* (New York: Union of Hebrew Congregations, 1977).

45. For fuller treatment of Jewish family education see Joseph Reimer, "Jewish Family Education: Evaluating its Course, Looking to its Future," *Journal of Jewish Communal Service* 67 (Summer 1991): 269–78.

46. The BJE's evaluation is in part reported in Susan L. Shevitz and Joan Kaye, "Writing for Sesame Street, Directing Traffic, Marketing a Product and Saving Souls: Jewish Family Educators Describe Their Practice," *Journal of Jewish Communal Service* 67 (Summer 1991): 279–89.

47. "Boston's CJP to be Honored in Montreal," *Jewish Advocate*, 8 October 1993, 1.

48. Ackerman, "From Past to Present," 26.

# The Smart Set:
# An Assessment of Jewish Culture

STEPHEN J. WHITFIELD

# *The Smart Set:*
## An Assessment of Jewish Culture

הולך את חכמים יחכם
"He who keeps company with the wise becomes wise."
PROVERBS 13:20

RECENT SCHOLARLY WORK that explores the back-woods folkways of white Southerners—from their penchant for bear baiting and livestock poaching to their recourse to family feuds and moonshining—is entitled *Cracker Culture,*[1] which sounds oxymoronic. It emits no air of mandarin elevation and moral seriousness, unlike such phrases as "Boston culture" or "Jewish culture." Especially when combined, these particular adjectives seem *meant* to modify a term that has become indispensable to the lexicon of the intelligentsia. Indeed "culture" has by now been stripped of its power to specify and enlighten, because the term embraces everything. (Consider, if only for the sake of alliteration, the tedium that acquisitions librarians risk when facing titles like *The Culture of Capitalism, The Culture of Compassion, Culture of Complaint, The Culture of Consent, The Culture of Consumption, The Culture of Contentment,* etc.) Overuse of the word should be a heuristic warning but not a deterrent, however; and the normative sense of "culture"—its denotation of excellence in the arts and sciences and humanities, its expression of the most exalted heritage of civilization—is what merits consideration in assessing Boston's contributions to American Jewish life.

The topic is daunting; and readers are therefore urged to be indulgent, since it presents challenges that are both conceptual and synthetic. For example, to situate the evolution of any culture within a metropolitan area is itself problematic—but even more so in Jewish historiography. How significant is an attachment to place for a people that has hallowed time (defining one day of the week as holy), that failed to record Revelation as occurring on its own land, that usually worked in the Diaspora with its bags packed? Jewish history has no analogue for the Socratic preference for suicide over exile. In a common room at Cambridge University, the

cosmopolitan biographer of the cosmopolitan Leon Trotsky once disparaged the
study of his own "roots." "Trees have roots," Isaac Deutscher, born near Cracow,
opined. "Jews have legs."[2] An unsettled people is not unsettling in an American
context, however, since mobility is an American trait from which Boston has hardly
been exempt. The Hub City has been a mecca as well. Unlike Mecca, which pro-
hibits infidels within its gates, Boston has lured a wide diversity of intellectuals who
have come there to learn, to write, to teach—that is to say, to help establish para-
digms as well as to express heterodoxy. How long does it take to make such residents Bostonians, or to be the custodians of its culture? How is the creativity of
those born elsewhere to be incorporated into contributions to Boston Jewish life?
Without evidence of fierce pride of place or an abiding sense of local affiliation, no
confident answers can be given.

Transience works in more than one direction, of course. Dating from 1920, a
notorious "Curse of the Bambino," in which the Red Sox sold a pitcher named G. H.
"Babe" Ruth to New York, has afflicted culture as well. The Boston Symphony
Orchestra ignored a musical genius who had been born in Lawrence, raised in
Newton and Sharon, educated at Boston Latin School and then Harvard, and
groomed at Tanglewood; so Leonard Bernstein went on to conduct and compose in
New York instead. Or take the case of the avatar of "the new historicism," Profes-

sor Stephen Greenblatt, who had been raised in "a passion-ately Jewish household" in Newton; he was turned down for admissions to Harvard College and became a superstar in cultural studies on the other side of the continent, at Berke-ley.[3] But the reverse route has been more common for Jewish intellectuals, who have come to Boston far more conspicu-ously than they have departed from it.

Does such mobility mean, however, that they are Bosto-nians? Would that category include, for example, two of the four living American laureates of the Nobel Prize for Peace? Henry A. Kissinger earned his doctorate at Harvard in 1954 and soon thereafter taught for twelve years on its faculty, where his fame in political as well as academic circles began. It was only during government service in Washington (1969–1977), including a Nobel Prize in 1973, that Kissinger became the nation's most admired citizen and (according to the Miss Universe contestants of 1974) "the greatest person in the world today."[4] After leaving the Department of State,

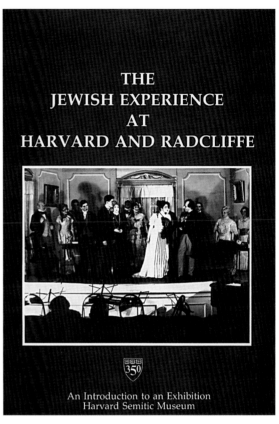

THE
JEWISH EXPERIENCE
AT
HARVARD AND RADCLIFFE

An Introduction to an Exhibition
Harvard Semitic Museum

FIG 2. "The Jewish Experience at Harvard and Radcliffe" exhibi-tion catalog from the Harvard Semitic Muse-um exhibition of the same name, 1986. *American Jewish Histor-ical Society.*

he returned to New York, where he had been raised after his family had fled Nazi Germany in 1938. Though Kissinger's work in international relations (as theorist and practitioner) has scarcely affected the formation of Jewish culture (other than to prove the openness of the American polity itself), he shares one trait with the most resonant and eloquent voice of the American Jewish community; for only by the most generous criteria can Elie Wiesel be considered a Bostonian. He has taught at Boston University since 1976, and a decade later won the Nobel Prize for Peace while on its faculty. But the wrenching path from Sighet through Auschwitz and Buchenwald, and on to Paris, has culminated in New York City, where he has for-mally resided. Writing mostly in French, Wiesel has set almost none of his fiction in America—much less in Boston.

If such figures illustrate the hazards of any attempt to define a Bostonian, the contributions of the community's thinkers and artists to Jewish culture entail risky definitions as well. The city has nurtured or attracted enough prominent Jewish intellectuals to dominate any Hall of Fame, if a Cooperstown for the U.S. intelli-gentsia existed. But how they helped shape Jewish culture requires close analysis. A book could easily be done—an exhibition and catalogue *were* done, in 1986—on the accomplishments only of Jewish students and faculty at Harvard and Radcliffe, tracing some features of their lives in what has arguably been—from an era before the United States even existed—its premier institution of learning. More than an essay needs to be written just on the influence upon Judaic scholarship exerted by faculty members at Brandeis University, which is by contrast less than half a century old. Yet the participation of academic figures in communal organizations and local culture varied very widely. The intellectual legacy of Boston has certainly been fostered by its more than four dozen institutions of higher education, and the Boston accent can be detected in the *Ursprache* of the nation's intelligentsia. But there is no single intellectual tradition to which the local Jews have subscribed, no common discourse which they have spoken.

Yet the ancient tongue of this people curiously unites two figures whose careers illustrate the sheer diversity that any chronicler of Boston's Jewish culture is forced to acknowledge. It is fitting that the first noteworthy Jew to settle in Boston was not a merchant but an academic: Judah Monis, the author of a Hebrew grammar (1735) and the recipient of a Harvard M.A. degree—the first college degree a Jew received in the American colonies. But Boston's first consequential Jew was also a terminal Jew, a convert, though Monis might not have been a Christian by choice. Baptism was a condition of employment at Harvard, where he had been appointed instructor in Hebrew as early as 1722 and would hold the post for nearly four decades.[5]

FIG 3. Caricature of Noam Chomsky by David Levine, drawn for *The New York Review of Books. Forum Gallery, New York.*

In terms of international reputation, the most consequential Jew in Boston since the 1960's also specialized in Monis's field of Hebrew grammar. A product of the Zionist movement and of an observant home in Philadelphia, Noam Chomsky had proofread when barely a teenager his father's edition of a medieval Hebrew grammar, and considered quitting the University of Pennsylvania in the late 1940's, "because I wanted to go to the Middle East to live on a kibbutz and work for Arab-Jewish cooperation."[6] Instead Chomsky moved to Boston in 1951 as a Junior Fellow at Harvard, where his work on transformational (or generative) grammar was "so unorthodox," he recalled, "that at the end of my three-year term as a Junior Fellow no one would hire me as a linguist. The only job I could find was teaching Hebrew at Brandeis for twelve hours a week, at $3500 a year."[7] Remaining instead at Harvard for another year and beginning his teaching career at Massachusetts Institute of Technology in 1955, he would soon shape a major branch of linguistics that was so innovative that his first book, *Syntactic Structures* (1957), had difficulty getting published—except in The Hague.

Chomsky was devoted to the active as well as contemplative life. His most famous manifesto against the Vietnam war, "The Responsibility of Intellectuals" (1967), had first been published in a local Jewish student magazine, *Mosaic*. Yet implacable anti-Zionism makes the relationship of this self-described "libertarian socialist" to Boston Jewry problematical. Perhaps no Jew—and almost no one else—in American academic life has been icier in his hostility to the state of Israel, as reflected in two books on the subject, *Peace in the Middle East?* (1974) and *The Fateful Triangle* (1983). The energies of an iconoclast and controversialist also made him, in 1973, "too busy" to attend the most distinguished of endowed academic lectures—named after Charles Eliot Norton at Harvard, in which Leonard Bernstein's *The Unanswered Question* tried to trace possible connections between music and Chomsky's linguistics,[8] which signifies the vibrancy of the culture of the Jews, which is not quite synonymous with Jewish culture.

Volume 1, Number 1          Spring/Summer 1986

FIG 4. *MOSAIC: A Jewish Student Journal*, revived by Harvard students in 1986. The original *MOSAIC* was published by Harvard-Radcliffe Hillel from 1960 to 1973. *American Jewish Historical Society*.

But what exactly does Boston have to do with it? Journalist Theodore H. White claimed that, except for New York City, "Jewish communities in America absorbed the ideas of their host cities";[9] and yet despite the inclusion of his hometown in that generalization, no proof is offered in his engaging autobiography. In documenting a case for local influences, White didn't have *bubkes*—and no wonder, since no unbridgeable fault lines divide one American Jewish community from another. Jews have surely been affected by their neighbors; but they have also *differed* from their neighbors by resembling their co-religionists elsewhere in the United States. Boston did not create a unique Jewish subculture but a variation on the American norm. When the Hebrew poet Ephraim Lisitzky arrived in Boston in 1900, he "felt like an alien," because "the learned and the pious . . . [were] a small minority." He could not forget "the impression of my first Saturday in Boston. I compared it to the Sabbath in Slutzk and my heart bled. . . . Slutzk, though poverty-stricken, dressed up in glorious raiment in honor of the Sabbath." But what Lisitzky lamented about Boston would have been applicable to any American community. The city of his adolescence was not unusual, in that "very few Jews observed the Sabbath. . . . Leaving the synagogue after the Sabbath service, the observant were confronted by a tumultuous Jewish quarter; shopkeepers stood in their shop doorways; peddlers on their wagons shouted their wares. . . . As I entered our house[,] it seemed to me that the Sabbath candles were bowed in mourning."[10] The standards of the *shtetl*, which linked learning and piety, could not be transplanted to Boston even by those who had so recently fled from the Old World.

There is nevertheless something to be said for the admittedly secularized intellectual *intensity* of Boston that almost no American community could surpass. Harry A. Wolfson could vividly recall the devout sobriety of the Lithuanian yeshivas of his own *fin-de-siècle* youth. But there was something intoxicating about Harvard, with the unsurpassed resources of its library, the tranquillity and openness with which esoteric learning could be pursued, the challenge he accepted of elucidating all of medieval philosophy from Philo to Spinoza—to say nothing of the freedom from the fear of what would now be called "hate crimes"; and the intellectual integrity of Cambridge that Wolfson idealized propelled him far from the certitudes and practices of the tradition to which Lisitzky was pledged. Or consider a native son like Theodore White himself, who was probably the brainiest reporter ever to work for Henry R. Luce's *Time* Magazine. White's flair for foreign affairs was hardly stifled at home or in the classroom. "The Boston Latin School had given me reading knowledge of Latin, German and French," he recalled. "Yiddish I understood from home. Hebrew was the language I knew I spoke best after my native English." At Harvard he was active in the Zionist Avukah Society and picked up Mandarin Chinese. White won a fellowship to China, from which he would send such compelling dispatches during the convulsions of the civil war and the Japanese invasion that *Time* broke precedent by bestowing a by-line—a couple of decades before he became the authoritative, if oleaginous, quadrennial chronicler of Presidential campaigns.[11]

An aura of intellectuality penetrated areas that have ordinarily been immune to its charms. It is rare enough for department store magnates to be reflective; but perhaps the *only* historical figure so inclined was Edward A. Filene, who founded the Twentieth Century Fund to support research on economic and social questions, befriended Lincoln Steffens, and wrote *Morals in Business* (1935) and other books, plus articles that appeared in the *American Economic Review,* the *Atlantic Monthly,* and the *Nation.*[12] Nor is it necessary for authors of science fiction to be scholars. But on the short list of the century's most influential practitioners of that genre was Isaac Asimov, an associate professor of chemistry who taught at Boston University Medical School from 1949 until 1958. (*The Foundation Trilogy* [1966] was only one of this polymathic graphomaniac's achievements, since he wrote—not edited—over two hundred books, mostly at his West Newton home. Asimov's speed as a writer was limited only by his speed as a typist.) It is also very peculiar for baseball players to earn advanced degrees; but Moe Berg, a catcher for the Red Sox (1935–39) and other teams, had also been a Doctor of Philosophy, a Doctor of Laws, an instructor of Romance Languages at Princeton, and an off-season student at the Sorbonne. Other Jews must surely have been affected by the value that local tradition placed upon learning, which an incident in 1921 revealed. Theoretical physicists are usually not treated with the indulgence of celebrities. But when Albert Einstein came to Boston to solicit funds for the Hebrew University on Mount Scopus (bringing Chaim Weizmann and other Zionists along with him), the German scientist's train was met with a brass band in the morning and with a kosher banquet in the evening.[13]

FIG 6. Moe Berg as a Boston Red Sox Catcher, from a baseball card. *Private collection.*

Surely it helped that the religious heritage of the Puritans and Brahmins was so austerely literate (rather than, as with "cracker culture," so casually anti-intellectual). Even though the Puritans' intolerance of heresy, blasphemy, and just plain orneriness is what the modern imagination still associates with colonial New England, and even though one Solomon Franco was banned in Boston as early as 1649 (and kicked back to Holland),[14] it did not discomfort the legatees of a people that had lived by The Book that the magistrates and ministers were so haunted by what they called the Old Testament. Governor William Bradford of Plymouth Plantation taught himself to write in Hebrew out of "a longing desire to see with my own eyes something of that most ancient language and holy tongue . . . in which God and angels spake to the holy patriarcks, of old time."[15] A century later the third endowed professorship at Harvard was established—in Hebrew. The patrimony of Puritanism lingered. Among the last Brahmins was an Associate Justice of the Supreme Court who not only took pride in the ancestry that shone in the cognomens of Oliver, Wendell, and Holmes; the "Yankee from Olympus" also found himself drawn to admiring younger Jewish intellectuals like Louis D. Brandeis, Felix Frankfurter, Harold J. Laski, and Morris Raphael Cohen, who knew *yichus* when they saw it.[16]

The enlightened liberal heritage of Boston's intelligentsia should not be romanticized, however, or rearranged to prefigure the pluralist standards of the late 20th century. Though Henry Wadsworth Longfellow's "The Jewish Cemetery at Newport" (1852) is tinged with awe for the historic grandeur of the people buried there, he took for granted the desuetude of the remnant, doomed to extinction. Another poet, Ralph Waldo Emerson, the anti-institutionalist apostle of individualism and free-thinking, cast his first vote as a member of Harvard's Board of Overseers in favor of compulsory chapel (abolished in 1886.)[17] James Russell Lowell veered from

pride in the possibility of Jewish ancestry to the flip-side symptoms of insecurity and snobbery, from admiration for the "universal ability of the Hebrew[s]" to concern for the loss of social status that their rise adumbrated. This "race in which ability seems as natural and hereditary as the curve of their noses," he observed, "made their corner the counter and the banking-house of the world, and thence they rule it with the ignobler scepter of finance."[18] The rancid antisemitism of Henry Adams, whom Lowell probably influenced in this respect, is too notorious to need elaboration here,[19] though it is worth noting that his bigotry went over the top only in the 1890's, while mordantly observing the Washington scene. That the outstanding scholarly biographers of Lowell and Adams should turn out to be, respectively, Martin Duberman and Ernest Samuels—both Jewish—is a delicious historical irony.

The administration of Lowell's distant cousin, A. Lawrence Lowell, has mostly accounted for the notoriety of Judeophobia on the Harvard campus; his discriminatory policies in the 1920's have been extensively investigated.[20] A national vice-president of the nativist Immigration Restriction League, President Lowell scarcely combatted the antisemitic feelings that many undergraduates harbored, and privately told an alumnus that equal treatment depended on the Jews' willingness to abandon their "peculiar practices." When once challenged to justify the quota policy, Lowell asserted that fifty percent of the students caught stealing books from Widener Library the previous year were Jews. But he must have felt sheepish when asked what the total number of students caught that year had been; the answer was: "Two."[21] Until the era of the Second World War, Jews found it extremely difficult to get tenure at Harvard. The Department of Philosophy admittedly managed to make room for Harry A. Wolfson, a scholar of almost frightening erudition. His achievements were duly recognized and honored. But it required the initiative of a Jewish philanthropist, Lucius N. Littauer, to create a chair in Hebrew Literature and Philosophy that paid Wolfson's salary. Another precedent was shattered only in 1939, when the Department of English hired Harry Levin and granted him tenure four years later.[22] Social and religious prejudice was hardly confined to the citadels of the Ivy League, but Harvard's acquiescence in putting such anti-democratic sentiments into practice encouraged others.

Jewish faith in the meritocratic ideal was eventually vindicated, and the most generous impulses of democratic Cambridge and Boston were eventually honored. The "City upon a Hill" never became a Forbidden City. But a price was often exacted—the abandonment of Judaic tradition. Perhaps those "peculiar practices" would have been jettisoned anyway, but the appeal that the residues of the Puritan culture exerted was undeniable. The impact of assimilation was perhaps especially pronounced in the sciences, which, as far back as Cotton Mather's promotion of vaccination against smallpox, was argued to be compatible with faith. In the intervening couple of centuries, however, such an assumption was undermined. Reason and revelation largely parted, forcing the historian to note how rarely scientists of Jewish origin can be included in the saga of an explicitly Jewish culture.

FIG 8. Norbert Wiener in his MIT classroom. *The MIT Museum, Cambridge, Massachusetts*

FIG 9. *Time* magazine cover of Edwin Land aiming the new Polaroid camera at the reader, June 26, 1972. *Copyright 1972 Time Inc. Reprinted with permission.*

Consider the generational difference between Leo Wiener, a remarkable Harvard philologist whose first book surveyed a language he preferred to call Judeo-German—*The History of Yiddish Literature in the Nineteenth Century* (1899)—and his even more remarkable son. Norbert Wiener matriculated at Tufts at the age of eleven, got his doctorate in mathematical logic from Harvard seven years later, and taught for over four decades at MIT. As the founder of "cybernetics" (a term he coined—just as Asimov invented "robotics"), Wiener was spiritually descended from the creator of the Golem, Rabbi Judah Loew of Prague, though the first volume of Wiener's illuminating autobiography records the delicacy with which his parents treated the misfortune of Jewish origins. These he could not, as a point of honor, repudiate. "Yet it was equally impossible for me to come into the fold of Judaism. I had never been there," he recalled. "It was emotionally impossible for me to hide myself in the great majority as a fugitive from Judaism; but it was equally impossible for me to hide myself and be consoled in a restrictedly Jewish community."[23]

As an absent-minded genius, Wiener was the stuff of legend;[24] so too was the career of a far more practical scientist. Edwin Land was in fact the most famous inventor to emerge in postwar Boston, though he had dropped out of Harvard as a freshman to work on cameras, telescopes, and sunglasses. In 1943, when his three-year-old daughter asked him during a vacation why she could not have snapshots right away, he did not reply to Jennifer in the classic manner of a Ring Lardner father ("'Shut up,' he explained"). Instead Land went for a stroll and figured out, in his head, the basic design of what

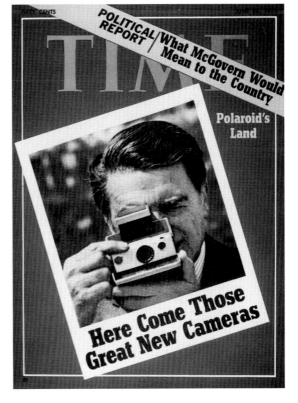

became the Polaroid Land Camera, which first went on sale at Jordan Marsh department store in 1948. Within a quarter of a century, Land's own Polaroid stock was already worth about half a billion dollars—a financial vindication of his devotion to "the art of the fresh, clean look at the old, old knowledge." The planet's richest scientist, he was also involved in classified defense work, including the CIA's scanning of Soviet territory from the U-2 spy plane, and thus personified the entrepreneurial achievements of high technology which were fueled by Pentagon contracts, which in turn contributed so decisively to Boston's postwar prosperity. (The military even funded Chomsky's linguistics at MIT.) Though Norbert Wiener had refused early in the postwar era to cooperate with the Department of Defense,[25] he and Land shared a resolute secularism that reduced Jewishness to a birth defect rather than an identity to be explored or a heritage to be cultivated. Looming large in any general account of how Jews have punctuated the nation's culture, such figures belong, however equivocally, to local Jewish history as well.

"In all countries where Jews have equal rights with the rest of the people, they lose their fear of secular science," according to Mary Antin, the author of perhaps the most endearing and influential, if indirect, case for frictionless integration into a hospitable society. Assimilation was a *condition* that Norbert Wiener and Edwin Land lived out. Assimilationism was a *program* that Leo Wiener inculcated and that Mary Antin advocated. Her roots were in Polotzk, Russia (near Vitebsk). But her legs took her to Boston, where she offered a deliberate response to the promise of American life with an autobiography dedicated to Josephine Lazarus—the sister of

Emma Lazarus, the first American Jew whom Emerson ever really met, and whose 1883 sonnet welcomed "the wretched refuse of your teeming shore." Antin's *The Promised Land* (1912) evokes the ordeal of pogroms and desperation in the Pale, where "Passover was celebrated in tears . . . In the story of the Exodus we would have read a chapter of current history, only for us there was no deliverer and no promised land." So at the end of the seder, instead of "Next year in Jerusalem," it was "Next year—in America!"[26] The promised land was not located in historic Palestine but in the New World, where a liberal democratic polity, a secular system of public education, and an expanding capitalist economy would bring redemption. The opportunities of a free society could be expected to terminate a long history of persecution; integration could be achieved so successfully, she implied, that the United States was no *Galut*.

It is not coincidental that her ideal of Americanization was brandished at the same historic moment that two other Bostonians devised other programs — Zionism and cultural pluralism — to address the novelties of the Jewish condition in the United States. *The Promised Land* was published three years before both Louis Brandeis's speech on "Zionism and Patriotism" and Horace M. Kallen's article in the *Nation* on "Democracy versus the Melting Pot: A Study of American Nationality." This cluster is suggestive. In the three decades before the outbreak of the Great War, huddled masses had landed in unprecedented numbers from Northern Europe, Southern Europe, Eastern Europe, and East Asia. Yet of all the immigrant groups, the Jews seemed to produce the most incisive writers on the topic of how such groups might be accommodated to American life. In this era Jewish immigrants were vacuum-packed into the impoverished neighborhoods of virtually every major city. Yet of all these bustling ethnic communities, Boston stimulated the most resonant ideas about the reshaping of America through the interplay of minorities.

When fresh questions about *e pluribus unum* were being posed (and nativists were giving the wrong answers), Antin, Brandeis, and Kallen pondered the destiny of Jews in an open society. Of course the three Bostonians (all born elsewhere) were hardly alone in defining—or championing—these particular variations on being Jewish at the dawn of the century. But Israel Zangwill, the melodramatist of *The Melting-Pot* (1908), was not an American; and Randolph Bourne, the author of "The Jew and Trans-National America" (1916), was not even an "ethnic," much less Jewish. Antin, Brandeis, and Kallen worked out the three models of Jewish identity that would be fulfilled, modified, and revised over the course of the 20th century—not only in Boston, but throughout the United States. Their gift for envisioning the meaning of the national experiment, and for specifying the place of their own minority, would be bestowed upon future generations of Jews who would opt for the only serious alternatives that America presented: assimilationism, Zionism, cultural pluralism.

Brandeis and Kallen became the most vocal prophets of the ideals of Jewish nationalism and ethnic pluralism, and stated most cogently how a liberal democracy could both sustain and be reinforced by Jewish communal continuity. How the leadership of Louis Brandeis, the local "people's attorney," affected American Zionism is recounted in Mark Raider's essay in this volume. Here another legacy that Brandeis inaugurated deserves to be traced—in the profession he adorned. This lineage is progressive, pragmatic, experimental; above all it defines the law as an instrument of liberal social amelioration, as a lever of enlightened and rational policy. This family tree also has roots, sunk into the pivotal institution of the Harvard Law School.

FIG. 11. Supreme Court Justices Oliver Wendell Holmes, Jr. and Louis D. Brandeis in the 1920's. *United States Supreme Court.*

FIG 12. Felix Frankfurter with Justice Brandeis. *Franklin Roosevelt Library.*

Brandeis had been in the audience when Holmes delivered his path-breaking Lowell Lectures on "The Common Law" (1880); and just as the recent graduate of the Law School had been something of a Holmes disciple, Brandeis was to transmit to other Jews a sense of the law that was uncommon. His was a capacious vision of its potential for remedying the social injustices that accompanied industrialization. His law clerks included not only a future Secretary of State, Dean Acheson, but also David Riesman, the co-author of one of the most influential works in the canon of American social science, *The Lonely Crowd* (1950), as well as Paul A. Freund, who taught Constitutional law at Harvard. But the jurist's most famous disciple was, of course, Felix Frankfurter, "half brother, half son," who shared Brandeis's proclivity for activism (though only briefly his Zionist commitment). From his perch as the first Jew hired to teach at the Harvard Law School, Frankfurter plunged into a host of causes, as a contributor to *The New Republic,* as a defender of the rights of aliens and labor unions, and perhaps most famously as a palladin for the procedural rights of Sacco and Vanzetti—in a case so internationally notorious that it was the subject of the first production of the Yiddish *Yung teater* in Poland; the play was entitled *Boston* (1933). Frankfurter also posted early warnings against Nazi barbarism and, in a very rare self-reference, described himself in a wartime dissenting opinion as a member of "the most vilified and persecuted minority in history."[27]

Frankfurter's progressive heirs could be said to take quite divergent paths. His compulsive kibitzing was replicated in the behind-the-scenes career of one of his clerks, Richard N. Goodwin, in whom Garry Wills discerned "a discriminating feel for where the action is going to be, an automatic way of slumping toward the action's center, and a gift for focusing everyone's attention on it." Born in Allston-Brighton as Richard Ginsberg, raised in Brookline, valedictorian at Tufts, first in his class at Harvard Law School, subsequently a resident of Concord, Goodwin was closest to the center of the action as an assistant and speech-writer to Presidents Kennedy and Johnson, and as a speech-writer in the 1968 primaries for both Eugene McCarthy and Robert F. Kennedy. Goodwin coined the phrase "Alliance for Progress" to revive FDR's "Good Neighbor" program for Latin America, and basically wrote LBJ's most soaring address on "the Great Society" (the phrase that the President briefly tried to claim was his own).[28] That 1964 vision is utopian ("The Great Society . . . demands an end to poverty and racial injustice. . . . But that is just the beginning. . . ."),[29] but was aborted by the escalation in Vietnam, which Goodwin also condemned, from within the Administration. Johnson "never talked to me again, and I never talked to him again," Goodwin recalled, his meteoric career as a Mr. Fix-It having gone down in flames. This "voice from the Sixties," lamenting the segmentations of "social, racial, and class division," as well as the curse of big money in politics, was largely stilled.[30]

FIG 13. Laurence H. Tribe. *Laurence H. Tribe.*

"We are teachers," Brandeis liked to say to his brethren on the Court;[31] and it is fitting that two faculty members at Harvard Law School, where Frankfurter had taught for a quarter of a century, faithfully embody the patrimony of liberal activism. Born in Shanghai to Polish Jews who were escaping from both Nazi and Soviet persecution, Laurence H. Tribe graduated *summa cum laude* in mathematics from Harvard College, and was midway through a graduate program in algebraic topology when he switched to Harvard Law School, where he has taught Constitutional law since 1969. Within six years of the publication of *American Constitutional Law* (1978), it had been cited in over four hundred court cases; and its author became an extracurricular champion of civil rights, civil liberties, and feminist causes, winning a series of victories in appeals to the Supreme Court. In representing the Korean evangelist Sun Myung Moon, the "Prophet of God" who had been convicted of tax fraud, Tribe sounded like Justice Brandeis: "It is exactly the people who are hated who ought to have the protection of the courts against mass hysteria. The issue in this case is not religion alone but rather how to protect minorities against oppression."[32]

FIG 14. Alan M. Dershowitz (right) with Natan Sharansky. *Alan M. Dershowitz.*

In Alan M. Dershowitz the various strains in this tradition of liberal advocacy recombined in a combustible fashion. His primary career has been, like Frankfurter's, as a professor at the Harvard Law School, where, at the age of twenty-eight, Dershowitz was the youngest person ever to get tenure. But a more vocal career has been carved out of a zealous representation of unpopular clients whose procedural rights or freedom of expression, he claimed, had been violated. Some of these figures have been so

gamy ("almost all of my own clients have been guilty," he conceded in 1982) that Rev. Moon looks savory. Unlike Dershowitz, Brandeis was primarily a conciliator and a keen student of social policy. Frankfurter was a controversialist, and thus more directly akin to Dershowitz, who has been a pump-up-the-volume Zionist sharply critical of Justice Frankfurter's failure to respond more effectively to the Holocaust. The title of Dershowitz's best-selling memoir would have made both Brandeis and Frankfurter blink: *Chutzpah*. Not exactly reclusive, Dershowitz insisted that, despite their comfort, American Jews still feared a backlash from vigorously pursuing their own interests—in defending Israel and in condemning antisemitism. *Chutzpah* concludes somberly, unsure about the future of Jewish identity in America. For the perils are "subtle: willing seduction, voluntary assimilation, deliberate abdication. We have learned—painfully and with difficulty—how to fight others. Can we develop Jewish techniques for defending against our own success?"[33]

In providing an answer, the Brandeis lineage of legal activism would not be helpful; and even the Zionist legacy was quite limited in nourishing cultural resources, in strategizing the seeding of creative cultural institutions. (Brandeis admitted his own ignorance of Jewish matters.) Nor does the historical record reveal any serious attempt on Frankfurter's part to articulate a positive sense of identity. No person had ever struck the Rev. Reinhold Niebuhr as more intelligent than Frankfurter, who nevertheless gave a woefully reductive definition when Walter Lippmann once asked him what a Jew is: "a person whom non-Jews regard as a Jew."[34]

FIG 15. Horace M. Kallen. *American Jewish Historical Society.*

The corrective was sanctioned by Kallen's theory of cultural pluralism, in which he proposed an America formally akin to "a federal republic; its substance a democracy of nationalities, cooperating voluntarily and autonomously through common institutions in the enterprise of self-realization through the perfection of men according to their kind." America's "common language" would remain English. "But each nationality would have for its emotional and involuntary life its own peculiar dialect or speech, its own individual and inevitable esthetic and intellectual forms." America was not a nation-state but a state composed of many nations. Kallen proposed the metaphor of an orchestra performing an unfinished symphony, in which "each ethnic group may be the natural instrument, its temper and culture . . . its theme and melody and the harmony of its dissonances and discords . . . the symphony of civilization."[35] (Perhaps not even Kallen had anticipated that, in an actual orchestra, one ethnic group would be *primus inter pares*, with conductor Arthur Fiedler personifying the

Boston Pops, along with its associate director, Harry Dickson, the father of Kitty Dukakis).

This is not the place to amplify either the praise or the criticism that Kallen's theory garnered, but to note that, however fertile, it was *only* a theory. It was up to the ethnic groups themselves to activate their particular traditions, to join (without the obstacle of auditions) the orchestra, to know the score. In this New World Symphony, there was room on stage for more players; but they themselves bore the responsibility for bringing their own sheet music. Kallen himself may have been the first Jew to receive both a bachelor's and a doctoral degree in Arts and Sciences at Harvard.[36] But three years later he moved on to Madison, and then New York City, where he would teach for the next five decades. There were signs that he had already left behind a vibrant Jewish culture in Boston that would help make his conception operational.

The Harvard Menorah Society had been founded in 1906 by, among others, Kallen himself, though its dominant figure was Henry Hurwitz of Gloucester, who also organized the Intercollegiate Menorah Association. It was pivotal to the perpetuation of "Hebraism" (or Jewish culture) for at least another generation; its monthly, *The Menorah Journal,* published Bourne's aforementioned essay, as well as Wolfson's non-scholarly writings, for example. Hurwitz served as chancellor of the Association and as editor of the magazine until his death in 1961, though by then any local orientation had disappeared.[37] The national successor to the Intercollegiate Menorah Association was, in effect, invented in the Midwest: the Hillel Foundation.

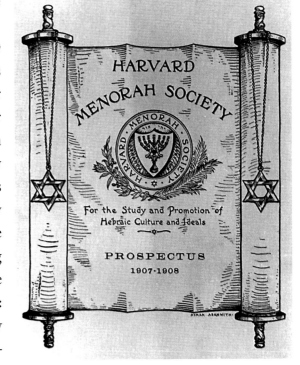

FIG 16. Cover of the prospectus for the "Harvard Menorah Society," 1907-1908. *American Jewish Historical Society.*

Its longtime director (and contributor to *The Menorah Journal*), Abram L. Sachar, came out of retirement to serve as first president (1948–68), chancellor and then chancellor emeritus of Brandeis University, whose history provides far greater evidence—despite its name—of cultural pluralism than of Jewish nationalism. Its visionary founder was a New York rabbi, Israel Goldstein, who saw the university as fulfilling an "essentially Zionist purpose" —which is why he expected to retain Einstein's support (deemed invaluable for securing the necessary funding). But when the founding trustees appointed Sachar, according to one historian, "the underlying purpose of Brandeis shifted subtly but crucially: from directly promoting Jewish objectives to indirectly strengthening the position of Jews by establishing an insti-

FIG 17. Abram L. Sachar. *Brandeis University Libraries/Mr. Ralph Norman, Brandeis University Photo Archives.*

FIG. 18. Marie Syrkin. *American Jewish Archives, Cincinnati, Ohio.*

tution of quality. . . . What Sachar's vision captured, with an unerring eye for gradations of social and academic prestige, were the educational ideas and institutional forms most closely associated with elite higher education in the late 1940s." In its first couple of decades in particular, the Brandeis campus became a leftist, egalitarian version of the New England Ivy League. "Sachar had an uncanny sense of intellectual quality; he couldn't quite sing himself but he knew good singing when he heard it." As a result, Martin Peretz '56 (later the editor-in-chief of *The New Republic*) recalled, there was "a cohort so intensely engrossed with ideas (and in battle over ideas) that I cannot believe that such intensity has been duplicated in any other institution, before or since. These were people, most of them, at least, who were convinced that ideas not only illumined; they also liberated."[38] Among them, from 1949 until 1973, was Max Lerner, a liberal columnist and wide-ranging celebrant of "the American Century." His would be the last single mind to apply itself to an attempt at the comprehensive exploration of *America as a Civilization* (1957). Another longtime faculty member, Lawrence H. Fuchs, not only specialized in the study of Jewish political behavior but also, in *The American Kaleidoscope* (1990), his most important book, came far closer than Kallen ever tried, to describing how the "civic culture" actually functioned in legitimating diversity within an expansive, adhesive polity.

But Brandeis University also sought to meet the responsibility to which the theory of cultural pluralism had entrusted it, and became the major North American center, in a secular and non-sectarian environment, for Jewish scholarship. Sachar himself had published an often-reprinted *History of the Jews* (1930) and had hired leading writers on Jewish themes, like Ludwig Lewisohn and Marie Syrkin. The Department of Near Eastern and Judaic Studies included foreign-trained scholars like Alexander Altmann, Nahum Glatzer, Simon Rawidowicz, and Nahum Sarna, as well as American-trained savants like Marvin Fox, Marshall Sklare, and Boston's Ben Halpern.

In 1969 a colloquium on campus inaugurated the Association for Jewish Studies in Boston, where its headquarters have remained. Several Brandeis students were also decisive in conceiving and editing *The Jewish Catalog* (1973), which had a couple of sequels and became so successful that, among the works of the Jewish Publication Society of America, only its Bible translation sold more on an

FIG. 19, *above*. Brandeis University, aerial view, 1994. *Photograph by Aerial Photos International, Inc.*

FIG. 20. Brandeis University, the Protestant, Roman Catholic, and Jewish chapels. Each is shaped in the form of a Bible partly open and the three together symbolize the harmony of faiths. *Brandeis University Libraries/Mr. Ralph Norman, Brandeis University Photo Archives.*

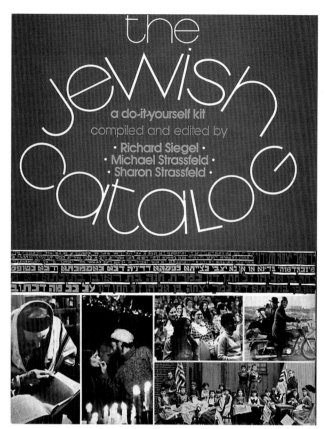

FIG 21. Cover of *the Jewish Catalog*, compiled and edited by Richard Siegel, Michael Strassfeld, and Sharon Strassfeld. Philadelphia: The Jewish Publication Society of America, 1973. *American Jewish Historical Society.*

annual basis. [39] A onetime professor at Brandeis (as well as MIT), Leonard Fein, served as editor and publisher of *Moment* magazine from its founding in 1975 until 1987. The independent monthly was devoted to the recovery of Judaism and Jewish culture, which was not separated from politics—liberal Democratic at home and Labor Zionist on the Israeli scene. At once critical and sentimental, *Moment* sought to ground identity in affirmations through both social activism and renewed ritual. Despite Fein's own talent as a writer and lecturer, his magazine failed to attract sufficient support from "a community linked together by a smattering of nostalgic rememberings (and misrememberings), an assortment of fears that have more to do with yesterday's traumas than with tomorrow's prospects, a handful of rituals, and frenetic activity on Israel's behalf." [40]

The efflorescence of Jewish cultural life in Boston by the end of the 1960's was partly a function of generational transference that was not yet exhausted a couple of decades later. To be sure, a renascence could be detected in other cities; but "the Hub of the Universe" is an especially apt setting in which to mark the historic rise of Jews to intellectual and artistic visibility. Here are some indices, some signs of the times:

American culture, the leading "confessional" poet observed in 1964, would not be "active. . . without the Jewish element. . . . It's a painful reality that a minority should have such liveliness and vigor." [41] By then the statement was almost a truism. But its interest lay in its source: Robert Lowell, the great-grand-nephew of James Russell Lowell and a distant cousin of A. Lawrence Lowell.

In the 19th century, Nathaniel Hawthorne had traced the consequences of adultery in Massachusetts in his most famous novel. In the 20th century, John Updike of the North Shore updated *The Scarlet Letter* with two novels. In *S.* (1988), the Arhat—the Indian fakir with whom the Hester Prynne character is smitten—turns out to be a faker named Art Steinmetz of Watertown. In *Roger's Version* (1986), which is Chillingsworth's side, the author acknowledges the assistance of a Harvard classmate, Jacob Neusner, a leading authority on the Mishnah and other religious texts. No references to any contemporary Jews appear in the American notebooks of Hawthorne, who privately admitted, while abroad, to a "repugnance I have always felt towards [t]his race." [42] In contrast Updike, by far the most important man of letters in the Boston area, can barely get Jews out of his mind, even writing two novels in the voice of Henry Bech.

In Saul Bellow's second novel, published in 1947, the antisemitic antagonist complains of seeing in a library "a book about Thoreau and Emerson by a man named Lipschitz . . . A name like that?. . . It seems to me that people of that background simply couldn't understand. . ."[43] In the postwar era Jews on the Harvard faculty would become authorities on New England's religious and literary tradition, including Sacvan Bercovitch on the Puritans (and Hawthorne), and philosopher Stanley Cavell on Thoreau and Emerson. An even more symbolic change occurred in the field of history. Charles Warren (Harvard '89), the descendant of a distinguished colonial family, had been important to the founding of the patrician Immigration Restriction League of Boston in 1894. Yet from 1965 until 1973, Harvard's Charles Warren Professor of American History and the director of the Charles Warren Center for Studies in American History was a product of one of those immigrant neighborhoods that such nativists regarded as sores on the body politic. Brooklyn-born Oscar Handlin, whom Senator John F. Kennedy hailed as "perhaps America's most gifted social historian," had once intended "to write a history of the immigrants in America. Then I discovered that the immigrants *were* American history."[44]

FIG 22. Cover of *Moment* magazine, volume 8, number 6, June, 1983. *American Jewish Historical Society.*

Before the Second World War, a versatile City College undergraduate had calculated that the only way that he might snatch an academic post was to make himself a specialist in a downright exotic field, like Sinology, that might be in demand. The idea was dropped. But starting in the little magazines as well as *Fortune*, Daniel Bell would eventually rank among the country's most influential intellectuals. A self-described "Old Testament Jew,"[45] he retired from Harvard in 1990 as the Henry Ford II Professor of Social Sciences (itself a chair named for the grandson of America's most mischievous antisemite), over a decade after the university had opened a Center for Jewish Studies (though before a chair in Yiddish literature was filled). Also symbolizing the greater prominence of Jewish culture was a new Hillel Foundation building, designed by the Israeli architect Moshe Safdie and named for Henry Rosovsky, an ex-dean of the Faculty of Arts and Sciences and the first Jew to serve on the Harvard Corporation. Plans were announced by president Derek C. Bok, whose wedding—a French civil ceremony—had been performed by a Jew, Pierre Mendès-France, and whose grandfather had been the Dutch-born journalist

FIG 23. Oscar Handlin. *American Jewish Historical Society.*

Edward Bok whose "Americanization" Kallen himself had criticized as "too self-conscious," "too little like a growth."[46]

In 1980 the Emerson Award of Phi Beta Kappa was presented to Frank Manuel, who had been born in Boston's plebeian West End in 1910, the son of a baker who had been involved in organizing the local Hebrew Bakers Union. A specialist on the utopian heritage, the Brandeis University historian (later at Boston University) had published an early book in diplomacy on *The Realities of American-Palestine Relations,* long before he would embody Emerson's "American Scholar."[47]

The first editor of *The Atlantic Monthly* had been James Russell Lowell, who had thrashed out the idea of the magazine over oysters at the Parker House in 1857 with Emerson, Longfellow, and Holmes, Sr. In 1980 a Montreal-born real estate magnate with the un-Brahmin name of Mort Zuckerman bought the venerable organ of the patriciate,[48] which in 1911-12 had published Antin's paean to *The Promised Land* before it appeared as a book.

Its counterpart in political theory, which took homogeneity for granted, had been formulated in *Federalist #2.* Americans were "descended from the same ancestors," John Jay had announced; they professed "the same religion" and were "very similar in their manners and customs." When one of his descendants, Theodora Jay Stillman, died in her Beacon Street home in 1968, her estate was left to her husband, Philip Rahv. The Brandeis University critic exemplified the cosmopolitan radical Jewish intellectual; his native tongue was Yiddish, yet his best work included exquisite essays on Hawthorne and Henry James. When Rahv died in 1973, the estate that could be traced back to a Founding Father was bequeathed to the state of Israel.[49]

Such scholars and numerous others benefitted from the trend toward greater tolerance that, throughout the United States, had gained momentum in the shadow of the Holocaust. Postwar Judaism became fully legitimated as one of the three great faiths in the American mosaic, even though the very tiny number of its adherents (in contrast to Protestantism and Catholicism) called to mind the elevation of Taiwan, conflated into "China," as one of the Big Five permanent members of the United Nations Security Council. Judaism had become one of the Big Three, and those born within its precincts were accorded equal footing. The openness of American society in the past half century vindicated the expectations of Antin as well as Brandeis and Kallen. Those who opted out of the Jewish people and for whom Americanization meant assimilation have indeed found a society that has almost entirely eliminated the barriers that Jews in some other countries had been unable to scale. But the faith of those who sought to make their citizenship compatible with their Jewish loyalties have also proven correct, for no other Diaspora society has been so receptive to communal claims and to the legitimation of Jewish choices.

*Some* friction with civil society may, however, be inevitable—and salutary. At the outset of his *Adventures,* Huckleberry Finn describes how the Widow Douglas took out a Bible "and learned me about Moses and the Bulrushers; and I was in a sweat to find out all about him; but by-and-by she let it out that Moses had been dead a considerable long time; so then I didn't care no more about him; because I don't take no stock in dead people." Huck fails to understand the Widow's fascination with Moses, "which was no kin to her." Judaism collides with the sensibility of the archetypal American kid, however. Its adherents *do* put stock in dead people; they *are* kin to Moses; and the challenge facing the custodians of American Jewish culture is how to (re-)establish the bonds of ancestry and continuity. The precariousness with which that challenge would be met could be said to characterize Boston's Jewry across the span of a century. Walter Lippmann was one of those detached intellectuals who was looking for love in all the wrong places. But for those driven by the dictates of peoplehood, the question that he posed in 1916 has lost little of its urgency. "If you get rid of the theology and the biological mysticism and treat the literature as secular, and refuse to regard the Jews as a . . . chosen people," he asked the editor of *The Menorah Journal,* "just what elements of a living culture are left?"[50]

# Notes

1. Grady McWhiney, *Cracker Culture: Celtic Ways in the Old South* (Tuscaloosa: University of Alabama Press, 1988), 92, 140, 161–62, 165–66, 167.

2. Quoted in Simon Schama, "Stopping by Woods," *New Republic,* 26 October 1992, 34.

3. Quoted in Adam Begley, "The Tempest Around Stephen Greenblatt," *New York Times Magazine,* 28 March 1993, 37.

4. Ted Morgan, *On Becoming American* (Boston: Houghton Mifflin, 1978), 110; Theodore Draper, *Present History: On Nuclear War, Détente and Other Controversies* (New York: Random House, 1983), 424.

5. Samuel Eliot Morison, *Three Centuries of Harvard* (Cambridge: Harvard University Press, 1936), 57–58; Henry Rosovsky, "Then and Now: The Jewish Experience at Harvard," *Moment,* June 1980, 20; Nitza Rosovsky, *The Jewish Experience at Harvard and Radcliffe* (Cambridge: Harvard University Press, 1986), 4.

6. Quoted in Ved Mehta, *John is Easy to Please: Encounters with the Written and Spoken Word* (New York: Farrar, Straus & Giroux, 1971), 186, 188–89; "Interview," in Noam Chomsky, *The Chomsky Reader,* ed. James Peck (New York: Pantheon, 1987), 7, 8–10.

7. Quoted in Mehta, *John is Easy to Please,* 189; Daniel Yergin, "The Chomskyan Revolution," *New York Times Magazine,* 3 December 1972, 112, 114.

8. Mehta, *John is Easy to Please,* 190; Charles M. Young, "The Rolling Stone Interview: Noam Chomsky," *Rolling Stone,* 28 May 1992, 45; Michael Steinberg, "The Journey of Bernstein from Chopin to Chomsky," *New York Times,* 16 December 1973, sec. 4, 19, 36.

9. Theodore H. White, *In Search of History: A Personal Adventure* (New York: Harper & Row, 1978), 13–14.

10. Ephraim E. Lisitzky, *In the Grip of Cross-Currents,* trans. Moshe Kohn and Jacob Sloan (New York: Bloch, 1959), 67–68.

11. Judah Goldin, "On the Sleuth of Slobodka and the Cortez of Kabbalah," *American Scholar,* Summer 1980, 395; White, *In Search of History,* 46, 51.

12. Saul Engelbourg, "Edward A. Filene: Merchant, Civic Leader, and Jew," *American Jewish Historical Quarterly* 66 (September 1976): 115–17.

13. Daniel J. Kevles, *The Physicists: The History of a Scientific Community in Modern America,* 2d ed. (Cambridge: Harvard University Press, 1987), 212, 213.

14. Isaac M. Fein, *Boston—Where It All Began: An Historical Perspective of the Boston Jewish Community* (Boston: Boston Jewish Centennial Committee, 1976), 1.

15. William Bradford, *History of Plymouth Plantation,* ed. William T. Davis (New York: Scribners, 1908), 17.

16. Edmund Wilson, *Patriotic Gore: Studies in the Literature of the American Civil War* (New York: Oxford University Press, 1962), 784–85; idem, "The Holmes-Laski Correspondence," in *Eight Essays* (Garden City, N.Y.: Doubleday Anchor, 1954), 236–37; David A. Hollinger, "The 'Tough-Minded' Justice Holmes, Jewish Intellectuals, and the Making of an American Icon," in *The Legacy of Oliver Wendell Holmes Jr.,* ed. Robert W. Gordon (Stanford: Stanford University Press, 1992), 216–28.

17. David Levin, *Exemplary Elders* (Athens: University of Georgia Press, 1990), 23.

19. Quoted in Louis Harap, *The Image of the Jew in American Literature: From Early Republic to Mass Immigration* (Philadelphia: Jewish Publication Society, 1974), 97; Martin Duberman, *James Russell Lowell* (Boston: Beacon Press, 1966), 307–10; Barbara Miller Solomon, *Ancestors and Immigrants: A Changing New England Tradition* (New York: John Wiley & Sons, 1965), 18–20.

19. Solomon, *Ancestors and Immigrants,* 38–42; Harap, *Image of the Jew,* 358–68.

20. Marcia Graham Synnott, *The Half-Opened Door: Discrimination and Admissions at Harvard, Yale, and Princeton 1900–1970* (Westport, Conn.: Greenwood Press, 1979), 26–124; Seymour Martin Lipset, "Political Controversies at Harvard, 1636 to 1974," in Lipset and David Riesman, *Education and Politics at Harvard* (New York: McGraw-Hill, 1975), 145–50; Rosovsky, *Jewish Experience,* 8–26.

21. Lipset, "Political Controversies at Harvard," in Lipset and Riesman, *Education and Politics,* 146.

22. Leo W. Schwarz, *Wolfson of Harvard: Portrait of a Scholar* (Philadelphia: Jewish Publication Society, 1978), 91–92; Rosovsky, *Jewish Experience,* 30.

23. Susanne Klingenstein, *Jews in the American Academy, 1900-1940: The Dynamics of Intellectual Assimilation* (New Haven: Yale University Press, 1991), 8–17; Gershom Scholem, "The Golem of Prague and the Golem of Rehovot," in *The Messianic Idea in Judaism and Other Essays on Jewish Spirituality* (New York: Schocken, 1971), 335-36; Norbert Wiener, *Ex-Prodigy: My Childhood and Youth* (New York: Simon & Schuster, 1953), 153–54.

24. Bruce Jackson, "'The Greatest Mathematician in the World': Norbert Wiener Stories," *Western Folklore* 31 (January 1972): 1–22.

25. Quoted in Michael R. Beschloss, *Mayday: Eisenhower, Khrushchev and the U-2 Affair* (New York: Harper & Row, 1986), 75; "Polaroid's Big Gamble on Small Cameras," *Time,* 26 June 1972, 81, 82; Mehta, *John is Easy to Please,* 192–93; Steve J. Heims, *John von Neumann and Norbert Wiener: From Mathematics to the Technologies of Life and Death* (Cambridge: Massachusetts Institute of Technology Press, 1980), 333–35, 342.

26. Mary Antin, *The Promised Land* (Boston: Houghton Mifflin, 1969), 111, 141.

27. Quoted in Melvin I. Urofsky, *Louis D. Brandeis and the Progressive Tradition* (Boston: Little, Brown, 1981), 156; Lucjan Dobroszycki and Barbara Kirshenblatt-Gimblett, *Image Before My Eyes: A Photographic History of Jewish Life in Poland* (New York: Schocken, 1977), 235; West Virginia Board of Education v. Barnette, 319 U.S. 624 (1943).

28. Garry Wills, *Nixon Agonistes: The Crisis of the Self-Made Man* (Boston: Houghton Mifflin, 1970), 500–17; Bo Burlingham, "The Other Tricky Dick," *Esquire,* November 1975, 122.

29. Quoted in Richard Goodwin, *Remembering America: A Voice from the Sixties* (New York: Harper & Row, 1989), 278.

30. Quoted in Tim Sandler, "Revolutionary," Boston *Phoenix,* 6 November 1992, sec. 1, 14, 18.

31. Quoted in Samuel J. Konefsky, *The Legacy of Holmes and Brandeis: A Study in the Influence of Ideas* (New York: Collier Books, 1961), 268–69.

32. Quoted in "A Prophet's Unlikely Defender," *Time,* 23 January 1984, 30; Peter Collier, "Blood on the Charles," *Vanity Fair,* October 1992, 159–60.

33. Alan M. Dershowitz, *The Best Defense* (New York: Random House, 1982), xiv; idem, *Chutzpah* (Boston: Little, Brown, 1991), 281–83, 353–54.

34. Quoted in Michael E. Parrish, *Felix Frankfurter and His Times: The Reform Years* (New York: Free Press, 1982), 6, 129.

35. Horace M. Kallen, "Democracy versus the Melting-Pot," in *Culture and Democracy in the United States: Studies in the Group Psychology of the American Peoples* (New York: Boni & Liveright, 1924), 124–25; Moses Rischin, "The Jews and Pluralism: Toward an American Freedom Symphony," in *Jewish Life in America: Historical Perspectives,* ed. Gladys Rosen (New York: KTAV, 1978), 65-80.

36. Rosovsky, *Jewish Experience,* 28.

37. Pearl K. Bell, "The Harvard Menorah Society," in Rosovsky, *Jewish Experience,* 48–50; Allon Gal, *Brandeis of Boston* (Cambridge: Harvard University Press, 1980), 149–62.

38. Richard M. Freeland, *Academia's Golden Age: Universities in Massachusetts 1945–1970* (New York: Oxford University Press, 1992), 185–89; Abram L. Sachar, *A Host at Last* (Boston: Little, Brown, 1976), 12–30; Martin Peretz, "Frank Manuel: An Appreciation," in *In the Presence of the Past: Essays in Honor of Frank Manuel,* eds. Richard T. Bienvenu and Mordechai Feingold (Dordrecht and Boston: Kluwer Academic Publishers, 1991), 1–2, 5; Louis A. Gordon, "Judaism and Jewishness at Brandeis University," *Jewish Spectator,* Spring 1993, 16–18.

39. Jonathan D. Sarna, *JPS: The Americanization of Jewish Culture 1888–1988* (Philadelphia: Jewish Publication Society, 1989), 281–85.

40. Leonard Fein, ed., "In All Its Parts: An Introduction," in *Jewish Possibilities: The Best of Moment Magazine* (Northvale, N.J.: Jason Aronson, 1987), xii.

41. Quoted in A. Alvarez, *Under Pressure: The Writer in Society: Eastern Europe and the U.S.A.* (Baltimore: Penguin Books, 1965), 173.

42. "'Plump and Bustling': John Updike Recalls Neusner," *Baltimore Jewish Times,* 9 February 1990; Harap, *Image of the Jew,* 107–17.

43. Saul Bellow, *The Victim* (New York: Signet, 1965), 131–32.

44. Solomon, *Ancestors and Immigrants,* 99–102; Oscar Handlin, *The Uprooted: The Epic Story of the Great Migrations that Made the American People,* 2d ed. (Boston: Little, Brown, 1973), 3.

45. William F. Buckley, Jr., *In Search of Anti-Semitism* (New York: Continuum, 1992), 6; Peter Steinfels, *The Neoconservatives: The Men Who are Changing America's Politics* (New York: Simon & Schuster, 1979), 164; Daniel Bell, Letter to the Editor, *Encounter,* July 1977, 96.

46. "A New Home for Hillel," *Harvard Magazine,* July–August 1991, 56; Kallen, "Democracy *versus* the Melting-Pot," 86.

47. Peretz, "Frank Manuel," in *Presence of the Past,* 2, 4–5.

48. "New Cash for an Old Bostonian," *Time,* 17 March 1980, 97.

49. John Jay, Alexander Hamilton, and James Madison, *The Federalist Papers,* ed. Garry Wills (New York: Bantam, 1982), 7; Dorothea Straus, *Palaces and Prisons* (Boston: Houghton Mifflin, 1976), 79, 87–88, 94.

50. Samuel Langhorne Clemens, *Adventures of Huckleberry Finn,* Sculley Bradley and others, eds.., 2d ed. (New York: W.W. Norton, 1977), 7–8; Walter Lippmann to Henry Hurwitz, 24 December 1916, in Horace Kallen Papers, quoted in William Toll, *Women, Men and Ethnicity: Essays on the Structure and Thought of American Jewry* (Lanham, Md.: University Press of America, 1991), 29.

# APPENDIX A

# *The Jewish Population of Boston*[1]

| DATE | ESTIMATED NUMBER OF JEWS IN BOSTON | ESTIMATED NUMBER OF JEWS IN GREATER BOSTON[2] | ESTIMATED POPULATION OF BOSTON | ESTIMATED POPULATION OF GREATER BOSTON[2] |
|---|---|---|---|---|
| 1790 | a few individuals and families | | 18,000 | |
| 1820 | a few individuals and families | | 43,000 | |
| 1845 | 40–100 | | 114,000 | |
| 1850 | 350–500 people; ca. 125 families | | 137,000 | |
| 1860 | 1,000–2,300 | | 178,000 | |
| 1870 | N/A | | 251,000 | |
| 1875 | 3,000 | | | |
| 1880 | 4,000–5,000 | | 363,000 | 798,000 |
| 1890 | N/A | | 448,000 | 1,029,000 |
| 1895 | 20,000 | | | |
| 1900 | 40,000 | | 561,000 | 1,313,000 |
| 1905 | 45,000 | | | |
| 1910 | 57,000–65,000 | 100,000 | 671,000 | 1,602,000 |
| 1920 | 80,000 | | 745,000 | 1,869,000 |
| 1930 | 85,000 | | 781,000 | 2,169,000 |
| 1935 | 115,000 | | | |
| 1940 | 87,000 | 120,000 | 771,000 | 2,210,000 |
| 1950 | 83,000 | 137,000 | 801,000 | 2,411,000 |
| 1960 | N/A | 150,000 | 697,000 | 2,589,000 |
| 1965 | 40,000 | 208,000 | | |
| 1975 | 33,000 | 195,000 | (1976) 618,000 | (1976) 2,862,000 |
| 1985 | 25,000 | 228,000* | 574,000 | 2,832,000 |

1. All numbers rounded to nearest thousand. Population ranges are provided based on the following statistical sources:

Jewish population estimates of Boston: Jacob Rader Marcus, *To Count a People: American Jewish Population Data, 1585–1984* (1990); archival sources; federal census statistics; *American Jewish Yearbook*; Combined Jewish Philanthropies demographic surveys of 1965, 1975, 1985.

Jewish population estimates of Greater Boston: Jacob Rader Marcus, *To Count a People: American Jewish Popula-*

*tion Data, 1585–1984* (1990); *American Jewish Yearbook*; Combined Jewish Philanthropies demographic surveys of 1965, 1975, 1985.

Total population estimates of Boston and Greater Boston: Federal census reports and *Statistical Abstracts of the United States.*

2. Standard Metropolitan Statistical Area.

* Includes entire CJP service area.

# Estimated Jewish Population of Roxbury-Dorchester[3]

| | 1910 | 1920 | 1930 | 1940 | 1950 | 1955 | 1960 | 1967 | 1970 |
|---|---|---|---|---|---|---|---|---|---|
| Roxbury–Dorchester | 12,000 | 44,000 | 76,500 | 74,000 | 70,000 | 58,500 | 47,000 | 25,200 | 15,800 |
| Elm Hill district (*including Grove Hall west*) | 2,700 | 14,000 | 19,000 | 18,000 | 16,000 | 10,000 | 5,000 | 500 | 300 |
| Grove Hall–Blue Hill Ave. district (*not including Grove Hall west*) | 7,000 | 10,500 | 10,500 | 10,000 | 8,500 | 5,500 | 2,000 | 200 | 150 |
| Franklin Field– Franklin Park– Mount Bowdoin district | 900 | 8,500 | 17,500 | 17,000 | 17,000 | 14,500 | 12,000 | 3,000 | 500 |
| Mattapan district: Franklin Field– Morton St. | 800 | 8,000 | 16,000 | 15,000 | 15,000 | 14,500 | 13,500 | 6,500 | 3,200 |
| Mattapan district: Morton St.– Mattapan Sq. | 100 | 2,000 | 12,000 | 12,000 | 12,000 | 12,500 | 13,000 | 13,500 | 10,200 |
| Other districts | 500 | 1,000 | 1,500 | 2,000 | 1,500 | 1,500 | 1,500 | 1,500 | 1,450 |

In 1980 there were about 1,000 Jews in Roxbury and Dorchester, most of them in the Morton Street–Mattapan Square area and in Dorchester's traditionally Catholic districts.

3. Population estimates prepared by Gerald Gamm, based on census reports, various population studies, and archival records.

# Estimated Jewish Population of Brookline, Allston-Brighton, Newton[4]

| | 1920 | 1930 | 1940 | 1950 | 1960 | 1970 | 1980 | 1990 |
|---|---|---|---|---|---|---|---|---|
| Brookline (*all*) | 1,000 | 8,000 | 14,000 | 19,000 | 26,500 | 28,500 | 28,000 | 24,000 |
| Allston–Brighton | 1,300 | 4,000 | 8,000 | 13,000 | 14,500 | 11,500 | 13,000 | 11,000 |
| Newton | 500 | 1,400 | 4,500 | 8,000 | 27,000 | 31,000 | 30,000 | 31,000 |

4. Population estimates prepared by Gerald Gamm, based on census reports, various population studies, and archival records.

# Combined Jewish Philanthropies, 1895-1995

## LEGAL NAMES OF THE COMBINED JEWISH PHILANTHROPIES

1895   Federation of Jewish Charities
1908   Federated Jewish Charities
1930   Associated Jewish Philanthropies
    1940   The United Jewish Campaign (for overseas rescue and services) and the Associated Jewish Philanthropies unite their fundraising in the nation's first Combined Jewish Appeal
1960   Combined Jewish Philanthropies

## SUPERINTENDANTS AND EXECUTIVE DIRECTORS

| | | | |
|---|---|---|---|
| 1895–1899 | Rabbi Solomon Schindler | 1945–1960 | Sidney S. Cohen |
| 1899–1911 | Max Mitchell | 1960–1970 | Dr. Benjamin B. Rosenberg |
| 1911–1917 | Martha Michaels Silverman | 1970–1981 | Bernard Olshansky |
| 1917–1919 | Morris D. Waldman | 1982–1987 | David Rosen |
| 1919–1929 | Dr. Maurice B. Hexter | 1987– | Barry Shrage |
| 1929–1945 | Dr. Ben M. Selekman | | |

## PRESIDENTS AND CHAIRS OF THE BOARD

| | | | |
|---|---|---|---|
| 1895–1901 | Jacob H. Hecht | 1962–1964 | Benjamin Ulin |
| 1902–1903 | Godfrey Morse | 1964–1966 | Sidney Stoneman |
| 1904–1908 | Lehman Pickert | 1966–1968 | Bernard D. Grossman |
| 1909–1918 | Abraham C. Ratshesky | 1968–1970 | David R. Pokross |
| 1919–1921 | Louis Baer | 1970–1972 | Hon. Matthew Brown |
| 1922–1924 | Louis E. Kirstein | 1972–1974 | Irving W. Rabb |
| 1925–1927 | Albert W. Kaffenburgh | 1974–1976 | Norman B. Leventhal |
| 1928–1929 | Judge Abraham K. Cohen | 1976–1978 | Leonard Kaplan |
| 1930–1942 | Louis E. Kirstein | 1978–1980 | Leo Dunn |
| 1942–1944 | Judge Abraham K. Cohen | 1980–1983 | Ruth B. Fein |
| 1944–1947 | Judge Jacob K. Kaplan | 1983–1985 | Sherman H. Starr |
| 1947–1950 | Milton Kahn | 1985–1987 | Arthur D. Katzenberg, Jr. |
| 1950–1953 | Reuben B. Gryzmish | 1987–1989 | Joel B. Sherman |
| 1953–1956 | Benjamin Ulin | 1989–1991 | Edwin N. Sidman |
| 1956–1958 | Benjamin A. Trustman | 1991–1993 | Alan R. Goldstein |
| 1959–1960 | Simon J. Helman | 1993–1995 | Michael J. Bohnen |
| 1961–1962 | Louis P. Smith | 1995–1997 | Michael B. Rukin |

## CAMPAIGN CHAIRS

| | | | |
|---|---|---|---|
| 1940 | Samuel Markell | 1946–1947 | Herman Gilman |
| | Sidney R. Rabb | 1948 | Louis R. Golden |
| 1940–1941 | Reuben B. Gryzmish | 1949 | Irving Usen |
| | Milton Kahn | 1950 | Harold Sherman Goldberg |
| 1942–1943 | Israel Friedlander | 1951 | Simon J. Helman |
| 1944–1945 | Louis H. Savage | 1952 | Isidor Slotnik |

| | | | | |
|---|---|---|---|---|
| 1953 | Matthew Brown | | 1982 | William R. Sapers |
| 1954–1955 | Louis B. Smith | | 1983 | Lester Gilson |
| 1956 | Philip W. Lown | | | Arthur D. Katzenberg, Jr. |
| 1957 | Lewis H. Weinstein | | | Albert I. Levine |
| 1958–1959 | Joseph M. Linsey | | | Mitchell J. Marcus |
| 1960–1961 | George Shapiro | | | William R. Sapers |
| 1962 | David Kane | | | Lee Scheinbart |
| 1963 | Bernard D. Grossman | | | Sherman H. Starr |
| 1964 | Roger P. Sonnabend | | 1984 | Steven Grossman |
| 1965 | Abraham Goodman | | 1985 | Joel B. Sherman |
| 1966 | Norman B. Leventhal | | 1986 | Edwin N. Sidman |
| 1967 | Mortimer Weiss | | 1987 | Alan M. Schwartz |
| 1968–1970 | Bert Rabinowitz | | 1988 | Ruth B. Fein |
| 1971 | Leo Dunn | | 1989 | Paula L. Sidman |
| 1972–1973 | George Katz | | 1990 | Alan J. Tichnor |
| 1974 | Mitchell J. Marcus | | 1991 | Robert L. Beal |
| 1975 | Sherman H. Starr | | 1992–1993 | Cynthia B. Shulman |
| 1976 | Lee Scheinbart | | 1994 | Jay L. Fialkow |
| 1977–1978 | Paul D. Slater | | 1995 | Michael G. Frieze |
| 1979 | Albert I. Levine | | 1996 | George Krupp |
| 1980 | Arthur D. Katzenberg, Jr. | | 1997 | Ted Bernard |
| 1981 | Lester Gilson | | | |

# About the Authors

WILLIAM BRAVERMAN received his A.B., A.M., and Ph.D. from Harvard University, where he was a lecturer in the History, and History and Literature Departments, and where he wrote his dissertation, "The Ascent of Boston's Jews, 1630–1918." He is currently at New York University School of Law, where he serves as the Review and Essay Editor of the *New York University Law Review*. He has published articles on both historical and legal topics.

SUSAN EBERT is the Assistant to the President of the Combined Jewish Philanthropies of Greater Boston. Previously she worked in the CJP Communications and Planning Departments. She received her Ph.D., M.A., and undergraduate degrees in comparative literature from the City University of New York. She has consulted to many community organizations on development and public relations.

GERALD H. GAMM is Assistant Professor of Political Science at the University of Rochester. A native of the Boston area, Gamm received his Ph.D. in History and Political Science from Harvard University in 1994. He is the author of *The Making of New Deal Democrats: Voting Behavior and Realignment in Boston, 1920–1940* (University of Chicago Press, 1989). He has recently completed work on a book, tentatively titled *Neighborhood Roots*, that examines local institutions and neighborhood change in Dorchester and upper Roxbury over the period 1870–1990.

SHERRY ISRAEL, a social psychologist, is an Associate Professor in the Hornstein Program in Jewish Communal Service at Brandeis University. She also currently serves as Research Director for the Combined Jewish Philanthropies' 1995 demographic study of greater Boston's Jewish community and was Senior Planning Associate at CJP prior to coming to Brandeis. She is the author of *Boston's Jewish Community* (the 1985 CJP demographic study) and of articles on group process, planning in Jewish education, and other subjects. She holds a B.A. from the University of Chicago and an M.A. and Ph.D. from University of California at Los Angeles.

LEON A. JICK is the Helen and Irving Schneider Professor Emeritus of American Jewish Studies at Brandeis University where he served as Dean of the College, Director of the Lown Graduate Center for Contemporary Jewish Studies, and Chairman of the Department of Near Eastern and Judaic Studies. He is the author of *The Americanization of the Synagogue 1820–1870* and of numerous articles on American Jewry and Judaism.

DAVID KAUFMAN earned his doctorate in American Jewish History from Brandeis University. His dissertation, "'Shul with a Pool': The Synagogue-Center in American Jewish Life, 1875–1925," is now being prepared for publication. While at Brandeis, he acquired an expertise in the history of Jewish Boston and became a popular lecturer and tour guide. He has held teaching positions at Hebrew College, Brown University, and the University of Massachusetts at Amherst.

SCOTT-MARTIN KOSOFSKY, the designer and producer of this book, is proprietor of The Philidor Company, Boston. His award-winning work includes *The Harvard Hillel Sabbath Songbook* (1992) and *The Christmas Revels Songbook* (1985), both with M. Sue Ladr; the folio edition of *The Aspern Papers* by Henry James, illustrated by Peter Milton (1993); his recent work includes Rudy Burckhardt's *Talking Pictures* (1994); and *Silver Torah Ornaments at the Jewish Museum, New York* (1995).

MARK A. RAIDER is completing a Ph.D. in Near Eastern and Judaic Studies at Brandeis University, writing on "The Impact of Labor Zionism in the United States, 1919–1948." His publications have appeared in *American Jewish History, YIVO Annual, The Journal of Israeli History,* and *American Jewish Archives.* Recipient of several academic fellowships, he is currently a Doctoral Dissertation Fellow of the National Foundation for Jewish Culture and a Research Fellow at the Tauber Institute for the Study of European Jewry, Brandeis University.

JOSEPH REIMER is an Associate Professor in and Director of the Hornstein Program in Jewish Communal Service at Brandeis University. He is the first author of *Promoting Moral Growth: From Piaget to Kohlberg,* a contributor to *Lawrence Kohlberg's Approach to Moral Education* and the editor of *To Build a Profession: Careers in Jewish Education.* He has written numerous articles on Jewish education and is currently completing a book on synagogue education to be published by the Jewish Publication Society.

JONATHAN D. SARNA is the Joseph H. & Belle R. Braun Professor of American Jewish History at Brandeis University and chairs its Department of Near Eastern and Judaic Studies. His many publications include *JPS: The Americanization of Jewish Culture* (1989); *The Jews of Cincinnati,* with Nancy Klein (1989); *The American Jewish Experience* (1986); *People Walk On Their Heads* (1982); and *Jacksonian Jew: The Two Worlds of Mordecai Noah* (1981).

ELLEN SMITH is Curator of the American Jewish Historical Society and an historian of American religion. Among her exhibitions, catalogs, and essays in history, science, and technology are *On Common Ground: The Boston Jewish Experience 1620–1980* (1980); *Send Us a Lady Physician: Women Doctors in America 1835–1920* (1986); and *"A Most Valuable Citizen": Moses Michael Hays and the Establishment of Post-Revolutionary Boston* (1990).

STEPHEN J. WHITFIELD holds the Max Richter Chair in American Civilization at Brandeis University, where he has also served as chairperson of the Department of American Studies. He has taught as a Fulbright visiting professor at the Hebrew University of Jerusalem. Professor Whitfield is the author of seven books, including *Voices of Jacob, Hands of Esau: Jews in American Life and Thought* (1984) and *American Space, Jewish Time* (1988).

# Selected Bibliography

The following introductory bibliography lists the key books and articles on the history and experiences of the Jewish people in the Boston area from the 17th through 20th centuries. Publications primarily about Jewish Boston, or with substantial references to Jewish Boston and issues affecting it, are included. Additional sources may be found in the endnotes to each chapter in this volume.

ABBREVIATIONS:

*JPS*  The Jewish Publication Society of America
*PAJHS*  Publications of the American Jewish Historical Society

## Primary Materials

Boston, almost uniquely among major American Jewish cities, does not have its own local Jewish historical society. Records of Jewish Boston have thus gravitated toward national archives. The most important personal, institutional, and congregational records are housed in the American Jewish Historical Society, Waltham, Massachusetts, and the American Jewish Archives, Cincinnati, Ohio. Relevant collections are also located at Harvard University and in Boston-area synagogues.

Boston's Jewish newspapers include:
*Boston Advocate*, 1905–1909, renamed the *Boston Jewish Advocate* and later, *The Jewish Advocate*, 1909–present.
*Boston Hebrew Observer*, 1883–1886
*Boston Jewish Chronicle*, 1891–1893
[Boston] *Jewish Herald*, 1893
*Genesis 2*, 1970–1989
*Jewish Times*, 1945–present

## General Histories of Jewish Boston

No comprehensive history of the Boston Jewish community has been written. *The History of the Jews of Boston*, and Schindler's *Israelites in Boston* featured individuals and their achievements through the mid- to late 19th century. In the 20th century, Fein's *Boston,* and *On Common Ground* provided popular overviews. Albert Ehrenfried died before his very useful but uncompleted history to 1900 could be completed, and it is published in a limited, private edition. Braverman's recent dissertation provides a good overview, but is unpublished, and ends in 1918.

Braverman, William. "The Ascent of Boston's Jews, 1630–1918." Ph.D. diss., Harvard University, 1990.

Ehrenfried, Albert. *A Chronicle of Boston Jewry, From the Colonial Settlement to 1900.* Boston: Privately Printed, 1963.

Fein, Isaac M. *Boston—Where It All Began. An Historical Perspective of the Boston Jewish Community.* Boston: Boston Jewish Bicentennial Committee, 1976.

*History of the Jews of Boston and New England. Their Financial, Professional, and Commercial Enterprises, From the Earliest Settlement of Hebrews in Boston to the Present Day. Containing a Historical and Statistical Record of Every Jewish Congregation, Fraternal Order, Benevolent Society and Social Club, Together with Biographies of Noted Men, And Other Matters of Interest.* Boston: The Jewish Chronicle Publishing Co., 1892.

*On Common Ground: The Boston Jewish Experience, 1620–1980.* Waltham: American Jewish Historical Society, 1981. [Catalog for exhibition of same name.]

Schindler, Solomon. *Israelites in Boston. A Tale Describing the Development of Judaism in Boston, Preceded by the Jewish Calendar for the Next Decade.* Boston: Berwick & Smith, 1889.

## The Colonial and Early Federal Periods

The interest in early American Jews and Jewish communities on the part of the founders of the American Jewish Historical Society (AJHS) yielded a large number of articles on colonial Jewry, including important publications on Boston. Lee M. Friedman, a Boston lawyer, fine amateur historian, and president of the AJHS led the way, and most of his articles are still reliable. Much valuable information is also found in Ehrenfried (above). A contemporary overview of the literature on Jews and Puritans can be found in the volume edited by Shalom Goldman.

Broches, Samuel. "A Chapter in the History of the Jews of Boston." *YIVO Annual* 9 (1954): 205–11.

———. *Jews in New England: Part I, Historical Study of the Jews in Massachusetts, 1650–1750.* New York: Bloch Publishing Co., 1942.

Librarian and social activist Fanny Goldstein (1888–1961) was born in Russia and emigrated with her family to Boston's North End in 1900. After attending Hancock Grammar School and taking classes at Simmons College, Boston University, and Harvard University, she became a librarian in the Boston Public Library's (BPL) North End branch in 1913. In 1917 she helped organize the Saturday Evening Girls Club for immigrant girls, and edited the group's magazine. From 1922 to her retirement in 1957, she served in the BPL's West End Branch, where she built and published collections of books of interest to neighborhood immigrants, pioneered library exhibitions, and initiated Negro History Week, Jewish Music Month, Catholic Book Week, Brotherhood Week, and Jewish Book Week. This latter event grew into the Jewish Book Council of America and the national Jewish Book Week program. She was the first Jewish woman to direct a branch library in Massachusetts. Her work developing Judaica holdings in the BPL system culminated in her 1954 appointment as the first Jewish woman curator of Judaica in the BPL. After retiring, she served as literary editor of *The Jewish Advocate*. Portrait by Sonia Mazer.

De Sola Pool, David. "Hebrew Learning Among the Puritans of New England Prior to 1700." *PAJHS* 20 (1911): 31–83.

Fingerhut, Eugene R. "Were the Massachusetts Puritans Hebraic?" *New England Quarterly* 40 (December 1967): 521–31.

Friedman, Lee M. "Biblia Americana." In *Pilgrims in a New Land*. Philadelphia: JPS, 5708–1948.

———. "Cotton Mather and the Jews." *PAJHS* 26 (1918): 201–10.

———. *Early American Jews*. Cambridge: Harvard University Press, 1934. [Essays relating to Boston Jewish history include "Jewish Residents in Massachusetts Before 1800," an update of his "Early Jewish Residents in Massachusetts," *PAJHS* 23 (1915): 79–90; "Judah Monis, First Instructor in Hebrew at Harvard University," originally in *PAJHS* 22 (1914): 1–24; and Appendices A–F.]

———. *Jewish Pioneers and Patriots*. Philadelphia: JPS, 5703–1942. [Articles relating to Boston include "Cotton Mather's Ambition," "The Dedication of Massachusetts' First Synagogue," "The Ten Tribes Lost Again," "Medford's Jewish Street," and "The Gideons," update of "Roland Gideon, An Early Boston Jew, and His Family," *PAJHS* 35 (1939): 27–37.]

———. *Pilgrims in a New Land*. Philadelphia: JPS, 5708–1948. [Boston-related essays include "Biblia Americana," "The Naturalization of Aaron Lopez," and "A Beacon Hill Synagogue, on the 19th century Congregation Anshe Libawitz."]

———. "Some Further Notes on Judah Monis." *PAJHS* 37 (1947): 121–134.

Goldman, Shalom, ed. *Hebrew and the Bible in America: The First Two Centuries*. Hanover and London: Brandeis University Press and Dartmouth College, Published by University Press of New England, 1993.

Hühner, Leon. "The Jews of New England (Other than Rhode Island) Prior to 1800." *PAJHS* 11 (1903): 75–99.

———. *The Life of Judah Touro (1775–1854)*. Philadelphia: JPS, 5707–1946.

Klein, Milton M. "A Jew at Harvard in the 18th Century." *Proceedings of the Massachusetts Historical Society* 97 (1985): 135–45.

Kohler, Max J. "Judah Touro, Merchant and Philanthropist." *PAJHS* 13 (1905): 93–111. [Includes a transcription of Touro's will].

Lebowich, Joseph. "The Jews in Boston Till 1875." *PAJHS* 12 (1904): 101–12.

Marcus, Jacob R. *The Colonial American Jew 1492–1776*. 3 vols. Detroit: Wayne State University Press, 1970.

———. *Early American Jewry: The Jews of New York, New England and Canada, 1649–1794*. 2 vols. Philadelphia: The Jewish Publication Society of America, 1951–1953.

———, ed. *Memoirs of American Jews 1775–1865*. 2 vols. Philadelphia: The Jewish Publication Society of America, 1955.

Meyer, Isidore S. "Hebrew at Harvard (1636–1700): A Résumé of the Information in Recent Publications." *PAJHS* 35 (1939): 145–70.

———. "The Hebrew Exercises of Governor William Bradford." In *Studies in Jewish Bibliography, History and Literature in honor of I. Edward Kiev*, ed. Charles Berlin, 237–88. New York: Ktav Publishing House, Inc., 1971.

Moore, George Foote. "Judah Monis." *Massachusetts Historical Society, Proceedings*, Vol. 52 (1918–1919): 285–312.

Silberschlag, Eisig. "Judah Monis in Light of an Unpublished Manuscript." *Proceedings of the American Academy for Jewish Research* 46–47 (1980): 495–529.

Shipton, Clifford K., ed. *Sibley's Harvard Graduates*. Boston: Massachusetts Historical Society, 1945. "Judah Monis," Vol. 7: 640–46.

Smith, Harvey. *Moses Michael Hays, Merchant—Citizen—Freemason, 1739–1805*. Boston: Moses Michael Hays Lodge, A.F. & A.M., 1937.

## The Mid-Nineteenth Century and Central European Jews

Steven Mostov's essay is essential reading for this period. Burton Kliman's senior thesis is also excellent; a copy is on file at the American Jewish Historical Society, Waltham. Ehrenfried (above) details the stories of many organizations and individuals in this era.

Cohen, Naomi W. *Encounter with Emancipation: The German Jews in the United States, 1830–1914.* Philadelphia: JPS, 1984.

*Germans in Boston.* Boston: Goethe Society of New England, 1981.

*History of the Jews of Boston and New England. Their Financial, Professional, and Commercial Enterprises, From the Earliest Settlement of Hebrews in Boston to the Present Day. Containing a Historical and Statistical Record of Every Jewish Congregation, Fraternal Order, Benevolent Society and Social Club, Together with Biographies of Noted Men, And Other Matters of Interest.* Boston: The Jewish Chronicle Publishing Co., 1892.

Kliman, Burton Samuel. "The Jewish Brahmins of Boston: A Study of the German Jewish Immigrant Experience 1860–1900." Senior thesis, Brandeis University, 1978.

Knights, Peter R. *The Plain People of Boston, 1830–1860: A Study in City Growth.* New York: Oxford University Press, 1971.

———. *Yankee Destinies: The Lives of Ordinary Nineteenth-Century Bostonians.* Chapel Hill: University of North Carolina Press, 1991.

Mann, Arthur, ed. *Growth and Achievement: Temple Israel.* Cambridge: Riverside Press, 1954.

———. *Yankee Reformers in an Urban Age.* Cambridge: Harvard University Press, 1954.

Moltmann, Gunther. "The Pattern of German Emigration to the United States in the Nineteenth Century." In *America and the Germans,* ed. Frank Trommler and Joseph McVeigh. Philadelphia: University of Pennsylvania Press, 1985.

Mostov, Stephen G. "A Sociological Portrait of German Jewish Immigrants in Boston: 1845–1861." *AJS Review* 3 (1978): 121–52.

Schindler, Solomon. *Israelites in Boston. A Tale Describing the Development of Judaism in Boston, Preceded by the Jewish Calendar for the Next Decade.* Boston: Berwick & Smith, 1889.

Winsor, Justin. *The Memorial History of Boston, Including Suffolk County, Massachusetts, 1630–1880.* 4 vols. Boston: Ticknor and Co., 1880.

## The Eastern European Migration and Settlement

Ehrenfried (above) provides helpful details of the period to 1900. The work of Robert Woods and his settlement house colleagues provides important contemporary views of the immigrant Jewish population in Boston, and Barbara Solomon's *Pioneers in Service* surveys charitable enterprises on its behalf. No single publication surveys the period in total.

Ainley, Leslie G. *Boston Mahatma.* Boston: Bruce Humphries, Inc., 1949.

Aurelio, Santo J. "'Land of Hope, Land of Tears': Jewish and Italian Immigrants in Boston, 1880–1914." Master's thesis, Harvard University, 1985.

Bamber, Golde. "Russians in Boston." *Lend a Hand Monthly: A Record of Progress* 8 (March 1892): 170–73.

Baltzell, E. Digby, Allen Glicksman, and Jacquelyn Litt. "The Jewish Communities of Philadelphia and Boston: A Tale of Two Cities." In *Jewish Life in Philadelphia, 1830–1940,* ed. Murray Friedman. Philadelphia: Institute for the Study of Human Issues, 1983: 290–313.

Baskin, Maurice. "Ward Boss Politics in Boston: 1896–1921." Senior thesis, Harvard University, 1975.

Buenker, John D. "The Mahatma and Progressive Reform." *The New England Quarterly* 44 (September 1971): 397–419.

Bushée, Frederick. *Ethnic Factors in the Population of Boston.* New York: Arno, 1970 [1903].

Friedman, Lee M. "A Beacon Hill Synagogue." In *Pilgrims in a New Land.* Philadelphia: JPS, 5708–1948.

Fuchs, Lawrence. "Immigration through the Port of Boston." In *Forgotten Doors,* ed. M. Mark Stolarik. Philadelphia: Balch Institute Press, 1988.

Gamm, Gerald H. *The Making of New Deal Democrats: Voting Behavior and Realignment in Boston, 1920–1940.* Chicago: University of Chicago Press, 1989.

Handlin, Oscar. *Boston's Immigrants: A Study in Acculturation.* Revised ed. Cambridge: Harvard University Press, 1979.

Huggins, Nathan Irvin. *Protestants Against Poverty: Boston's Charities, 1870–1900.* Westport: Greenwood Publishing, 1971.

Joseph, Samuel. "Jewish Immigration to the United States from 1881 to 1910." In Faculty of Political Science of Columbia University, ed. *Studies in*

*History, Economics and Public Law* 59. New York: Columbia University Press, 1914.

Kaganoff, Nathan, Martha Katz-Hyman, and Michael Strassfeld, eds. "Organized Jewish Group Activity in 19th Century Massachusetts: A Check List Recording all Groups Identified, Their Purposes, Years of Existence, a Listing of Prominent Individuals Connected With the Program, as Well as Eventual Disposition When Known." Typescript manuscript, American Jewish Historical Society, Waltham, 1979.

Kaufman, David. "'Shul With a Pool': The Synagogue-Center in American Jewish Life, 1875–1925." Ph.D. diss., Brandeis University, 1993.

Kopf, Edward. "The Intimate City: A Study of Urban Social Order: Chelsea, MA, 1906–1915." Ph.D. diss., Brandeis University, 1974.

Kuznets, Simon. "Immigration of Russian Jews to the United States: Background and Structure." *Perspectives in American History* 9 (1975): 35–126.

Linenthal, Arthur D., M.D. *First a Dream: The History of Boston's Jewish Hospitals 1896 to 1928.* Boston: Beth Israel Hospital in association with The Francis A. Countway Library of Medicine, 1990.

McDonald, R.C. "The Jews of the North End of Boston." *Unitarian Review* 35 (May 1891): 362–69.

Meagher, Timothy J. "'Immigration Through the Port of Boston': A Comment." In *Forgotten Doors*, ed. M. Mark Stolarik. Philadelphia: Balch Institute Press, 1988.

Neusner, Jacob J. "The Impact of Immigration and Philanthropy Upon the Boston Jewish Community (1880-1914)." *PAJHS* 46 (December 1956): 71-85.

———. "The Rise of the Jewish Community of Boston, 1880–1914." Senior thesis, Harvard University, 1953.

Reznikoff, Charles. "Boston's Jewish Community: Earlier Days." *Commentary* 15 (May 1953): 490–99.

Solomon, Barbara Miller. *Ancestors and Immigrants: A Changing New England Tradition.* Chicago: University of Chicago Press, 1972.

———. *Pioneers in Service: The History of the Associated Jewish Philanthropies of Boston.* Boston: Court Square Press, 1956.

Warner, Sam Bass, Jr. "Mary Antin." Chap. in *Province of Reason.* Cambridge: The Belknap Press of Harvard University Press, 1984.

Wieder, Arnold A. *The Early Jewish Community of Boston's North End. A Sociologically Oriented Study of an Eastern European Jewish Immigrant Community in an American Big-City Neighborhood Between 1870 and 1900.* Waltham: Brandeis University, 1962.

Woods, Robert A., ed. *Americans in Process: A Settlement Study By Residents and Associates of the South End House. North and West Ends, Boston.* Boston: Houghton, Mifflin and Company, 1902.

———. *The City Wilderness. A Settlement Study by Residents and Associates of the South End House.* Boston: Houghton, Mifflin and Company, 1898.

Woods, Robert A. and Albert J. Kennedy, eds. *The Zone of Emergence: Observations of the Lower Middle and Upper Working Class Communities of Boston 1905–1914.* Abridged and edited with a preface by Sam Bass Warner, Jr. Cambridge: Harvard University Press, 1962.

## The Twentieth Century

Ackerman, Walter. "From Past to Present: Notes on the History of Jewish Education in Boston." *Jewish Education* 51 (Fall 1983): 16–26.

Beatty, Jack. *The Rascal King: The Life and Times of James Michael Curley (1874–1958).* Reading: Addison-Wesley Publishing Co., 1992.

Burnes, Jacob M. *West End House: The Story of a Boys' Club.* Boston: The Stratford Company, 1934.

Engelbourg, Saul. "Edward A. Filene: Merchant, Civic Leader, and Jew." *American Jewish Historical Quarterly* 66 (September 1976): 106–122.

Feingold, Norman S., and William B. Silverman, eds. *Kivie Kaplan: A Legend in His Own Time.* New York: Union of Hebrew American Congregations, 1976.

*Fifty Years of Jewish Philanthropy in Greater Boston, 1895–1945.* Boston: Combined Jewish Appeal, 1945.

Fisher, Sean M., and Carolyn Hughes, eds. *The Last Tenement: Confronting Community and Urban Renewal in Boston's West End.* Boston: The Bostonian Society, 1992.

Fowler, Floyd J., Jr. *1975 Community Survey: A Study of the Jewish Population of Greater Boston.* Boston: The Combined Jewish Philanthropies of Greater Boston, 1977.

Fowler, Morris, Floyd J. Fowler, Jr., and Arnold Gurin. *A Community Survey for Long Range Planning: A Study of the Jewish Population of Greater Boston.* Boston: Combined Jewish Philanthropies of Greater Boston, 1967.

Fridkis, Lloyd Alan. "A Community Divided: An Analysis of Synagogue-Federation Relations in America, with Particular Reference to the Boston Jewish Community." Senior thesis, Brandeis University, 1980.

Gal, Allon. *Brandeis of Boston.* Cambridge: Harvard University Press, 1980.

Gamm, Gerald H. "Neighborhood Roots: Exodus and Stability in Boston, 1870–1990." Ph.D. diss., Harvard University, 1994.

Ginsburg, Yona. *Jews in a Changing Neighborhood: The Study of Mattapan.* New York: Free Press, 1975.

Gordon, Albert I. *Jews in Suburbia.* Boston: Beacon Press, 1959.

Herlihy, Elizabeth M. and others, ed. *Fifty Years of Boston. A Memorial Volume Issued in Commemoration of the Tercentenary of 1930.* Boston: Subcommittee on Memorial History of the Boston Tercentenary Committee, 1932.

Hyman, Paula E. "From City to Suburb: Temple Mishkan Tefila of Boston." In *The American Synagogue: A Sanctuary Transformed,* ed. Jack Wertheimer. New York: Cambridge University Press, 1987: 185–205.

Hurwich, Louis. "Jewish Education in Boston (1843–1955)." *Jewish Education* 26 (Spring 1956): 22–34.

Israel, Sherry. *Boston's Jewish Community: The 1985 Demographic Study.* Boston: Combined Jewish Philanthropies of Greater Boston, 1987.

Joselit, Jenna Weissman. "Without Ghettoism: A History of the Intercollegiate Menorah Association, 1906–1930." *American Jewish Archives* 30 (November 1978): 133–154.

Kantrowitz, Nathan. "Racial and Ethnic Residential Segregation in Boston 1830–1970." *The Annals of the American Academy of Political and Social Science* 441 (January 1979): 42–54.

Klayman, Richard. *The First Jew: Prejudice and Politics in an American Community, 1900–1932.* Malden: Old Suffolk Square Press, 1985.

Klingenstein, Susanne. *Jews in the Amerian Academy.* New Haven: Yale University Press, 1991.

Levin, Richard. "The History of the JF&CS" [Jewish Family and Children's Service of Greater Boston]. Boston, 1987.

Levine, Hillel, and Lawrence Harmon. *The Death of an American Jewish Community: A Tragedy of Good Intentions.* New York: Free Press, 1992.

Lupo, Alan. *Liberty's Chosen Home: The Politics of Violence in Boston.* Boston: Little, Brown, 1977.

Margolis, Daniel J. "The Evolution and Uniqueness of the Jewish Educational Structure in Greater Boston." In *Studies in Jewish Education and Judaica in Honor of Louis Newman,* eds. Alexander Shapiro and Burton Cohen. New York: Ktav, 1984.

Phillips, Bruce A. *Brookline: The Evolution of an American Jewish Suburb.* New York: Garland Publishing , Inc., 1990.

Rosovsky, Nitza. *The Jewish Experience at Harvard and Radcliffe.* Cambridge: Harvard University Press, 1986.

Sachar, Abram L. *A Host at Last.* Boston: Little, Brown, 1976.

Schwarz, Leo W. *Wolfson of Harvard: Portrait of a Scholar.* Philadelphia: JPS, 1978.

Segal, Robert E. *The Early Years of the Jewish Community Council of Metropolitan Boston.* Boston: The Jewish Community Relations Council of Greater Boston, 1985.

Stack, John F. Jr. *International Conflict in an American City.* Westport, Conn.: Greenwood Publishing, 1979.

Steiner, M.J. "Hebrew Teachers College of Boston (1921–1951)." *Jewish Education* 23 (Winter 1952): 30–35.

Strum, Philippa. *Louis D. Brandeis: Justice for the People.* New York: Schocken, 1984.

Synnott, Marcia Graham. *The Half-Opened Door: Discrimination and Admissions at Harvard, Yale, and Princeton, 1900–1970.* Westport, Conn.: Greenwood Publishing, 1979.

*Temple Bnai Moshe Dedication Book.* Brighton, Mass.: Congregation Bnai Moshe, 1954. [Contains excellent essays on aspects of Boston Jewish history.]

Thernstrom, Stephan. *The Other Bostonians: Poverty and Progress in the American Metropolis, 1889–1970.* Cambridge: Harvard University Press, 1973.

Ueda, Reed. *West End House 1906–1981.* Boston: West End House, 1981.

Warner, Sam Bass, Jr. *Street Car Suburbs: The Process of Growth in Boston, 1870–1900.* 2d ed. Cambridge: Harvard University Press, 1978.

Whitehill, Walter Muir. *Boston: A Topographical History.* 2d ed. Cambridge: Harvard University Press, 1978.

Whyte, William Foot. "Race Conflicts in the North End of Boston." In *The Many Voices of Boston,* ed. Howard Mumford Jones and Bessie Zaban Jones. Boston: Little, Brown, 1975.

## First-Person Narratives

Alpert, David B. "The Man from Kovno." *American Jewish Archives* 29 (November 1977): 107–115.

Angoff, Charles. *In the Morning Light.* New York: The Beechhurst Press, 1951.

———. *Journey to the Dawn.* New York: The Beechhurst Press, 1951.

———. *When I Was a Boy in Boston.* New York: The Beechhurst Press, 1947.

Antin, Mary. *From Plotzk to Boston.* Boston: W.B. Clarke & Co., 1899; reprint New York: Markus Wiener, 1986.

———. *The Promised Land.* Boston: Houghton Mifflin, 1912; reprint Princeton: Princeton University Press, 2d ed., 1969.

Bernstein, Burton. *Family Matters: Sam, Jennie, and the Kids.* New York: Summit Books, 1982.

Brudno, Ezra S. *The Tether.* Philadelphia: J.B. Lippincott Company, 1908. [fictionalized]

Carmen, Kevie. "Recollection of the Early Years, 1887–1926." Typescript, American Jewish Historical Society, Waltham.

Chyet, Jacob Maurice. "From Rovno to Dorchester." In *Lives and Voices: A Collection of American Jewish Memoirs,* ed. Stanley Chyet. Philadelphia: JPS, 1972: 360–368.

Goldberg, Isaac. "A Boston Boyhood." *American Mercury* 17 (1929): 354–361. Reprinted in *The Many Voices of Boston,* ed. Howard Mumford Jones and Bessie Zaban Jones. Boston: Little, Brown, 1975.

Hentoff, Nat. *Boston Boy.* New York: Knopf, 1986.

Katzman, Jacob. *Commitment: The Labor Zionist Life-style in America: A Personal Memoir.* New York: Labor Zionist Letters, 1975. [on Chelsea]

Lisitzky, Ephraim E. *In the Grip of Cross-Currents.* Translated by Moshe Kohn and Jacob Sloan and revised by the author. New York: Bloch Publishing Company, 1959.

Mirsky, Mark. "Last Bleak Echoes of a Thousand Years: The G&G on Blue Hill Avenue." *Boston Sunday Globe,* 7 March 1971, Section A.

Pratt, Walter Merrian. *Seven Generations: A Story of Pratville, and Chelsea.* Norwood: Privately Printed, 1930.

Rubenovitz, Herman H. and Mignon L. Rubenovitz. *The Waking Heart.* Cambridge: Nathaniel Dame & Co., 1967.

Russell, Francis. "The Coming of the Jews." *Antioch Review* 15 (March 1955): 19–38.

Viscott, David S., M.D. *Dorchester Boy: Portrait of a Psychiatrist as a Very Young Man.* New York: Arbor House, 1973.

Weinstein, Lewis H. *Masa: Odyssey of an American Jew.* Boston: Quinlan Press, 1989.

White, Theodore H. *In Search of History: A Personal Adventure.* New York: Harper and Row, 1978.

# Index

N.B. Illustrations are indicated by (*fig.*); endnotes are referenced by *n*. Unless otherwise noted, places and organizations are in and of Boston. The historic spelling of many organizations' names varies, and may differ within chapters depending on the authors' sources.

# Colophon

*T*he *Jews of Boston* was designed, composed, and produced by Scott-Martin Kosofsky at The Philidor Company in Boston. The text typeface is Montaigne-Sabon, made by Mr. Kosofsky in 1992. It is a typeface of French Renaissance heritage, though more directly influenced by the work of the distinguished 20th-century typographer and book designer Jan Tschichold. Rudolph Ruzicka's Fairfield italic, a typeface with a long connection to Boston, was used for the titles. The Hebrew quotations were set in Mr. Kosofsky's own Soncino, based on the font made in 1494 for Gershom ben Moses Soncino, the great Italian printer and publisher.

The entire book was created on a Macintosh computer, in Quark XPress. Photographs and documents were scanned at The Philidor Company and at Aurora Graphics in Portsmouth, New Hampshire. Mr. Kosofsky did the retouching and made the duotone separations using Adobe Photoshop. All the images were incorporated into the page files which were output directly to film at Aurora Graphics.

The Nimrod Press, Westwood, Massachusetts printed the book on eighty pound Sterling Satin, an acid-free sheet made by the Westvaco Corporation. Acme Bookbinding, in Charlestown, bound the book with Record Buckram, made in Tennessee by Holliston.